BEHIND THE Masks

Discovering Your True Self

JEAN BOND

GATEWAY BOOKS, BATH, UK

First published in 1993
by GATEWAY BOOKS
The Hollies, Wellow,
Bath, BA2 8QJ, UK

Distributed in the USA
by Atrium Publishers
11270 Clayton Creek Rd
Lower Lake, CA 95457

Laserset in 9.7/11.5pt Palatino by
Ann Buchan (Typesetters)
Shepperton, Middlesex

Printed and bound by
Cromwell Press of Broughton Gifford, Wilts.

British Library Cataloguing in Publication Data:
A catalogue record for this book is
available from the British Library

ISBN 0-946551-98-7

To my father, Edgar Anderson and my brother Cyril Anderson, who believed in me.

Contents

Acknowledgements

I am totally indebted to my husband, Tim, for his openness and courage in allowing me to reveal so may details of our personal life in writing this book. I know he is totally committed to my work, but this goes, I feel, 'above and beyond the call of duty'. I also want to thank him for his faith in me and in my courses and my writing. He is my staunchest supporter.

If I were to write a list of all the people who have contributed to this book it would be a book in itself, so I have to content myself with giving my heartfelt thanks and love to all the people who have had the courage to work with me and walk with me, and all the people who have encouraged me in my writing and in developing my courses. A special 'thank you', also, for the people whose contributions to the courses I have used in the text. There are some people who have assisted many times in a voluntary capacity on my courses and who have done sterling work in running support groups. My love and thanks to Max and Mike Elkins, Pete and Lesley McBreen, Howard and Beverley Gwatkin, Maggie Sawkins, Annie Murphy, Eileen and Ken Allcock, Steph Lambert, Sophie Drabik, Tony Grenville, Julie Mills, Paul and Martin Topham, Catherine Benfield, Dianne Lyons, Justin and Wendy Smith, Gabriel Hearst, Betty Woods, John Mills, Maureen Flick, Chrissie and John McGrath, Denis Hanlon, Russell Makin, Richard Cole, Sandra Mawdsely, Sandra Lofthouse and all the rest of you who put in so many hours of your time out of your love and commitment to humanity. I am sorry there is not the space to name you all.

I have had some professional teachers too, the most influential of these being Werner Erhard whose 'EST' training allowed me to begin to remember who I really am. Also James Holland who demonstrated different approaches to healing and growth. He frightened me, not to death, but to life. And more recently, Emmanuel, courtesy of Pat Rodegast, who is pure love and whose words delight my soul.

In particular I want to say to Liz Carroll and Pippa Southcott, thank you for all you taught me by allowing me to understand, and for your courage in living with your pain.

I also want to acknowledge my friend Lin Southwell for her secretarial help and her commitment to my clients and to me.

I especially want to thank my dear friend Margaret Cowgill for growing up with me and putting up with me for so many years. She has given me her unfailing loyalty and support through thick and thin. Through her I learned what friendship is.

I also want to acknowledge my family, past and present; my great nephew, Michael, who has lived with Tim and myself through the writing of this book and endured much in the process; my sister whom I took a long time to get to know; my ex-husband (number 2) for being a lovely, and forgiving man, and for providing me with a wonderful step-son and step-daughter. I am grateful to Sue for her amazing capacity to forgive and for her courage in allowing me to use extracts from our conversation on the course, not to mention having a delightful son, Ben who is a joy to have around.

Last but not least I thank my mother for making the mistake of having me and for being my first teacher.

Other acknowledgements

I am grateful to Bantam Doubleday Dell Publishing group for permission to use material from Emmanuel's Book by Pat Rodegast and Judith Stanton, and to Pat Rodegast for permission to use extracts from tapes of Emmanuel recorded at Bromsgrove, by Living Dharma Tapes.

My thanks also to HarperCollins Publishers for permission to reproduce extracts from Motivation and Personality by Abraham Maslow.

Introduction

This is the true joy in life, the being used for a purpose recognised by yourself as a mighty one; the being a force of nature, instead of a feverish, selfish little clod of ailments and grievances complaining that the world will not devote itself to making you happy.

I am of the opinion that my life belongs to the whole community, and as long as I live it is my privilege to do for it whatever I can.

I want to be thoroughly used up when I die, for the harder I work the more I live. I rejoice in life for its own sake. Life is no brief candle to me. It is a sort of splendid torch which I have got hold of for the moment and I want to make it burn as brightly as possible before handing it on to future generations.

(George Bernard Shaw)

This book is an account of a journey undertaken by almost one thousand 'ordinary' people who came to the conclusion that there must be *more to life than this*! It is an exploration of the steps we need to take to create a paradigm shift in our experience of ourselves, and thereby to enable us to participate in life at a different evolutionary level. It is a moving and inspirational account of the life experiences of some of those people and the insights they gained, by undertaking a course which required them to make a total commitment to doing something about the quality of their lives and to being authentic in acknowledging the pretences and facades they had perfected.

They found the courage to identify the defensive structures they had put around themselves, and to begin to take them down, and learn how to be vulnerable and therefore *real* with others. They discovered the fear, the pain and the joy that is an inevitable concomitant of this process, and they learned that life, lived from the perspective of the evolved individual, can be a daring adventure, a *shared journey towards meaning*, as Marilyn Ferguson (1982), put it, which could put an end to those experiences of emptiness and the despair of loneliness that so many of us have lived with for so long.

I invite you to share that journey, and hope that this book will enable you to realise that you do not have to stay locked in hopelessness or be resigned to the way your life is right now, that you can break through the limits you have set on your relationships, your aspirations, your beliefs about your capabilities and your capacity to love and be loved.

It is an often heart-rending and poignant search for the truth about the human condition. Those who read it will realise that they are not alone in their suffering and their need to be known, loved and acknowledged for who they *are*. The reader will recognise him/herself in those who appear on these pages, and feel less isolated with the thoughts and beliefs they might have about themselves.

In my view there is no simple, mechanical solution to life-problems. I have been working on my growth for ten years and I know I will continue to do so for the rest of my life. I have never read any book, no matter how good, that showed me how to solve the problem. What I hope people will discover from reading this book is that there are several steps in the growth process, the first being *awareness* — knowing why we do what we do; the second being to make a *commitment* to doing something about it — taking a growth-choice rather than a fear-choice; the third being *acknowledgement* — being able to share that knowledge with other people and to stop being ashamed of it; and the fourth is to *forgive ourselves and others for the mistakes we have all made*. These steps should lead to the development of *self-acceptance* and the ability to *face up to the problems that life presents us with*, rather than running away and hiding from them. Having done all this we need to create for ourselves a *purpose for living*, that is, as G B Shaw put it, *mightier than ourselves*.

In one of the case studies in the book I have tried to show that taking the growth-choice in life *is* difficult and painful, but the alternative, operating in a way which is designed to alleviate fear, is worse. After reading this book I hope you will be minded to get support with your growth from courses, books and perhaps individual therapy or counselling. There are many different approaches to personal growth available, and many journals and source books that can be consulted to find out which one you would find most compatible with your needs.

I am sure that it will take more than this book to heal the damage we incur in the passage through life, particularly in the early part of it but, until we can identify that damage and see that there is a way to heal it, we are stuck.

I hope that reading this book will open up for you a new realm of possibilities — a different dimension of existence that will enable you to begin to free yourself from your psychological processes and become a fully actualised human being.

The Abyss

by Val Blomfield

The terrain's very tricky here, you know.
You go for miles, untroubled till you find
You feel a sense of danger and you see
With one false move that you could stumble in . . .

I'd say it's even worse than death, you know,
With such a drop and with that lurching fall
I call it the abyss and spend my time
Devising ways to keep me from its threat.

I'm always very busy here, you know.
I work till I'm exhausted and I drop
Because that leaves me with no time to think
About that place of emptiness and gloom . . .

I met this woman walking here, you know,
At first I thought her mad, but I'm not sure.
She told me she was scared of the abyss
Until she had this very strange idea

That you could jump right in — and live, you know,
And even face that dreadful, endless drop
And come out safely at the other end
Where you would find a better place than this.

The woman talked about that land,you know
The one you'd get to if you risked that jump.
You'd feel the earth there firm beneath your feet
And know your inner rhythm and the world's

There's free and open country there, you know,
Though that could lead to danger too, of course.
But she believed you'd find that you could cope
If you had faced the abyss and survived.

So in a way she tempted me, you know,
To jump into the abyss and be free
And find my own good country and my truth
And be in touch with my reality.

But I 'm so scared of that long fall, you know,
I would not care to take that chance myself,
Although that woman really made me think
About the land where I could find some rest.

But then it is a most grave risk, you know,
And I don't feel I can be so strong,
Although my life is weary here and strained
I think I'll try the jump another day.

And I'll keep on in my old way, you know,
And I'll stay busy and keep on my track.
I'll close my eyes and eat my flower dreams
And hope I'll rid myself of this dull ache.

1. *There must be more to life than this!*

Fifteen years ago I had everything that anyone could possibly want in order to be *happy*. I had a *good* husband, who had a well paid job; we had a detached house, two cars; I had an interesting and remunerative career, and we had a wonderful relationship. There was nothing more I could possibly need or want, but it was not enough. I had frequent feelings of emptiness and noticed that the thought *what's the point*?, would often sneak into my mind.

I used to feel very ungrateful. When, I wondered, would I ever be satisfied? Would it take more money, status, love? What else could I look for that would fill this hole in my existence? People kept telling me how *lucky* I was, but I didn't feel lucky, I felt cheated — but of what? I felt a great deal of empathy with Macbeth's famous soliloquy:

Tomorrow, and tomorrow, and tomorrow,
Creeps in this petty pace from day to day
To the last syllable of recorded time,
And all our yesterdays have lighted fools
The way to dusty death.
Out, out brief candle!
Life's but a walking shadow, a poor player,
That struts and frets his hour upon the stage,
And then is heard no more; it is a tale
Told by an idiot, full of sound and fury,
Signifying — NOTHING!

It took me several years of searching and a broken marriage, plus several more futile relationships, to find out why I felt cheated. Both I and many people were hurt in the process. I did it the hard way for a long time, keeping my feelings and thoughts to myself and changing the circumstances of my life, in the vain hope that this would be the key to happiness. It was not. I believe, now, that I have found the key, not to happiness, as such, but to a life that is full and rewarding where I welcome each day and live every moment of it to the full.

I feel now, that life does not have to be a 'brief candle'. It can be a 'splendid torch', and the brighter we make it burn, the more it will lighten the darkness of our journey through the jungle of the world.

I believe the time has come for humanity to grasp this torch, before the light of the world goes out for ever, and we destroy ourselves and the future of the planet with our greedy demands for love, security and feelings of grandeur. We need to address our arrogant disregard for the future of the human race and the evolution of our species. The time has come, but how do we move to a different plane of existence, one that does not encourage us to gobble up precious resources and literally eat ourselves out of house and home?

I realise now that although I was secretly miserable in my respectable and cocooned state, I was reluctant to admit this because it might have *rocked the boat*. Why put a good thing at risk — and for what? If I'd told my husband I was unhappy, he might have been offended and stopped loving me. I don't suppose he would have known what to do anyway. I didn't, so why should he?

There are so many pressures upon us to maintain the status quo, to believe what we are told through cultural channels. Many of us live in a state of comfortable hibernation, developing various strategies to defend ourselves from hurt and pain, and to keep ourselves free from risk of failure and exposure to the judgements of others. Using readily-available pain-killers, such as TV, alcohol or sleep, we deaden our emotions, close down communications and cut ourselves off from intimacy in relationships. Eventually we reach a state of anaesthetised tranquillity, which must seem much better to many than the unsatisfied hunger of the *je ne sais quoi* that we felt before.

One of the images that frequently comes to mind in describing my own 'jump into the abyss' is that of the transformational process from caterpillar to butterfly. The caterpillar knows only cabbage. It is a life of endless consumption and narrowly focused attention. For the butterfly to emerge in all its splendour it must go through the darkness and confusion of the chrysalis, the shedding of the old self, the discovery of the new, the pain of expansion, the daring of flight.

Why doesn't life work?

How do human beings come to this stage of realising the necessity to evolve? In my own case it started with a weekend spent with people who had seen through the culturally-created reality we live in, and had begun to question the assumptions upon which we base our actions and relationships. The weekend was a workshop entitled *Openness in education.* I have to laugh at my naivete at the time: I thought I was going to a workshop about teaching in Open Plan Classrooms! I now have only a hazy memory of the content of that weekend, but it was nothing to do with open plan classrooms! I was amazed by the passion of the people there who spoke of cultural conditioning and the expectations of ourselves and others that this generated. They spoke of *the manipulation of the oppressed by the oppressors,* and used phrases like *Freire says . . . ,* and *the medium is the message . . .*

I felt totally confused and ignorant and spent a lot of the time desperately wishing I could understand what on earth they were talking about. After all, I was a college lecturer (at that time), I *should* know what they were saying. Some years later I began to read the powerful works of Paulo Freire and grapple with the ideas he was expressing about freedom and education, but at the time I felt embarrassingly inadequate. Something began to sink in, however. I became aware of the hidden messages of our culture and the sub-cultures within it, referred to by Marshall McLuhan, and once I had seen them I wondered how I could have been so blind to the powerful effect they have on the behaviour of the individual and the views they have of themselves.

These messages from the culture come in the form of agreed *norms* that everyone knows they should be aspiring to meet. Not that this is ever actually spelt out to anyone, we just pick it up from TV and other media sources. Fairy Tales and children's stories are a powerful source of cultural conditioning. The pretty girl always gets the prince (*eg* Cinderella; Snow White). Not only are they pretty, but they are *good.* Males are always heroes, or villains, the former being dashing, handsome and rescuing types. Stepmothers are always wicked. These are the role-models held out for us to live up (or down) to. Later on it is the TV soap operas that mould our ideas of how we should be — the dripping-rich glamour girls or the go-getting, ruthless, business men.

If these role-models don't fit the bill then you can always aspire to the hard-hitting, hard-drinking, tough and rugged Western or War heroes. Quick-on-the-draw and able to face up to any odds and wipe them out single-handed, you can be the invincible machine. So women work out how they should be, and men work out how they should present themselves, and woe betide you if you are not quite the right shape or size!

When I was in my late teens and early twenties, Marilyn Monroe was in vogue. My bust being practically non-existent, with hips to match, I resorted to deceit. I bought thickly foam-padded, circle-stitched bras from a well-known department store which, (almost) gave me the desired dimensions. Unfortunately between the real me and the end of the bra cups was about three inches of space. If I danced with anyone who held me tightly the ends of the bra would cave in. With dextrous squeezing of the arms and a slight wriggle I could make them pop out again — hoping that no-one would hear the 'pop'. I managed to solve this problem to some degree by stuffing cotton wool in the ends. Then I lived in an agony of anxiety, hoping my 'date' would not get too familiar and end up with a handful of foam rubber and cotton wool. Add to this the fact that I was short-sighted and, *'men never make passes . . .'*, my chances of meeting Mr Right seemed very slender — even if I actually noticed him when I met him, as I usually left my glasses off when *man hunting*!

Now this may all sound very humorous to you — and looking back, even I can manage a wry smile, but at the time the 'messages' I was getting were clear; *you haven't made it! Not for you the Clark Gables of this world. You will have to settle for the also-rans.* And I did — lots of them; never making any commitment in case one day I (the ugly duckling) should turn into a swan and be in line for a prince. I didn't want to get stuck with a defective frog.

Actually, after waiting for this miraculous transformation until I was 25, I did settle for a sweet frog, as I subscribed to the other cultural message that *if I waited much longer I would be out of the marriage market altogether and* (dreadful fate) *on the shelf*! Then, would you believe it, the miracle happened! Along came the Prince. He was everything a man should be. A little fuller in the face perhaps; a bit short in the leg, but, otherwise . . . We had a whirlwind, secretive, and hence exciting, love affair, and I ended up getting married, *again*.

Up to the point of my involvement in the *Openness* course mentioned above, it looked as though we had found the perfect relationship. My husband was pleasant, generous, fun-loving, socially competent and affectionate. He never forgot my birthday, took care of all the finances, arranged holidays, hauled me up mountains — which he assured me I loved, so I believed him — and bathed my feet afterwards when I was complaining about the effort I had put in. He worked hard, wanted only me and sang my praises to everyone. I was the perfect wife — look how I could sew, cook, paint, walk, join him in his sports and hobbies! I might be a little funny face, but I had a lovely bum, a sporting physique, I was intelligent and lively — in short I was everything he ever wanted.

There were one or two minor *flaws*. I did have very working-class origins, and had to watch my pronunciation of one or two words. My dad was a manic depressive, *which should not be mentioned* in public, and I must never eat chip butties, even in the privacy of my own home. Providing I kept these embarrassing details hidden, then I was the perfect wife, and all that was necessary to make his life complete. In fact, other people were an intrusion. We were all we needed.

Although something inside me was peeved about this elimination of all things working-class, I could see that my husband was entitled to feel embarrassed about them. After all, I was embarrassed by my lowly origins, my mother's accent, my father's mental illness, my council-estate upbringing.

There were also other pluses to the relationship. My husband was a well-known figure in his particular field. He was wonderfully encouraging and lived for a year in a tiny caravan so that I could go to university and take an advanced qualification. Yes — *all in all I was very, very lucky to be so much in love and have such a wonderful, strong, successful adoring partner.* What on earth did he see in me? *I should thank my lucky stars and make sure I kept him,* which, of course, meant that I had to try to please him and be cheerful, to try to be as he liked me to be.

So why did I feel so miserable? Why did I dread sex? Why did I want to find fault and be nasty to him? Why did I find it so intolerable when his daughter came to live with us? Why was I so ungrateful, so mean, so nasty, such a failure as a stepmother? Was I going mad, like my father? Was I just a naturally nasty person? How could I tell anyone about this underlying current of unhappiness when I had everything the world thought necessary to ensure perfect bliss? *There must be something radically wrong with me,* and I should keep quiet about it, otherwise everyone would think I was ungrateful and insatiable.

The weekend on *Openness* proved a revelation and an immense release. The scales rapidly fell from my eyes. I began to see that I was trying to be the person my husband wanted me to be — to live up to his expectations of the perfect wife, the passionate lover, the ideal mother, the playful partner, the sporting friend, the interested and intelligent colleague, the diligent housewife, the perfect hostess. It occurred to me that the reason I persistently left my shoes in the middle of the bedroom floor, where he was sure to fall over them, knowing that this would make him angry, was my way of getting back at him for all the pressure I felt from him to be the perfect woman. And I was so innocent and contrite about it! *Oh! Gosh! Have I done it again? I'm so sorry!* I saw why I was so irrationally irritated when he would ask "would you like me to clean the windows, or wash the dishes *for you?*". *The hidden message was, these areas are your responsibility, not mine, but I might, magnanimously, help you out.*

Of course his attitude was no more conscious or deliberate than my response — which was to try, most of the time, to live up to these expectations (with the odd rebellious incident thrown in). No doubt I had subtly communicated my expectations of him, which he too was trying desperately to live up to. In fact we became caught in a vicious trap of *well if I have to live up to your expectations, I am going to make damned sure you live up to mine!* Both of us were trapped in a prison of culturally-conditioned attitudes which were subliminally operating our responses to each other.

In my case, I was making it impossible for me to live my life the way I wanted to live it — to be who I wanted to be, to express my inner rhythm. Instead I had to strive constantly to fit into the culturally-indoctrinated role-models — a futile and spiritually-crippling way of being. One of the prime examples of this was my husband's belief that a couple who were really *in love* and had a *good* relationship should have sex at least three times a week. If this did not happen, then he began to get moody and say that I was making him ill because he was frustrated and that changed his personality. I then became enormously guilty, even though I could see, at one level, that I was not responsible for supplying his sexual demands. I realised I must be frigid, that I clearly had a *problem* in this area.

I felt, after my releasing weekend on the course, as if I had been living my life in a dark cage surrounded by bars, unable to see where they were. I frequently bumped up against them and was totally puzzled by the experience — like a bird who does not realise that it cannot fly through glass, and who beats itself senseless trying to find freedom beyond an invisible and impenetrable wall. It feels the pain of impact and is not able to make any sense of what is happening. Freedom is there, visible and accessible, but something indefinable stands between it and its goal.

The effect on me of realising what stood between me and freedom was electric. I wanted *out*! I rejected all I had previously thought wonderful: the pastimes, my husband's friends, social events, and ultimately my husband. I thought *if I could get away from all of that — then I would be free.*

WRONG! — I made one fundamental mistake: I took *myself* with me!

Let's all pretend we're okay

It is impossible to overcome years of brainwashing by changing one environment for another. The whole framework of our culture produces the conditioning, not just one small part of it. The messages contained within love songs, novels, magazines, soap operas; the historical inheritance; the social sculpturing of beliefs and values by parents, peers and teachers, these all serve to predetermine our behaviour and form our personality.

If we exchange one culture for another there may seem, initially, to be a sense of freedom, but this is quickly overcome by a feeling of *déjà vu*, as other, different expectations make themselves felt. This became clear when I went to USA for a year and lectured at a university in Michigan. At first, I felt totally accepted by everyone. No-one wanted to know which school my father went to, or what he did for a living. Having lowly origins and then *coming up in the world* was something to be admired: lowly origins in this context were a bonus. Everyone *loved* my accent: I didn't have to watch how I said things. They thought I was 'cute'. I basked in admiration and began to gain confidence in myself.

However, the honeymoon was soon over. Students resented my setting them term papers (essays), and did not see why I could not give the multiple choice questionnaires which other professors gave out. Some of them were appalled when I criticised the USA for its international and domestic policies, whereas, in Britain, speaking out against governments and policy is a legitimate game. So once again, I began to find myself up against the cultural conditioning of the environment. At least now, however, I could see what was going on. I could now decide whether to make myself unpopular or not. I decided on the former course. "To thine own self be true" began to make a lot of sense to me. It also took on new meaning: *Thou canst not then be false to any man.* This meant that I could not present myself falsely, I had to drop my *act*. This, of course, presented me with a different set of difficulties. I became vulnerable and open to attack.

My flight from prison to the relative freedom of the USA presented me with other valuable learning experiences. Away from the pressures of my relationship, I was free to experience the terror of loneliness. Sitting alone and TV-less in my one-bedroom student apartment, 5,000 miles from home, I sorely felt the need for security and someone to *love* me. I telephoned my husband often and insisted he called me. This, I was to learn later, was a big mistake! I was simply trying to crawl back into the nice safe cage.

When X rang one morning at seven and invited me to go out for 'breakfast', despite my initial suspicious reaction to this culturally-incompatible (and slightly immoral) suggestion, I leapt at the opportunity to escape from my solitary confinement and homesickness, and off I went. X was an attractive man and seemed a pleasant enough character. In fact he insisted on telling me his whole life story from birth to that day, in great detail. At the time I could not believe that anyone could be so self-centred and so utterly uninterested in anyone else. *Never again* I promised myself.

But something strange and wonderful occurred. Because of the detail he had gone into about his early childhood, which was, by the way, incredibly sad, I could see what a damaged individual he was, and my intolerance gave way to understanding and the fairly unconscious thought that I could probably *save* him. *Maybe if I could understand him enough and love him enough I could turn him into someone less egocentric and more responsible.* In fact, he told me later that he had got the idea of telling me his whole life story from meeting someone who had invited him to do just that, and then did the same himself. He said that he then felt closer to this person than anyone else in his life. Unfortunately he did not give me the chance to do the same!

If only I had read Robin Norwood's book, *Women Who Love Too Much* (a book about women who come from dysfunctional families, and the addictions they form to men who are 'impossible'), before em-barking on this episode — it might have saved me a great deal of time and trouble. But I hadn't and it didn't, and maybe this was an experience I had to go through in order to grow. And grow I did, since X was one of the most (unawarely) manipulative people I had met, and learning to resist his tactics was a strengthening experience. At least I felt he needed me more than I needed him, and of course I thought, mistakenly, *I still had my husband to fall back on.* X did have good points, and we did have some good times together, but I was not sufficiently aware and awake, then, to support him, and to avoid getting pulled into games with him.

I see now that this whole episode constituted what Kelly (1955) calls a *slot rattle.* I will explain this more fully in a later chapter, but for now suffice it to say that, in order to survive we try out one strategy, and if that does not work, or give us what we need, we simply employ a different one, which is the exact opposite of the one we tried in the first place. In my case, having looked for someone who was a complete contrast to my father, I then exchanged him for someone who had very similar tendencies. A friend of mine pointed this out to me several years later, when she said one day *Why do you keep going out with all these lunatics?* I gaped at her in amazement, considered the men I had 'dated' since going to the USA, and realised that she was not far wrong. I did keep seeking out very unstable and zany-type men. I realised later that I was clearly attempting to work out my relationship with my father — but more of that later. As it was, eight years after leaving my husband, I was still trying to work out how to have a satisfactory relationship with a man!

David Smail (1987), clearly illuminates the problem for people who are attempting to change, when he explains that therapy often has only a temporary effect on people who have been psychologically scarred by their life experiences, because it is impossible to heal those scars if we are simply going to put people back into the environment that caused them in the first place. That environment consists, he says, of a culture where people, from the time they are born, are constantly exposed to the judgements of others. Comparisons are made by themselves and others of the speed of their developmental progression, their success, attractiveness, physique and so on, measured against that of their peers or the rest of the population. We cannot escape the *gaze of the other*, as Thomas Szasz (1972), puts it.

We are frequently graded, examined for flaws, assessed, judged and usually found wanting in one capacity or another. Now, in England, after education changes from 1989, the implementation of the National Curriculum, and assessment at the ages of seven, eleven and fourteen, this pressure on the individual to *keep up with the Joneses*, especially in the area of academic success, will be even stronger than before. How many children were psychologically damaged by failing their examinations at age eleven, and became the victims of selection into a 'Secondary Modern' school instead of a 'Grammar' school? People who attended the former were in no doubt that they were the 'second class' citizens of Britain. I recently spoke to the mother of two children, the younger of whom 'passed' her selection test at 11, after her older sister had 'failed' it. This has aggravated problems between the two sisters, and between the older girl and her parents, because she never feels adequate when she compares herself with her younger sister. How many more children might suffer a similar execution of their identity, and see themselves as being *no good* and *not able* at the tender age of seven, and have this impression reinforced four years later and three years after that?

I have a student at university who 'failed' her school examinations, largely because they terrified her. Now they terrify her even more, so despite handing in brilliant essays in termtime, she goes to pieces at exam time and suffers the torment of hell. Whatever she does is *never good enough*. If she receives an excellent grade for her work she justifies it by saying that the lecturers *are just being kind*. She wonders if it is worth all the agony she suffers trying to get it *right*.

Schooling has much to answer for in terms of assaulting the individual's sense of worth. In the course of my work I see many five- or six-year-olds furtively trying to hide the fact that they are on a 'lower' reading book than the other children in their class, or on their table. They say to me *I'm thick, Miss, or, I'm on the bottom table*. The subtle message of failure and inadequacy and therefore *not rightness* has already been transmitted, and it will be reinforced as the child goes through the school system. Good and Brophy [1972] noted how often teachers group less able children on one table, usually in a corner of the classroom. The less able children are called on less frequently than brighter children to answer questions and, when they are asked, the teacher waits only briefly for a reply before asking someone else. Usually, brighter pupils are given twice as long to think of an answer to a question and are prompted with another question if they do not respond correctly. The subtlety of these messages is programmed into the psychological processes of the child at a deeply unconscious level, reinforcing beliefs they may already have about their intellectual ability (or apparent lack of it). For those who get to university, even the *créme de la créme* of the population have had much of the stuffing knocked out of them by schooling — and they are supposed to be the *success stories*!

This damage to our nation's elite becomes evident when I ask university students a question, and no-one wants to volunteer an answer. "I know", I tell them, "you are playing the game called *if I sit here long enough she will answer the question herself* — well, you will wait a long time — I'm not going to do that". Embarrassed grins tell me I have hit the mark. "So why is it", I continue, "that you do not want to answer my questions?" Out it all comes: *In case people argue with me*, or *In case it's the wrong answer*, or *I'm frightened in case people laugh at me*. I encourage them to explore how this state of affairs arose. Why do we live in such fear all the time?

Soon my students get used to my directness and apparent ability to read their minds, and begin to take more risks, becoming more questioning and more willing to offer suggestions, to own up to their fears and inadequacies and to talk about personal problems — but it takes me to do it first. "Do you know", said one of them, "how much you blew our minds? You actually looked directly at us when we spoke, and waited for us to answer questions. You explained things to us and really didn't mind if we couldn't understand. You were honest about yourself and told us details of your personal life. We couldn't make you out at first". Eventually they begin to feel safe to be themselves and to talk about how they feel, perhaps for the first time in their educational history. And these, as I said, are society's *successes* — our *failures* fare even worse.

Schooling, however, is not the only influence on our lives. We have parents who influence our early development. Whether they over-protect their offspring, are cruel and negligent, or just *terribly nice*, no-one escapes without being affected by the experience (*eg* see Alice Miller, 1989). Many people who take my course were sent to boarding school by their parents, often for the best of motives. The damage that this can do will become clear in a later chapter.

Then there are the scars left on the psyche by the treatment of peers. Are there any among us who have not been bullied, laughed at, name-called, left until last when being selected for teams, and so on?

Unfortunately our culture keeps quiet about the crushing effect all these phenomena have on our self-esteem. We think that the upbringing we had was *normal*, and if we were unhappy it was because we didn't *fit in*, or were *stupid*. So we try desperately to look, and be, as *good* as the next person, not realising that the rest of the population is doing the same thing. Humanity is suffering from an insidious disease — that of denial of the truth. Scott Peck (1991) calls people who do this *People of the Lie*, and maintains that they are *evil*. I was rather shocked when I read this. I thought that to call them *evil* was overdoing things a bit. However, as I read on I began to understand what he was saying. As a priest who once took my course said, *lying* is *evil*.

In order to preserve the elaborate pretence of their lives, people have to draw others with them into their conspiracy, creating ever more victims in the game of *Let's pretend we are okay, and life is wonderful*. I could see how this applied to my own life when I was living a lie with my ex-husband, pretending we had a wonderful relationship, and absolutely no problems. When my step-daughter came to stay, she provided the perfect reason for my covert unhappiness. I no longer needed to look at its true source. She was an unhappy child whose mother had not been supportive, and she expressed her unhappiness the way teenagers do. She was rebellious, capricious and careless. All my resentment about feeling trapped was projected onto this convenient scapegoat. Of course, at the time, I had no idea what I was doing. I felt perfectly justified in feeling angry with her and pouring out a catalogue of complaints. There were times when I could not face going home, and drove round and round the block to delay my entrance — all this I ascribed to her being there.

One evening I lost my temper with her so completely that I grabbed her by the hair and banged her head against the wall. All the despair of my own situation went into that act, and I wanted to break her skull open. Later I was bitterly ashamed and frightened by the extent of my viciousness. This was what Scott Peck was driving at. Even if we do not go to the extremes of becoming physically violent, we will use other people to help us preserve the lie we are living, no matter what cost to them or to ourselves. In my case, there is a happy sequel: eleven years after I left my husband, my step-daughter rang me, and we had an initially apprehensive, but subsequently therapeutic and joyful reunion. I still stay in contact with her. In fact, she recently took my course, and this has enabled greater depths of relationship to open up.

Below is a transcript of the interaction that took place between us, after course participants had completed a process of looking at their relationship with their mothers. The session was particularly moving, with people getting in touch with a lot of pain and sadness about their childhood, and the inadequacy of the parenting they received:

Jean: *I could take any group of 50 people off the street out there, and they would all tell the same story. Rarely have I seen such courage in people, such a capacity to just go on, despite what they have had to endure — it has blown me away. I teach these courses a lot and over the space of many years I have got used to sharing people's suffering, but I have been moved to tears many times during this week-end. I feel as though someone just put me through a mangle. But you see, all it does is make me more resolute to put an end to all this, to do something about the fact that human beings inflict such suffering on each other, such hurt, such damage. It has got to stop, hasn't it? Don't you think it is time it stopped? And I don't know any better way to do it than this. If I did know a better way, I would do it.*

I found it particularly painful to watch . . . (sobbing) *I found it particularly painful to watch Sue go through that pain. I felt it was* me *going through it. I guess Sue was the only child I ever had, really, and I didn't appreciate her when I had her at all. I am so incredibly grateful that she rang me up two years ago, and at least made some effort to communicate with me, because she gave me the opportunity to clear up the mistakes I made with her, and I hope I will be able to have a loving relationship with her now, because I wasn't up to having that relationship with her when she needed it. I really regret that very much. And I love her dearly . . . I never thought I would have to do the 'Mother Process' from the other angle of being a mother!*

Sue: (sobbing) *I wanted to speak to you all day, but I didn't think I should because I thought I might waste your time, because there were people in here with so many problems who needed your attention. I didn't want to waste your time, so I just kept it to myself. You are so brilliant at this, I wanted them to have you and I didn't want to be greedy.*

Jean: *You are not being greedy, and perhaps this will make up for all the times you couldn't have me, when you should have done.*

Sue: *You have helped me speak to my mother. I felt quite angry towards her and I thought I had cleared it up, and it has opened it all up again. I still have the problem and I don't know where to start. My mum didn't seem to like me. She didn't want to show me any affection. She showed all the affection to my brother. I understand why. My dad had left her in a right mess, and I look like my dad, and when she sees me, all the things he did come back. And I even knew that when I was eight. It just hurts so much because I never got any love at all. To be honest, I feel she used me as a skivvy. I did all the work in the house, but I could never do anything right. I haven't said that to her yet, but I will. I came to live with you and my dad. Oh, I have missed so much out — in the meantime I had been abused, and my mum didn't believe it.*

Sue had been abused by a family friend over a two year period, and kept it to herself, because, like most sexually-abused children, she was afraid of the problems it would cause. Eventually, however, this all came out, and her mother, like many women in her situation, did not believe her; she could not believe her, because if she did she would have had to let go of the only means of love and security she had at that time. This is a terrible predicament that many women find themselves in. Of course we can all sit in judgement on them, but who amongst us has not turned a blind eye to injustice, cruelty and exploitation when it suited? How much do we care about exploitation of children in the third world, and other ethical and moral issues? In truth we are all *People of the Lie.*

Sue: *She called me a liar, and said that I was doing it to hurt her, and I kept it to myself for two years. I have talked to her about it now, and she feels so guilty that she didn't do anything about it at the time.*

And I came to live with you (Jean), *and I needed some love so desperately and I didn't get it. My dad found it so hard to show affection. He is a typical man* — I don't need to love anybody — *what I feel happened to me is that in all my relationships I want so much love, and I don't get it — even now I don't get it and so what I do is, I just want to go and screw around. I used to go and have affairs here and there, and talk about 'bonking', and I am fanatical, and I like to make people laugh about it, and I know deep down inside it is because I am just desperate for some attention. When I organise affairs I am in complete control. I am the* persecutor, *not the victim. But it's not right, and I was still not happy with it and not contented, and I am back to square one, and I don't know what to do. And it is affecting everything.*

I have not got any confidence in myself and I come across as being very brave. Other people have said how brave I am, and it's crap, I'm not at all, and I have to teach kids, and I'm very frightened of them, and if I allow them to see that, they just mince me up, and I just can't afford to have that happen any more. I don't know what to do or where to go.

Jean: *If I had a fairy godmother right now I would say, "Please turn the clock back".*

Sue: *I wish you could, because I know you could help me now.*

Jean: *But I didn't know then what I know now. I wasn't up to it. Do you know what: I could be listening to myself talking too, because I used to screw around and that was about getting love too. And I hated myself for it. And I even don't want sex any more because of what it has come to mean.*

Sue: *I tell a lot of people about all this, but I don't think I ever realised how I really felt about it. I don't think I think about it deeply enough.*

Jean: *No, you see, up to now you have told it like a story. I used to do exactly the same, but I never really got in touch with how I felt about things, and I never let anyone else really know it either, because it was too bloody painful.* (We hug for a long time and cry together, along with everyone else in the room, who are moved by the experience).

Jean: (To the group) *So you see, what you have just seen happening between me and Sue is possible for anybody!*

In other words, it is possible for anyone to achieve true intimacy and a deep sense of total love and compassion with another human being. It is possible to wipe away all the mistakes of the past and form supportive and powerful relationships that are nurturing and healthy, but it takes tremendous courage and the willingness to endure the pain and heartbreak of looking honestly at the mess we create in our own lives, and that of others, in order to clean up the mess.

Most of us have never found an environment which enabled us to find that kind of courage, or which made us feel sufficiently safe and trusting to experience that depth of pain — so we live our lives by the formula *If you can't make it — fake it*. Pretend that life is wonderful and everything is *just fine*. Own up to the fact that you might be experiencing a *few minor problems*, but otherwise everything is terrific. Alternatively, you can blame the things that go wrong in your life on the circumstances — there is a familiar list of these: the government, the tax system, the cost of living, teachers, the boss, the other woman/man, your children, the weather, your arthritis/asthma/poor digestion. Only when we stop pretending is there a possibility of beginning to heal the damage we have suffered, and have been carrying round with us, but it is a frightening process. When you begin to examine the fabric of pretence you have woven, you may have to face the possibility of giving up all that goes with it.

And what does go with it? Why are we so insistent on pretending that all is well? We think we will lose security, love, consistency, control, status, respect and so on. The reason I say why we *think* we will lose it is twofold: 1. this is not a necessary outcome and 2. we probably never had these things in the first place — it just felt that way, temporarily.

The first steps to growth

If you want to grow and open up possibilities in your life, the first requirement is that you begin to tell the truth about the way life really *is*. When people decide to take the first level *Emergence* course, they are asked to take the first step in this direction by filling in a questionnaire under various headings. The following are some of the typical responses that people make. These might serve to illustrate the type of fears and frustrations that people keep hidden, in the belief that to have these *inadequacies* makes them different from, and inferior to, others.

Things you can't do, or would like to do better:
Be more in control of my job or career; learn to drive; find a suitable life partner; be more in control of my temper and emotions; more understanding; be more capable; learn more quickly; settle for the good things my life offers; be organised and purposeful; learn to say No, as a parent; make friends; communicate; more confidence in my work; choose suitable partners; make lasting friendships; handle money; express myself when angry; get on with women; relax.

Things that worry you:
Failing; rejection; my bad temper; being used by others; death; the unknown; job security; racism and sexism; my own sexuality; am I wasting my life? jealousy; being late; getting old; inadequacy at work; looking a fool; the future; being on my own; not being good enough; being left out; boring people; what people think of me; arguments; being hurt emotionally; meeting people; money — lack of it; my children's future; environmental issues; personal health; no direction in life; lack of confidence.

Things you would like to change:
Leaving things to the last moment; feeling 'got at'; longer concentration

span; being extremely suspicious; me; my husband's feelings; my intelligence; to be confident and spontaneous; to be committed to a task; my job; be less selfish; be less hypocritical; be more ambitious; find more direction in my life; to have better academic qualifications; to be less of a martyr; to be more assertive; my size; stop worrying what people might think; increase number and quality of friends; ability to mix with people; be more creative; be efficient; be articulate; stop procrastinating; be more tolerant; drifting with no positive direction; to worry less; understand myself; to become more outward-looking.

The above questions are only a sample of three from twelve on the questionnaire, and are responses taken randomly from people on but one of the courses, but they are fairly representative of the type of answers people give. Not all responses are so searching, and some people put very little down. Some look at the questionnaire and decide at that point not to take the course after all! It looks too risky!

There is no doubt that those people who are attached to keeping things just the way they have always been, or to the way that seems to keep them safe, will stop short at this point and decide to opt for the *house-boat* mode of being: stay put, drop anchor and don't go anywhere, and then perhaps, the boat will not get rocked. Sadly, however, for the house-boat dwellers living in the backwaters of life, the rest of the world bustles by them, and all they get is the backwash of those who are going somewhere — and a very restricted outlook.

WARNING!! **If you decide to read on, this book might change your life. You may never again be satisfied with backwater living!**

2. *The road-blocks of fear*

Fear is not a private affair, because it stands like a road-block between the individual and reality ... Again , fear is not a private affair, because, long sustained, it breeds a sense of helplessness that is out of keeping with the responsible practices of freedom.

(Overstreet, 1962, pp104, 107)

Today when I woke up I was feeling pretty low. I had a headache hovering; I felt reluctant to get out of bed. When Tim (my husband) put his arm around me, I felt resentful — *he was intruding on my space! Why couldn't he leave me alone? He was always wanting sex from me when I wasn't in the mood!* I did not respond to his friendly gesture, simply lying there, inert, and not speaking. He then said he would like a cuddle. I was outraged. How *dare* he make demands on me when I was feeling like *this*! I just about managed to keep these thoughts to myself and told him that I was feeling miserable, and did not want to cuddle him, putting my arm around him, to show that he should not take it personally. His next move was to offer to bring me breakfast in bed. I declined this grumpily. He then said that I didn't need to feel miserable, and would I like to talk about it. I told him that I obviously did need to feel miserable, since I had no intention of talking to him, or of getting out of my mood. He asked me if I knew why I wanted to be miserable. I began to reflect on this.

I realised that I was deliberately making myself angry and making him the source of that anger. Why was I making myself angry? This is my way of coping with fear. You perhaps will not be surprised to learn that it was the way my mother coped with fear too. Other people repress their fear with drugs, alcohol, cigarettes, or chocolate, but I have to be angry with or about something or somebody, and who better than Tim, who is around all the time?

I also had the startling and painful realisation that, when I get angry with Tim, he becomes very fearful of that anger, thinking that it means he is going to be rejected. Now Tim uses a totally different strategy to cope with fear from the one I use. He becomes withdrawn, almost like a tortoise: he pulls his head back into his shell and switches off. He becomes ineffective, leaves things around, forgets to do things and doesn't hear what I am saying to him. At this point I have a legitimate reason to be angry with him. The anger escalates and he deteriorates — and so it goes on — a vicious downward spiral of relationship.

Once I had seen what was happening, I was able to stop feeling angry and be loving with Tim. We could laugh at the fact that, in order to appease or placate me, and divert the anger, he had offered to bring me breakfast in bed, or make me a drink — all of which only makes me more of a tyrant. After the laughter had stopped and I got out of bed and started to get on with my day, I then experienced the huge amount of anxiety that my anger had been designed to suppress.

I sat down and did some 'flow writing'[1], and came to the conclusion that my fear revolved around leaving my nice secure job at the university, thereby losing two thirds of my income and, on top of that, embarking on a project of buying a house in France. In my usual way I wanted to buy the house, have it all renovated and to borrow money in order to modify another building belonging to the property, to make it habitable. This entailed making important decisions, taking a financial risk and giving ourselves a great deal of work — all in French! All this was going to take a long time and, since my French is extremely limited, it was fraught with difficulty.

Once I had identified the source of the anxiety, I did something about it. We decided to take it in easy stages and forget about the mortgage. The feelings of intense fear faded away — and the migraine came along instead! Ah well, at least a migraine is short-lived and, in my case, usually signifies the *release* of extreme tension.

So why I am telling you all this? To illustrate, graphically, the quotation that begins this chapter. My fear of buying this house stood like a road block between me and the reality of my relationship with Tim. Fear is not a private affair, because it drastically affects our health and wellbeing, and those of people around us. My fear has a devastating effect on Tim's ability to function effectively, and subsequently on my attitude towards him. My fear, and his, kills our ability to relate to each other — and we are not unique in this respect.

The survival functions of the mind

Most of us live in abysmal ignorance about the mechanism we call *mind*.

[1]Flow writing is a good way of getting to the bottom of unspecified anxiety or identifying the source of upset. You simply write down anything and everything that comes into your head for about twenty minutes, without editing your thoughts in any way.

All of us seem to accept that there is such a thing, that it resides somewhere in the brain, but further than that we do not go. Scientists have spent much time, money and effort attempting to discover how the mind works, and yet it is still a mystery to most of us, even those who are experts on the subject.

Michael Talbot's book is a pertinent exploration of the unexplained phenomenon relating to the mind — extra-sensory perception, telepathy and poltergeists, to name but a few. The most fascinating aspect for me was the reference it contained to some work by Lorber (in Smith), who investigated the brain-capacity of people suffering from *hydrocephalus* (water on the brain). Lorber initially became aware of two children who were victims of *hydrocephalus* — a condition which leads to an abnormal build-up of cerebro-spinal fluid in the brain. Neither of these children appeared to have any cerebral cortex, which according to scientific theory about the functioning of the brain should have completely disabled them. However, their mental development appeared to be normal. Although one of them died at the age of three months, the other was still continuing to develop normally at twelve months, despite repeated medical examinations that could detect no evidence of any cerebral tissue.

Later Lorber came across an even more fascinating incident. He was put in touch with a student at Sheffield university who had a head that was slightly larger than normal. After running a CAT scan on this boy he discovered that, although this student had an IQ of 126, and had gained a first class honours degree in mathematics he had "virtually no brain" (Smith). "Lining his skull was only a thin layer of brain cells a millimetre or so thick, and the rest of his cranium was filled with cerebro-spinal fluid . . . The boy continues to live his life normally, except for the fact that he possesses virtually no brain" (Talbot, 1988). According to psycho/physiological evidence of how brains function, this should be impossible.

Although this research has been carefully documented and reported in reputable scientific journals, it has attracted little interest or attention from the medical or scientific world. Those who have commented upon it, like Kenneth Till, a former neurosurgeon at the Great Ormond Street Hospital, London, dismissed it by stating that Lorber is being *overdramatic*. Lorber himself admits that interpreting brain scans is not easy, but adds, "I can't say whether the mathematics student has a brain weighing 50 grams or 150 grams, but it is clear that it is nowhere near the normal 1.5 kilograms" (in Lewin, p.233). So why is the medical/scientific world disregarding this work?

One of the reasons for this, I feel, may well be that human beings hate to have their views of reality challenged, and scientists are no exception to that. Fear of discovering that they may have been operating under false assumptions, and may have been fooling themselves, leads many otherwise brilliant *minds* to reject possibilities that might open up huge new fields of knowledge. The fear of losing status and respect is very strong in eminent people. Those who have challenged existing truths, like Socrates, Galileo or Einstein, have been not only verbally attacked for their discoveries, but also physically endangered or destroyed.

Most studies of the brain and mind are conducted on a cause-and-effect basis. "If I stimulate this, and the person does that, then this means that stimulating this is responsible for what occurs next." This is a perfectly legitimate way to think, and might frequently be correct, but perhaps it does not always necessarily follow. Perhaps the brain and, therefore, the mind, are still mysteries to us and the only way to unravel the mystery is by applying, as Krishnamurti (1974) put it, *constant vigilance.*

In other words it requires human beings to develop the capacity to observe and explore the mechanisms and functions of their own minds, in order to begin to understand the complex and powerful instrument that they have at their disposal: we must be our own scientists. Until we begin to do this, it is like having access to an incredibly complicated computer which could, if you knew how to operate it, run your life completely effectively. It could communicate perfectly, allow you to express yourself authentically and lucidly, enable you to be in touch with what you really want to do with your life — in short it would serve to make you a truly powerful human being who could make your mark on life and contribute to the development of the human race.

Instead of this, the powerful instrument often seems to function of its own accord, without our being able to do anything about it — in fact without many of us even being aware of the fact that we have it! How many of us, for instance, have ever considered where *thoughts* come from? Yet the mind churns them out incessantly. We can't seem to switch them off when the thoughts are irritatingly repetitive — such as when songs run repeatedly through your head — or self-destructive. A friend of mine was unable to sleep, because she kept monitoring her performance of the day, criticising herself for what she had said to people, wondering if she had been inappropriate, wishing she had not said some of the things she had said. Her internal critic would not keep quiet and let her rest.

Nor do we seem to be able to make the mind work whenever we want it to. Sometimes it works wonderfully, but we don't quite know what we did to make it operate that way. Sometimes it crashes and self-destructs. Like the most horrific science fiction film, the instrument takes over and gets completely out of control of the person who designed it — YOU!

Until we can begin to get back into control of our minds we are virtually powerless. We rely entirely on this instrument, and if it malfunctions we are completely at its mercy. At best we discover perhaps half the functions of the machine, and under-use even this bit considerably. We need to learn what affects the functioning of the mind — what makes us decide to develop one view of life rather than another, or believe certain things about ourselves and dismiss other thoughts? How did we develop the identity that we have adopted? In what ways are we influenced by the culture and the people close to us?

In order to breach this gap in our education, I developed the *Emergence* course referred to earlier. Participating in courses of this nature entails having your view of reality frequently challenged, and this people find uncomfortable and confronting. In order to deal with these vague feelings of discomfort people develop various strategies which are designed to defend them from the danger surrounding them.

Enter the caterpillars

"The unmoved human being is as unaware of his evolutionary possibilities as a caterpillar might be said to be unaware that it may become a butterfly". (Moore)

As I watch course participants coming into the room on the first day, it is interesting to observe where they choose to sit. Do they hide at the back or go straight to the front? Do they avoid other people or find someone to talk to? Do they talk nervously or present a laid-back and cool demeanour? Do they look hostile, or nervous? How do they perceive themselves and others, and interpret the situation they find themselves in? Do their minds detect danger and switch into *survival mode*, and how does that manifest itself in terms of their behaviour? Each person copes with the uncertainty of embarking on a two-weekend quest for growth and personal power in a unique, and often quite humorous way — to the people observing, that is!

"Excuse me", says Alice loudly, when the group is all assembled, and I settle down to give my introductory talk. *"I don't like the way these chairs are arranged. I think they should be in a circle."*

Jean: *Oh! Why is that?*

Alice: *I feel a bit hostile actually. It feels to me like a revivalist meeting, like I'VE SEEN GOD you know and I find that a bit unpleasant. I was talking to Jack just now — well actually I didn't raise it — he felt it was like being back at school when we walked in. I have had very unpleasant experiences at school. This set up seems very formal to me compared with some other kinds of groups. It all seems very much the school audience and that sort of authoritative figure and those watchers at the back* [assistants]. *It makes me feel very uncomfortable actually. I am trying to be open minded about it, but it raises my hackles a bit. The last group I went on we were in a circle, and that was a very good course.*

Jean: *OK. So maybe this course is not like the other courses you have been on.*

Alice: *No well it obviously isn't I appreciate that.*

Jean: *I have got the seating arranged this way at the moment because it is less intimidating for people that way. Maybe this is a useful incident to use to start to explore the question,* 'Is the way I see things necessarily the way it is?'

Alice: *Well that's fine, but I like it less formal.*

Jean: *Maybe it doesn't have to be 'formal' this way.*

Alice: *I would find it less intimidating to have the chairs in a circle that's all and I've talked to other people who think so too.*

Jean: *Who else agrees with that?*

Only one hand is raised. Alice looks amazed.

I went on with Alice to explore with her the possibility that her mind was comparing the situation she had walked into with a similar situation in her past, that she had found very threatening to her identity. Maybe she had been made to feel stupid, ridiculed, or had her self-image damaged in similar ways. Mind, being the guardian of our safety and our identity, compares the situation with the one that did the damage in the past, and sends out warning signals: *this place is dangerous*. Notice that Alice then looks for some way to try to make it feel safe for her. She attempts to persuade me to rearrange the room so that it looks less like a school and more like a therapy group, or workshop, where she had felt much safer. Teacher and taught are on a more equal footing and the leader is devoted to the nurturing and wellbeing of the group.

Once Alice had realised that she was actually distorting reality, filtering what was happening through the framework of her past experience, she was able to sit down and accept the way the chairs were arranged. But it took her about twenty minutes to arrive at this position. Of course she still had other fears which came up from time to time during the course and affected her participation, but this initial encounter enabled her to be more open to the possibility that things were not always the way they seemed to her to be.

If we take Claxton's view, that the mind is a mechanism for survival, and has a capacity to compare any new situation with past traumatic or threatening experiences — a facility to produce automatic, pre-programmed reactions to cope with the perceived threat, then Alice's reaction could be explained diagrammatically as follows:

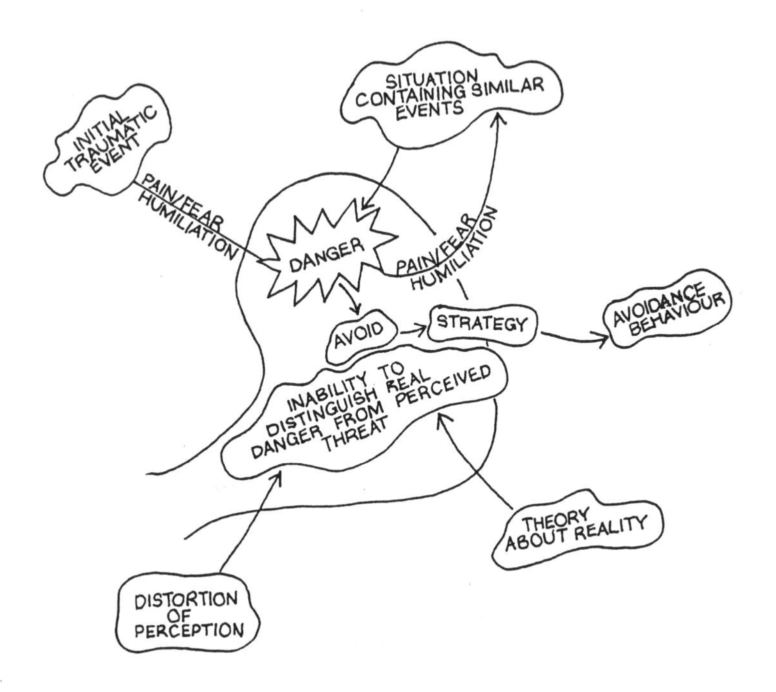

Had I reacted to the hostility shown by Alice, by becoming defensive and attempting to repress or dominate her, she would have been confirmed in her belief that she was going to be treated like a child at school and that I was, like her previous teachers, out to get her, thereby reinforcing the whole mind defence system. I asked Alice to suspend her judgement if she could, by simply observing her emotional and intellectual responses to what was going on, and by noticing how often she interpreted people's actions as being attempts to dominate her.

Alice has told me since that she found this a very valuable experience. So too did other people on the course, who then began to realise that maybe the way they saw things was not always the way things *were*. Their fear was standing, like a road-block, between them and reality. In this case the *road block* that Alice was using to defend herself was *distortion*. Other means of avoiding situations perceived by the mind as *dangerous* are, physical avoidance, regression (retreating into childish behaviour like temper tantrums, sulking, thumb-sucking *etc*), rationalisation, justification, projection, displacement and denial, (an absolute refusal to admit that anything is going on at all — *this isn't happening*).

When we start to feel uncomfortable, we tend not to stay with the feelings (which are signalling *danger* to our nervous system) and explore them to see what they are really about. Instead we allow our dislike of this discomfort to drive us into one, or more, of the strategies mentioned above. Erich Fromm, in his book *Fear of Freedom*, points out how limiting and restrictive to growth this response is. He says, "You can either have your feelings, or they can have you". In other words, most people allow life-decisions to be determined by how they feel, rather than being able to look at what will best serve their interests and their growth.

When people come to the courses I offer they are usually operated by their feelings — as indeed most of us are, when it comes to making decisions or doing what we know we need to do, in order to be effective, or to keep to what we promised others we would do. The problem is that most of our feelings are based on fear and threat to our survival. Alice's feelings were based on the threat to her identity which she experienced at school, and the erosion of her sense of worth and significance, which can ultimately lead to a feeling of annihilation and non-existence, the death of self. Below is another example of someone who is run by her feelings. In this case it is anger which seems to have her, and she found this very difficult to understand.

Beth: *My anger seems to be expressed in a very bizarre sort of way. The big things I can get angry about, and I get quite angry, but I am in control. But the little things I go absolutely completely beyond the pale about. I know they are stupid things: there are two which come to mind. Whenever my children have knocked a drink over and it's sticky on the floor or sticky on the table, I absolutely hit the roof. And the other is even more stupid: when I have a garden full of washing and it rains. And I will shout and swear at the heavens and I am totally neurotic about it. And everybody disappears, and then I go and calm myself down and think what a total idiot I was. I really don't know why I do this stupid thing.*

Jean: *Did your mother ever get angry when you knocked things over?*

Beth: *I don't remember that she did. She may have done.*

Jean: *Or about the washing?*

Beth: *Possibly. I seem to remember that getting washing dry was a big priority. We didn't have tumble driers then. It was all brought in in front of the fire.*

Jean: *So was washing day a big deal to your mother?*

Beth: *Yes it was. Yes, my grandmother came over and it was all in the hall on a Sunday night.*

Jean: *And did your mother get irritable?*

Beth: *Possibly. And I used to come home on a wet day and hate it 'cause the house was full of steam. And I used to be really miserable. I am neurotic about rain anyway. It is really stupid.*

Jean: *Absolutely, because have you noticed that however angry you are with it it just carries on anyway?*

Beth: *Yes. It just doesn't get through [to me that I am incorrect].*

Jean: *It doesn't get through because you are not relating to what is going on in the here-and-now. You are having a stack attack.*

The mind is like the most incredible recording machine there ever was. If you were to be put under powerful hypnosis you would (theoretically) be able to recall in minute detail everything that ever happened to you since you were born — or perhaps even before that, if the Buddhists are to be believed. The mind is a continuous linear recording of successive moments of now (Hubbard, 1980). It is like having a stack of recording discs in the brain. If a traumatic incident happens to you, this incident will be recorded on a special disc marked *danger*. At some later point another similar incident will occur which will reinforce the danger message of the first incident, so that now you know that this really is a dangerous situation. A bit later on another similar incident occurs and reinforces it even more.

This phenomenon was explored by Watson who was a very early behavioural psychologist. Watson experimented with a small child (whom he referred to as 'Little Albert'), in a way that would be ethically unacceptable by modern standards, giving the child a white rabbit to hold and simultaneously administering an electric shock. The child quickly learned that *white cuddly rabbit = pain*. However it did not stop there. Watson observed that the child generalised his fear-response to anything that remotely resembled the rabbit — anything white and fluffy, fur rugs, furry slippers or gloves all became objects of terror to him. I believe that Watson then reversed the process and so the tale ended happily for Albert. Unfortunately for most of us the ending is not so happy. The process is not reversible, because we are barely aware that it is going on and we certainly do not know what created the fear in the first place.

Jean: *I would suggest that your anger about the rain has something to do with your mother and the way she was on washing days. And it could be that it goes back to an even earlier situation where your mother panicked about something to do with rain, or something unpleasant or dangerous happened to you with regard to rain. Maybe you went out and got wet and your mother was very angry with you for getting wet. Maybe she once got into trouble for getting wet. She has probably passed her stuff (conditioning) on to you. Your anger has nothing to do with rain; it has to do with something that happened to you very early on, which for you was a very traumatic, or distressing experience.*

Beth: *How do we find out these things?*

Jean: *Only by asking the question* why am I so angry about rain? *You will get to the point where you will feel the anger coming up, and you can say Ah, this is my conditioning about rain coming up.* Eventually you will laugh at yourself, but now it is still running you.

All of us have been conditioned in this way. We all over-react very unreasonably to issues and experiences in our lives, and it is probably because some element in the current situation will have sufficient connection with an early life-threatening, or identity-threatening incident to trigger off a *stack attack.* It is like pressing the button of a juke box. Something happens and the mind says, *This is a number 28 incident,* and onto the turntable the record goes. It plays right through while you wonder what it is all about. There are probably millions of these records in the stack of the mind. That is why it is important to start becoming educated about what the stack contains. First of all it is important to notice when you are reacting to situations, or, in fact, not reacting at all.

Jean: *Who is thinking* 'That never happens to me. I never have extreme reactions?'

Anthony puts up his hand.

Jean: *That is an extreme reaction. To never have an extreme reaction is an extreme reaction. How Beth copes with it is panic/anger. How you cope with it is to suppress it, cut it off?*

Anthony looks sceptical and shakes his head.

Jean: *You cannot say whether I am right or wrong. Because I say this and it is not in your experience, you assume it is not correct, but it is very hard to truly know because our mechanisms for suppression are so effective.*

It is difficult to communicate with people honestly when most of them (and ourselves) are operating out of unconscious fears. It is also difficult to trust other people not to harm you when you are unknowingly generating expectations of them, which are based on the way you were treated by other people in the past. This presents a major problem when setting up a course which is designed to be supportive and allow people to start to take risks with each other for the first time. If people are going to be encouraged to identify and drop their defences and avoidance-strategies, in order to discover how to embark on their own growth, then they need to be able to rely on the willingness of others to explore their fears and examine their reactions.

First steps to awareness

Using a strategy which I first saw adopted by Werner Erhard and his team, I have put together a number of conditions that I felt would be necessary in order for people to begin to trust each other and feel that they could be safely vulnerable. People are asked to examine these conditions (seventeen in all) and consider whether they are willing to give their word that they will keep to them for the duration of the course. This requirement is the first structured opportunity on the course that people are given, to become aware of their own psychology.

As soon as people are asked to make a public commitment to something there is a strong possibility that their survival mechanisms (or defence strategies) will come into play. It is almost as though the mind cannot tolerate being pinned down, in case an unforeseen and dangerous situation arises. It needs a *get-out clause.* This became very clear as I talked to Annabel, a young person who had had many problems as a teenager and was still in the process of rebelling against her mother (and most other things in life). Her avoidance strategy was *regression.* This involves behaving like a little child and abdicating responsibility for what is happening. In this case the major theme was *you can't make me!*

Annabel: *I can't promise I can participate fully, as I've no idea what we're going to do.*

Jean: *Are you willing to trust that I won't ask you to do anything that is going to be damaging to you?*

Annabel: *Yes, but even so . . .*

Jean: *What will stop you?*

Annabel: *Don't know.*

Jean: *What does it take to trust someone?* (To the group:) *Who trusts me?* (lots of hands are raised).

Participant: *We know you wouldn't do anything to hurt us.*

Annabel: *But it might be something I don't want to do.*

Jean: *And that might be the very thing you need to do.*

Annabel: (Angrily) *But I'm not going to do something I don't want to do!*

Jean: *You will need to relinquish that right in here — give it up. It is going to be very hard for you. I know that because I see me over there — I recognise myself in you.*

Annabel: *We were told, right from the beginning that it's your right to say* no.

Jean: *You must have had a different type of mother from mine! By committing yourself to being here, on the course, you have already said* yes. *It is about doing whatever it takes for you to be in control of your psychology, even when you don't feel like it — particularly when you don't feel like it, because when your mind perceives some threat to its survival it will definitely not feel like doing anything. This will be an opportunity to find out what it is like to make choices in life, rather than by being run by your feelings.*

It was clear that here was someone whose survival-strategy in life was based on regressing, in an attempt to be totally in control. Like a three year old, *No* and *I don't want to* were her favourite words. No one was going to tell her what to do or how to do it. Annabel's background was interesting. She had been brought up almost entirely by her mother, who was a writer. Her mother had very liberal views about raising children and did not believe in imposing her views upon them. The net result was what Winnicott (1971) refers to as 'the omnipotent child'. This particular defence-strategy produces a person who needs to be totally in control at all times. The lack of clear and consistent boundaries early in childhood produces a deep-rooted insecurity which can, according to some experts, (*eg* Coopersmith, 1976) lead to the development of schizophrenia and which frequently leads to 'maladjusted' behaviour.

Many of the pupils at a school for emotionally and behaviourally disturbed girls had similar early childhood experiences. Their parents were intimidated by their temper tantrums and, under these circumstances, children very quickly learn that there is no control unless they impose it. For a child, however, that is far too much responsibility and a high anxiety level is developed.

Cleo also adopts the strategy known as regression. She becomes three years old — the stage at which she seems to have become emotionally arrested. Interestingly enough it was at this point in her development that her younger sister was born. Three year olds toddle — they lisp out their words and demand a lot of attention. Unlike the previous case Cleo relies on getting other people to tell her what to do and look after her, so that she does not have to take any responsibility for her life. She is still doing this at age sixteen. Unless she develops a deeper understanding and awareness of her own psyche, she will still be doing it at forty.

I also had a great *little girl* act around men. I would put my head on one side and use a baby voice to ask them for something, or to get them to do something for me. It worked brilliantly to get my own way, but it was totally self-disempowering, putting me in the category of *helpless female*. I gave it up when I realised that it was costing me my autonomy and self-respect.

This fear that we all carry around with us, of annihilation, of losing our identity, of becoming totally isolated and alone, had created problems for another course participant. Bert attempted to cope with his fear by trying to please everyone, but he was beginning to experience the cost of doing this.

Bert: *I'm happy to do what I'm told. I can't ever do what I really want to do.*

Jean: *What is the price you pay for doing what you are told?*

Bert: *Having to do what I don't want to do. I feel unfulfilled. There is a great sense of loss and lack of worth. I don't feel valuable.* (Crying:) *I don't feel I have a right to say "This is how it should be done". When I'm proved right I still feel bad. I feel stupid and bad.*

Jean: *It is difficult to assert yourself when you feel worthless, and if you don't assert yourself you feel more worthless.*

Bert is trapped in a vicious circle of behaviour that eats into his feelings of self-worth and creates yet more anxiety. He desperately needs to feel that other people find him acceptable and lovable. To avoid the fear of rejection, he spends his life being compliant and trying to please people; in so doing he has to deny his own expression. It is impossible for him to develop a sense of his own power, since he abdicates this all the time, in order to placate and please others. His identity is continuously suppressed and denied and gradually he becomes totally confused about who he is, what he stands for in life and what his life is about. Life becomes meaningless and empty as he waits around for the crumbs from the tables of others. He cannot choose from the menu of life to create his own feast.

Bert then *depresses*. Notice I do not say he *becomes depressed*. This is not a grammatical or typographical error — it is an expression used by William Glasser to emphasise that depression is not an illness. It is an extreme strategy used by the mind to suppress fear, and one that, paradoxically, can lead to self-annihilation. It is the inevitable outcome of the helpless and hopeless position that Bert's survival-strategies have led him to. That which we devise to enable us to survive the terrors of isolation actually leads us further into the pit! It is a tragic human paradox.

The driving force of fear

What is it that Bert hopes to achieve by denying himself his wants and wishes in favour of other people's? In Maslow's terms Bert is attempting to meet his *deficiency needs*. Maslow believes that if certain basic necessities are not met early in life, human beings will continue to seek them throughout their existence, and this is the underlying motive behind the majority of our actions and decisions. Seldom are we conscious of these driving forces, although we frequently find apparently reasonable explanations for what we do. These *rationalisations* mask our true motives and lead us to follow paths which do not serve our best interests, since, as with the example of Bert, we are looking for something we feel we do not have, and are attempting to find it from outside ourselves, rather than expressing our true selves, or our true potential, by finding it within us.

In other words, if I want to experience being loved, I know of no better way — indeed I know of no other way than to give love. Only in giving of yourself will you discover who you are. Only when you discover who you are, will you relate authentically to others, and only when you can do that will you experience being in a true relationship. If you relate *in*authentically with others then no-one is in a relationship with you — they are relating to your *act*. You therefore never experience being loved or liked for who you truly are, and so you are convinced, as are many people who come on my course, that, if you were really yourself with people, no-one would like you or want to know you. In this case the fear that you will not be liked is the road-block that stands between you and the development of deeply intimate and powerful relationships.

When I ran a singles group several years ago, one of the members would never commit herself to attending any social events in advance, in case, to use her own words, she 'got a better offer'. In her case the better offer was an invitation to go out with a male. Her need for love frequently led her to avoid commitment to anything, losing her opportunities to take part in interesting activities, and alienating her female friends.

Other people are not so honest and simply let you down if a better offer comes along. As a result you stop trusting them (perhaps eventually you stop asking them) and at some level of consciousness they feel guilty and bad about themselves, further eroding their own self-esteem and losing the very thing that they were desperate to find — love and friendship.

People let you down not only because something better has turned up, but because they no longer feel like doing what they agreed to do, or because their fear of being inadequate or unpopular is too great for them to handle. Not that they are aware of this, of course, because they have already repressed the fear and found a reasonable excuse for not doing what they had said they would do.

It is this inability to rely on the word of others that creates huge problems for human groups. If we cannot rely on people to keep their word to us in relatively harmless situations, how can we rely on them when we are feeling really defenceless and vulnerable? We cannot and we do not, and as a result of this we feel crushingly alone in times of crisis and despair. Can we trust people not to take advantage, to keep confidences, not to gossip about us, to come when we need them? Oh yes, they said we could, but then they said they would come on holiday with us and, at the last moment, they let us down, because they didn't feel like going — they'd changed their minds.

For me this experience began in childhood when, countless times, I would end up weeping with bitter disappointment because my friend had broken promises to go somewhere or do something with me, and I was then faced with the prospect of an empty and companionless day to fill. Even more painful was the sense of rejection and unlovableness that accompanied this. That was what made it difficult to bear.

As I continue my work with groups, it becomes clear that people have very little awareness of the effect their actions have on others. Much of this stems from a total belief that they are not significant, and it could not possibly make any difference to anyone else whether they are there or not. We are so bound up in our own reality that it is difficult to see it otherwise. I know the devastating effect that other people's unreliability had on me as a child and I see it more clearly when working with groups. If one person leaves, the whole group feels bereft, and it takes time for people to recover their trust. In fact, if one person breaks their word or reneges on the commitment, the integrity of a large part of the group seems to be affected, and people revert back to their self-interested approach to life.

Usually fear is at the bottom of broken promises: fear of losing love, fear of losing control. On a recent course nine people were late coming back to the last session of the second day. I had told them beforehand, clearly, that the session was to be on mothers. When they came back I asked them if any of them wanted to say anything about being late. Dora stood up.

Dora: *Well, I was told I was going to be late, but I decided it (the break) wasn't long enough.*

Jean: *So you feel it was okay to keep everyone waiting and to break your word to people?*

Dora: *Well I thought you would just close the doors and I would just miss a bit. Actually I thought you might be angry with me and throw me out.*

Jean: *So you didn't mind missing the bit on mothers?*

Dora: *Oh, I didn't realise that we were doing mothers.*

Jean: *You didn't hear me say so?*

Dora: *No . . .* (pause) *Perhaps I did hear it but I didn't take it in.*

Jean: *Perhaps you took it in but you didn't want to hear it?*

In fact Dora experienced huge upset during the process on relationships with mothers, and realised that her deliberate lateness beforehand could well have been an unconscious tactic to miss this process, by being kept outside the room until it was finished. Physical avoidance is a good way to ensure that you escape from danger.

People who do not turn up for the course or drop out at some point are clearly operating a physical avoidance strategy. Despite having given their word that they will not drop out, without communicating that they intend to do so, they cannot bring themselves to communicate, and simply stay away. Some of them remain in ignorance as to why they are doing this, rationalising it away by stating that their problems are insignificant compared with *all those poor people in the room*. The course is not *for me* because, they say, *I have no problems, my life is wonderful. I just don't need it.* These are the people that Scott Peck refers to as *People of the Lie* — people who, when tragedy occurs in their lives, look hastily around for a convenient scapegoat to blame for the disaster. After all people who have no problems cannot have their lives going wrong. Someone else must have done it to them!

Such a person is the mother of one young girl who was referred to me recently. This child ended up in psychiatric care and later was referred to special education. The parents were told that she was *handicapped*. They were relieved to hear it. After all, if her genes are defective, then what could they do? When the other daughter began to show signs of becoming first of all disruptive and then positively delinquent in her early teens, the parents put the cause down to the elder daughter's *handicap*, despite the fact that she was not at the same school and was rarely at home.

It is an *evil* act to look for a convenient scapegoat. It disempowers the scapegoat and those doing the scapegoating. It is a lie. It was obvious to all impartial observers that the way the parents treated their children had contributed mightily to their behaviour. Being constantly preoccupied with their business, giving in to the younger daughter's whims, failing to discipline her, giving her privileges that a younger child would not ordinarily expect (such as having the biggest and best bedroom) and drawing hastily on the social services when their children were difficult, instead of dealing with the situation themselves, all contributed to their children feeling unloved. An emotionally distant father, and a mother who put her social engagements before the needs of her offspring, were further factors in this tragic story. When the elder child went into hospital for an operation, the parents went on holiday, and yet, her mother insisted, "She knows I love her!". How — how on earth could anyone know *that* when it seems as though they have been deserted in a situation where they are frightened and in pain?

I am not seeking to condemn these parents, because they too were victims of their parents' ignorance and lack of education about the rearing of children and the psychological processes of human beings. No-one really wants to damage or destroy anyone else, but we certainly will do so, until we can take responsibility for what is happening around us, and stop trying to find something or someone else to blame for it. Unfortunately people are just too afraid of admitting their inadequacy, of owning their mistakes, of recognising their blindness and ignorance.

Other people are too afraid of being judged, of telling the truth about their lives, in case the glittering facade they have built tarnishes and disintegrates before their eyes, and they have nothing but their pain, loneliness and emptiness to share with others. As a rule the step into the abyss of fear is too great, and they retreat into their bunkers, put on their tin helmets and settle down to wait until the war is over and it is safe to come out. They will probably wait a long time and die wondering where their lives went.

Slot Rattling: *or, if one way doesn't work, try the opposite direction*

Sometimes, when a defence-strategy becomes too obviously painful and self-defeating, people realise the folly of what they are doing and look at the alternatives. This often leads them to what George Kelly (1955) calls a *slot rattle.* I love this phrase, as it so aptly describes both the tactic and the futility of it. The slot is a channel or line connecting two ends (or poles) of what Kelly calls a *personal construct.* Without each end of the pole the phenomenon perceived or constructed by the mind cannot exist: for example, 'up' would not have any meaning unless there were a 'down' to fix it in the physical plane. 'Up' only exists in relation to 'down'. In similar ways all other phenomena can only be identified in comparison to their opposites; male/female, right/left, kind/cruel, *etc.* Even items which apparently have no verbal opposite, for example 'red', can only be identified by comparing them with that which they are not, such as 'not red'. (For further information Fransella and Bannister give a useful and lucid account of Kelly's theory.)

Kelly uses the word *construct* because it denotes that in this way we build, or devise, our own unique view of the world — we construct reality. The simple construct, however, is only one level of a complex interconnecting network of meanings that enable us to relate to the world around us.

Exploring these networks of meaning can startlingly illuminate our defence-strategies and give us a clear view of what we are defending, or striving to achieve. The following conversation might serve to illustrate Kelly's explanation of human behaviour and the strategy he calls *slot rattling*:

Clive: *I've had depression for the last two years. Not just ordinary depression, but clinical depression, and I'm not sure I can relate to all of you here. From my point of view you all seem to have pretty mundane sort of problems. I am not belittling your problems, but I find it hard to relate to them.*

Other participants reacted rather angrily to this statement. It is very easy to imagine, when we are locked in misery, that our problems are greater, and even of a different calibre than those of anyone else. It reminded me of a passage in Postman & Weingartner, where a teacher in a very deprived area of New York points to a black child from a particularly deprived background and says to him, "How many legs has a grasshopper got?" The reply comes back, wistfully, "Gee man, I wish I had *your* problems."

One of Clive's problems was that his condition had been labelled in a particular way, *clinical* depression. Now he has an *illness*, rather than just a frame of mind. There is something *wrong* with him. Everyone else on the course is, in his view, *normal*, and he is not. This was a problem for Clive because he immediately felt that something was needed to make him better — something that was different from everyone else. I corrected this view:

Jean: *No it's exactly the same for you, Clive. You just have different avoidance-strategies. Your problem is exactly the same as Dave (another participant). It's fear. I know you find this hard to believe, but it is exactly the same — he is using the avoidance-strategy of denial, and you are using depression.*

The fact that Clive has been labelled *clinically depressed* causes him, and the medical profession, to look for chemical solutions to the state of his mind. He has a *chemical imbalance* in the brain. I do not believe that this is a useful way for the medical profession to construe reality, but suffice it to say that Clive is now depending on chemicals (drugs) to put things right for him. He has also been told he has to change his attitude, or thought patterns. I maintain that this is actually impossible for a human being to do. How can you not think what you think? Most of the time we are not even aware of what we are thinking because it goes on at a subliminal level, so changing what we are thinking is difficult, if not impossible. Attempts to think positively can serve to reinforce the negative thoughts we had in the first place. *No — really, I* am *okay*. Only someone who believes they are *not okay* needs to convince themselves they are okay, and paradoxically this confirms that they are not.

So if we cannot change our thoughts, what can we do?

Jean: (to Clive) *You are unhappy — very unhappy. You feel helpless and stuck in some situation that you cannot get out of, and you have not the courage to get out of it or do anything about it, and you have* depressed. *And you are doing that and you can stop. And I am not saying you are bad and wrong, and you shouldn't be doing it. I am trying to empower you — to let you know that I know that it is an avoidance-strategy that you are using. You will think yourself into a depressed state and when you get aware enough of your thoughts you will be able to watch yourself doing it. You will be able to recognise those thoughts that you use to do it with. Can you tell me some of them now?*

You are lying in bed and you wake up: what is the first thought that comes into your head?

Clive: *It's to do with controlling my thoughts, something like that.*

Jean: *But that is what your whole fear is about. It's about not being in control.*

Your whole thought-pattern is about being in control. What are you afraid will happen if you lose control?

Clive: *I just get very frightened.*

Jean: *Frightened of what?*

Clive: *Frightened of thoughts.*

Jean: *Why are thoughts frightening? What can thoughts do? Let's say you have the thought* I should kill myself. *That is a frightening thought — if you listen to it. If you see that a thought is only a thought and it only has power if you give it power, it is not frightening. You have millions of thoughts and you don't do a thing about most of them. You have a thought* — I wish it wasn't raining.

Clive: *That isn't the position at the moment. At the moment I can't control my thoughts.*

That is a very basic human problem. We cannot control our thoughts.

Try this simple experiment: **stop thinking, right now . . .**

Did you stop? Or were you thinking *See, I've stopped thinking!* Consider those times when you are thinking about something that you no longer want to think about, something embarrassing, or something that happened that did not want to happen. You go over and over the incident in your head, changing it around to the way it should have been, until, eventually, you see that it is futile — and you decide to stop. But you go on, and on.

Certainly meditation can be an effective way to discipline the mind, enabling us to notice when the mind strays onto subjects we do not want to address, and to bring it back to something less destructive or futile. But usually, the more we try to stop thinking, the less we can. So is there anything we can do?

Paradoxically the answer is — *stop trying*. A frequent phrase used in the EST Training was 'What you resist, persists'. It is so with thinking. Clive is resisting his thoughts; he is also making judgements about them. They are *bad*, and he *shouldn't be thinking them*. All this serves to increase the fear that generated the thoughts in the first place. Now he feels more out of control and more helpless than he did to start with. Once we attach significance to our thoughts, they grow in power and can become overwhelming. Most insanity is based on the fact that we consider our thoughts to be real and of incredible significance.

Jean: *You think that what you are thinking is significant. It isn't. It doesn't mean anything. Where are your thoughts coming from?*

Clive: *Most of it is guilt from my past. I don't know how to get rid of it.*

Jean: *You can't.* (To the group:) *Who else has got guilt from the past?* (Lots of hands, including mine). *How do you get rid of it? Notice that you feel guilty and it is just a thought you have. Accept it. Guilt is a thought. You need to feel guilty for some reason.*

At this point I decided to *ladder* Clive's construct of *bad*. Laddering is a technique devised by Hinkle from Kelly's theory, which enables people to make sense of their own apparently nonsensical or self-destructive behaviour. Clive is actually having obsessive thoughts about having harmed someone and is needing to check constantly to see whether he has or not.

Jean: *Why do you need to feel guilty?* (He shakes his head). *It is not immediately obvious to you, but when I ask you a question I want you to explore something. I want you to stand up and explore something. I know you feel conspicuous, but I want you to know that it is okay with everyone, whatever way you are in this room. So you feel guilty because you are bad.*

Clive: *At the moment yes. I haven't always felt bad.*

Jean: *What is the opposite to bad?*

Clive: *Good.*

Jean: *Which would you prefer to be?*

Clive: *Good.*

Jean: *Why do you prefer to be good rather than bad?*

Clive: *Well, because it is the right way to be — I always thought it was the right way to be. As opposed to the wrong way.*

Jean: *Why is it better to be the right way rather than the wrong way?*

Clive: *Don't know.*

Jean: *Look and see. What happens to people who are bad?*

Clive: *They get punished.*

Jean: *What happens to good people?*

Clive: *They are in control.*

Jean: *And why is it good to be in control?*

Clive: *They are in charge of themselves.*

Jean: *As opposed to..?*

Clive: *Being out of control and not in charge of themselves.*

Jean: *And what is good about being in charge of yourself? What can you do that you couldn't do if you were not in control?*

Clive: *Live your life to the best of your ability.*

Jean: *Do the things you want to do.*

Diagrammatically Clive's construct can be laddered in this way:

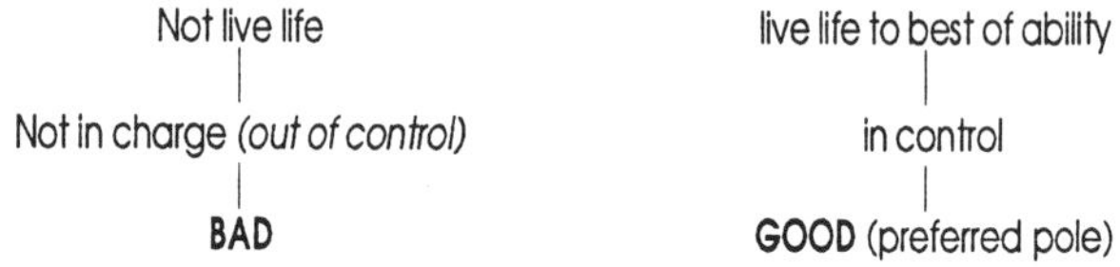

Not live life	live life to best of ability
|	|
Not in charge *(out of control)*	in control
|	|
BAD	**GOOD** (preferred pole)

According to Kelly, construct-systems depend on, or can be traced back to, some very core constructs. These core constructs usually bear a strong resemblance to the deficiency needs and growth needs described by Maslow, and referred to earlier in this chapter. In this case what Clive has arrived at is not, in fact, a deficiency need, but a growth need — the need to be true to himself. This is essential to his well- being. So why doesn't he do it? Why does he not just be good, and then he can do what he wants to do? The answer might become clear as the conversation continues.

Jean: *Can you see any disadvantages of being who you want to be?*

Clive: *Not from where I am standing.*

Jean: (To the group:) *Can anybody else see any disadvantages to that?*

Participant: *You might not be what other people want you to be.*

Jean: *And then what might happen?*

Participant: *They might not like you any more.*

Clive: *Who are you suggesting the other person is?*

Jean: *I'm suggesting that initially it was your parents. If you had been* good *— did as they wanted you to — they might not have allowed you to be who you wanted to be. If you think that being good means obeying your parents (and most children do) then you know actually that being good does not get you what you want. You want desperately to be the person you want to be. You want to live your own life the way you want to live it, and you think if you do that, your life will fall to bits.*

Clive: *No. NO.*

Jean: *That you are going to alienate somebody or get rejected or lose love. And so, if it isn't* good *people who can do what they want to do it must be* bad *people who can do what they want to do, so if you are* bad *it might get you to be able to live your own life. However, if you are* bad, *you are going to lose everything. There is a big part of you that wants to be bad. You are sick of being good. You are tired of it. A large part of you needs to be bad so that you can be who you want to be, except you are terrified of being bad, because that will lose you love. You are stuck in a huge dilemma and you feel completely helpless because there is no way to win in this construct.*

(To the rest of the group:*) He cannot win. Whatever he does he loses.* (To Clive:*) You don't need to be good anymore Clive. Give it up right now. And you don't need to be bad. All you need to do is have courage and be you. And you will not lose love — if you do it wasn't love in the first place. If you lose love just by being yourself, they never loved you, or if they did, then what they are showing you is not love, it is possession and control or domination. It is not love. People who reject you for being true to yourself do not know how to love you. In here you will experience what love is.* (To the group:*) Can any of you identify with him? Put your hand up if you can.* (Lots of hands).

Are you beginning to realise that you are no different from anyone else in here? Some of you are bad guys in here. Some of you chose to be bad. There is one sitting next to you. He chose the other end of the slot. *Sod this — good guys never get to do what they want to do, so I am going to be a bad guy.* But that doesn't work either, does it Dave? (*speaking to another participant*).

Operating in that whole construct of reality does not work. There is another place to come from, but few of us have ever experienced coming from our true selves. The whole purpose of this course is to give people a sense of who they really are outside this invented reality.

Jean: *So when you have all those thoughts, Clive, it is because you want to believe you are bad. You are not bad and you're not good either. You are just a human being and you are probably not cut out for sainthood. Few of us are. I have decided to withdraw my application for sainthood — I don't think I am ready for it.*

It is extremely difficult to see who we really are, or even who we want to be, when we are caught up in our suffering and our fear. It is also difficult to see that we are not the only people suffering; to avoid thinking that there must be something badly wrong with us if we are feeling this way, because everyone knows that if you are normal *then you do not suffer, unless a* real *tragedy has occurred in your life, and then you put a* brave face *on it all and* get over it *as soon as possible. Since we cannot be open about our suffering, we become very alone with it. Whether we are alone with it in the way that Clive is and depress or become ill to justify it, or whether we do what Dave does, refusing to look at the fact that he is suffering, and denying it, jovially, all the way to the pub, it still has the same destructive effect. I ask Dave:*

Jean: (to Dave:*) Is that right?*

Dave: *Rightish — yes.*

Jean: *You deny your suffering with a smile on your face. 'Just get a few pints down you and you'll be all right'. Is that the story?*

Dave: *Something like that.*

e is busy being one of the boys. I had an interesting conversation recently with another man, similar in age to Dave, who had developed the same behaviour. He was beginning to see that this behaviour, of needing to get approval from his peer group by being part of the drinking, joke-telling, woman-ogling culture, was destroying his marriage and impeding his ability to manage his workforce.

Jean: *What is the opposite of being one of the boys?*

Eddy: (after much thought) *A 'stiff'.*

He explained that a 'stiff' is someone who has no fun, is boring, can't enjoy themselves — is, in fact, a 'straight' man.

Jean: *So in that construct of reality you don't have a lot of choice, do you? It is either* be a boring creep *or* be one of the boys?

Eddy: *Dead right.*

Jean: *So it is almost superfluous to ask you why you prefer to be one of the boys as opposed to a stiff?*

Eddy: *(Laughing) I suppose it is really, but you have a* with it *sense of humour and you are at ease in situations.*

Jean: *As opposed to?*

Eddy: *A stiff wouldn't understand humour. You'd have to be a* goody, goody.

Jean: *And what is the advantage of having a good sense of humour?*

Eddy: *You fit in with people. You are comfortable.*

Jean: *So the other type does not fit in?*

Eddy: *No.*

Eddy then told me that he had been sent to a boarding school as a child, and when he came home in the holidays he felt alienated from his peers, because they were telling in jokes, based on things that had happened while he was away. They seemed to have a different set of interests and values to him, so he felt left out and very uncomfortable. He did not fit in. At boarding school he had not felt left out, but this was due to relating to the more rebellious elements in the school — being, in fact, one of the boys.

Eddy found academic work difficult and was afraid of failing. This was partially connected with his having a very dominating and pushing mother who was very anxious for him to succeed. Although he desperately wanted to please her, he was also desperately afraid of displeasing her by failing. He therefore used a well-tried defence-strategy of avoidance — *if I do not try, I cannot fail.* He could not now fit in with those pupils who did apply themselves and work hard, and so had to develop a laid-back and nonchalant image. This was very self-defeating when it came to developing a career. However it was also very hard to give up, because, in his construct-system, the survival of his identity depended on his continuing this way of life.

This pattern did not fit in too well with being a father and a husband either, since it entailed him staying out late at night and often going straight to the pub from work, leaving his wife to cope with all the domestic problems. So his marriage and his career were at risk — the cost was enormous. Although he could see this, there was still a reluctance to give up this image, since the alternative looked so unattractive.

Jean: *But is the alternative really to be so straight-laced and boring? Are there people you know who are not one of the boys who do have fun?*

Eddy: (Thoughtfully) *Yes, I suppose there are.*

Jean: *This is just a construct. It is thoughts that you have about the way life is, and they are not true. You made them up. You need to stop being one of the boys.*

Eddy: *But what do I do instead?*

This is a very real dilemma that faces all of us who recognise that our behaviour is self-defeating. What do we put in its place?

Jean: *You need to live in that question. Don't try to put anything in its place. Just notice that you want to be one of the boys, and then don't do it, and see what happens. Think of something you could do instead that you consider to be really worthwhile.*

This brings me back to the importance and significance of the quotation by George Bernard Shaw with which I opened this book. Unless Eddy has a purpose in his life, considered by himself to be a mighty one, then it will not seem possible for him to give up his destructive survival-strategies, because he will have nothing else to live for. Also he will have nothing to motivate him to cope with the fear that giving it up will generate.

It should, by now, be clear that it is extremely difficult for human beings to become aware of and identify their fear because: (a) in the culture's view of *normality* they are not supposed to have fear, and (b) they don't like it when they get it. And so they flee from it, using the methods described above, and it never gets handled. Herman Hesse addresses this phenomenon in a very powerful passage in his diary in 1918, and he suggests a solution.

> Suffering only hurts because you fear it. Suffering only hurts because you complain about it. It pursues you only because you flee from it. You must not complain, you must not flee, you must not fear. You must love. You know all this yourself, deep within you, that there is a single magic, a single power, a single salvation and a single happiness, and

> that is called loving. Well then, love your suffering. Do not resist it, do not flee from it . . . It is only your aversion that hurts, nothing else.

I remember walking up a mountain in Ireland many years ago with a group of people. It was drizzling and the going was steep and difficult. Most of us were complaining about the fact that our legs were aching and we were out of breath. The man in front, who was a tough, outdoor, athletic type, turned round to me at one point and said, with a totally unsympathetic grin on his face, "It's only pain". I remember feeling furious at his crass insensitivity and his smug superiority. What a stupid remark to make — 'It's only pain!' What an idiot!. And then, "What does he mean — it's only pain? *Only* pain? But surely pain is significant, dangerous?" This was a moment of freeing realisation for me. I did not have to let this pain assume horrendous proportions. I could treat it as what it was — only pain. I did not have to add anything else to the experience, I could simply experience it — and carry on walking.

I could 'love my suffering', but loving it did not need to mean giving in to it, or mollycoddling it, it could simply mean acknowledging it and then allowing my legs to go forward. As I continued up the mountain the physical struggle continued, but the psychological struggle ceased. I was going to the top and it would hurt. It would not be pain-free and easy. I believe that most of us flee from suffering because we do not believe it should be there. Once we understand the inevitability of pain and suffering, it becomes much easier to accept.

3. *Fear choice or growth choice*

The person who gives up his individual self and becomes an automaton, identical with millions of other automatons, need not feel alone and anxious, but the price he pays, however, is high; it is the loss of his self. His neurosis is always to be understood as an attempt, and essentially an unsuccessful one, to solve the conflict between that basic dependency and the quest for freedom.

Erich Fromm (1984), p154.

Do you believe in fairy tales?

If this were a magic book full of spells that could enable you to have, be or do anything you desired, what would you wish for? This is not a flippant question. For me many books have been *magic*, leading me to discover depths and qualities within myself, like finding an Aladdin's cave of treasure.

Perhaps the tale of Aladdin has something to tell us: Aladdin was very frightened when the genie appeared; he wondered what on earth he had unleashed, and at first, he did not know what to ask for. Finding out your inner power is frightening too, especially if you really do not know what you want. For many of us it is too frightening. We do not want to unleash the powerful genie who can bring us our heart's desire and enable us to become the people we are capable of being. We might have to stop being ordinary, insignificant people and become Princes (influential people) who have to take responsibility for what goes on in the world.

I met a 'genie of the lamp' once. He didn't look like one at all. In fact he looked completely harmless and insignificant. This man gave me the opportunity to become the sort of teacher I really wished I could be. I was struggling hard in an open-plan primary school, having come from a job as a physical education teacher in a secondary school. Adjusting to the different age-group, with a very wide spread of ages, and an even wider range of reading ages and IQs was difficult enough, but I was also attempting to put into practice various philosophies that I had come across while studying for an advanced diploma in education and then for a Master's degree.

I knew that I was not catering for the needs of each pupil and that what I was doing was not what I wanted to do, but the question was, what did I want to do? And then there was Mr D on top of all this.

Almost every time he walked past my teaching area he would say, "Oh, that's interesting, why are you doing that with them?". Most of the time I could not give him an answer, or certainly not one that satisfied me — or him! Why was I doing it? Because I had seen it done by someone else, or because it had been done to me. He made me think deeply about my purpose as a teacher, the motives behind my relationship with children, the way I organised my classroom, what I was asking children to do — in fact everything about the work I was doing. It was extremely uncomfortable, but I found him incredibly stimulating and talked to him about what I could be doing, and why, for hours. He taught me more about teaching than anyone else ever has. He also began to teach me about myself. I liked and admired him tremendously, but most of the other teachers disliked and avoided him.

At the time I did not explore the fact that the other teachers found his questioning offensive. I assumed that they found him intrusive. But later I wondered how something which I found such a contribution could appear as such a huge threat to others. Come to think of it, Socrates had the same effect on people in power — and he was eliminated!

Maybe, on reflection, the others were right to be frightened. In order to learn new ways of doing things we have to give up the tried and tested methods, and this, to most of us, is very frightening. Without it, however we cannot grow. I reached a point, half-way through the first term at that school, where I could not do anything without wondering if it was the right thing to do. I had to discard most of my teaching strategies, and almost all of the material I had been using, because I could not, in educational terms, justify its use. I felt completely adrift and very inadequate. The bonus was that I created something quite unique and extremely effective, that eventually led to my securing a lectureship in teacher education. Had I been more aware of what was happening to me at the time, and what all the fear and feelings of panic were rooted in, I might have found this experience a little less traumatic — but that's another story!

That's another story is a phrase which is used consistently in Michael Ende's (1985) brilliant children's book, *The Never-ending Story*. My life has been, up to now, an adventure, in the course of which new vistas and different worlds of experience have opened up for me. It will be, I hope, a never-ending story of many possibilities. Michael Ende's novel was, for me, a brilliant allegory of the development of human potential. It also contains a moral, which is something like, *make sure that which you wish for is based on pure motives and not on the needs of your ego, otherwise you will come to a sticky end*. Such was almost the fate of Balthazar Bastion Bux, the hero of the tale.

The Never-ending Story of Abraham Maslow

Bastion is an unattractive, fat little boy — a classic target for being bullied and tormented by his school-mates. His mother had died, and his father, overcome by the loss, had become very remote and cold with Bastion, who now had no-one with whom to share his misery, loneliness and fear. One day he escaped from his tormentors into a bookshop, and there picks up a strange and magic book which enables him to escape into a world of fantasy — Fantastica. How often I did that as a child! He becomes the Messiah that the people of Fantastica have been waiting for, to save them from an evil presence that is destroying their country. He basks in their love and admiration and makes an intimate friend of one of the natives.

Soon, however, he loses sight of his purpose (to save Fantastica and its ruler, the Childlike Empress, from death and destruction), and develops a lust for power which drives him to destroy those who question him. He loses all trust in his friend, whom he then attempts to kill. Only when he loses almost all he has gained, and all he had, including the memory of who he was, does he begin to realise that what he really wants is to give his father the love that he so desperately needs, and to go home again and face up to reality.

It is a brilliant story which, for me, illustrated the theory of another man who has greatly influenced me in my journey through life, Abraham Maslow. I certainly would not have found reading *The Never-ending Story* such a powerful experience had I not been familiar with Maslow's work.

Had Maslow been interpreting Bastion's behaviour he would have said that his journey into Fantastica arose from a longing to find some meaning in life, and to gratify his basic psychological needs, since these had not been, and were not being, met by his current circumstances.

At the beginning of his journeys in Fantastica, whatever Bastion created in his mind manifested itself in reality. He found this disconcerting at first, but soon began to enjoy his control over his environment, thereby satisfying his safety-needs, his needs for security, stability, dependency, freedom from fear, anxiety and chaos[2].

Bastion discovered a 'luck dragon', who could take him wherever he wished, and extract him from any kind of danger, and an amulet that protected him and gave him great power. He passed laws and created order out of chaos. Or, as Maslow would say, he satisfied his need for 'structure, law and order, limits, strength in the protector, and so on'[3].

[2]Maslow, (1987), p181.
[3]*ibid*, p18.

He then realised he was deeply and unconditionally loved by the ruler of Fantastica, (who was wasting away, as the evil 'nothing', which people kept falling into and disappearing, crept across the land), and by his friend, Atreyu. He then began to lust for more and more status and power, what Maslow refers to as the *esteem-needs*:

> the desire for strength, achievement, mastery and competence, confidence in the face of the world, and independence and freedom. Second we have . . . the desire for reputation or prestige, status, fame and glory, dominance, recognition, attention, importance, dignity or appreciation.

Of these needs, however, it appeared he could never have enough — but that's another story!

Maslow believes (as stated in Chapter 2) that most human beings spend their lives attempting to gratify basic physiological and psychological needs. He states that these needs are organised hierarchically — that is, that lower-level needs must be gratified before higher-order needs emerge. The theory is usually represented in the form of a pyramid. (see fig 2). If some of these needs are lacking within a family environment, then the children will suffer from this experience and display behaviour which is designed to produce the fulfilment of these needs.

The different strategies people develop in order to fulfil these needs are not necessarily the same — which might explain why children from the same family can be extremely different from each other. Very often one child is very *good* and another very *bad*, but bad and good are both strategies developed to fulfil the needs in which these children are deficient. The younger sibling will often adopt the reverse strategy to the older child, since they are intuitively aware that their sibling's strategy has been

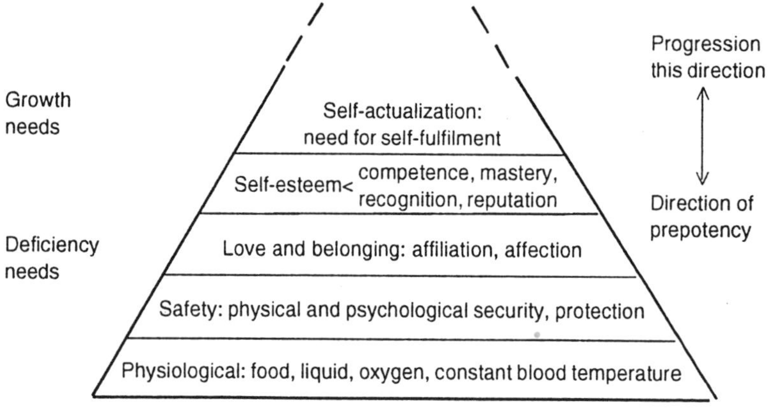

Figure 2 Taken from Child, 1986

ineffective in providing what they want. So 'if X doesn't work, try Y', says the scientist in the mind. If the elder child tried being bad then the younger will try out being good, and vice versa. This could explain the *black sheep of the family* syndrome.

Frequently, however, children raised in a similar environment do develop the same strategies in order to fulfil their basic needs. Until I read Abraham Maslow's theory I was tempted to believe, as do many teachers, that children who were *disruptive* or *disaffected* were simply *naughty* children who had *defective* personalities, or that they were *acting out* their anger at being treated badly or ineptly by parents. Now I realise that their behaviour might be simply an attempt to solve a problem — that of how to feel safe, wanted and respected.

These children make it obvious that something is wrong. In most human beings it is not so obvious, largely because we see the striving for the fulfilment of deficiency-needs as *normal*. Indeed the culture we live in probably would not survive economically if people were not lacking in these basic needs! If you want to know what I mean, look carefully at the advertisements on television. Do they not attempt to persuade you that if only you used the right aftershave or talcum powder, then you would get love? Do they not tempt you with status and power if you buy the right car? Do they not guarantee you the love of your children if you use the correct washing-up liquid? Advertisers know all about deficiency-needs, and they try to persuade you that, if you buy their product, your dreams will come true!

Your every wish is my command: *unconscious commitments and your 'fairy godmother'*

Let me be clear though, that for most of us all of this goes on at an unconscious level. The majority of us are quite unaware that we have these needs, or that our lives are devoted to their gratification. How would we know? Is self-actualisation part of the National Curriculum at school? Consequently our behaviour is often inconsistent with our stated intentions, since the gratification of these needs overrides any conscious commitments to our goals and aspirations.

According to Maslow we move up the pyramid or hierarchy gradually — gratification of one level of need will release us to attend to the gratification of another level. If the need is not met then we are stuck and cannot grow. This theory is not popular with most academics: I guess because most of them are operating at the level of esteem-needs and striving for recognition. Maybe that is what I am doing in writing this book; except that I know that fame, in itself, is empty and futile. Marilyn Monroe obviously discovered that. So many academics are stuck in chasing more prestige and further recognition, and they never have enough of it. The same is true of other 'successful' people.

Many of the people who attend my courses do so because they feel stuck in some area of their lives. Perhaps they are stuck in a damaging relationship or in a dead-end job. Telling the truth about this is a first step to changing the situation but another vital step is to become aware of what is keeping us in that situation, when we know that we should get out.

In order to enable people to uncover the unconscious commitment that is stopping them from progressing, or a way of getting out of self-defeating situations, the following exercise has been devised. It is more effective to do this with a partner (and it's more fun), but you can do it by questioning yourself and writing the answers down:

If you had a fairy godmother and could ask her for three wishes that could enable you to live your life exactly the way you want to, what would they be? Write them down.

It is not a good idea to ask for something that is not a human possibility (*eg* 'I'd like to be able to fly'). It is also rather a waste of a wish to ask to win the football pools, although making a lot of money would be a legitimate request, if you think that would make a significant difference to your life.

Take the first wish off the list of three and state it aloud.
Now ask yourself, or get your partner to ask you: What will stop that happening?
Reply to that.
(There is a danger that really smart people will say *me*. Well — don't. Obviously it is probably you, but if you know that, then look and see what is it about you that will stop it happening).
Now ask, What else will stop that happening?
Keep asking this question until you feel you have got to the bottom of the problem.
Then take another of your wishes off the list and repeat the process.

These are some of the responses that course participants came up with:

Sandra: *I'd like to be successful at work, but what is stopping me is fear of rejection* (affiliation-needs).

Jenny: *I want to change my job, but I'm afraid to, in case I don't make a success of the next one, and I lose everything* (security-needs).

Doug: *If I go and try it, and fail, it will be my responsibility. 'Yes, me, the one who didn't do it. I tried and didn't get there'* (self-esteem-needs).

Jane: *I want to get a degree but I am afraid of failure.*

Jean: *Fear of failure: is that really what it is about?*

Jane: *Fear of other people's judgements if I fail* (esteem-needs)

Eddy: *I want to have a real relationship with people I go down to the pub with. My fear is of approaching people, fear of not being able to communicate with these kind of people. Basically fear of rejection* (affiliation-needs).

The paradox here is that, in order not to lose love, Eddy does not risk expanding his relationships, and so misses the opportunity to become affiliated with a group from fear that he will lose everything. People do not want to end up like the dog with the bone, in Aesop's fable, who sees what he thinks is a bigger bone reflected in the water and lets go of the one he has got, only to find that the other was an illusion and he ends up with nothing.

Perhaps we have taken the moral of this tale too much to heart; or perhaps it fits in with the fear surrounding our deficiency-needs. Of course we must recognise that it is possible to chase illusions, and it is not in our interests to do so. We need to be able to distinguish between illusion and reality. Not easy when you have a mind! It is usually much easier to see when someone else is chasing an illusion. It was not difficult to see this in Lydia's case:

Lydia: *I want to get out of this relationship. I wish I could make up my mind and then stick to it. That was my wish, but the mind says, 'you won't survive this way', and then I am back in the trap again* (security-needs). *But then I say to myself, 'perhaps I do love him'.*

This is a classic example of rationalisation on the part of this woman, who was being consistently physically and psychologically abused by her husband. How many times have I heard, 'But I love him', as the reason for someone staying in such a relationship. It brings up the whole question of *love* — that will be addressed in a later chapter.

Even if this person does love her husband, she certainly does not feel loved by him — she feels invalidated and demeaned. So we see someone who sacrifices her love-needs in order to satisfy her security-needs, despite the fact that, at times, her life is threatened. Or it could be that this is the only expression of love she recognises, having been beaten and abused by her father — so is it better than the lack of love she might have if she leaves?

The conversation with Lydia is very useful since her stated intention is to get out of the relationship, but her unconscious commitment is to staying in it. No wonder she stays! Only when her fear of staying outweighs her fear of leaving will she leave, and that has not happened, even though she can see that her life is actually at risk. One of the problems for her was that she was convinced her husband would kill her if she did leave, so staying looked like the lesser of two evils.

If she did pluck up courage and risk leaving she would probably, like many other women in this predicament, end up finding another destructive relationship, since she will be operating out of the same unconscious commitments, and so her life will not change (see Robin Norwood, 1986, for further reading on this issue). However, as my conversation with Lydia progressed it took a direction which eventually did enable her to find the courage to leave her husband, and find a home and a job for herself several months after completing the course:

Lydia: (Still talking about her relationship) *I don't think I have ever taken responsibility for my own life.*

Jean: *It's a lack of belief in yourself. You seem to need to keep putting yourself through this emotional mill! It provides you with tremendous stimulation, and it keeps you safe from risk. You sacrifice all your esteem-needs and love-needs for security-needs. You do not know where you are going. If you get away from him, what are you going to put into your life?*

Lydia could not really answer this question. When we feel worthless and unlovable it is not even worth addressing it. That is a common problem with many human beings. Their lives are empty and meaningless because they do not, at a deep level, feel they are worthy of a life that means something, or are capable of having one. They have not, they think, got what it takes.

Self-actualisation

Maslow's theory occupies an important place at the beginning of the *Emergence* course I run: according to Maslow, it is the fact that human beings spend their lives operating at the level of their deficiency-needs that limits the exploration of their true potential. Our full capabilities can only be expressed when we operate from the top level of the triangle: the level of growth-needs or self-actualisation. At this stage the human being is free to explore, extend themselves, take risks, love unconditionally, drop their defences, be truly intimate, or experience ecstasy:

> My people (*self-actualised people*) report that they can be themselves without feeling that there are demands or expectations upon them; they can feel psychologically (as well as physiologically) naked, and still feel loved, wanted and secure. These conclusions are further supported by the greater freedom of hostility- and anger-expression in our subjects, as well as in their lowered needs for conventional politeness with each other . . . The fact is that self-actualising people are simultaneously the most individualistic *and* the most altruistic and social and loving of all human beings [Maslow, 1987].

When describing self-actualised people, Maslow warns that it is easy to confuse their behaviour with that of someone who is entirely selfish and self-interested. This is the conclusion some of my clients reach. In fact, it is just the reverse: people who are operating out of deficiency-needs are selfish, although it might not appear to be so — for instance, in order to get love, they appear to be extremely self-sacrificing and helpful. It is, of course, simply a means to an end, that they are not aware of attempting to attain. Furthermore, if they were to aspire to becoming self-actualised they would realise that they would have to stop living their lives to please other people — which would, in their expectations, lose them love. Maslow maintains there is a distinct difference between the self-interest of the person operating at the lower levels of the hierarchy and those who have transcended those needs.

I have noticed that when I insist on taking time to do those tasks I have set myself, which to me hold great meaning and satisfaction, I am far more likely and willing to support and serve those whom I am close to. Since I have devoted a lot of time to writing and to my other work, and this is producing results, I have much more empathy and compassion for Tim, my husband, and for the other people around me. The way I talk to them is different: I am more patient and observant, much less critical. This is because I am no longer carrying resentment about my not doing what I feel I must do for my own and others' growth. When I give in to the demands or needs of others and martyr myself I am *not* compassionate — just the reverse! So, if I act as a martyr, I am doing things for them, but I am not really with them, since my heart is not in it.

Self-actualised people (those who no longer experience the need for love, security and status, etc) are, Maslow says, independent of their environment, and this means:

> . . . a relative stability in the face of hard knocks, blows, deprivations, frustrations and the like. These people can maintain a relative serenity in the midst of circumstances that would drive other people to suicide; they have also been described as *self-contained*.

Wouldn't we all like to be less tossed about the circumstances of life? Is not this true control?

As soon as many of my students hear about Maslow's theory I can see them thinking 'Well, I don't want to be one of those people who is always at the effect of their deficiency-needs. I want to be self-actualised, that is a much more superior way to be'. The next question, of course, is *how do I get there*? There is no simple answer to this, unless it is the answer that Maslow comes up with, which is the *transcendence of the ego*. This does not really mean much to most of us anyway. And, although the answer might be simple, the execution of it is not!

The question usually arises from the ego-state anyway, since the mind sees the transcendence of the ego (or deficiency-needs) as a more effective way of meeting the deficiency-needs, and of being really somebody. Someone self-actualised really is in control, and, since they are part of only 4-6% of the population (Maslow's estimate), then they would be very *superior* to most other people. Of course this type of thinking would be very alien to someone who was self-actualised. It is, in Alan Watts' terms, the ego 'trying to pull itself up by its own bootstraps'.

Maslow stresses that it is not *inferior* to be operating at the level of deficiency-needs, since these needs are legitimate and fruitful. Indeed he believes they could, and should, be regarded as basic human rights, since the fulfilment of them is necessary in order to avoid illness and pathology. For instance, Maslow points out that deficiency in security-needs can be at the bottom of obsessional/compulsive behaviour which, he says, is a frantic attempt to order and stabilise the world so that 'no unmanageable and unexpected or unfamiliar dangers appear'.

This was certainly true of Bill, who developed such behaviour when his marriage broke down. He could not leave a room without switching the light on and off several times. His marriage obviously gave him feelings of security, but he was not secure within himself. This had presumably been caused by the fact that he was sent away to school as a young child, and had never recovered from the total loss of safety that this invoked. He was subjected to cruel and harsh treatment from teachers and peers — on several occasions being suspended from a window high up in the building, and dangled over a terrifying drop! The departure of his wife no doubt invoked the emotional memories of that other time of perceived abandonment, with its consequent horrific experiences, and his mind tried desperately to hold on to some semblance of security and stability.

Identifying where we are operating from in the hierarchy: *some apparent contradictions*

As I said earlier, the ego is the mechanism for survival of the organism. In order to operate at the growth level of Maslow's hierarchy this must be transcended. This does not mean, however that we must simply suppress our basic needs, pretend they do not exist. This can sometimes give the impression that the person is indeed self-actualised, but it might not necessarily be so. The following is a conversation I had with one of the participants on my course. At first he sounds as though he is operating at the growth level of the pyramid, but something does not sound quite right:

Steve: *I don't feel I need love and belonging. I feel there is an obligation to have it, and I suppress that need.*

Jean: *You could be describing my brother. He had a very high opinion of himself and he didn't need other people. But when he did this course the first thing he said was, 'In all my life no-one has ever really appreciated me'.*

Steve: *I have the substitution of appreciation in that I am appreciated for my career, for what I do. And maybe I'm not appreciated, but I feel that I am. I don't feel lonely.*

Jean: *Why should you — you don't feel anything, do you?*

Steve: *Yes I feel compassion. I find I feel compassion for a group or maybe for an individual. I felt compassion for the people talking today.*

Jean: *How did that feel?*

Steve: *Sadness, so painful, how could people do such things to people? How could they be so unthinking? Obviously people were not thinking 'let's be cruel'. How can they go through and feel that? And not see what damage they are doing?*

Jean: *Do you feel emotional pain yourself?*

Steve: *No I can't feel . . .*

Jean: *No, you cut yourself off from it. You are going to make sure you never put yourself in a position where anyone could get at you and hurt you. Do you live on your own?*

Steve: *Yes, and all my pleasures are solitary ones.*

Jean: *Do you know what* lonely *feels like?*

Steve: *No.*

Jean: *No. Because you never felt it?*

Steve: *I don't feel a need to have people. I feel an irritation. If people come to stay, I can take about two days and then they have to go. They disrupt my life.*

Jean: *In what way?*

Steve: *I'm doing what I want to do. If you live on your own you become self-obsessed. I can indulge their every whim for a while, and then I get fed up.*

This sounds very much as if, according to Maslow's criteria, Steve is a self-actualising person. And yet I somehow felt that it was not so in his case. So he enjoyed being solitary (a condition of self-actualised people), and he did not need love. Was he really choosing to be solitary, or was this an expression of a lower-level deficiency need? The conversation continued:

Jean: *If you get into a relationship, you think you will have to give up doing what you want to do?*

Steve: *Definitely. Give up everything.*

This was the clue! The self-actualised person would not be afraid of having to give up everything in a relationship. They would be immune to manipulation. Their need for growth would over-ride their need for approval and for security in relationship. They would have sufficient belief in themselves and their capacity to generate other relationships to eliminate the need to defend themselves from intimacy with others.

> They (*self-actualised people*) have the power to love and the ability to be loved . . . *They* at least know how to love, and can do so freely and easily without getting wound up in conflicts or threats or inhibitions. (Maslow, p151.)

There might be several reasons why Steve is avoiding relationships: one might be that, in this way, he gets to be totally in control of his environment. He can do exactly what he wants to do (*safety-needs*). A self-actualised person would know that he could do that anyway. Steve might also be protecting his self-esteem:

Jean: *So living on your own, you can be totally in control. You are living out of security-needs, because your need to be in control is your dominant motivation.*

Steve: *I think so. Self-esteem is also very important. I am confused by the way the triangle is organised.*

Jean: *It's very easy to esteem yourself when you are the only person whose opinion you rely on. It is probably what Coopersmith would call a* defensively-high self-esteem. *You have to believe in yourself because all you have is you. You have to be okay, otherwise you have nothing.*

Fromm (1984) may provide some insights into Steve's confusion about the way the triangle is organised when he says:

> Other mechanisms of escape are withdrawal from the world, so completely that it loses its threat, and the inflation of oneself to such an extent that the world itself becomes small in comparison.

I can see now that this was precisely how my brother coped with his fear of life. He withdrew into himself completely and developed the utmost contempt for people. Happily, two years before he died, he realised what he was doing, and was able to experience love for others and for himself, and develop a true sense of his own worth.

Steve had an alternative explanation. He felt he had simply given up the need for love, having been satiated with it as a child. Wouldn't life be simple if we could?

Steve: *I would say I have stopped wanting to be loved.*

Jean: *Not out of choice though. You haven't really stopped needing to be loved. But I think you are suppressing your need for love.*

Steve: *You could be right. I came on the course because friends talked me into it. I'm safe already, I feel. The thing I am missing . . . I feel I am missing . . . is a relationship.*

Jean: *You may say that your friends talked you into coming here, but I think there is something in you crying out to be recognised, to be expressed. I think you have a capacity to love that is not being expressed. Is that true?*

Steve: *Yes, I think I could love — it's the needing of love that comes back.*

Jean: *You don't love because you would be in a position where love would come back to you, and you can't handle it.*

This seems to illustrate Maslow's comments about people who appear to have skipped one of the levels in the hierarchy. When we are satiated with love, or security, we quickly underestimate the necessity for them, and so concentrate on the attainment of higher-level needs (in Steve's case, self-esteem). After a sustained period of deprivation of that which we once had in abundance, the lower-order need re-emerges.

I can see this clearly in myself when I decide to go on a diet. Normally I am not obsessed by food, or the need for it — I simply eat when I am hungry, and I eat what I like. As soon as I feel that my hunger is in danger of not being appeased, however, because I am now *dieting*, I am hungry all the time and I want to eat incessantly, which is defeating the object of the exercise. Perhaps that is one of the reasons that diets don't work!

This movement up and down the hierarchy seems to explain Mark's behaviour — and perhaps demonstrates why he has had two failed marriages. He fluctuates between trying to please his wife, by paying more attention to his responsibilities as a husband and father, and spending his time at the rugby club, thereby meeting his esteem-needs:

Mark: *My story relates around the rugby club. I am one of the few white-collar workers that play there, and they said 'You must be earning a packet!'. Eventually they were saying, 'This is one of the wealthiest men in town . . . ' That must have boosted my self esteem.*

Jean: *So must the fact that you are captain of the team. And you have got a very strong attachment to that. It is very important to you?*

Mark: *Yes.*

Jean: *Do you know what it costs you to have that attachment to that group?*

Mark: *It probably costs me my relationship with my wife and my kid, and I'm perhaps too committed to the rugby club. I was going to retire, but the lads said, 'Please come back', and I went back.*

Jean: *Why?*

Mark: *Because it gave me a hell of a lot. I enjoy the camaraderie down at the club.*

Jean: *You wouldn't risk your wife and child for that. What is it? I enjoy eating Mars Bars, and people enjoy drinking alcohol and do it until their liver rots and their brains cease to function properly. So you don't make such sacrifices just because you enjoy it. Obviously there is something more to it.*

There are two possible interpretations of this conversation. One is that Mark is concentrating on esteem-needs, feeling that the love-needs are catered for. Threat to the love need — his wife saying she will leave — sends him back down the hierarchy again. Or could it be that the continuity of the rugby club offers him more security than the married state, because this has broken down twice before? Whatever it is, Mark needs to give up his involvement in the deficiency-need game before it destroys yet another marriage and seriously affects his son's development. Our unconscious commitments and actions do have effects on other people as well as ourselves.

I became aware very recently that I was employing a strategy to encourage my husband's growth, which was actually pushing him back down the hierarchy of needs, and so producing the opposite result to that which I intended. On several occasions, when I see that he cannot, or dare not, pursue his own life and do what he needs to do in order to become self-actualised, I have threatened to leave him. Now this is a genuine threat, since when he is intent on pleasing everyone and daren't say *No*, I lose all respect for him and fall into the habit I learned so well from my mother — that of despising men.

The fear that I will leave him can throw Tim out of his need for love and approval, back into his need for security — for our relationship represents security to him. This means that he lets go of the need to please everyone else and tries harder to do what I ask of him.

Of course this strategy of mine does not work. I was not even conscious that I was doing this. It was quite instinctive. It does not work because it is still manipulating Tim via his deficiency-needs, merely ensuring that he stays dependent on them. What would work, I am sure, would be to offer Tim unconditional love and acceptance so that he would begin to love and accept himself without having to prove to himself (and everyone else) that he was worth it. I find that very difficult. In fact, becoming self-actualised *is* very difficult. It demands, as Krishnamurti (1982) puts it, *constant vigilance*. So why bother?

Living out of deficiency-needs: *the pay-off and the cost*

Often when people realise that there might be effort involved in evolving, they insist that they like being the way they are. Their lives are okay. They are quite happy. Like Steve, they cannot really see the point in emerging from their safe bunkers and joining in the war.

If the lack of love in Steve's life was due to him having been satiated at an earlier stage, and therefore taking it for granted or devaluing it, this can be, according to Maslow, a *form of pathology*. Presumably, for a human being to mock or devalue what it depends on for growth is a form of psychological sickness. However, it might be tempting for Steve to stay in his bunker and not risk emerging. He had managed so far without being self-actualised and was, in the eyes of the world, a successful person. Why spoil a good thing?

> To be able to recognise one's own needs (*ie* to know what one really wants) is a considerable psychological achievement. This is doubly true for the higher needs.
>
> (Maslow, p57)

Many people, in fact, balk at the idea of living out of growth-needs, especially when they realise that it can be a painful process. Furthermore it is a journey that has to be based on faith — a bit like those voyagers who first set out to sail around what they believed to be a flat earth. They had no way of knowing when, or if, they would fall off the edge and into nothingness.

Transcending the fear of the unknown and setting off led these early explorers to whole new worlds they never could have dreamed existed. The journey to self-realisation is very similar. It requires faith in there being something available to us which is beyond our current experience, and yet is well worth the risks involved in getting to it. It might even require falling into *nothingness* (as Val Blomfield's poem implied). So it is easier for people to see the benefits of living at the level of deficiency-needs — they do get to feel safe, comfortable, loved and so on — than it is for them to see what they would gain from becoming self-actualised. Similarly it can be easy to see the problems of becoming self-actualised, while the benefits are more obscure.

For people who have been seriously deprived of their basic needs in early childhood, the growth experience can be extremely painful, and I am sure that we all know this at some level of our consciousness. That is, I think, why many people want to avoid growth. Doing so, however can have serious consequences.

Ruth was a student who came to me one day in great distress. At first she found it difficult to speak. Her manner was strange, I thought. She looked at me almost hostilely, as if she was expecting a fight. Her face was covered in dark red blotches and she was fighting back tears. In fact she was terrified of my rejecting her, or not wanting to listen to what she had to say. Ruth struggled to tell me that she was finding my course difficult — a university course on pupil-disaffection. I had been talking about Maslow's theory and the views of Carl Rogers, and how important it was for teachers to be authentic in their relationships with pupils. I spoke about the necessity to transcend our ego-needs if we were to avoid damaging other people. She felt that, if she were to be authentic, no-one would want to know her.

Ruth had an excellent student-teaching record. She was a first class student, she had a very attractive fiancé who had a good job, and she was popular with her fellow students. I could not believe that this distressed, painfully embarrassed, inarticulate girl was the person I had observed in the lecture sessions. She had come across then as a lively-minded and interested person who was very committed to teaching. She managed to say that she had to see someone and talk to someone, otherwise she felt she would snap. She felt unreal, unlovable and that she did not know how much longer she could keep her *act* together. She was getting married in the summer and she wanted to have children, but did not feel she was fit to be a parent, or a wife, because she felt so empty, so false. She lived in fear of people finding out what a horrible, unconfident and *nothing* person was really there. Her life, she felt, was *plastic* and meaningless. She frequently felt suicidal.

My first instinct, especially since she said she felt suicidal, was to advise Ruth to see the university counselling service — my own instinct for survival with the university authorities came to the fore, because I did not want to be blamed if she did kill herself! That was me taking the *fear choice*. I also had a very busy schedule and knew that working with Ruth would take a lot of time. But I saw it had to be me. I had something to learn and Ruth offered me the gift of learning it. We have worked together for 1½ years now. It has been a painful, sometimes frightening and turbulent, but loving and growing relationship. I might have been Ruth's guide and therapist, but she has been my teacher, and we have both learned a great deal about love and trust in the process.

The secret that Ruth found it so hard to reveal was that she had been sexually abused by her father as a small child. At the time she came to see me she was not 100% sure if this was the case. Certain incidents she could not get out of her mind could only add up to this conclusion. Ruth knew that she had been deeply damaged by something so severely that, to put it in her own words, she felt 'so filthy, disgusting, depraved and destroyed'. Ruth knew that she had to find out exactly why she felt so annihilated. Why had her mother been so consistently cold, rejecting and cruel to her, eventually locking her out of her home one Christmas and selling all her possessions to a charity shop? Was she really such an evil person? What had she done to deserve this? Ruth now knows what happened that almost destroyed her will-to-live and her ability to feel loved and connected with people. She knew that it was vital that she did know, and, for reasons that I will explain later, why others should know too. At her request, therefore, we share this with you.

I took Ruth back to that incident she could remember when she was four years old. She recalled lying on her bed in terror, covered in blood, her genitals having been ripped apart in the act of rape committed by her father. She whimpered at first and then, as her fear grew, her cries for her mother became louder. Her mother came into the room, angry at having been disturbed, but instantly horrified at the sight of her young child, haemorrhaging profusely. She picked her up, and then *threw her down* back onto the bed and rushed out of the room. From that moment Ruth knew that she was totally alone, and that she had done something terribly wrong.

She was taken to hospital and kept there for 'a long time'. She recalled being happy in the hospital. People were nice and gentle with her. A neighbour took her home, and from that point on she cannot remember her mother, or many other people, being nice and gentle with her again. Her mother never kissed her, hugged her, or had any physical contact with her, over and above what was necessary. She became the family scapegoat. Nothing she could do ever pleased her mother. Her father had left home when she got back, and her mother divorced him. However her father had regular monthly access to her and her brother and sister, and despite her constant pleas to be left at home and not to see him, she was made to go.

You may think that this would be sufficient to cause Ruth some problems in her life, but there was much more. Eventually Ruth recalled many incidents of sexual abuse by her father from the age of approximately nine months onwards. The final one had been merely the tip of the iceberg. She realised, during a recent asthma attack, that her recurring illness had been caused by having to perform *fellatio* with her father when she was very tiny.

When she was telling me this she wanted to cry, but was too afraid to do so. If as a child she tried to shout or cry while her father was assaulting her, he would only push his penis further down her throat to shut her up, and making it impossible for her to breathe, hence the asthma attacks in later life. What a lesson for a small child to learn! *If you cry you get severely punished. Look happy about something that is actually threatening your life, or it will get worse!*

Unlocking all these horrifying memories was terrifying for Ruth and agonising and frightening for me. It was almost too much to bear, especially when she was reliving the agony and pain it caused her. She was also terrified that I, like her mother, would not be able to cope with it, and she would be thrown aside, yet again.

Her greatest fear, however, I will let her state for herself:

I might have found it bloody difficult to live my act *with all that agony and pain inside of me, but I was my act — successful in my degree, and at teaching, popular, sewn up. That is why the growth-choice is so terrifyingly difficult — to risk letting go and shattering everything. 'What if I couldn't function?' was one of my biggest fears. I needed to strive hard, to suppress the pain and earn some love and recognition — yes — but what if, after I let the pain out, there was no motivation left?*

Her other major fear related to her relationship with me and with other people.

Would you, could you still find it possible to love me, having done all of the things I had done — would anyone in the world still love me? Those sessions with you have released the most dark and evil experiences of my life — that was, and is, a huge risk to take, especially since I was so totally rejected last time.

So why did Ruth take the growth-choice, and what has she gained from taking that huge risk? She has realised, after many months of work, that she was not to blame for what happened; that she is not dirty and disgusting. I know that everyone else can see that, and would never dream of thinking it so anyway, but the child cannot. The child cannot see the parent as evil. The parent is the source of safety and love. If they punish you, shout, or withdraw their love, you must be to blame, not them.

You cannot afford to reject your parents and you cannot afford to have them reject you. Therefore you do what you can to please them, even if it is killing you. I cannot really do justice to the whole issue of child abuse here — in the next chapter I will be making it clear, as does Alice Miller's writing, that it does not always take such obvious forms, and that most of us suffer abuse in one form or another. That is why we feel deficient in the area of basic needs.

The rejection of Ruth by her mother, and the other negative messages she received throughout her childhood from her were, in some ways, far more damaging than the sexual abuse she suffered from her father. The denial — which is still going on — that anything wrong had occurred leaves the child unable to work out the emotional distress and psychological damage which has been caused. It is the same for many more of us and, like Ruth, we have buried our knowledge deep in our unconscious, of the various types and degrees of abuse we suffered, because the pain of knowing it, and the fear that we will be *found out* is too great.

The risk Ruth took in taking the growth choice was and is painful, but it is paying off. She is able now to express anger with people when she needs to and to assert herself. She is beginning to trust people and she has realised that she was innocent and was vilely defiled. From here the seeds of love and self-respect are beginning to take root, and death does not look like the only viable option. She is starting to acknowledge the courage and tenacity it took her to keep on going and stay alive. She is recognising her bravery and her capacity to suffer and still function capably.

It is dawning on her that she is a beautiful and attractive person who deserves love and respect, and she has found the courage to choose an elegant, yet pretty, wedding dress, despite residual thoughts that one like that is too good for her! She is forming an authentic and powerful relationship with her colleagues and her pupils, and she feels *alive*, not dead, inside. She has taught me not to be afraid of reaching in to the dark recesses of the mind and sharing the deepest agony of human experience. I have walked hand-in-hand with someone through a living nightmare of brutality and degradation. She has given me yet another lesson in love and commitment.

Ruth wanted me to write this and was angry at my first attempt. I made it too clinical, too easy for people to miss the horror that child abuse is. We are too familiar with the expression to be in touch with what it really denotes. My first draft in no way indicated the courage it had taken her to leap into the abyss, nor would it have communicated to others why it was necessary to take that leap, despite her fears.

She has survived the abyss. She is growing and learning to laugh and have joy in her life. She is becoming *real*. She wants to make this opportunity available to every human being. Few could find the journey more terrifyingly painful than she did, many will find it much easier — why not take the fear-choice? The cost of staying safe is too high. It is the death of the self. Only from the basic core of our being can we begin to rebuild a whole and complete self.

The *Primal Scream* is a gripping account of people searching for the truth about their lives. One of Arthur Janov's (1976) patients describes his experience:

> So days like this are sad, because they remind me of the great lie that has been perpetrated on me, on my brothers and my sisters and on humankind. There is quite simply nothing, nothing at all. I'm happy that I have the freedom to feel the nothing. For were I still so extremely sick, I would be struggling to feel meaning, to get approval for my gift-bearing childishness, to struggle to get the love that was never there for me, to struggle to stay sick. Nothing isn't very pleasant. Nothing is. That's about it.

In *The Neverending Story* (Ende, 1985), the childlike empress of Fantastica is looking for a new name so that she can get well. "Why do you need a new name to get well?" Atreyu asks her,

> "Only the right name gives beings and things their reality", she said. "A wrong name makes everything unreal. That's what lies do." "Maybe the saviour doesn't yet know the right name to give you". "Oh yes he does", she assured him. "I know it all right", said Bastion. "I knew it the moment I laid eyes on her. But I don't know what I have to do".

This must be the dilemma of everyone in the healing profession. We can all see who the person really is. It is knowing what to do in order to have them see it that is difficult.

What is unreal is the belief we develop — from being deprived of our basic needs — that we are not secure, lovable and valued human beings. However, if it is not possible to compensate for the lack of these basic needs, we must recognise (become aware of) the lies we have believed, and then the truth of who we are will be revealed.

So healing is a painful process, and if we don't heal, what then? Does it really matter that much if we cannot express our true natures? Look and see! Look at the world around you and estimate the price the human race is paying for attempting to be *comfortable* and walled up in our bunkers. The price is high — too high. The pay-off for becoming self-actualised is joy, a great deal more energy, aliveness and mastery of life — the power to express ourselves fully. The ultimate cost of living out of deficiency-needs is destruction: the death of the soul.

Deficiency-needs and global destruction

At the time of writing this, the Gulf War is in its sixth day. Apart from the obvious costs of war, in terms of the senseless destruction of life, this one could threaten humanity on a much greater scale than ever before. Pollution and environmental imbalance is inevitable. The spread of deadly disease by germ warfare is a distinct possibility. So what drives human beings to this level of insanity?

I know little about the background history of Saddam Hussein, except that he was probably abandoned by his father, and was, according to one daily newspaper, abused by his brutal step-father. He also had a fanatical uncle with whom he lived for a large part of his life, who seemed to influence him greatly. There seems to be some doubt as to the veracity of this report, but I am sure of one thing — he is living out of his deficiency-needs. He has had his innate need for growth thwarted. He has risen to great heights of power, but he is not satisfied, because a true sense of power, the power to *be himself*, rather than the power to dominate and control, has never developed.

> It would seem that the amount of destructiveness to be found in individuals is proportionate to the amount to which expansiveness of life is curtailed. By this we do not refer to the individual frustration of this or that instinctive desire, but to the thwarting of the whole of life. The blockage of spontaneity of the growth and expression of man's sensuous, emotional and intellectual capacities.
>
> (Fromm, 1987.)

Which of course, cannot be expressed if we are frantically striving to fulfil our basic needs. Fromm goes on:

> Life has an inner dynamism of its own. It tends to grow, to be expressed, to live. It seems that, if this energy is thwarted, the energy directed towards life undergoes a process of decomposition and changes into energy directed towards destruction. Destructiveness is the outcome of unlived life.

This was certainly true of Hitler. Alice Miller (1990b) illustrates, with horrific clarity, Hitler's childhood experiences, at the hands of a brutal and totally autocratic father and a weak mother who, despite being over-protective in other ways, failed to protect him from his father's beatings and derisive comments.

> Adolf lived in daily jeopardy, in a hell of continual fear and severe trauma. He was forced, at the same time, to repress these feelings in order to rescue his pride, or it is possible that he did not show his suffering and had to split it off.
>
> (Miller, p157.)

Maslow states that basic needs can eventually be satisfied by giving people sufficient access to them, but that the lust for power, which is often a manifestation of the deprivation of respect and autonomy in childhood, can never be satiated by giving people the power they are craving. This kind of power is simply a substitute for one's own sense of worth which, when it is established, needs no confirmation from the outside world.

> We know that giving gratification to neurotic needs does not breed health as does gratification of basic inherent needs. Giving neurotic power-seekers all the power they want does not make them less neurotic, nor is it possible to satiate their need for power. However much they are fed, they still remain hungry (because they're really looking for something else). It makes little difference for ultimate health whether a neurotic need be gratified or frustrated. It is very different with basic needs like safety or love. Their gratification does breed health, their satiation is possible, their frustration does breed sickness.
>
> (Maslow, 1987.)

Bullies and tyrants are more to be pitied than reviled since they are simply demonstrating their neurosis, which in the case of Hitler and of Saddam Hussein, they did, or are doing, on a very grand scale:

> The jubilation characteristic of those who declare war is the expression of the revived hope of finally being able to avenge earlier debasement, and presumably also of relief at finally being permitted to hate and

> shout. What didn't the son (Hitler) do to forget the trauma of beatings his father gave him; he subjugated Germany's ruling class, won over the masses, and bent the government of Europe to his will. He possessed nearly limitless power. At night, however, in his sleep, when the unconscious lets us know about our early childhood experiences, there was no escape: then his father came back to frighten him, and his terror was boundless. Had he made the entire world his victim he would not have been able to banish his introjected father from his bedroom, for one's own unconscious cannot be destroyed by destroying the world.
> (Miller, 1990b.)

The conditions which prevailed at Auschwitz and Belsen bore a striking similarity to the circumstances of Hitler's childhood. People were deprived of their dignity, humiliated and tortured. They were treated as sub-humans — just as Hitler was by his father. There were regular beatings, and the uncertainty of never knowing when you would be singled out for brutal treatment — just as in Hitler's childhood. The massacre of six million Jews was, Miller believes, a result of Hitler projecting his hatred of his father (whose own father was believed to be a Jew) onto a whole race of people.

Alice Miller is clear, however, that Hitler could not have risen to the heights he attained, had not the majority of the German population been suffering from the same neurotic needs. Child-rearing practices which emphasised the breaking of the child's will by harsh and unrelenting punishment were very common at that time, perhaps more so in Germany than elsewhere. People perhaps saw in Adolf Hitler the attainment of a dream that they so longed for: the rise of the weak and powerless to the pinnacle of power and control. If this is so then we all have a responsibility to become self-actualised and put an end to senseless destruction, by refusing to follow those who would lead us into such power-struggles.

Self-destruction

At a more individual level it is something other than life and freedom that can be destroyed by our striving for the fulfilment of basic needs: it is our whole sense of ourselves — the self which is sacrificed on this altar.

John: *I had to please my parents all the time, and through pleasing them I could not show emotion. As soon as I showed any emotion they did not like it. And so I went around trying to please them by being* happy, *and what it did was totally suppress me from showing any emotion, in terms of sadness, and so I did not know how to express anything else. I was a blank face, just not experiencing life at all. And I didn't know it. I thought I was coping with it. I was dealing with it and* pleasing *everyone. I look back now and see there was something I was missing. It was costing me my relationship with people.*

John went on to say that he had never been able to find out what he wanted to do with his life, since he was devoted to keeping his parents happy. That was how he tried to get love, but of course this is not love. This is conditional love: *I will love you only if you are happy*. He knew, at some deep level of knowing, that if his parents had really been offering him love, then he would have been able to express any emotion, wish or feeling, and they would have still accepted him and given him love. So the love-need was never satisfied, and never will be, by his parents, or any one else's parents, unless and until they can see what they have been doing.

Of course his parents are not to blame for the way they have treated their son. How are they to know any differently when, presumably, they received the same treatment from their parents, who received the same treatment from their parents? As Kemp (in Leidloff, 1986) says, we are all victims of victims. In failing to reach self-actualisation and live out of their growth-needs they came close to destroying their son's sense of identity, of who he is, or could be.

The problem for John was even more complex, because his parents seemed so loving and caring. The damage done to him was very subtle. After all, *all they wanted was his happiness*. This problem of the *wonderful parent* will be discussed more fully in the next chapter.

Other people become self-destructive directly out of the thwarted need for growth and self-expression, what Victor Frankl refers to as *existential neurosis* — the fact that life seems empty and meaningless. This was the situation in the case of someone I recently got to know. I realised, shortly after meeting her, that she was an alcoholic. At first she denied this vehemently. She definitely did not drink, only a little when she went out socially. When I persisted she admitted that she did drink, frequently and, in a very puzzled voice, asked me why I thought she did so. I said I thought that she was very lonely, and that she had reached middle age without doing anything with the intelligence she so obviously had.

She was a really lovely, bright and perceptive person who was damaging her brain and her liver with alcohol, because she could not bear the pain of feeling that she had done nothing with her life. She had such a low opinion of herself, both socially and intellectually, that she took for granted that people would not want to be friendly with her, and that she would not be capable of holding down a satisfying job.

So, alcoholism, drug addiction, self-mutilation, and, of course, suicide (the ultimate form of self-destruction) can all be traced back to the frustration of the basic needs and the development of neurotic attempts to satisfy them. Unless we can recognise what the needs really are, we will look in the wrong direction for their fulfilment. All we are aware of is a craving that has to be satiated somehow, *anyhow*! Anything that takes away the craving, even momentarily, will be seized upon as *the* solution.

In the EST training this was illustrated by comparing the intelligence of rats with the intelligence of human beings. When rats are being trained, cheese is used to entice them up the correct tunnel in the maze. If the cheese is moved the rat will, after several abortive attempts to find it down the same tunnel, look elsewhere. The difference between the rat and the human being, Werner Erhard maintains, is that the human being will never stop going down the same tunnel. He/she will never be convinced that the cheese is not there. This is the explanation offered for our self-defeating patterns.

Destructiveness in relationships

We can also be destructive of our relationships with others. Bernard's insatiable need for love caused him to behave in a possessive and clinging way with his wife. The more she tried to have some autonomy and space for herself within the relationship, the more he demanded her attention and time. He came to see me because his wife had threatened to leave him if he did not sort himself out. He knew perfectly well that his jealousy and possessiveness were destroying the relationship, but he felt he could do nothing about it.

I started to explore with him the reasons why he felt so terrified of losing his wife, and so angry when he thought she was being looked at and admired by other men. It turned out that he felt she would be comparing them with him and he would not compare favourably.

Jean: *Why do you think that?*

Bernard: *Because I don't like my body. I always used to get laughed at by the kids at school. I was very thin, all skin and bone, and I had a very big head and my ears stuck out.*

Jean: *So you feel physically unattractive.*

Bernard: *Yes, at one level I know I am not (*at the level of reason*), but at another level I just feel that my wife will obviously find other people more attractive.*

Despite many assurances from his wife that this was not the case, and even if she did find other men more attractive she would not be tempted to leave him, he was not convinced. I was struck by the fact that Bernard usually appeared to be very self-assured. The picture he presented on this occasion was quite different to the one he presented publicly.

I decided to try some *Voice Dialogue* work with Bernard — a technique developed by Stone and Winkelman (1986). Many of us are aware that we have different ways of presenting ourselves in different situations. For instance, at one time, when I went North to visit my family my accent would change, and I would become quiet and aloof. If, on the other hand, I went out to dinner with my husband's employer, I would 'watch my Ps and Qs' and be on my best behaviour (most of the time). I was definitely acting a *part*, and I knew it, vaguely.

Around my husband I had a wonderful little-girl act which I had perfected to a tee. This I was not even slightly aware of. The little girl would appear at strategic moments and cajole and lisp until she got her own way. In *Voice Dialogue* terms these acts would be known as *sub-personalities*. James Holland (of *Creative Interactions*) refers to them as *dis-ease entities*. He is not implying that we are sick, merely that these different personalities emerge when we are in situations in which we are not at ease — which is usually those times when our basic needs are not being met, or are being threatened in some way. It was interesting to see how Bernard deployed his sub-personalities, in order to get his need for love attended to.

One way that Bernard coped with his vulnerability, when he was a schoolboy, was to go home and get a lot of sympathy and comfort from his mother. He elicited this sympathy by being pathetic and helpless. I asked him if he could put himself into that role, recall the feelings and emotions and the thoughts that he had when he behaved that way.

Bernard co-operated with my suggestion, shutting his eyes and concentrating on the way he would feel. His body posture changed and his face took on a pathetic appearance. I began to question him about this sub-personality and how he felt. He felt, he said (in a very thin, high voice), very scared and very vulnerable. He did not want to be on his own. I asked him if he could find a name for this character. Without much hesitation he decided to call him by the nickname he had been given at school, *Mr Bones*. I asked him to describe himself as Mr Bones. He was, he said, all skin and bone. He had a big head and glasses. He felt terrible most of the time. I asked him how he felt about himself. 'Well, disgusted, really'. He didn't like this personality at all.

I asked him if he did have a personality he liked. Yes he did. Could he describe him and give him a name? Yes, he would call this one *Mr Muscles*. This guy was athletic and physically okay. He could stick up for himself and was arrogantly confident. He could find his own way of dealing with things, was able to push through fear and could therefore be independent and a *non-victim*. I then had a conversation with Mr Muscles, asking Bernard to walk over to another chair and get into that personality as he did so. His face, voice and body posture changed once again. He adopted a nonchalant position in the chair and grinned at me confidently.

Jean: *What do you think about the way Mr Bones was treated.*

Mr Muscles: *Well I feel really sorry for him, 'cause he's not a bad little chap.*

Jean: *Does he ever annoy you?*

Mr Muscles: *I'll say he does. He's so pathetic, such a wimp.*

Jean: *Does he ever stop you doing things?*

Mr Muscles: *Well he tries, but I don't let him.*

The conversation proceeded with Mr Muscles becoming increasingly critical of Mr Bones. I then addressed Mr Bones and asked him what he thought of Mr Muscles. He thought he was a great guy and really admired him, but he did get scared by him. He took him frequently into situations he could not cope with, and he kept trying to warn him that he would be annihilated, but Mr Muscles would not listen.

The result of this dialogue between the two sub-personalities was quite dramatic. Bernard was amazed at the conflicting interests expressed by these two characters, and wondered how, between them, he had managed to function at all. No wonder his wife was exasperated by him at times — dealing with two such distinct aspects of the one person must be very confusing! Clearly Mr Muscles emerged when Bernard felt loved and safe. Then the esteem-needs emerged, and in order to attain his objectives of being admired and respected, he projected a confident, almost over-confident image.

Lurking beneath that, however, was Mr Bones, ever watchful for the prospect of getting out of his depth and being exposed as a pathetic weakling. So if Mr Muscles wanted to swim, Mr Bones went through agonies about his physique and was terrified, in case he was laughed at and rejected. When the situation became really threatening, Mr Bones took over and Mr Muscles was shut in the closet. Between the two of them, his wife had quite a hard time.

Bernard's first reaction to the emergence of his two sub-personalities was one of dismay and shock. 'I'm not schizophrenic, am I?' he asked me anxiously. I assured him that it is normal for human beings to develop several different personalities; only when these personalities split off from each other and become totally separated is there need for alarm. (A dramatic example of this can be found in *Sybil*, by Flora Rheta Schreiber — Sybil actually lives out her life as sixteen separate individuals).

Now that Bernard could see these two personalities quite clearly, he had more chance of over-riding their demands and becoming more authentic in his communication. He could now hear his Mr Bones voice and his Mr Muscles voice, and could see that neither of them was able to tell other people how Bernard was really feeling, or what he wanted. In case there is some confusion about whether *Bernard* really exists, in his own right, there is no doubt that there is a part of him who can observe all the sub-personalities. In *Voice Dialogue* work this is referred to as the *aware ego* — but I prefer to call it the *observer*, since I feel, as does Maslow, that the ego is the instrument of expression of the deficiency-needs, therefore the sub-personalities are the ego, which other aspects of the self can learn to observe and transcend.

Only when we learn to develop the *observer* can we become authentic in our relationships and our communication with ourselves. The aware observer within us can acknowledge the fears and needs of our sub-personalities and restrain, for example, the impulsiveness of the part of us that is sick of being held back.

One of my sub-personalities is my *omnipotent child*, who will not be told, or shown what to do. She has to have her own way. I have no doubt she developed that way in order to resist being crushed by a dominating mother, who needed desperately to feel in control of her life, and so attempted to control everyone else around her. These sub-personalities certainly have their uses at various stages of our lives. My *omnipotent child* saved me from losing my will and my sense of myself, but it also got me into trouble and would have led me more astray if it were not for my *charming little girl* entity, who did not like the *omnipotent child's* tendency to upset people.

We should not be alarmed at our many-faceted *selves*, but realise that they are expressions of our desperation. They have, at some time, made life bearable, but we need to recognise that we have probably outgrown them. We do not need to let them have their head any more. We need to learn to identify and accept each and every one of them without allowing them to take us over any more.

Other aspects of destructiveness

Bernard's sub-personality, Mr Bones, emerged to protect him from the traumas of school. James, another course participant, had developed a different *dis-ease entity*. He maintained that he had come on the course to 'get some motivation to do something'. He was 'searching for a goal'. But his whole attitude to life and the way he presented himself projected complete indifference to everyone and everything, except his football team. Apparently the goal he was searching for was not the one on the pitch, and yet almost all of his conversation and his life was devoted to analysing, enthusing about and watching soccer. When not in the *dis-ease entity* of *Football Fan*, he usually presented the *I'm not bothered* personality.

I explored with him what had led him to wall himself up inside this castle of indifference, which he emerged from only to cheer his team. He had, he said, been accepted on a course of higher education, but failed his exams because he had been too intent on getting his third-level needs met, those of *affiliation*. He had not put any energy into his work, concentrating instead on drinking with his friends and spending his time socialising.

This is a very familiar phenomenon in universities and colleges. Many a very capable student throws away their degree in order to be *one of the boys*, or in the case of women, to meet the needs of some male she is involved with. This *one of the boys* syndrome was a repetition of something that had happened to James at school. Within the school culture it is not 'cool' to work hard and concentrate on studies. Pupils, particularly boys, can become very unpopular if they do so. Few children have the level of psychological maturity to enable them to cope with the ridicule and rejection that they see others going through, by sticking to what they want to do in the face of opposition from their peers — and so they sacrifice their esteem-needs for the lower-order needs. Other people, as I have stated above, strive to satisfy their esteem-needs and destroy their capacity for self-expression and growth.

Most of the schools and teachers I am familiar with would not know how to encourage and cater for the growth-needs of pupils. Motivation to work always revolves around gaining status and recognition, usually denoted by concrete rewards (stars, merit marks *etc*). There seems to be a tacit assumption that pupils will not engage in study and learning for its own sake. There has to be some external carrot, rather than the creation of internal satisfaction. Of course, as Margaret Donaldson (1982) says, the snag with this is that pupils come to see the end result as the important aspect of the learning situation, rather than the process of learning itself. It is a product-orientated, rather than a process-orientated experience.

This, of course, fits in with the value-system of a capitalist society where profit (end result) is the only criteria for success. This is not a condemnation of capitalism, but rather an observation that our education system replicates the values of society, and all of this is going on at an unconscious level, in that no one ever spells out for us precisely what is happening in such terms as these. And we do have to live, so we have to subscribe to the bribery and go for the hand-outs from other people, rather than seeking our own inner motivation. This makes it very difficult to live our lives from a different, self-expressive, level. In James's case, participating actively in life had become too dangerous. He preferred to live out his adventures vicariously through the people involved in the game. He sat on the sidelines and watched the action in safety, while his team took all the risks.

It should be obvious, by now, though that it is essential that we begin to stop being passive spectators of life and start to participate to the full, so that we are *thoroughly used up when we die*, not atrophying from watching television! The first stage of this process is, obviously, that of exploring our relationships with our parents, since this is where the problems all begin. We need to find out the messages we picked up, the beliefs we developed, the strategies we devised and the *dis-ease entities* that we created. These early years, as the Jesuits well knew, provide the building blocks of the adult human being and determine our future character:

Give me the child until he is seven and I will give you the man.

4. *Parents: the fundamental relationship*

All children are born to grow, to develop, to live and to articulate their needs and feelings for their self-protection. For their development children need the respect and protection of adults who take them seriously, love them and honestly help them to become oriented in the world.

(Miller, 1990a)

After I took the EST Training in 1982, my mother was initially astonished and subsequently delighted at the transformation that occurred in my attitude towards her. Previously I had *tolerated* my mother, resenting her for many reasons — the basic one being that she was not how my mother should be. It seemed to me that my mother had always been angry. She was angry with my dad (permanently), angry on washing days, ironing days and cleaning days (she was always cleaning!). She was angry with the weather, the price of food and (during the war) the lack of it. And she was angry with me. She hated me reading because I had perfected the art of losing myself in books and replying to whatever was said to me without registering a word of it, or allowing it to distract me from what I was doing. If I was indoors I was *under her feet*. If I was playing with toys I was *making a mess*. If I had friends in I was ruining her polishing, and so on.

I developed an effective fantasy to escape from this constant tirade and provide me with some solace. My favourite fairy story was *The Princess and the Pea*. I knew that I must be a princess because I could not sleep on lumpy mattresses, and there were plenty of those around in those days. I had never attempted the real test, that of detecting a pea under six — or was it thirteen? — mattresses and becoming bruised all over in the process — but I suspected this would be the case if I tried it out. I also had thin (*aristocratic*) ankles and small feet, so this was ultimate proof to me of my royal blood.

I explained the discrepancy in status between my so-called parents and myself by deciding that I was a changeling. Kidnapped by gypsies, I had been planted on my parents in this dump, and their real child was swanning around in the lap of luxury in the palace, which is where I rightfully belonged. There were times when I truly believed this.

While the fantasy helped to make life a little more bearable, by holding out the hope of being rescued and restored to my birthright, it did not stop me developing a very negative self-image, underneath the *princess* pose. It took me a long time (44 years to be precise), to realise that I had interpreted my mother's anger as a reflection of my *badness*. If someone is always angry around you then the obvious conclusion to come to is that you must have deserved it, and therefore you are a *bad* person. This all happens at an unconscious level of course. The mind adds one and one and comes up with four.

The conscious mind may rationalise and resist, but the message is firmly grooved. The realisation, forty years later, that this had occurred, coupled with the recognition that my mother's anger was simply a mask for her fear and feelings of resentment towards her difficult and impoverished life, freed me from my *bad* self-image and made me feel far more compassionate towards the woman who had struggled so hard to feed, clothe and provide for us over all those lean years. It was a large step forward in the process of self-healing — and healing my relationship with my mother.

If my mother's anger made me decide I was a *bad* person, then my father's mental state made me feel an extremely insecure and worthless person. I lived in constant fear that other kids would find out my father had been in a 'loony bin', or that they would call round when he 'had it on him' (which is how my mother described his manic phases). When he was in that state, I never knew how he would behave or what he would say.

I learned to fear the way in which my father's behaviour would affect people's judgements of me, and I learned to despise and resent him because of the risk he exposed me to (affecting my esteem needs).

Because of his inability to take responsibility, and his incompetence at most practical tasks, I decided at an early age that he was 'useless, and more trouble than he was worth'. That has caused me profound problems in my relationships with men. I am inclined to have the utmost contempt for men, and the deepest need to find one who will take care of me and make me feel worthwhile and safe. There has been something radically wrong with every man I have had a relationship with — and they have been many. When I found the one who was respectable, reliable, responsible, stable and caring, I found reasons to despise him too. He was too narrow, intellectually limited, and he was a workaholic. I also made sure he wasn't much good in bed and that he got to feel inadequate in that area.

The sins of the father

Only when I had finally disposed of him, and started looking around for a replacement, did I realise that I might have thrown away something good, someone who really had my best interests at heart and who had some sterling qualities that did not seem to be around in other men I met. I began to wonder what on earth had possessed me to reject him so easily. It took me a very long time to work it out.

For the next eight years, I met and attempted to have relationships with men whom a friend of mine, in a moment of utter frustration, pointed out to me were *raving loonies*. This was a somewhat exaggerated statement, but, when I considered the behaviour of the men she was referring to, I had to admit there was truth in it. Certainly many of them were odd, to say the least. Two of them had suffered quite severe breakdowns, and the rest definitely had peculiar quirks of personality.

With hindsight the explanation for my behaviour is obvious. Having found and discarded my ideal father I had sought out replicas of the one I had — but why would I want to do this?

My father died whilst I was married to my second (*ideal father*) husband. He died a lingering death, so I was well prepared for the event, which I did not think would affect me very much. The moment he died my mother was frantic to have him 'laid out properly'. I rushed around to find the local woman who performed that service. She came, all efficiency and gaunt righteousness to 'do for the deceased'. After a time she appeared at the door of the living room, where I was busy being a tower of strength to all, and announced that we could now all 'view the deceased'. I was horrified. No way did I have any inclination to look at a dead body. However, hypnotised by her insistence on the correct protocol — that I must see him — I allowed her to almost push me into the room.

On the bed was a carcass — an empty shell — a husk. I had the horrible realisation that my father had gone. There was no-one in there. I was utterly distraught. "That's not my father in there", I said, and rushed out of the room, sobbing. I ran outside, beside myself with loss. I was inconsolable and all I could do was repeat over and over again, "That's not my father in there". I could not explain what was happening to me because I did not know.

I could not explain the extent of my own grief and pain. I thought, at the time, that it was the shock of seeing a dead body, but I now know that was not the case. My relatives assumed that I was denying that this was my father's body, and were seriously concerned for my sanity. They suggested giving me an injection, which, fortunately, I refused to consider. Eventually they sent for my husband and I calmed down. I would not/could not go to his funeral and stayed behind to prepare food for everyone instead.

Even now, as I write this, I find it difficult to find any rational explanation for my reaction to his death. Was it unexpressed love — deep regret that

I had never allowed myself to see who my father really was — never shared his pain and recognised his fear of life? I never had a 'proper' relationship with my father, and now the opportunity was gone. Furthermore, in the last few hours of his life, I saw how much he loved me. Barely able to speak, he reached for my mother's hand as I stood at the end of the bed and, looking at me with absolute love he said "Our child". There was something in his eyes that said "Your existence has made my life, my suffering, worthwhile".

Maybe he knew then what I would do with my life. Certainly he saw who I really was, and I saw total, unconditional love for the first time. I am sure now that I had made an unconscious commitment to having a meaningful relationship with my father, and that every man I have shared my life with since has contributed to my completing that relationship.

It is not only men who have assisted me in this task. When I met Denise she was obviously in need of some immediate and intensive intervention. I felt very drawn to her and started to spend a lot of time with her when she was depressed and unable to cope, which seemed to be most of the time at that point. I then discovered that she had been diagnosed as a *manic depressive*. Tim and I invited her to share our home, and we lived, and learned, together for two-and-a-half years. During this time I developed a profound understanding of the syndrome known as *manic depressive psychosis*, or *bi-polar depression*, but the story of how Denise learned to control her mood-swings without the use of drugs must wait.

Will I ever be able to put my father to rest? I believe I am getting there, but it is a slow process which can be damaging and painful if there is no awareness of what is going on.

Robin Norwood (1986) gives a clear account of 'women who love too much', and understand too little about the influence their parents have had on their feelings about themselves, and their attitudes to men. We have a responsibility to ourselves, our family, friends and colleagues to become aware of the effect that our relationships with our parents has had, and continues to have, on our development and on our relationships with men and women.

Conspiracy and deceit

It was fairly obvious in my case that I could not escape being damaged by the way my parents tried to handle their fear of life. In other cases it is not so obvious. I grew up realising that my parents had somehow failed in their task and had not provided me with what I needed, but some children never arrive at that realisation. Even where it is clear to an outside observer that children are being neglected or inappropriately treated by parents, the child will distort, deny or repress their own experience in order to collude with the parents' view of reality.

The only way they can then account for their feelings of inadequacy, self-hatred and shame is by blaming themselves for the way their lives turned out. Idealising their parents, they turn their frustration in upon themselves and decide that they must be, at best, *bad*, and at worst, *evil*, people, to have brought all this misery down upon their heads. They see their lives as a punishment for their failure to be the ideal offspring that their parents wanted.

This has occurred over and over again in some, if not all, of my clients. In my case, although much of my anger at the situation was directed at my parents, I still developed a feeling of being *bad*, as a result of my mother's continuous anger. Children who are sexually abused can only think that they must have done something terrible to merit the punishment (as they see it) that was meted out to them. In the case of Ruth (cited in the last chapter) her father would begin the whole ritual by saying that she had been naughty, and he was going to punish her.

This also happened in another sexual abuse case where the uncle would make sure that the child remained silent by telling her that her mother would think that she was very wicked, and then would die. Her mother was very ill at this time. He also said that her father would be very angry with her if she told him what was happening. The child went through the tortures of sexual abuse weekend after weekend because she thought it must be a punishment for her wickedness. There was no-one she could turn to because she felt she had to protect her mother and she was afraid of her father's anger. The abuse continued for four years before she plucked up the courage to refuse to visit the uncle any more, and risk her father's wrath. Prior to that she had cried and protested that she did not want to go, only to be told not to be a *silly* girl because her uncle and aunt *adored* her (and, incidentally, it suited her father's convenience to pack her off there).

When my client eventually confronted her uncle with what he had done, and presented her father with what had happened, the uncle, of course, denied it, and her father, although he said he believed her eventually, still visits the uncle and aunt on a regular basis and is resentful of the fact that what his daughter had revealed has strained their relationship. I had a conversation with the father and told him precisely what devastating results the years of sexual abuse had had on his daughter and, although he was upset at the time, he quickly rationalised the whole affair and decided he must let *bygones be bygones*. The daughter, needless to say, felt doubly betrayed by his complicity.

In another case the child, reared by parents who shamefully neglected their children's hygiene and health, idealised her father, describing as a *saint* a man who had used her as a subject for child pornography, exposed her to sexual conversation and sexual scenes that she was not mature enough to cope with. She struggled to keep herself and her clothes clean, never took friends back to the house, and was deeply ashamed of the home she lived in, which was indescribably filthy. She complained to no-one because she was desperately afraid that she would be taken away and put into care. Her sister had to be bathed at school and her hair was so matted that the knots had to be cut out of it by a school teacher. They never had sheets or pillows on the bed and the house was always freezing cold, because windows were broken and never replaced.

The father was a highly-respected member of the community. His children were kept like animals. It took many weeks of patient coaching to enable my client to see that all the anger she had towards her husband and the world in general was all related to her suppressed anger with her parents. She would not, *could* not blame them. If she did she felt *evil*. She felt that God would punish her in some way. Part way through our sessions she would wake up in the night, convinced that something terrible was going to happen because she had betrayed her father. Of course, this was the position she was in as a young child. Had she exposed the neglect and abuse, she would have been removed from her parent's care (or lack of it) altogether — and she did get a lot of attention and affection from her father, which she did not want to lose, despite the price she had to pay for it. It was all she had and all she knew. How was she to know that her experience was not usual?

This person's experience with her parents has also had a devastating effect on her attitude towards her own body and to sexuality generally. At one time she did not trust her own responses towards children, fearing that she might get some sexual stimulation from seeing their naked bodies, or be impelled to touch them inappropriately. Thankfully that fear has now gone. She has also stopped having relationships with men who beat and abuse her. This person is working hard to become aware of, and heal, the damage that she incurred, and she is making progress.

This client's attitude to her parents corresponds precisely to Alice Miller's statement:

> Till now society has protected the adult and blamed the victim. It has been abetted in its blindness by theories, still in keeping with the pedagogical principles of our great-grandparents, according to which children are viewed as crafty creatures, dominated by wicked drives, who invent stories and attack their innocent parents or desire them sexually. In reality, children tend to blame themselves for their parents' cruelty and to absolve the parents, whom they invariably love, of all responsibility.
>
> (Miller, 1990a, p169)

Not only do children absolve their parents from blame because they love them, they do so because they need their protection (such as it is) and are desperately afraid of being abandoned. This is not so unreasonable as it might sound. One person who took my course had been given money to go to the cinema by her mother and felt, halfway through the film, that she must go home, and returned, only to find her mother half-way down the garden path with her suitcase in her hand. Despite her desperate pleadings she never saw her mother again. She was eight years old at the time. Her story of abusive and neglectful parenting by her own parents and the foster parents in whose 'care' she was placed would have made a moving and horrific film. She is still suffering from the effects of these experiences.

Unless and until the victims of abuse, neglect and repression get in touch with the reality of their childhood and re-experience the despair, fear and hopelessness they felt as children, they will continue to either eat themselves away with guilt and self-recrimination, or to destroy others in their need to redress the injustice they suffered. Unfortunately the others that they destroy will probably turn out to be their own offspring, or those that they consider to be inferior to them or weaker than they are.

A school teacher who took my course was totally dominated and manipulated by her mother, who constantly rebuked and criticised her. If she could not manipulate her daughter any other way she would resort to crying, leaving the child with enormous guilt feelings. When this participant's son came to the next course, he said he had realised how manipulated he had been by his mother, since she would cry if he did not do what she wanted him to do. He is now very wary of forming a relationship with any female. Who can blame him?

The same teacher saw how she controlled her classes in the same way as her mother had controlled her, with sarcasm and constant criticism. After she had completed the first weekend of the course, her relationship with the pupils in her classes changed dramatically. The former 'dragon' apologised to her pupils for her previous treatment of them, and explained that she had treated them that way because she was scared to death of losing control, and of appearing to her colleagues to be *useless*. She acknowledged that her behaviour was very damaging and made a commitment to treating them differently in future. The class (fifteen year-olds) was spell-bound by her honesty and her courage. One or two tittered with embarrassment, but were soon quietened by the others. One particularly difficult pupil approached her in the next break and said "I admired you for doing that, miss. It must have taken a lot of guts". The dragon had turned into a human being. Released from the tortures of her childhood she is now able to stop herself from inflicting on those around her the patterns of control she learned so well.

If only parents really knew what they are teaching their children! How often I hear my mother's critical and angry voice issuing from my own mouth! She taught me everything she knew. However, I know that my mother did not have a blissful childhood herself. My mother's mother was a *termagant* (overbearing). She went through seventeen pregnancies and reared thirteen surviving children. From what my mother has said I gather that her husband (my grandfather) was a charming, self-made man, who was rarely at home to help his wife with her considerable domestic responsibilities. Even if he had been at home more often, the existing social values would not have permitted him to lend a hand domestically.

He abandoned his wife and three young children when my mother was a teenager. My mother hinted, not so long ago, that the way her father kissed her felt *wrong*. She also told me that he had sexually abused one of her sisters, who had ended up in a mental hospital for most of her life. My mother married the first person who took an interest in her, to get away from the misery of her home situation, but she merely re-created more misery (although of a different kind) in her own domestic life.

Alice Miller (1989) points out that, in Germany, a whole race of people suffered because Hitler did not understand what had been inflicted upon him as a child. So for generation upon generation we repeat the traumas of our childhoods in the theatres of our lives.

Are there any who escape, who grow up to be loving, well balanced, self-expressive people? According to Maslow only 4% of the population achieve this — and that, I feel, is a generous estimate. I do have people on my courses who say they had *wonderful* parents. They have a harder time than others in realising how they have been damaged by their early childhood experiences.

Killing with kindness

One of my course participants was appalled at how cruelly other people on the course with her had been treated. Her mother had been *wonderful*, and had done an amazing job of bringing her up single-handedly. However, from what she said, it became clear that her mother had been grossly over-protective with her, with quite devastating consequences.

Penelope began by saying that she could not bear to be in the room with people who were in pain. She could not stand unpleasantness. She did not watch the news or read newspapers because it was all too horrible, and she did not want to know that it happened. There was nothing she could do anyway, so it was better not to know. She hated violence and could not see how or why people should be that way. When her children were small she had not allowed fairy stories like *Hansel and Gretel* in the house, because they were *nasty*, and she did not think children should be frightened by those sort of stories.

I could see that the other people in the room were beginning to feel impatient with this ostrich attitude. Although I understood the basis of her phobia about suffering and violence. I too began to conclude that she was incredibly selfish — a 'porcelain china person' was the phrase that came to mind. One who was so delicate she had to be protected from anything *nasty* — and yet she was a nurse! How did she cope with that? Well, she was *cheerful* and *practical*. I wondered whether her mother had been the same when her daughter was in pain, and whether there had been any room for her to express and experience suffering: probably not.

The irony was that, having been protected from all this knowledge of violence and nastiness, her son had joined the army at the age of sixteen, and had been subjected to a great deal of brutality and bullying. His mother and father had bought him out of the army (rescued him), only to discover that he is now intent on joining the SAS (Special Armed Service). This is what had brought her onto the course.

She continued to express her amazement, and be appalled at other people's suffering, without sharing any of her own, but in the end, away from other people, she broke down and sobbed and told me the truth about her life, both professionally and privately. She too has since become more human and compassionate in her profession. For years she had lived her life feeling that it was wrong to impose suffering on anyone, and that pain and anguish should be avoided — including her own. Her son had given her the opportunity to learn that we cannot avoid the pain of life, and yet we try to do so, not only at our peril, but at the risk of the lives of people around us. In talking to Penelope I was reminded of the oft-quoted phrase, "All the good man has to do in order for evil to prevail is — nothing". But the main point here is that a parent's unacknowledged hidden agendas will tend to be played out by the child.

It is often difficult for people to discover the truth about their experience as children. As Alice Miller (1990b) says, repressing their feelings about their parents is the only way that children can sustain a relationship which they see as vital to survival. Many children feel, she maintains, 'guilty, bad and damned, if they go to bed at night bearing a grudge against their parents'.

This reminds me of the prayer many of us were encouraged to say last thing at night. I am sure you will remember it:

> God bless mummy, God bless daddy, God bless . . . (*add others*)
> Make me a good boy/girl,
> For Jesus Christ's sake — Amen.

Quite a powerful message! God didn't have to bless me — he had to *make me a good girl*! It seemed to me on many occasions that God had a mammoth task to undertake, if all my mother said about me was to be believed, which it certainly was — by me, at least.

Alice Miller continues, 'The child will have to believe that the cruelties he suffered were for his own good, and later, as an adult, he will be unable to recognise the untruth for what it is . . . '.

Repressed, unconscious hatred has a destructive effect, whereas relived hatred is not a poison, but one of the ways out of the trap of pretence, deceit or over-destructiveness. And the patient really does get well when he stops sparing the aggressors by harbouring guilt feelings, when he finally dares to see and feel what they have done.

The process that people undergo on the course with respect to their parents does allow them to relive their experience at the hands of their parents. It releases a great deal of emotion, anger sometimes, but mostly pain, anguish and sadness about the betrayal of trust that they experienced (and repressed) as children. They are asked to think of any anger or resentment they have against their parents. If they can't think of anything, they are asked to think of things they want their parents to forgive them for. If they still can't think of anything they are asked to look at what it costs them to have no conflict in the relationship with their parents.

This last request often releases those people who had really *nice* parents, who apparently didn't do anything to them, and were really loving. I am prepared to believe that this is possible but I usually know, by the way the person relates to others and deals with issues on the course, in which instances this is not really the case. A typical example of this is Clare, who always thought her parents had 'done the right thing' in sending her to boarding school at a very early age (four, in her case):

Clare: *I think I bought their argument that I was getting a good education at a high price, but now I think I am very angry.*

Jean: *It is fine to be reasonable, but you need to get in touch with the damage that was done.*

Clare: *I cannot talk to my mother about this problem. We all (*brothers and sisters*) went through this phase of alcoholism and drug-addiction. My mother saw it all. She just ignored it.*

Rod's parent's are typical of those described in Skynner and Cleese (1984) who hide certain unacceptable emotions behind a screen:

Rod: *There are a whole lot of charades going on. My father thinks that everything's okay. "We have a fine relationship, Rod, what's wrong with it?" There is such hypocrisy! We have a lousy relationship, and he doesn't see that. "Be nice to your mother, be nice to your sister, be nice to your grandma". But my response was, "Why should I be nice? Why can't I be how I am?" He even changes his speech when guests come round. My parents have a social graces thing. I think its false: "Don't say this, don't say that". I feel very angry about that. Things have happened in my family, and I hate the secrets. I hate the fact that my sister has had an abortion, and my parents don't know that at all. There are secrets all over the place. Abuse in your own family, and my parents . . .* (breaks down sobbing)*. My sister had to have an abortion, and she couldn't tell my mother. Because "You've got to be in control, got to do the right thing". I didn't find out until a year later, and it really upsets me that there are secrets in the family. My sister was abused by my grandfather. Everyone pretends there is nothing wrong.*

Jean: *There is a conspiracy of secrecy, and you feel part of the whole thing.*

Rod: *My father is going to die not knowing the truth about what is going on. I went to see him and told him how bloody angry I was with him. He said that he accepted he got some things wrong, but he just laughed the whole thing off. I accepted the part I played. I am a really angry person, just furious, and I pretend everything is okay, that I'm* just the nice Rod. *I feel angry that our society is geared up to having to find a partner so that you feel secure, "Got to buy a house for comfort", and my family life is geared to getting those things, to being comfortable and avoiding things. I'm not convinced . . . I want to be convinced that getting those things isn't the way to go. I want to be secure. I don't want to give all those things away. I want to do something with this anger. I want to put it onto you and get angry and scream my head off.*

A woman in the room had a major insight about her family as a result of this interaction:

Donna: *Everything that he has said reflects the situation in my family. It has not just affected me, but my mother and sister too. They try to put on social graces and parade us in front of our friends. We were always brought up to be very honest and open about things, and I realised that everything we had been brought up to be, our parents weren't.*

Donna then talked about becoming pregnant and not being allowed to have the baby, or talk about it. Her father cut off from her after this event and wouldn't speak to her, after being very close to her for most of her childhood.

The problem with this is that children receive double messages. *Be honest and open,* but *Don't talk about things that are not nice,* and *Pretend that embarrassing things just did not happen.* This means that the child has no opportunity to express its pain, or expiate its guilt about the events that occurred. Added to this is the pain of knowing that your parents are lying, which you have been told is *bad* — and having to go along with it.

Children are very clear about things and can be painfully honest. Parents often repress that. I am not saying they should not repress matters in some instances, where what they say might hurt someone else's feelings, but it presents us with a dilemma: how do you socially-condition children without suppressing them and encouraging them to be deceitful? Part of the child knows that it is living a lie, and that it is part of a conspiracy of silence. And while that silence continues, the abuse persists.

Another example of parental manipulation and repression came from Duncan. He could not understand why he had difficulty in his relationships with women, because his parents had been very loving and upright people. If Duncan did anything they did not approve of, or if he demonstrated his love to them, they did not punish him, nor were they ever cruel in any way. They were *upset*. This ultimately destroyed his capacity to live his own life and sent him underground in his dealings with people.

Duncan: *You were saying earlier about learning to be accountable. My parents are too accountable. I was brought up a Catholic, and a few years ago I joined the Pentecostal church, and they were so upset and grieved! Ever since then I have kept up the pretence that I still go to Mass. I can't tell them; they would take it that it was their fault, and that they had gone wrong somewhere.*

Jean: *Do you do this with other people?*

Duncan: *I suppose I do.*

Jean: *You have entered into the conspiracy!*

Duncan: *Yes, I find out what time Mass is, and I tell them which Mass I went to. Otherwise she* (mother) *can't sleep, and gets very upset.*

Jean: *She needs to look at why her inability to control your life causes her to lose sleep. If she can't let you grow up and live your own life she has a serious problem, and you should not make it yours. She manipulates you, and she has done so all your life. You have no relationship with your parents.*

Duncan went on to talk about his relationships with women, His previous partner left him because they had arguments. He could not think what the arguments were about at first, and then he recalled that several times it was about the fact that he felt he had to go to Sunday lunch with his parents, even if he had made a prior arrangement with his partner, because he couldn't upset his mother.

Jean: *Are you surprised your partner didn't want to stay in the relationship?*

Duncan: *I don't think she* (mother) *tries to manipulate me.*

Jean: *Of course not. It is not conscious. It is something she has learned. If she gets upset, it gets her what she wants from you. Loving someone means letting them do what they want to do with their own life, and loving them anyway. It's difficult to let your kids make mistakes. But you have to let them do that and love them anyway. You can say,* I don't condone what you did, I don't like what you did, and I love you anyway. *Not* I'll only love you when you are good. *Your parents are not having a relationship with you, because you are deceiving them. They think you are a totally different person than you are. Don't you all feel betrayed when you find out something about somebody you thought you knew, and you discover they have been deceiving you? You find out something they haven't communicated with you? Don't you feel,* Who the hell was I having a relationship with?. *When your parents die you will regret bitterly that you did not have a real relationship with them. You cannot have a relationship based on a lie. None of us can.*

Pat was another person who bent over backwards to please her parents, but in her case it was impossible. Even lying did not work, because the only way she could have pleased her mother was to have been born a boy:

Pat: *My parents manipulated me.* (Crying) *My mother wanted a boy. She never took any notice of me. She totally ignored me. I spent my life trying to please her and get her to love me. My dad was the only person who ever loved me, and when I was eighteen I wanted to leave home and go abroad to get away from the pain of it, and he said that if I did that he would have to side with my mother, because he could not afford to lose her, so he would have to lose me. And I have never had a real relationship with him ever since. And I married someone just the same. I did everything to please him — it was never good enough. I have always tried to please my children too. I didn't want to marry my husband, but my mother said,* When are you ever going to do something right?, *so I married him anyway.*

The above examples are a selection from hundreds of people on my courses who have spent their lives trying to work out how to please their parents, losing their own identities on the way. For Pat the task was totally impossible, but she still tried hard to find some way of compensating for the crime she had committed at birth — not being what her mother had wanted. She then married a man who was, similarly, never satisfied with her the way she was, and criticised her endlessly.

Already endowed with *existential guilt*, Pat fell readily into this unconscious game. Her sense of worth became non-existent; she ceased to exist as an individual and became a chattel to her husband and her children. When she came to an information evening about my course she was at rock-bottom. She was *depressed*, always crying for no reason. In reality she was grieving for the loss of her *self*, suffering, as Viktor Frankl would put it, from *existential neurosis*.

In other words, she was nobody and nothing, and life was empty and meaningless. Her one goal in life had been to please her mother (or anyone else she related to) and she had partially succeeded, since her children did appreciate her, despite taking her for granted and expecting her to put herself out on their behalf. The price she had paid for this marginal appreciation was enormous. By her mid-fifties she had sacrificed her life

— her self-expression, her true self — to a hopeless cause. She had become an empty shell.

This is the story of hundreds of women (and men) who re-enact the relationship they had with their parents throughout their lives, trying to win the love and appreciation they were never given as children. They cannot get off this self-destructive treadmill, because they do not know what motivation keeps them on it. Their memory of their childhood is, as several clients put it, *like being in a fog*, or they assume that the guilt they feel about not pleasing their parents really does belong with them — they feel they really did fail their parents in some way. Most of them assume that they had *reasonably happy* childhoods, since nothing *terrible* happened to them. It is not the case. The most terrible thing that can happen to any human being is the suppression of their self-expression, the crushing of the emerging identity, no matter how this is carried out.

Another participant was a very sad case of crushed identity. Keith was a typical bachelor. Very shy, inconspicuous and apologetic, he was very lonely and felt unable to have relationships with people. He began by expressing his guilt about saying anything

Keith: *My parents were very loving. I felt as though I was being thoroughly disloyal, putting down* (in an exercise we did on the course) *anything I resented about my parents, but my mother had been brought up in a very wealthy Edwardian family. And she was always talking about her childhood, and she was always saying, "Remember your station in life. You are middle-class, never forget it". I was very hurt because I was sent to a secondary modern school. That wasn't right — I should have gone to a grammar school. I made friends and took them home for tea. Afterwards I was put through the third degree, "Exactly what do you have in common? Why do you want to be friends? You must have something in common with them". And eventually it would end up, "Well they are very nice, but they are not your class. Please don't bring them to this house again". And I lost several friends that way. I hated that. The penny only dropped this week. If we had a party or something at work, and we all paid so much for the food, even though I have paid for it and put things in towards it, I can't sit down and enjoy it — I think I have got to get up and serve everyone else. I am afraid to be made the centre of attention. Even at my twenty-first, I had a limit on the friends I could invite, because I had to invite all my relatives. I was being chivvied all the time. "Keith, go and see to this person, that person". I hadn't had anything to eat at all. And it was* my *party. Thinking about it, my mother didn't mean it, and she didn't consciously think of it, but in her young days she had servants, and the men went round serving food and drink. She couldn't afford that, so I,* muggins, *was the servant.*

Jean: *You could not make decisions. You could not experiment with relationships.*

Keith: *There was a boy down the road, and I couldn't stand him, because he was a creep, but my mother approved of him.*

Jean: *He* was *a creep, but he was the right kind of creep. Your experience with your mother is as damaging an experience as those which other people have described. You totally abdicated your own personality in order to serve people. You got the message you are* not good enough. *You are not the right class of person. You are not good enough for your mother. Nothing would have been good enough. You could never win with her.*

Keith went on to cite further instances where his mother indicated that he was not living up to her expectations of how he should be, and what he should achieve.

Jean: *Your mother invalidated you all the time. You believe you are incompetent and incapable. Your whole presentation is an apology.*

Keith: *I'm sorry for that.* (Lots of laughter).

Jean: *If you walk into a room and you are an apology, people will think you are not good enough. This is not the case. Who you are is a worthwhile and valuable human being.*

I don't know whether Keith will ever be able to escape from the mould that his mother poured him into; whether he will ever connect with people in anything other than a superficial and very *polite* way, but he has more chance of doing so now than he did before. Unfortunately, this type of destructiveness can produce more severe problems than those manifested by Keith who did at least manage to hold down a job, albeit one that he felt was demeaning — and certainly one that his mother did not feel matched his *station in life*. He also managed to function reasonably well in other ways, despite feeling cut off and isolated from people.

For other clients of mine, the outcome of having parents who crushed their identity had more serious repercussions. I am beginning to suspect that many so-called manic depressives may have this experience in common. Ken went from an over-protective, mollycoddled existence at home to a relationship with a much older woman who totally dominated his life. He became a manic depressive. Other clients I have worked with, who have been given the same label, have, without exception, had *nice* parents, who were overwhelmingly protective. The parents never gave them the opportunity to think for themselves, or to stand on their own feet. The outcome of this treatment is an adult who is totally lacking in confidence, because they have become so dependent upon the judgements and advice of their parents. They also lack any sense of individuality — any separate identity — because, in order to make sure that they continued to remain under their parent's wing, they have had to sublimate their own will, and hence their sense of self.

It is this *will*, issuing from a strong inner sense of self, that enables us to become powerfully effective, self-expressive human beings. May (1958) calls it the *will-to-power*. Power, in this sense, meaning, to use Fromm's words, 'the power to act'. Without it, human beings suffer from feelings of helplessness, incompetence and a total lack of control. The manic depressive behaviour is a desperate attempt to overcome this devastatingly powerless state. The depression is a result of giving in to feelings of hopelessness, and the mania is an attempt to convince oneself that one really can control one's life and be regarded as a person of some significance.

One person who had been identified as having *bi-polar* (or manic) *depression* used to buy black opals in his manic phases. These stones, to use his own words, are "unique, extremely rare and precious". They are also incredibly expensive. His desire to possess such gems is no coincidence. He wanted to feel unique, beautiful, rare and precious. The next best thing was to own something that would make him the envy of others. He would have something that other people admired.

Insanity is not, I maintain, an *illness*, any more than any of our survival-strategies are illnesses. It is an attempt to compensate for the terror created by living in a world where those whose main concern should be the healthy and whole development of their offspring devote themselves instead either to trying to meet their own needs at their children's expense, or to attempting to cushion children from the reality of life. Of course they think that doing this will produce healthy and whole human beings — how would they know otherwise?

Even if the over-protectiveness of parents does not lead to psychosis, it is still extremely disabling. Phil wanted to come on the course because he was "completely lacking in confidence". However, he said he could not afford to take the course, because he had bought a new house and had to get a lot of furniture for it. I pointed out to him that this furniture would not do much for his confidence, and perhaps he might take a look at his priorities, since this might be one of his problems. It turned out that his priority in every circumstance was to avoid upsetting his parents. He felt his parents would be annoyed if he spent money on a course instead of spending it on furnishing his house.

He was 26 years old. The conversation demonstrated to him his fear of his parents, and his dependency on them. He took the course, but lied to this parents about where he was going. His special homework for the first week of the course was to tell his parents where he had been, and stand up to their disapproval, letting them know that from now on he was going to decide how he spent his time. He could not do it! He did not manage it during the second week either, and although he promised me he would do it the following week, I am not sure whether he did. I think, in this case, that 'no news was *not* good news'.

ital that he overcomes this fear, because the incident mentioned as not an isolated one. Desperate to study music at university, ad never fulfilled his dream, because his parents had told him he ood enough to become a musician. His parents were working-ople who no doubt felt that getting a white-collar job was as much le like them could hope to aspire to. My parents had similar views y mother thought that being employed by a bank was more than g ough for me. What more could I possibly want? University was no the likes of me.

If children take on the limiting aspirations of their parents, they will settle for safe mediocrity, and repress their natural desire to reach for the stars, settling instead for the limiting restrictions of the garden fence. Thankfully I met people fairly early in my life who encouraged me to reach for the stars, my ex-husband being one of them. Also my favourite reading was about the lives of people who were *above my station*. We later went to live in a middle-class area, where my mother was a housekeeper to a bachelor, and I made friends with a lot of middle-class little girls. I soon decided that I was not going to settle for mediocrity. There were other things in life.

Being male and mollycoddled, Phil has problems relating to people. He was bullied at school for being a *mummy's boy*. He does not communicate well, because the only defence he has against every thought of his being controlled and monitored by his parents is to conceal from them what he is thinking and doing — so he has to conceal everything from others too. And he knows his parents love him! Don't they tell him so all the time? Sadly they do not know how to love — few of us do. We know mostly fear. Fear of our loved ones dying, getting injured, leaving us, turning out to be a person who does not reflect well on the way we brought them up, becoming more successful than we are, failing in life . . .

It so demeans people to treat them as if they were incapable invalids! Unfortunately it can also destroy them. I have had to become ruthlessly compassionate with my mother to stop her developing into a helpless little old lady, which part of her would dearly love to do. She has to struggle with arthritic pain and loneliness, and it looks like an uphill struggle, but I know that *looking after her* is the way to drive her to senility and to dying, much sooner than she needs to. So I tell my mum she is as tough as old boots, and I love her too much to see her give in and sink into the coma of mindless uselessness.

Roots of alienation

There is another problem that people experience in their relationship with parents, which I have not as yet mentioned. It seems to be a two-way process. I am referring to the child's feelings of not being able to communicate or relate to a parent, and the parent's reciprocation of those feelings. Usually neither party wants this state of affairs to exist, but it does. No-one is sure how it arose, and neither person can bring themselves to address the problem, feeling that they are unwanted by the other for reasons they cannot figure out.

In my experience of working with various ages of client, and hearing this from both the parent and the child, it is likely that the problem arises at, or very soon after, the moment of birth. I am certain that my own predisposition to become anxious in many situations began when I was in the womb. This statement is confirmed by Alice Miller (1990a):

> But infants also experience feelings and hurt, even pre-natally, that set the course for later life, yet these facts have not attracted the attention of many scientists.

My mother was in a state of constant and acute anxiety when I was in her womb. I was, she tells me, *a very nervous* baby, jumping at every sound and screaming every time I was moved. This was, at the time, put down to my personality, but I am convinced that it was mother's upset state that created this. At the time I was born she had *Alopecia*, and lost most of her hair. There was not a lot my mother could have done about this. My father was going through a manic phase, as he did with every pregnancy she had, and lost his job. No wonder she could not cope! But intervention on the part of health professionals could have made a huge difference to my mother and to my subsequent development.

Stephanie was another baby whose introduction to life had unfortunate repercussions, especially with respect to her relationship with her mother. Again, had informed intervention been available, Stephanie could have been saved from developing a very distant and difficult relationship with her mother, a relationship which resulted in her developing *maladjusted* behaviour, and ending up being taken away from home and placed in a residential school. Stephanie is a likable, lively and interesting young person. Members of her family are upwardly-aspiring, hardworking, *respectable* people. Stephanie is the middle of three girls. At first there seemed to be no reason why Stephanie should have developed emotional and behavioural difficulties. Her two sisters do not seem to have similar problems. Her father is a pleasant, easy-going man, her mother is caring and concerned for her children.

On talking to her mother, however, certain factors emerged which made sense of Stephanie's current and past behaviour. Her mother had a difficult pregnancy and a long and hard labour. Two midwives who attended her were totally unsympathetic, and her mother became more and more alienated from them as the labour progressed. As Stephanie emerged into the world, she thought she heard one of them say "she's dead". They then hastily took Stephanie off and she was put in an incubator for several days. The mother had minimal contact with her baby during that time. Eventually mother and baby were allowed home, but Stephanie developed feeding problems, and within a very short space of time was back in hospital. At that time it was not considered vital for parents to be in constant touch with young babies, and so again there was a long, six week separation between mother and child.

Stephanie's mother told me that she had always felt it difficult to be physically close with Stephanie and that her daughter seemed to have the same sort of problem, not wanting or welcoming physical contact. The simple explanation of this is that *bonding* had not taken place. But let us look at what this could really mean. Stephanie is born into a climate of fear and hostility (emanating from the relationship between mother and midwives). Mother then thinks the baby is either dead or about to die. She probably decides at some unconscious level that she had better not become attached to this child since she might have to lose her. This is reinforced by the later hospitalisation and feeding problems.

As for Stephanie, she is snatched away from her life-support system almost instantly, and put into a cot far away from any living, breathing creature. Jean Leidloff graphically outlines her theory about the terror this produces in the newly-born infant in her book *The Continuum Concept* (1986). The newly-born infant has no concept of time. It lives, as Jean Leidloff says, in an endless moment of *now*. It cannot reason that someone will be here in a moment, or in another hour or two. As far as the conceptless mind is concerned, the moment is eternity, and without human contact it will die. What can the infant do except retreat into a helpless apathy? In this apathy it learns that it has to rely on its own resources and hope that somehow it will survive.

Leidloff believes that all of us in Western civilisation have suffered from this experience to some degree, because of the 'civilised' tradition of putting babies in separate cots, and often in separate rooms, and leaving them to cry out their terror unattended. Maybe there is some truth in that. As far as Stephanie was concerned, however, the situation was exaggerated, and she went through a similar experience only a few weeks later. This child was likely to build up a high level of anxiety. She then had the added problem of being with a parent who was afraid of becoming attached to her, thereby being unable to provide the necessary degree of affection, warmth and physical closeness that Stephanie would have needed, to start to be able to control her anxiety. No one is to blame in this drama of life. There is only the victim of a victim.

When I explored the circumstances of Stephanie's birth and development with her and her mother there was a huge release on both their parts

— the shedding of a burden of guilt and fear that they were unable to love and be loved. Stephanie was able to phone her mother and say "I love you", although it took her two hours to work up the courage to do so, so sure she was of the rejection that it would evoke. In fact her mother told her that she loved her too, and all of us were moved to tears by the possibility that opened up for both of them at that moment.

Stephanie's mother had never talked to anyone about her feelings for her daughter, or her guilt about not being able to express love for her. She had not been counselled after the difficult birth, and had therefore been left with the feeling that she should be able to cope with it normally and alone. Stephanie had never realised that she might have started life with more fear than other children: she did not understand that her emotions and behaviour stemmed from this fear, and therefore she had no means of controlling her reactions to various situations.

Great rivalry sprang up between her and her sisters, particularly the younger one, since this was a further threat to the very limited love that seemed to be available from her mother. This jealousy of the younger sister was projected onto other girls who bore any resemblance to her sister, and the relationship was acted out over and over again — an endless rehearsal of a search for security and love.

The problems between Stephanie and her mother, and Stephanie and her survival-strategies, are not over but they both are becoming more competent at detecting their defence-strategies and overcoming them. Stephanie has worked with me individually, and she has also taken my course, and this has given her more tools and awareness with which to tackle her psychology.

Another woman who never felt that her mother loved her, had never been physically touched by her mother:

I had spent my whole life trying to really, really love people, in the hope that they would love me back, and I don't feel that I have the right to say this about my mother because I really, really love her and I know she loves me, but somehow she didn't have the capacity to show me the way I needed to be shown . . . I tried so hard to love her.

At this point another participant stood up, already in floods of tears:

Laura: *In about ten years time my daughter, who is eleven, will be standing here saying the same things about me as the last person said about her own mother. I cannot demonstrate any affection for her: I don't like her touching me, I don't like to touch her. She is bright, responsible — I couldn't ask for a better daughter. I don't want her to touch me and she must know it (*anguish in her voice*). The other children climb all over me, and I want them to, and if she sits down and puts her arm on me, I make an excuse to move. I* *understand why it has happened. I know theories about it but it doesn't alter how I feel. Understanding is the booby prize. When she was a baby it was fine, and then when the other two were born I didn't want her any more. When she was born, I was in a sterile atmosphere. The other two were born at home, and they were put onto me straight away. I never made that bond with her.*

Laura's feeling that it was the fact that her daughter was born *in a sterile atmosphere* which caused the problem, is corroborated by Alice Miller (1990a):

> In most hospitals normal births resemble operations on sick patients . . . it is in those first few minutes and hours after birth that the presence of the infant arouses and encourages the mother's caring capacity, so essential for her bonding with the child.

I urged Laura to tell her daughter why she thought the relationship was the way it was. She asked indignantly "How on earth can I tell her that?"

Jean: *She knows it anyway. And if you tell her the way you are telling me, she would understand. You know she knows, don't you?*

Laura: *Oh yes, I know she knows.*

Jean: *Then tell her. You know it is very common, don't you?*

Laura: *No.*

Jean: *How many other people feel this way?* (Several hands are raised; I then told Laura about Stephanie; then:) *Lack of communication is like bricks in a wall, and the only way through is to communicate. It is very frightening to tell an eleven-year-old the way you really feel. You don't know how she will receive that, but at least she will know what is really going on.*

Laura did not look convinced. She felt that this would only make matters worse. I then told her about another course participant, Pam,who had taken my course several years earlier. When she came to the course she was having difficulties with her eldest son (then aged ten). She could not get close to the child; like Laura she did not want to hug him or show him any affection. The child, however, was crying out for her love and attention. He made constant excuses to come downstairs after he had gone to bed and was always hanging round her. When she came in from work he found endless ways to make her notice him, asking him to talk to her, look at something he was doing, and so on. Pam was tired when she came in from work and found his constant demands very draining. The more he demanded, the more she drew away from him, and so the game developed.

During the course Pam realised that the problems with her son had happened at the moment of his birth. He had been born with a defect in his throat, which had necessitated immediate surgery. Not only had this interfered with the bonding process, making it difficult for the mother to connect emotionally with her son, but it triggered off, in the mother, a reinforcement of her feelings of inadequacy and failure. Pam disclosed that she had to do everything perfectly. She had to be the perfect wife, mother, daughter. At her work she had to be superb, faultless. This had stopped her from entering a profession as she could not afford to fail, and therefore did not dare to attempt to subject herself to the necessary training. It also put her under a great deal of strain, constantly checking to see whether she had missed anything or left anything undone.

The disability her son was born with indicated to her that she had failed in her capacity as a mother. A *perfect* mother would have had a perfect child. This child was not perfect, he was weak and defective. As she wheeled him around in his buggy she felt no sense of pride, only shame that she had produced this less-than-perfect person. She suffered guilt and feelings of humiliation. What an impossible context within which to begin a relationship! The revelation she had on the course was startling to her. She could see instantly all that was stopping her loving her child but, like Laura, the next question was "What do I do about it?" I urged her to go home and communicate with her son. She did.

When she arrived home, very late that night, her son, as usual, came downstairs, crying. He had forgotten to feed the rabbit. The rabbit would die. Normally Pam would have been very angry and shouted at him and made him go back to bed. Instead she took him on her knee and told him that she understood what he was trying to say: that he needed some love and he was lonely. Wasn't that it? The child sobbed with her arms around him, safe in his mother's loving arms, and truly connected with her for the first time in his life. He cried for a long time and she cried with him. She told him that she had found it difficult to love him, and she told him why. He said that he understood.

Since that moment Pam's relationship with her son has blossomed. He is also a different child. He is no longer fretful and difficult, although the change did not come overnight. He still has some problems at school because he is small for his age, and still unsure of himself at times, but now he has a loving parent who can hear his pain and share it with him, and he feels that he is *known*; that he is loved for being himself, imperfect though he might be. That is an essential condition for the healthy development of human beings. Incidentally, his mother is now training to be a teacher.

Conclusions

So far I have dealt with over-loving, distant, neglectful or sexually-abusive parents, and the effect that those experiences create. I have not mentioned much about physical cruelty, or emotional deprivation, where children are ignored and never touched by their parents.

Nor have I dealt with the effects in later life on children who are totally abandoned — taken into care at very early stages of their childhood. Children who have been brought up in institutions obviously have different types of problems. No bonding there, with anyone in particular, unless they were in a very enlightened institution. I know someone who was abandoned by his mother when he was a few weeks old and put into an institution, and later farmed out to foster-parents, who treated him appallingly, never giving him a sense of belonging to the family, and depriving him of almost everything he needed from them. He has found the greatest difficulty in sustaining close and intimate relationships. As soon as he begins to feel close to people he retreats, making it impossible for him to feel loved. It is almost as if he must repeat his childhood experience over and over again for eternity.

Perhaps I do not have to say that in all the cases cited in the paragraphs above most of the children *survive*, but it is often at the expense of their growth, and it seriously impairs their ability to form healthy relationships. I could relate numerous examples of severely-impaired functioning in adults caused by unimaginable cruelty in childhood. Some of these people, I am sorry to say, may never recover from their experience, not because it is impossible for them to heal the damage, but because the type of support and healing they need is not available.

It requires someone who will listen and validate the true experience, expose the lies that they have been told, and enable them to adjust their view of themselves as being deserving of positive treatment. Instead of this, those who do seek help are often treated as if they are sick, which only reinforces their sense of culpability, since they are confirmed in their feelings that there is something *wrong* with them. They are given drugs, and (according to Alice Miller), if they visit psychoanalysts, they are asked to understand that their parents were only 'doing their best', and they should be *reasonable* about the treatment they received.

Such treatment is not reasonable, even if it is understandable. I agree with Miller that the person should be allowed to express their rage and pain about the treatment they have suffered. They cannot do this by being *reasonable*. This simply keeps the pain repressed.

My clients often express confusion about this: should they forgive their parents, and why should they do so? I tell them to be in no hurry; to make sure that they are fully in touch with the damage they have incurred. They need to have accessed and expressed most of their own pain and anger before they get around to forgiveness if, indeed, they ever do.

Unless they do unlock all the pain, they will repeatedly choose partners who will continue the abuse, domination, over-protectiveness, neglect, or whatever. They will damage their own children by treating them in the same way, or going to the opposite extreme of the treatment they received. For instance, if they were neglected as children they might be over-loving with their own offspring.

I can see this already in one of my clients, who is determined her child will not be deprived. She is showering him with far more of everything than he wants or needs. She is in danger of rearing a spoiled brat, who thinks the world is there to devote itself to fulfilling his every wish. Despite the fact that she has begun to unlock the pain of her childhood, she has not reached the end of the road — because, perhaps, the end of the road is the realisation that, in this type of cultural setting, it is not possible for people to go through life without incurring some pain and damage.

She cannot protect her child from life. She must allow him to learn how to handle adversity responsibly and responsively. In order to do this we need parents who will listen, share our confusion, suffer with us in our distress, but firmly support us in standing on our own feet and confronting our own fears, coming to terms with our frustration. They need to be able to help us to recognise that life is frequently unfair and difficult, and equip us with the fortitude to carry on. As Rudyard Kipling says:

> . . . when there is nothing in us,
> Except the will that says to us, Go on . . .
>
> (Rudyard Kipling, *If*.)

The best we can manage, perhaps, is to recognise the damage, and experience and express the pain. But there is something else we need to do: we need to hold people accountable for the damage they do to us in order to create the opportunity for them to own up to their mistakes, and we need to clean up the mistakes we make in our dealings with others. Then, in order to move towards self-acceptance, we need to forgive ourselves our trespasses *and* forgive those who trespass against us. Then perhaps we will indeed create heaven on earth!

Postscript

My own learning process about the effects of my early childhood on various aspects of my life continues. I have long asked myself the question, "Why did I get involved in this type of work?" I never came up with any really satisfactory answer. Maybe I never realised what the true nature of my work is. Recently I participated in a *Group Dynamics* course, and there I saw what drives me to devise courses and work individually with people. I saw that I have an absolute determination to enable people to communicate and relate to each other in an open, caring and nurturing way. This may sound very *saintly*. I was beginning to think it might be!! Alas I have discovered the truth. I am no saint, only a neglected child.

On the *Group Dynamics* course, I happened to be placed in a group of people who were reluctant to, unable to, or scared to, open up with each other. There were long, long periods of silence, or attempts to discuss impersonal topics. The aim of each small group was to 'study its own behaviour in the here-and-now and for each member to observe both his/her own behaviour and that of others, and to consider the dynamics of interaction which emerge within the group'. This I attempted to do by sharing my observations of my own behaviour, attempting to draw attention to what the group was doing. My efforts fell on stony ground — or that is how it felt.

Eventually I did what I normally do in a group situation when it does not go the way I think it *ought* to go — I sulked. I put my feet on the chair and became extremely interested in the books on the bookshelf. The consultant pointed out to me that I was withdrawing and giving up on the group process. I felt grateful for her observations and let them sink in, but I was suddenly overwhelmed with an immense feeling of sadness, amounting to despair. I began to sob uncontrollably. No-one spoke. I sobbed for about ten minutes. Where was all this terrible grief coming from? Don't tell me that I was really so distraught because, at this particular moment, people would not relate to each other? There had to be more to it than that.

I began to realise that the depth of feeling I was experiencing was how I had felt as a child. When I was little there was no-one to relate to, no-one to communicate with, no-one who could help me to understand and handle my own feelings, my rage, frustration, loneliness and despair. My mother was too concerned with her own problems, my father was in a world of his own, and communication with him was not allowed by my mother. My sister saw me as a rival, my brother was completely shut off from the world. What could I do? I was alone with my emotions and my hurt. The pain of that must have been intolerable. I recaptured a sense of it that day as I sat in that group, surrounded by people and feeling utterly alone and unheard.

So that is why I am writing this book, and that is why I run my courses. I want a world where I can be heard, where I will not be alone, where I will be supported in making sense of myself and of life. And I want that for others too, otherwise there will be no-one for me. How many more people suffered as I did as children? How many of them are as unaware of that suffering and its consequences as I was? How much more am I unaware of, and how does it affect what I do and how I react to various situations?

I expect it will take me, and everyone else, a lifetime to learn. My childhood experience has had what might be seen as a positive effect on my work and my orientation to people — but I can see it could have been different. I could have coped with it the way my brother did. Saddam Hussein's childhood experience did not lead him to want a caring, nurturing world. Maybe there, but for the grace of God, go all of us.

5. *Revenge may be sweet, but forgiveness heals*

It is not a leader's role to play judge and jury, to punish people for bad behaviour. In the first place, punishment does not effectively control behaviour . . .
The wise leader knows that there are natural consequences for every act. The task is to shed light on these natural consequences, not to attack the behaviour itself . . .
At the very least the leader will discover that the instrument of justice works both ways. Punishing others is punishing work.

Heider, J, (1989).

Forgiving those who despitefully use you

I am aware that any parents reading this must, by now, be feeling pretty uncomfortable about the damage they might have inflicted, or might still be inflicting on their offspring. I know from my own experience with my stepdaughter that it is incredibly painful to realise that we have made mistakes in our relationships, and recognise the damage that has ensued as a consequence of those errors.

Sometimes it is so colossal a responsibility that we feel unable and unwilling to simply own up to what we have done. There is always the need to justify our actions or rationalise our deeds. *Well, I did it for her/his own good.* Or *I was only doing my best.* Or *I was so young when I got married and had children.* Or *We had waited so long for a child.* The simple unvarnished truth is that we did not know what we were doing. We re-enacted our childhood dramas and tragedies in total ignorance that we were doing so, and other people were damaged, and will play out their dramas on the next generation — and so it goes on.

The perpetuation of what John Bradshaw (1991) calls the *family system* seems inevitable. The family, he says, is a social system, governed by its own laws and operating on a principle of balance. If one member does not fulfil their function, other members must compensate by taking over that person's role. Bradshaw maintains that in unhealthy family systems the roles are 'frozen and rigid'.

It might be perfectly healthy for someone to take on another family member's role if that person is sick and unable to function, but there should be an awareness of what is happening, and an agreement between all family members that this is the best way to proceed. However, where one member has always been incapable of fulfilling their function, due to their being *emotionally* damaged, an unhealthy imbalance occurs with those family members who *are* capable carrying those who are not. Once we are born into this system we will sustain it, unconsciously, unwittingly, for all we are worth, unless and until someone or something frees us from the darkness of our ignorance, and throws some light on what we are doing, or have done.

According to John Bradshaw, if parents are irresponsible, the children, or one of them, has to become ultra-responsible. Bradshaw's father was an alcoholic, and so John became the surrogate husband to his mother and the surrogate father to his siblings. This not only affected John, but was passed down, *via* him, to the next generation, although not in the same way. Children who were inadequately parented attempt, in parenting their own offspring, to compensate for that which they missed. In this case it would probably result in John taking too much responsibility for his children, so that they would not have to do what he had to do.

A close friend of mine experiences great anxiety, often leading to panic attacks, when she takes on responsibility. If she finds herself taking on more than what she considers to be *her share* of responsibility, she becomes extremely resentful because, as a child, she had a mother who was great fun as a playmate, but rarely met her responsibilities as a parent. My friend had to handle the housekeeping budget, plan meals and cook and clean the house, otherwise nothing got done.

Not only did she worry about the chaos that would ensue if she did not take on these tasks, but it was also an attempt to keep the peace between her mother and father, and retain some sense of order and control. If meals were badly-cooked or late appearing on the table, if laundry was left around for an interminable length of time, her father would fly into a rage, throwing plates of food or teapots full of tea at the walls or onto the floor.

My friend, the eldest of two girls, took it upon herself to take charge of the domestic arrangements, but she did not choose it freely — she chose it from fear of the destruction that would ensue if she did not take over the reins. Not surprisingly, when she had children of her own, she did not expect them to make any contribution to the household chores, nor did she expect her husband to lend a hand. Just as she had done in her childhood, she took on the sole responsibility for running the house, adding to the already massive repository of fear and resentment that she had stored from her childhood.

She was totally unaware that this was the source of her frequent and deepening depression. She put it down to many other external causes — the place they lived in, her husband, her lack of career — and some of these were contributory. Valium, prescribed by her doctor, enabled her to stay locked in her ignorance for many years. Coming out of it was very painful, since not only did she have to cope with the withdrawal symptoms of valium deprivation, she also began to see how she had damaged her children. She had, by that time, left her husband and watched her children waste their potential and, in one case, get mixed up in the fringes of delinquency.

It has taken her a long time to clean up the damage, but it did not happen soon enough for the next generation. Her daughter's child is now in danger of becoming the *omnipotent child* of Winnicott's case-studies, because her mother is projecting onto her what she wanted and did not get as a child — the undivided attention and adoration of her mother. Special schools for EBD [Emotionally and Behaviourally Disturbed] pupils are full of such *over-loved* children.

This experience in her family system still causes my friend problems, despite many years of work on self-awareness. For many years in teaching she has avoided taking on any job that carried extra responsibility. This is a great pity since she denies the world her competence, which is considerable. She has recently begun seriously to tackle this whole issue, and is making great headway, but it has taken a great deal of commitment and perseverance.

So should we punish our parents for the way they treated us? Should we wreak revenge on them, withdraw from them, hate them for what we suffered, and for our deprivation? Or should we be *reasonable*, and recognise that they were only doing their best, and they didn't mean it and, after all, we didn't turn out too badly, did we? *Or did we*?

Alice Miller takes the view that we should not forgive our parents, because we need to allow ourselves to experience and work through the abuse that was inflicted on us. Forgiving parents and taking a lenient attitude towards their behaviour stems, she believes, from Freud's philosophy. Originally, she claims, Freud discovered that many of his patients had been abused as children, but having made this known, he was shunned by his fellow psychiatrists, who did not wish to embrace this theory. Miller (1990a) continues:

> Freud could not bear this isolation for long. A few months later, in 1887, he described his patients' reports on sexual abuse as sheer fantasies attributable to their instinctual wishes. Humanity's briefly-disturbed sleep could now be resumed.

According to Miller, Freud's closest confidant, Wilhelm Fleiss, did not support Freud in his initial interpretation, but it was later disclosed by

Robert Fleiss (his son) that Wilhelm had sexually abused him at the age of two, and that this coincided with Freud's renunciation of the truth. She also maintains that another famous psychoanalyst, Wilhelm Reich, asserted that he was sexually abused as a child because he wanted it and needed it! Freud, therefore, with his *sexual drive theory*, lent scientific weight to the already-established Victorian view that children are born *bad* and *wicked*, and must be corrected and shown the error of their ways by the *wise* and *kind* adults.

While I respect Alice Miller's position and can see why she is adamant that parents should not be seen as well-meaning and essentially innocent — because this, as a consequence, makes the child the problem — I also feel that she has *slot-rattled* — that is, in realising that Freud's position was misleading, she has concluded that the opposite position must be the correct one, that parents are bad and wicked, and children are essentially good and innocent. In fact it would be difficult to find the true villain of the piece unless it was the serpent in the Garden of Eden, because we are all victims of victims, or victims of an established family system. It might, however, be interesting to explore the allegory of the Garden of Eden to see what the Bible is trying to tell us.

If we see the 'tree of knowledge' as the ability to formulate concepts, make judgements, categorise, label and look for the *right answers* (the development of the ego), we can see that there was potential evil in the eating of the forbidden fruit. Someone who is not attached to the survival of their identity — because they have not formulated one — would not see other people as a threat, or be ashamed of their own inadequacy. They would not be determined to have children who reflected well on them, nor would they desire to control or feel superior to others. But, eat the fruit we did, and we are all suffering from that first step into ego-identity: mortality. The tragedy is that most of us do not realise what we have become — we can only know when we have evolved to the point of becoming observers of our identity from the space of our higher selves.

When we can do this we can see that, as Heider (1989) says, to punish others is to punish ourselves, because the desire for revenge keeps us stuck in our ego-state, and does not permit evolution. Revenge is about needing to be right and needing to be in control, to dominate, to get the better of somebody.

The mind seems to have developed a theory which goes something like *if I can make someone else suffer, I will suffer less myself.* This was certainly the way the mind of one of my clients was operating when he came to consult me. His reason for arranging a session was that he had suffered from acute depression for about eighteen months. He had been to various therapists, and spent a lot of money, but he could not shake off these feelings of despair and blackness.

Within a short space of time, the reason for his misery became obvious. He could not let go of his feelings of resentment, bitterness and anger towards his wife for breaking up the marriage. He wanted revenge, and the law appeared to be on the side of his wife. Not only had she rejected him, but it looked as though she might end up getting more out of the divorce settlement than he would.

He told me the sad and unfair story, and looked at me expectantly, waiting for me to tell him how to even up the score and get the better of her. I told him he needed to *forgive* her. He was somewhat taken aback. It was not what he wanted to hear. "Why on earth", he wanted to know, "should I do a stupid thing like that? She does not deserve it!" I suggested that he could go on holding on to all his bitterness and his depression, or he could stop carrying this dead weight around with him, going over and over it in his mind, expending massive amounts of energy trying to work out how to manipulate the law to give him what he thought he deserved. He could put it down, or he could let it kill him. It was his choice.

Although I'm sure he thought I was mad, he did follow my suggestions, and gradually he let go of his need to punish her. Later in this chapter I will describe the steps he took to let go of this. But forgiving his wife was the first step to ending his unhappiness and feelings of helplessness. First he had to generate a lot of compassion and attempt to understand his wife's behaviour and her reactions to him. Secondly he had to stop being afraid of what she might be able to do to him — of the apparent power she had over him.

As Jerry Jampolski (1979) says, there are only two ways to interact with life — one is out of *love* and the other out of *fear*. Revenge is an act of fear. Only when we can love those who despitefully use us and *trespass against us,* will we fully experience our own power. It is also the only way to enable those people who are enmeshed in their own deficiency-needs to be set free, but this requires another act of love also — that we hold them accountable. Forgiving people is an act of love, and this encompasses committing ourselves to the growth of others. In order for people who are inflicting damage on others to evolve, we need to love them *and* we need to hold them accountable for what they did — or are doing.

So people need to be held accountable for their mistakes, and experience the consequences of their actions, if they are to evolve from their unconscious patterns, and have any chance of becoming the people they, in their hearts, want to be.

A close friend of mine had three children, two of whom had always been very reasonable about the way their mother behaved when they were small. My friend married a selfish and incredibly self-centred man who prided himself on his appearance, loved his dog and physically abused his children. My friend, a product of a 'dysfunctional' family, tolerated his irresponsibility, his cruel treatment of her children and of herself, because she was afraid of him. Although she complained about it, she put up with it, rather than face up to leaving him and trying to cope with her three children on her own. Only when she met someone else did she find the courage to leave. This is very understandable, but not conducive to a joyful existence — and it certainly had adverse effects on all her children.

The man she left her husband for was probably worse that the other. He inflicted psychological abuse on all the children and sexually abused the two girls. My friend only found out about the abuse several years after the event and, although she confronted him with it, she was still too afraid to leave him. The psychological abuse of her son seriously eroded his sense of worth, and left him desperate for love.

As a consequence of this her son has frequently been in trouble and my friend has persistently bailed him out. She has tried desperately to win the love and approval of her eldest daughter for years, to no avail. The son continues to make many errors in his life and the daughter remains cold and aloof. It has taken her a long time to see what she was doing and why. She was driven by guilt at her complicity in the crimes that were perpetrated against her children, but she could not fully take responsibility for allowing this to happen. Why do we punish those who are 'accessories before and after the fact'? Because *not* stopping someone who is committing a crime renders one as guilty as the criminal, even though fear might be the reason for the lack of intervention. To fail to hold someone accountable for what they have done is tantamount to being an accessory to the crime.

It was only when her son became enraged at something she said to him, that he finally accused her of allowing the abuse to persist. At first she wanted to defend herself, but then she saw it was all true. She apologised to him for not being brave, and for putting her own self-interest before that of her children. She insisted that he listen and accept her apology, not just say it did not matter, because to her it did. It was the laying down of a heavy and wearisome load.

I can see both sides of the issue. I suffered for her children, but I also love my friend, and I know how she suffered as a child. Shall I not forgive her? Should her children hate her for ever? It took courage for my friend to confess her complicity. It was also a very healing process for her. She could have done it a long time ago, but her children had not held her accountable, so she could not see what she had done. If people are willing to be held accountable it seems easy to forgive them.

The other reason my friend constantly intervenes to rescue her son relates to another aspect of John shawis a *co-dependent*. This means that we need around us someone who will depend upon us but we, in turn, depend upon that person's dependence. "Depend upon it for what?", you may ask. According to Bradshaw and other writers, we depend upon it for our sense of worth. Bradshaw maintains:

> Helping and giving up one's self for others can often be a way to attain moral superiority. Helpers are always helping themselves. Taking care of others is a way to feel powerful, and in the moment of helping one can overcome one's feelings of emptiness and powerlessness.
>
> (Bradshaw, 1988, p170.)

Bradshaw recognised that, in helping and taking care of others, he was disguising his own need for self-glorification.

True love, in the case of my friend, and in the case of all other co-dependents, would be to allow her son to experience the consequences of his own behaviour, so that he could see that the cost of what he was doing outweighed the gains. Then he might have a chance of adopting behaviour that was less self-defeating and destructive of others. She might help him to do this by holding him accountable for what he was doing. She might have done this with her spouses too, had she not been so afraid of standing on her own feet.

Don't forget compassion!

I hope I have made it clear that we hold people accountable out of love, and it also needs to be done with great compassion. My mother has recently begun to realise the damage caused to generation after generation, by her decision (a fear choice) to stay with my father, and by the treatment she meted out to her children as a result of her unhappiness in that relationship. During a huge family row, when skeletons began to rattle out of the cupboard, my mother suddenly saw that she had to accept responsibility for what was happening four generations down the line. Sometimes I feel relieved that I will never be in that position. My mother is now a great-great-grandmother, and she can see the damage she produced going on and on and being repeated in every generation.

In the aftermath of the family uproar she felt *very ill*, and could not stop crying. She went to the doctor who, predictably, gave her sleeping tablets, and told her that she should not be expected to cope with *upset* at her age — it was too much for her. When she told me this I suspected that there was much more to it than the doctor had suggested, and that sleeping tablets would do nothing to ease her pain — rather, the reverse.

I asked her if she was upset because she felt she was, in some way, responsible for what had happened. Her tone changed and she said, in a very tearful voice, "Well, I do, because if I had left your dad, or not married him, none of this would have happened". Her pain was obviously considerable, so I let her cry for a while and then I reminded her that, if she hadn't married my father she would not be having this conversation with me, because I would not be here to have it with. She brightened up at this and said, "Well, I must have got something right, because you have turned out all right". I also reminded her that she did the only thing she could manage at the time, and if she was wrong to do that, then she just needed to accept that and forgive herself.

I notice that my mother, although she did accept, at one time, that she had damaged me, is now wanting to change the whole story of my early life. It is as if she cannot bear to die feeling that she harmed me. I think she knows what she has done, but cannot accept the responsibility for it, because she blames herself for what happened. She cannot forgive herself for what she did, even though I certainly have, because I know that, given her state of awareness (or unawareness) at the time, she did the best she could.

I find it difficult not to contradict her when she tells me how much she wanted another baby (me), and how she definitely planned to have me, when I know this is a lie. But I realise that she wants me now, and had she known how I would turn out, and how our relationship would be, she would have wanted me then, so perhaps it is not so much of a lie after all. I also realise that she cannot cope with the pain of how it really was. However, I wonder if I should let her die having rationalised the whole thing and not having forgiven herself?

When I see my mother's pain I can forgive her everything — and I also remember that she gave me the gift of life. So I cannot agree with Alice Miller that it is not necessary, or perhaps even advisable, to forgive our parents. However, I did find a way to unlock my pain and to realise that I was the unwitting victim of someone else's scarred existence. I recognised the damage I had incurred, identified what it had cost me and located the source of the problem. I know I will bear the scars and react (perhaps even forever) to people and events that press the painful spots but I can, at least, recognise that they are not really hurting me — only reawakening old sores. Perhaps in order to heal we need to let these sores weep a little.

An effective way to enable this healing to take place is through *bodywork* — not of the cosmetic kind. Painful memories, locked away by the mind, can be reached through deep body-massage or physical movement. All our experience is stored away somewhere, and everything can be accessed or retrieved by various methods.

You could look at this question of forgiveness another way too. I have recently been reading a book written by the Friends of *Emmanuel*. Emmanuel is a spirit-guide who speaks through a channel. The channel is a woman called Pat Rodegast. Ram Dass, another person whose talks and writings have enlightened me greatly on my road to self-discovery, has a great deal of respect for the words of Emmanuel, and so do I. Whether they come from another plane of existence, or just a sub-personality of Pat Rodegast is almost irrelevant. They certainly make me think.

Emmanuel, as do other sources of this kind, tells us that we chose our parents very carefully, in order to learn the next lesson in the curriculum of life. *Emmanuel's Book* can take the sting out of life by letting you see that everything that happens is an opportunity to learn and go on to the next lesson.

> You create your distortions and you create your truths. This is how you learn.
>
> You chose the childhood environment that was the most effective catalyst to bring into focus those distortions that you have selected to work on in this lifetime. It is a masterpiece of planning, construction and tactic that you have put into forming your body, your mind and your emotions. Trust the wisdom of your soul that chose the infant circumstances that formulated your concept of life.
>
> (*Emmanuel's Book*, 1987, p8.)

If this is true, then how could I *blame* my parents for being the way they were? I can only feel compassion for their predicament, and hope they learn as much from me as I did from them.

Another reason for forgiving our parents is that *we need to forgive ourselves*. It is another step on the road to self-acceptance. I am clear that I *become* my mother: I have *introjected* (taken into myself) her anger and her determination, her intense will to win. Everything I don't like about myself I see in my mother. If I cannot have compassion for her — accept her, forgive her — how can I love those parts of me that *are* her?

The process of forgiving my mother has been long and painful for both of us. The culmination of it was very recent. My mother is becoming progressively more infirm and dependent on others to help her. She decided she wanted to go into residential care. While we were looking for a suitable establishment she came to stay at our home. I had to help her constantly to dress and go to the toilet. This was not too bad until she was feeling particularly feeble one day and frequently called on me to help her. I was attempting to concentrate on my work and became more and more irritated by the distraction. She called me for the *umpteenth* time to help her to get up off the toilet. Her voice was really weak and pathetic. Suddenly I was swept by feelings of rage. Had I gone to 'help' her at that moment I might have done something I regretted. I had to ask her to wait while I calmed myself down. The strength of my feelings was a great shock to me. What was this all about? Surely I was not such a monster that I could not help my own mother?

I realised that my intense anger was related to the times when I had been ill as a child and my mother had been intolerant and impatient with me. I remember when I was eleven an occasion when I was sick in the night and could not get to the bathroom in time. I felt ill, frightened and miserable, but my mother shouted at me for vomiting on the floor. All of the hurt I felt at that time was re-activated by my mother's present state of dependency and weakness. I wanted to exact revenge for all the times she had made me feel guilty and bad for being ill.

Recognising the source of this intolerant rage seemed to release me from the urge to get my own back. From then on my resentment faded. I finally lost it altogether following a conversation I had later with my mother.

After spending a long time examining various establishments I finally found a Care Home that I felt would suit my mother. I was very choosy and my mother seemed happy with the one we finally selected. The quality of care seemed excellent and my mother seemed to settle down well. After the honeymoon period was over, however my mother began her usual routine of complaint. She managed to get the cook to the point of resigning and I felt that enough was enough.

I told her that this behaviour had to stop. "As long as you have lived," I told her, "you have moaned and complained about everything. Has this made you any happier? Has it ever changed things for the better?" She looked at me thoughtfully and said, with an element of surprise, "No". "Then," I said, "it is time to give it up. You made my life a misery with it as a child and it has got to stop". To my amazement my mum replied, "I did?" This was stated calmly and with acceptance. I then hastily added, to take the sting out of it, "Of course I know you were very unhappy yourself . . . " but before I could go any further my mother said, in a lost and penitent voice, "Yes, but that is no excuse." I was astonished. For the first time my mother had allowed me to hold her *accountable*. She had taken *responsibility* for what she had done, and *blame* did not come into it. At that moment I forgave my mother everything. I no longer feel any resentment or desire to do anything other than love her.

My mother appeared to be able to see I was not blaming her; in fact I was attempting to improve the quality of her life by pointing out to her how self-defeating her behaviour was, and she was able to to accept responsibility for her mistakes. Since then she has been able to talk about the guilt she has about the way she treated my father. She is also aware that she did not show her children enough love and that this had quite a drastic effect on us all.

This conversation enabled me to point out to my mother that, if she had not treated me the way she did I probably would not be doing the kind of work I am doing now. She cheered up considerably at this news. What a relief that my mother has communicated all of this and can continue to clear her mind of all the guilt and upset she has stored there, instead of continuing to feel bad about herself and her life!

Drawing the distinction between responsibility and blame

Most of us become confused by the word *responsibility* and do hear it as *blame*. The following illustration might make the difference clearer.

If a group of children were playing football outside your house and one of them, very excited and determined to score a goal, kicked hard at the ball, which broke your window, would she be to blame — would you blame her for it? Of course she would be *responsible*, because it was her own actions which caused the damage, but she did not *intend* to do so. It was her lack of skill which caused it. Of course, you might say that it was irresponsible of her to play so near a house when she had a low skill-level. That might be true.

If the girl, or boy, accepted her responsibility, and offered to make good the damage, then presumably she would be forgiven, despite the fact that you would have to live with a broken window until it could be repaired. If the child attempted to say that they did not do it, or that they couldn't help it, then you might find yourself getting very angry. If she didn't do it — who did? Who is going to take responsibility for it?

Such is the position that many people find themselves in, who know their parents have damaged them, but cannot get any acknowledgement of that. This is an extremely frustrating and painful place to be. The offspring is faced with a double betrayal: first the abuse, neglect, and damage itself, and then the denial of it. It is relatively easy to forgive someone their trespasses, if they own up to their mistake or misdemeanour, and offer to make good any damage caused, but if they deny their responsibility, it seems to magnify the crime. We can all make mistakes, but it is a deliberate decision to lie about something, or make light of what has happened. Didn't *they*, our parents, set the standards for integrity? Didn't *they* tell us that it didn't matter what we had done, as long as we didn't lie about it? Doesn't it imply that they have no faith in our goodwill, our capacity for forgiveness?

Parents who lie to their offspring about the errors they have made inflict further damage on their children, and dig themselves deeper into the pit of denial and self-deception. They leave no room for therapeutic communication — for contrition on the one hand, and the lifting of guilt and forgiving removal of shame on the other.

John Bradshaw's (1988) revealing explanation of the shame experienced by neglected or abused children is very useful. Children are ashamed of their parents, and they introject these feelings of shame, becoming ashamed of themselves. They are ashamed to be associated with evil acts or embarrassing behaviour. I was terribly ashamed of my parents — but I was also, therefore, ashamed of myself. Wasn't I, after all, a product of those people — that environment? It is this shame that keeps many people from revealing to others, to groups or therapists, friends or lovers, the terrible experiences they encountered as children. They feel in some way responsible — that they created it, or that they will be seen as inferior for having such inadequate, destructive or irresponsible parents.

It was this deep sense of shame which had kept Ruth (mentioned in chapter three) from seeking help concerning the abuse she had suffered at the hands of her father. Even when she had found the courage to come and tell me about it, she could not be completely open with other people when she took my first-level course. She did have another chance, however. Ruth was assisting on a later course and, realising that she had missed an opportunity to let go of all her guilt and shame about the abuse, by not addressing it on the course she took, she volunteered to partner one of the course members on the 'father' process.

Taking her courage in both hands she managed to share with the group about the abuse she had suffered from her father from the age of nine months. An older (mid-fifties) male participant found it difficult to believe that anyone could recall incidents that took place at such an early age, and questioned the accuracy of her story. He suggested that she might have been confused about this, and advised her to contact her father and re-institute her relationship with him.

It is no coincidence that this man looked very like her father. She was filled again with self-doubt and shame. *Had she made it up? Was she mad, evil?* She was devastated. Needless to say I was extremely aware that this participant had inflicted pain on my protégée. I knew it had taken considerable courage to talk about the abuse, because of the shame and guilt she still experienced and could not release — largely due to her parents' denial. It is difficult to sustain your sense of reality in the face of your parents refutation of it. They were the ones who always validated or refuted your world view right from the beginning.

I was angry, in fact: so angry that I knew I could not address the issue objectively. I had to sit on it for a while, leaving all those in the room who had always assumed responsibility for their parents' anger quaking with the certainty that they were the cause of my rather obvious upset. During the next break I spoke to Ruth and told her that she should address the issue with the person who caused her the upset, for two reasons. One, that she must not put me in the position of ideal mother, who would pick her up, soothe her hurt and defend her from the danger — she must experience her own ability to defend herself and hold her 'aggressor' accountable. As adults, we look to our partners or some significant *other* in our lives, to fight our battles for us. We are still looking for an ideal parent who will fulfil our need for them to play a role as protector.

The second reason for requesting Ruth to address this issue herself was that, had I attempted to hold this person accountable, he would have probably seen it as an attack, or as an attempt to justify myself. He needed to experience the consequences of his actions directly. It is to Ruth's credit that she agreed to confront the person herself.

The following transcript is, I feel, a brilliant and moving example of the possibility created by holding someone accountable, making room for forgiveness and relationship to come out of the deepest hurt. I have to say also that the man concerned demonstrated great courage and humility in his response to this communication. I think this illustrates the depth of relationship that can be achieved between two human beings who are, after all, relative strangers with no obvious commitment to each other, when the intention and context of the communication is love and support rather than judgement and revenge:

Ruth: *I want to share with everybody that I feel let down, because over the two weekends of the course Jean shared things about my life which I have found very distressing, and very hard to hear her talking about. I said I found it very hard, but I have a commitment in life to other people's growth, and if it is going to help somebody, it is okay, I can handle how I feel. I feel very let down because I felt what has been shared was questioned, and I feel that has invalidated my experience.*

I'm very hurt that I should have to justify something in this room, because the agreements are that we don't make judgements. Why should I have to justify myself when nobody knows what I have been through? And yet I am having the courage to share what I have been through with people. I walked away after the break, and I didn't want to come back, but I did, because I can only expect of people what I am willing to do myself. And I don't want to do this because I am making myself vulnerable in here again now. I don't trust people in here now, and I don't want to make myself vulnerable, because it is tough enough in the real world.

People do things with what you say anyway, especially with sexual abuse. Too many people can't handle it, and they want to deny it, and that is why it is allowed to happen, because if people really got the reality of it, people would do something about it. I kept it to myself for seventeen years, because I thought no-one would believe me, and you can't trust anyone anyway, and it is like being in a prison, because you are trapped within yourself, and you cannot share yourself with anyone, because the risk is that they will invalidate you, they won't believe you.

Adrian: *I have to confess, when you* (Jean) *said you were angry I immediately leapt to the right conclusion. It didn't seem at the time that I had any intention of its causing damage, or whatever. Over what she shared with us I wouldn't say I was disbelieving, but curious, and I thought long and hard as to whether I should pursue my thoughts and queries about how certain conclusions had been reached. I did wonder whether I should bring it up in the group. The idea was not to cast doubts on what happened, but to confirm in my own mind a reality that I have never suffered, and had difficulty in believing that of anybody.*

I now have no doubt that it does exist, and I think you were very courageous in sharing with us what you did. In my blundering efforts to convince myself of the horrible reality you have faced, I should have followed my first inclination and kept my trap shut. Although it obviously hurt you and made you wary of the group, the fault is entirely mine, and in my seeking after truth I went too far, and for that I am truly sorry.

Jean: *Why did you need to do that? Why did you need to question Ruth? I am totally aware of the danger, once you have dealt with this sort of thing, of seeing it where it isn't, and I think I expressed that when I suggested to Lin (*another person in the group*) that the root of her problem might lie in some form of early abuse. Now why do you need to question my expertise?*

Adrian: *Perhaps I should have spoken to you, or something. I found the kind of behaviour that creates that situation most distasteful. I don't want to believe it.*

Jean: *How many other men don't want to believe it? (*All the men raise their hands*).*

Adrian: *It's a slur on the males.*

Participant: *Could the rest of us do it?*

Adrian: *I wanted to know more.*

Jean: *I don't think you wanted to know more. That would have been different.*

Ruth: *(*To Adrian:*) Why should I have to justify my life to you?*

Adrian: *If I have no right to question anybody, I should not have come to this group. The only way I can find out is by questioning.*

Jean: *Yes, but Ruth did not pay you to work on her case.*

Adrian: *That is true.*

Ruth: *Nor are you in any position to pass any opinion, because you know nothing about it.*

Adrian: *I was seeking, selfishly, to establish, for my own peace of mind . . . I found it so disturbing.*

Jean: *Well, why didn't you say that? I want to give you the opportunity to learn something. I want you to learn how to communicate with people.*

Adrian: *That is why I came here. I can't apologise too much to Ruth.*

Jean: *You were reinforcing in Ruth the denial that anything had happened to her. Even though her mother picked her up in a very injured state, she has never spoken of that incident, or mentioned it ever since. When Ruth spoke about it to her mother she totally denied it. And now denial has happened again.*

Adrian: *I didn't deny it.*

Jean: *You were saying people can't remember things from nine months old. How do you know you can't? But I will tell you, if something traumatic happened to you at nine months old, you would be able to access it under certain conditions. It is all in there. There are ways in which you can access that knowledge. It is a well-researched, well-documented fact. The reason your communication with people breaks down is that you have got the kind of mind that cannot accept a reality different to yours. So your opinion has to be the* right *one.*

Adrian: *My reason for approaching Ruth was to shape my mind more in that way.*

Jean: *That is not how you came across to her. I don't think that is what the* unconscious *motives are. You cannot bear your view of reality not to be correct, and so you are always trying to prove that your view is right. Even at the expense of other people.*

Adrian: *But I found out this morning I was wrong.*

Jean: *Yes, but look what your need-to-be-right did. You questioned Ruth out of a need-to-be-right.*

Adrian: *A desire to be right yes, and I didn't want to accept at face value what I was told.*

Jean: *And in doing that, you not only invalidate her, you invalidate me. You invalidate the person teaching you, and that way you don't have to listen to me either.*

Adrian: *I have questioned you during the course.*

Jean: *I know, because you find it very hard to have teachers. I do too. I work out in advance what I have got to learn, and then I tell the teacher what it is. I make sure I am good at it. There is nothing worse than learning something that you did not know, especially when you think you need to know everything. That is why I go to someone for coaching. He slices me down the middle with a Samurai sword. It is the only thing that is going to flatten my arrogance. It is the only way I am going to grow.*

Adrian: *Do you accept at face value all their statements?*

Jean: *No. I question them with respect and with humility. I ask them,* with *respect and humility,* Why do you say/think that? *I might say I find that hard to believe, but I never say I don't agree. Because I am aware of the fact that I don't know what I don't know.*

Adrian: *I perhaps feel I know more than I do. That is why I question. I do change my views.*

I confessed to Adrian that I used to be very similar, and still can be, when I relax my vigilance. I think what I needed to learn, in order to stop alienating and upsetting people with my arrogance, was this: I have learned to *live with the question* — not to need always to know the answer. And that is a very uncomfortable place to live. A very out-of-control place to live. But actually, asking the question, and not needing the answer, is the key to growth. The first step is asking the question — the second step is to explore it. In exploring, you find something out and it might not be what you wanted to know. Most of us, when we get the answer we don't want, discredit it. We wait until we find the answer we want, the answer that fits in with our construct of reality. Some of us wait a long time — we waste a lifetime looking for the answer we want to hear.

Jean: (continuing) *It is hard to let go of control. I have been down that road and I am still on it!*

Adrian: *I can't take back what I have done, and whatever I may have inadvertently caused you* (to Ruth) *I hope it is not permanent. No way should you have to suffer the pain that you suffered. I don't know whether you can forgive me. It was a personal thing that I did. I can assure you that I have not discussed, and have no intention of discussing, what has gone on within the walls of this group.*

Jean: *I want to acknowledge Adrian for having the humility to say he has made a mistake. It takes a big person to say that. It is very moving to see people really communicating and really being authentic in their communication. It takes a lot to do that. So we all learn. There are no mistakes, only lessons. This was just another lesson.*

Ruth did forgive Adrian. It took her to the end of the day, but she did give him a hug, and she did see how damaged he had been by life. For Adrian it was the key to a shift from resistance to realisation. He recognised that he had probably hurt his wife in similar ways. He also began to see how damaging the domination of his mother had been, leading him to strive desperately for total control in every area of his life. Ironically enough he had contracted a disease which left him almost completely out of control of his own movements and speech.

'If we don't learn the easy lessons, they get harder!' (Millman, 1984). When I saw Adrian several weeks after the course, he looked considerably younger, softer, more approachable. I know this interaction made a considerable difference to his relationship with others. I know it was a painful experience, and that it took Ruth a great deal of courage to

contribute to Adrian the way she did, by holding him accountable.

Another brilliant example of the process of holding someone accountable, but not blaming them or making them wrong, is given below. Frank was sexually abused by a close friend of his parents as an adolescent boy. His mother and father are loving, responsible and honest people — I know them well. They trusted this man with their son, and that trust was betrayed. When his parents did find out, their anger — and guilt — were intense. It was a devastating shock to them. I am grateful to Frank for his permission to reprint this letter, and I do so without editing it in any way, other than to retain anonymity.

Dear G . . . ,
It is about two years now since I told Mum and Dad about the sexual relationship you had with me when I was a child. As you must know, you have been in my thoughts a lot since then. I have experienced many different emotions relating to when I was abused, particularly my anger directed at you and Mum, and thoughts and images of you as the Monster.

I have talked to many people about what happened to me. My feeling was that the more I could share my experience of being abused, the greater the awareness that I could inspire in others — perhaps so that they could identify abuse or potential abuse that they suffered as children.

Looking back, the worst part of what happened was the perpetual guilt, because you frightened me by talking about what would happen if anyone found out, and because I knew at a deep level that what you were doing was wrong. This guilt taught me to hide my true feelings from other people, and myself — and taught me to deceive both myself and others for most of my life. In recent years I have experienced great pain through my difficulties in opening up emotionally to people and to be honest with myself.

Fortunately I have had the love of many friends, and particularly my life-partner, to help me to learn to really express my feelings, to trust *enough to be vulnerable, and to start to get to know my true self — this had been hidden behind a great defensive barrier which I feel I erected when I was eight. In fact I spent the latter half of 1989 feeling a deep sense of sadness within me, which I related to a part of myself that had never been allowed to develop — the innocent eight year old boy that was confused by what you did with him. I still feel sad that I lost the innocence of my childhood so soon.*

In December last year I was diagnosed as being diabetic and I am now on regular insulin injections. I have thought about the underlying cause of my illness. From a metaphysical point of view I feel that just as holding anger within the body can cause cancer, my diabetic condition has resulted from the deep sorrow that I have been holding in my body.

Becoming diabetic has been a life-changing experience for me. At first I believed that I could control the illness by diet alone, but it turned out that I did need insulin. This chronic dis-ease has forced me to confront issues in my life that weren't comfortable and had been carefully hidden: did I really want to continue to live? *(which has been a real toughie, and I do!). And I was forced to really express my emotions, because of the physical damage that I now experience when I hold them within my body.*

Through my macrobiotic diet I have experienced being 100% committed to my own health, and come up against my own limitations again and again. I have now learned to put my scientific career into context, instead of being obsessive about it, which may well have saved my life! I no longer worry about what other people think about me, because I do now have a sense of my own worth.

I have experienced true inspiration from living with D; she is a wise and loving person who has shown me the true meaning of compassion. D has supported me as only a soul-mate can. Also my life has been transformed through my relationships with many friends, therapists and counsellors. Learning to be honest with my brother and sister, with Mum and Dad, has been incredible too. I have felt so much love for my brother and sister and my remarkable Mum and Dad, and I have received great support. It has been a real release for me to express my inner self with my family, and to begin to know who they really are.

I feel deep gratitude to all those people who have been there when I needed them, and shared this part of my journey.

The last two years has been an amazing, terrible and wonderful time for me. I can see that I have grown both mentally and spiritually through the pain of my experience of being abused — this has helped me to become closer to people and to start to live a truly fulfilling life. I have developed a deep interest in healing and I'm in the process of learning to practice as a healer myself. Recently I have realised what little experience of joy I have in my life, and I'm now learning to experience joy and to share it with others.

This acknowledgement of the incredible changes I have made in my life is written as much for me as for you, G . . . It is to put the sexual abuse into context. Abuse is a terrible thing because it is the ultimate betrayal of trust — a rejection of the responsibility, which all adults have, to care for and nurture children. You treated me as a sexually responsible adult when I was eight years old, and I believe that was wrong.

However I will no longer hold a grudge against you, G . . . To do so would continue to lock pain and sadness in my body and prevent me from healing myself. I forgive you G . . . completely and unreservedly. I do not want you to die feeling that you are a terrible person. We are all human, and I extend the love and compassion that has changed my life, to you.

Writing this letter has been a freeing experience for me.

Peace and love to you G . . .

An Exercise on resentment and accountability

Assuming that you now see the value of forgiveness and the cost of holding onto the past I suggest that you try the following exercise:

Take a large sheet of paper and divide it into five columns. You are going to make a list of people you are holding a grudge against, or towards whom you feel some resentment. Look hard and deep — it is not always obvious. Be very clear about what they did to you.
Next, see if you need to hold them accountable — not in order to get *revenge*, but to free yourself and them from the past. Write down the names in the first column, what they did in the next column, and then write down the consequences of their behaviour/actions in the third column.
If you find any of that difficult get another sheet of paper and write down on that all the reasons why you do not want to do this exercise. If any of the reasons include *I don't want to hurt them*, realise that they will suffer more and longer if you don't do it. When you have written down everything you can think of that is stopping you, throw it away. Have this symbolise throwing away your considerations and getting them out of the way.
Now go back to your original list. In column four, make sure that you have 'owned' your part in the drama. Acknowledge your mistakes/responsibility, etc. Then forgive yourself for all of that. If necessary talk to someone else about it who will be empathic and compassionate — not someone who will collude with you and tell you 'not to be silly'.
Finally, in the last column, write down the action you need to take in order to hold the person accountable and enable yourself to forgive them.

I decided I ought to carry out this exercise to give you an example. However, I personally had a great reluctance doing so, because I was reluctant to look for someone I needed to forgive for something. I realise now that there is someone I need to carry out this exercise with, and I definitely don't want to do it. Here is my list of why I am avoiding this process with him.

* I believe if I hold him accountable and forgive him for what I think he has done I will have to get involved again in something I do not have time for, and which I find difficult to cope with. Being angry with him gives me an excuse not to participate. I realise this means I do not trust my own ability to say *no*;
* I can feel superior to him while I hold the view that he is an insensitive, chauvinist dictator;
* I might find out that I was wrong, and may owe him an apology (horror of horrors!);
* It's a waste of time anyway because he will never change, and until he does I don't want anything to do with him. However, having written this, I

realise I am withholding from him the opportunity to change;
* There is something else, but I can't quite get to it. I think it is something pretty important. I do know that while I am holding onto my grudge, I am controlling the situation. That is a pretty familiar scenario for me.

I could go on with this list, but there is a limit to how long this chapter can be, so I won't! Instead I will give you an example of an incident that happened a few years ago, where I did complete this exercise, so that you can see the results that can occur from carrying it out.

Who	For What	Consequences	My misrakes etc.	Action
X (Male)	Insulting me/ putting me down	Made me doubt myself. Caused others to mistrust me. Almost ruined my reputation	Arrogance. Undermining colleagues with students. Doiing my 'own' thing. Being subversive.	Tell him consequences of his actions. Tell him how hurt I felt. Own up to my arrogance

The results of carrying out the action of holding him accountable were quite remarkable. When I got around to telling how him hurt I felt and how I felt he put me down, he told me, very angrily, that everything I did was a *load of rubbish*. I did not have to tell him how hurt I had felt by his opinion — it was obvious, because I spontaneously burst into floods of tears. All the hurt I had felt for all those years of being invalidated and *rubbished*, not only by him, but by other colleagues, came out in an uncontrollable rush of emotion.

His reaction was amazing. He looked at me in amazement and said, *Oh, dear, I didn't mean to hurt you*. Looking back I am quite incredulous that someone can tell you that all you have ever done is rubbish, and not think that will be hurtful — but I have to take his word for it. He then began to open up to me about his fears and where he felt vulnerable in life, and I was totally taken by surprise. Someone I had always seen as hard, uncompromising, arrogant and uncaring revealed himself to be frightened, unsure of himself and very susceptible to any slight criticism. He had felt attacked by me, and so had attacked me in return. I left his office feeling lighter and very loving towards him.

I still find him a difficult person to deal with, but he no longer intimidates me, and I do not let his caustic criticisms affect me any more. I am free of him.

Forgiving ourselves

So you can see that while we definitely forgive others for our sake, a necessary beginning to that process is to forgive ourselves. We cannot hold other people accountable if we feel secretly guilty about what happened. To hold people accountable is to make it clear to them that they damaged you, and that there have been, or will be, consequences to that act. Sometimes it is not always possible to make sure that people experience the consequences of their behaviour — in the case of the man cited above, he lost the friendship of Frank's parents as a results of Frank finding the courage to tell them what had happened.

Thirty years ago I was a victim of rape, and I regret very much that I never held the man involved accountable for his actions. I was too afraid to go to the police at the time, because I thought they would not believe me. I was also advised by a close friend of mine who was a lawyer that the best course of action was to do nothing. He told me that I would probably end up feeling humiliated and demeaned by the experience. I took his word for it, but I later found out that this man had raped another woman shortly after this incident. Not only did I experience the cost of not holding him accountable, but someone else suffered for it too.

As Ron Smothermon (1980) says, you need to forgive people, but you need to hold them accountable, otherwise 'you are asking for it, and you might have noticed that you are getting it!' In fact, a couple of years after the rape incident another man attempted to rape me. He did not succeed because I was absolutely determined it was not going to happen again, even if I had to die first. This time I did go to the police, but they did not prosecute him, giving me the same reasons as my lawyer friend had given me — I might come off worst, and so on. However, they assured me that they would make sure he did not try it with anyone else, and they would keep a watch on him. He was also excluded from the club where I met him.

Despite all this, or perhaps because of it, he followed me several times when I was riding my motor-scooter, and I was terrified that he was going to run me down — so again I can see that I should not have been satisfied with the inaction of the police, and insisted that they prosecute. I certainly would not make this mistake again. Part of the reason I did not pursue it in either case, however, was the feeling that I must have brought it about. Also, I knew that the way I dressed was designed to attract men — to look *sexy*. I had a lot of guilt about the promiscuous phase I had been through earlier in my life. My mother's judgements about my *immoral* behaviour had become internalised, and I felt that I must have deserved what this man did to me. I must have *asked for it*, mustn't I? Of course, I now see that dressing attractively, or even *suggestively*, as they say, gives no-one the excuse for rape or sexual abuse. It is not an invitation to take what you want regardless of other people's wishes, and without their permission.

I think women are in a particularly difficult cultural trap here. On the one hand they are encouraged by the media — advertisements for female products, page three spreads etc. — to be *sexy* and alluring. On the other hand some males in this society view this behaviour as a licence to abuse the trust women place in them and justify their lack of restraint. I had no idea that men would interpret my attempts to make myself look attractive as a 'come on'. I wanted only affection. I paid a high price for it. I think many women are innocent of any calculated attempt to seduce the male of the species, but they are frequently judged to be seducers and are only too ready to accept that this might be the case.

In a similar way, so many sexually-abused children grow up feeling worthless and guilty about participating in something that was *wrong*. There is a deep sense of shame, and sometimes a feeling that they are not like other human beings — that they are not human at all, otherwise this terrible thing would not have happened to them. Because our culture stresses that only those who deserve it are punished, children believe they must have deserved the treatment meted out to them, and are therefore bad and wicked. This applied to all of us who were, in some way, abused by our parents, or by other adults. Since this would also include teachers, few of us escape.

Frank was able to forgive himself by trusting others to accept him and to listen to him with compassion. When he realised that other people felt only the deepest love and sadness for what had happened to him, and that they placed the responsibility firmly on the shoulders of the man who had abused him, he was able to begin to adjust his perceptions of himself and of the part he played in the relationship. He saw that he was an innocent and frightened child, who thought he had no power to stop what was happening, and so did not. In fact, had Frank told his parents, the nightmare would have been over — but he did not, because he had been convinced that his parents would be displeased with him for allowing this to happen. So his shame was compounded because he did not tell them, and then, as it went on, it became more and more impossible, for, would they not have said, *why didn't you say something before*?

It usually takes a lot of courage to hold people accountable, but it is vital, because it constitutes an acknowledgement of your worth. The thinking behind letting people off the hook is that I must have deserved it, or it doesn't really matter, or even *they won't like me any more*. The thinking behind holding people accountable has to be that *no-one is going to damage me without realising it and having the opportunity to repair that damage, or make recompense for it, because I deserve love and respect not abuse and invalidation*.

The next step for Frank was to have compassion for himself and forgive himself — and then, as he says, he was able to extend that same compassion and understanding to the man who had betrayed him. Frank was able to stop carrying the man around with him. Forgiveness is an important aspect of growth. We can stand on the past and use it as a stepping-stone to the future, but we must not hold it before us as a barrier to our progress.

Maybe we cannot hold people accountable until we have forgiven ourselves, so this is an essential act.

An exercise in self-forgiveness

I suggest you make a list of things you are not forgiving yourself for right now. Make the list, and look at what you need to do in order to forgive yourself for them. My own list might look something like this:

* Being nasty with Tim and eroding his sense of worth;
* Not seeing my mother often enough;
* Not bothering to go to the university to see if my students had turned up, because they hadn't bothered contacting me;
* Not totally loving my brother when he was alive, because I was frightened he would become too intrusive in my life;
* Allowing my fear of losing my closest friend's friendship to stop me truly supporting her.

These are a few things that come to mind as I sit writing today. A lot of them I was not aware of until I started to compile the list! They have been sitting in the dark recesses of my mind, simmering away and dissipating my energy. Suppressing these feelings of guilt takes a lot of energy.

So what do I need to do in order to forgive myself for these things? I need to have compassion for myself and see that I am human. Let me start with the first item: I do not want to harm Tim. I am, in fact, committed to his growth and well-being. I do not want to be destructive with him — I have learned this reaction from my mother. It will take me a long time to eradicate it from my behaviour. I need to give myself time, and acknowledge Tim for giving me the space to learn how to do this. I must not beat myself up for doing it, otherwise I will not be able to stop — *what you resist persists*. I must simply acknowledge that it is not how I want to be, every time I do it — even if it takes me a while to get round to it. I need to understand that I am damaged. I need to heal my inner child. I need to forgive my father for not being the way I wanted him to be. I need to have compassion for Tim, and see that he is human and is also very damaged. I need to forgive Tim for not being the way I want him to be. I need to love him unconditionally.

Right now, this seems like a tall order, but I can see that it gives me somewhere to start, and it takes away the feelings of helplessness, and despairing thoughts that things will never change and there is nothing I can do about it. I also realise that changing any behaviour requires an enormous amount of self-discipline and persistent practice. Forgiving yourself is an important step in the process of self-acceptance.

One of the areas I have been working on recently is that of sex and intimacy. I will say more about this in a later chapter, but I want to say something here, which I think is related to forgiveness. I have realised recently that, in order to be able to have a deeply fulfilling sexually-intimate relationship, I have a lot of work to do on forgiving myself for all the times I have *performed* with men, and never really been truly present to the experience, and for all the times I have used sex to get what I wanted — namely *love*. I also need to do a lot of forgiving of males for the way in which they have used and abused me sexually. I need to forgive my mother for developing my early constructs of sex as something shameful, dirty and unpleasant. I need to let go of my sexual past and live in a newly-created experience of what it really is and can be — if I let it.

One very important aspect of forgiving yourself is to be able to tell the truth about the item around which you have a lot of guilt. For a long time I did not experience having any guilt around sex. I had rationalised it wonderfully. I had realised I needed to be authentic, and authentic, for me, meant that I could say I was not interested and didn't need it. This was huge step forward from my *act*, which was to be sexy and pretend I was having a great time in bed. It has taken me a long time to sort out the truth, which is, *I don't even know what 'sex' is!*

Nor did I realise that I could be involved in sex at different levels: the level of *having*, (*let's have sex* — or, more recently in my life, *let's not have it!*), and the level of *being*. It has taken me perhaps ten years to recognise the unconsciousness I had around sex — how I had repressed a lot of fear, guilt and shame about it. It took me longer to come clean about the strategies I was using to avoid it because, knowing a lot about the mind, I had developed some pretty subtle strategies.

Forgiveness is an essential ingredient in the process of growth. It is synonymous with self-acceptance and acceptance of others — it is synonymous with love. Without forgiveness there is no love. Without love there is no growth. When we cannot forgive others for their destructive behaviour, we cannot forgive ourselves. And destructiveness is only a matter of degree. Who is to say which is the most damaging: sexual abuse, or the abuse of a parent who destroys their child's identity, by insisting that the child becomes the person they want them to be, and crushing the child's spirit, and squeezing them into a mould not designed for their being. It doesn't really matter how the destructive process is begun, or carried on. Destruction is destruction. In a way it is a more insidious form of destructiveness to be *over-loving* with a child, because the child has no sense that they have been harmed. At least physical abuse and obvious nastiness are easier to deal with, more palpable.

I destroy Tim's sense of worth by constantly finding fault with him, and this is tantamount to murder. It is abuse of the soul. But for a long time I really convinced myself, and him, that it was for his own good. I wonder if many people are often so vindictive in their desire for revenge and their need to condemn, because it makes them feel better about their own misdeeds. By finding *monsters* in our culture, our crimes against humanity (and ourselves) pale into insignificance.

Jimmy Boyle, cited as the 'most dangerous criminal in Scotland', found his salvation in the trusting act of a prison officer, who handed him a knife, against all prison regulations. This act enabled Boyle to free himself from his bitterness and hatred against authority, and eventually become committed to supporting young offenders and drug-abusers. One small act of trust and love — one huge release of potential in another human being. Boyle changed from being almost totally destructive to being extremely creative and committed to humanity.

So we need to forgive, in order to learn how to love ourselves and others. We need to forgive, because without forgiveness we can do nothing about creating a society where monsters, in the shape of multiple murderers, sex-offenders and the like, do not exist. Only when we can relate to people with love and compassion have we any chance of understanding what drives people to such behaviour. Only when they can trust someone have they any chance of reforming — or transforming themselves.

This does not mean that we ignore the fact that they have damaged someone else. They must be held accountable for what they have done, otherwise they cannot tell the truth about it, and thus begin the process of forgiving themselves. Society must also ensure that others do not fall victim to their destructiveness before this transformation has taken place. I am sure that people who are destructive need to be contained, but I am also sure that punishment does not heal, and these people, like all of us, need healing.

As it is, such people are not encouraged to take the first step in the process of self-healing. If they tell the truth about what they have done, they condemn themselves to punitive retribution. Nobody acknowledges them for coming clean about it. They are not given any help.

Ian Brady (the multiple 'Moors murderer') was not considered to be insane and in need of therapy. He was considered to be in need of *punishment*. Ian Brady was consistently abandoned as a child. He was special to no-one, and never experienced being loved or wanted. He now exists in total isolation because, if he were put with other prisoners, they would tear him apart. Once again he has been abandoned and rejected. Once again he is totally unloved. It has been said that Brady experienced no remorse for his crimes, but who experienced remorse for the crime that was committed against him as a child?

I do find it extraordinarily difficult to understand how anyone can justify mutilating and torturing innocent children, but I am sure they do justify it in their own minds, otherwise they could not do it. And I am sure that I have justified my cruelty to children I have taught and helped to rear, not to mention the adults I have married or had relationships with. We are all capable of cruelty, and we probably practice it in one shape or form. Some of us are just much more subtle about it, so subtle that we cannot even see what we are doing — so subtle that our victims do not know that we are damaging them.

I was fascinated with the scene in *Jesus Christ Superstar* where the crowd are about to stone Mary Magdalene, and Jesus asks them about the sins they have committed against each other, their wives, their children. He then utters the famous statement, *Let he who is without sin cast the first stone.* I really saw what that meant for the first time, although I had heard it many times. They wanted to stone the woman to death to deflect their own guilt, and endow themselves with feelings of righteousness. It is tempting to do so. Don't be tempted. I would like to share with you another extract from *Emmanuel's Book,* which sums up perfectly what I have been trying to say:

> Murder, violence, cruelty, viciousness, wickedness — yes, this all exists, just as kindergarten exists before first grade. Violence is painful for you who look from a level beyond (not better than, but certainly wiser than), and see with anguish the anguish that creates the anguish. Do not be afraid of terror. Do not react violently to violence. Do not feel pain about pain. By doing so you perpetuate what you are seeking to avoid. When you pass judgement on such things you are limiting God's reality to your human understanding.
> From where you are, there is right and wrong, and from where I sit there is truth.
>
> (*Emmanuel's Book,* p94).

I know from my own experience that failing to forgive yourself and hold yourself accountable is a heavy burden to carry around. I recently wrote a letter to my ex-husband's ex-wife, whom I once replaced. In this letter I was able to acknowledge my lack of integrity and responsibility in having an affair with her husband. It took me twenty years to write that letter! I never even considered writing it, until someone on one of my courses was talking about the fact that her husband had left her for another woman. I realised that I was feeling very uncomfortable, and I said so.

I came to the conclusion that I was still feeling guilty about the part I played in the break-up of my ex-husband's marriage, despite having always justified my actions by saying 'If it hadn't been me it would have been someone else', and protesting that he did all the running in the beginning — in other words, I did not pursue and seduce him. I suddenly saw that all that was irrelevant. The truth is, I did not support him in getting to the bottom of the problems in the relationship and working them through if possible, to whatever conclusion. I colluded with him in believing the marriage could never work, and in running away. I needed to clean that up, and I did. I feel much lighter for having done so.

I recently shared this with a friend who was being harassed by her former lover's wife, who had found out about the relationship — after it had ended. I encouraged her to own her part of the deceit and apologise to his wife for her lack of integrity. I think she was rather taken aback, but realised eventually that it was the way forward for her and for the woman concerned. It allowed her, finally, to put the whole thing down.

I mentioned earlier in this chapter a client who could not forgive his wife for rejecting him. I have described the way in which he started the process of forgiving her. In a later session he was given an opportunity for another breakthrough. He had found it hard to swallow when I told him he had to forgive his wife, but there was worse to come: I told him he needed to forgive *himself*. 'FOR WHAT?!' he indignantly wanted to know. 'For the part you played in the breakdown of communication and relationship', I told him. What a lousy therapist I was turning out to be!

I then suggested that he tell his wife about a course I was running for families, and invite her to join him and their two children on the weekend course. It is to his great credit that he did that. At my suggestion he wrote a letter to his wife in which he had to come clean about his fragile ego and his lack of communication. The first letter he wrote carried out my instructions exactly, but he managed to make it clear that *it had been suggested to him that he write to her and say . . . .* I pointed out that there was a certain lack of responsibility in the wording of this letter, and so he re-wrote it, not without some effort.

At this point I do not think he really owned his own mistakes and his other misdemeanours, but he is gradually coming round to realising that it does not have to be a battle of who is right and who is wrong. This process of forgiving his wife for what has happened (and not happened) between them is gradual, but I notice that he has lightened up considerably, and is getting far more out of life than he has done for several years.

And, having forgiven, what then?

Let us suppose that my client forgives his wife completely and she forgives him. What then? Should they be re-united in the same type of relationship? Maybe — and maybe not. It depends what is right for them. What will contribute to their well-being and that of their children? There is no cut-and-dried answer.

Should Ruth forgive her parents? And if she does, what then? Should she be re-united with them? I think not. Although, again, it might depend on their response to her. If I were to meet the Hungarian refugee who raped me, I think I could look at him with compassion — I would like to think I would let him know what he had done, and the consequences it had. I would want to give him an opportunity to clean up his actions, but I am really clear that I would not accept an invitation to spend an evening with him alone in his flat! Not unless I was absolutely convinced that he was a reformed character, and that would take some doing.

Nor should Ruth attempt to re-establish a relationship with her parents based on a lie. Although Smothermon maintains that forgiving someone means that your relationship with that person 'will clear up remarkably', and Jampolsky asserts that forgiving means, 'correcting our misperception that the other person harmed us', I feel these statements are too simplistic. I was definitely harmed by the rapist and so was Ruth harmed by her father, both physically and mentally. I have certainly forgiven my parents, and I can have a relationship with my mother, and I feel she can no longer harm me. Ruth does not feel that way. Her mother can still invalidate her; her father fills her with fear. She feels he is a dangerous man. If people are dangerous, perhaps we should give them plenty of space. It is a little stupid to deliberately stand in the path of a rogue elephant on the loose.

Martin Luther King (1959), on the question of forgiveness says,

> We love the person who does an evil deed although we hate the deed that he does.

In his powerful book, *The Strength to Love*, King gives an inspiring motive for loving our enemies. 'Hate', he says, 'multiplies hate'.

> Darkness cannot drive out darkness, only light can do that. Hate multiplies hate . . . the chain reaction of evil — hate, begetting hate, wars producing more wars, must be broken, or we shall be plunged into the dark abyss of annihilation.

So if we forgive, we must not forgive because we *should*, or because it is *wrong* not to love people. If we forgive, it must be for our sake and for the sake of life itself, for the evolution of humanity. We must forgive in order to stop the cycle of destruction. We must also, with regard to parents and other people in our lives, give them the opportunity to clean up their mistakes and remove the wall of guilt from their relationship with us.

I do not feel, however, and I must emphasise this clearly, that people should remain in destructive and harmful relationships. Most of us have not aspired to the stage of enlightenment (or altruism) attained by the Ghandis and the Martin Luther Kings of this world. I, personally, am not willing to put my life at risk in order to save another's soul, although I might, in an emergency, put it at risk to save their body. Perhaps one day I will be able to reach the level of forgiveness and trust expressed by Martin Luther King, but right now I think I am too attached to staying alive! I do not consider myself to be built of the stuff that martyrs and saints are made of.

6. *Don't be fooled — towards self-acceptance*

Please hear what I'm not saying

Don't be fooled by the mask I wear, for I wear a thousand masks,
And none of them are me.
Don't be fooled, for God's sake don't be fooled.

I give you the impression that I'm secure,
That confidence is my name, and coolness my game,
And that I need no one. But don't believe me.

Beneath dwells the real me in confusion, in fear, in aloneness.
That's why I create a mask to hide behind,
To shield me from the glance that knows -
But such a glance is my salvation.

That is, if it's followed by acceptance, if it's followed by love.
It's the only thing that can liberate me
From my own self-built prison walls.

I'm afraid that deep down I'm nothing and that I'm just no good,
And that you will see this and reject me.
And so begins the parade of masks.

I idly chatter to you —
I tell you everything that's really nothing
And nothing of what's everything, of what's crying within me.

Each time you're kind and gentle and encouraging,
Each time you try to understand because you really care,
My heart begins to grow wings, very feeble wings, but wings.

You alone can release me from my shadow world of uncertainty -
From my lonely prison.

It will not be easy for you,
The nearer you approach me, the blinder I may strike back.

But I am told that love is stronger than strong walls
And in this lies my hope, my only hope.

Who am I, you may wonder?
I am someone you know very well,
For I am every man you meet, and I am every woman you meet,
And I am you, also.

(Anon)

Every time I read this poem I am moved to tears — and I have read it many times. Perhaps I weep for the pain that it expresses — the pain of the *normal* human condition; the pain I suffered for so many years, that of not being *known*. Why is there such a fear of letting people see who you really are? I think I can best answer that by looking at the process of writing this book.

The further I get with this, the more considerations I have about people reading it. I know some people will be threatened by it. They will need to invalidate it so that they can ignore what is in it. They will, consequently, invalidate me (by inference). My whole life is in here: my ego hates that. I may become an object of curiosity, someone who is seen as a weirdo, a freak, a fringe person. At the university my outspokenness and ideas threatened some people. I was contained and controlled by being regarded as the *token renegade*, the pet oddity (as if all departments should have one).

This set me outside the group, it isolated me. It was a high price to pay for trying to express myself authentically. Sadly, my attempts to be authentic never really worked. Although I told myself I was honest because I did not pretend to be someone I was not, in the academic world, I *did* pretend that I did not care about the isolation, the labelling, the lack of partnership and connectedness. I *did* care very deeply, but pretending just dissolved the pain a little. It made me feel less vulnerable, even if I wasn't. And it made me ill.

I sought for all sorts of reasons for the illness and all sorts of solutions. I saw acupuncturists, took thyroxine, consulted a homoeopath, went on high-energy diets — all to no avail. Finally my homoeopath, Jeremy Sherr (a very perceptive and skillful healer) said, "You should leave the university; your heart isn't in it". I thought he was mad. I loved my work with the students. But he was right. The person I felt I had to be at the university was not *me* — even after all the work I had done on myself, I dared not be *me* there. I was not *known*, and it was killing me.

Much of the anger and anguish that people express on the course is realisation that their parents do not *know* them. In order to of their parents, they have hidden behind their masks, and might have gained their parents' love, they know that it is empty and meaningless, because the only love that really counts is the love that comes to you for *being yourself* — for being *real*. Paradoxically though, as Margery Williams says in *The Velveteen Rabbit*, 'When someone loves you, really loves you, for a long, long time, *then* you become real'. It seems to be a circular process.

Most of us are afraid to be real around our parents — or anyone else. As it says in the above poem, we are afraid that, deep down, we are *nothing* and *no good*, and that, if anyone sees that (especially our parents), they will reject us — and so begins the parade of masks.

This next bit of information is so important, I wish I could write it miles high in the sky for every human being to see and understand:

Until someone loves every part of you, accepts you totally, just the way you are, you cannot love yourself and you cannot ever know love.

Until the day you know who someone else really is and totally accept them, just the way they are, you will never know what loving is.

When I took the *EST Training* I revealed my darkest side — my innermost weaknesses — to 301 people. I experienced only compassion and love. Something very fundamental shifted. I felt beautiful, known, recognised. People acknowledged me for my courage and told me they understood. I was accepted. Having taken off all the masks, I had survived, I belonged, I was *real*. It gave me the courage to be real with other people, too.

I realised that this was probably the most important aspect of growth-work, and one that was not accessible, on this scale, from individual therapy. In Frank Masson's book, *Against Therapy*, he argues that a good therapist only provides what any true friend gives us — love and acceptance. This is probably true, but I know that a true friendship is very precious, and most of us would be loath to risk losing the person we most value. It is a powerful experience for a client when a therapist is totally accepting. It is perhaps the first time they have ever known love in that sense. But when a large number of people are totally accepting, it enables us to really grasp that we are acceptable *just the way we are*.

Although many people do find the courage to be very open about themselves on the course, there are those who are too afraid to take that step even in that safe environment. They have many reasons for remaining silent: *someone has already said what I was going to say*; or *what I feel is too trivial to mention, for other people's problems are much worse*; or *it's too awful to tell anybody*; or *I will break down and never stop crying*; or *it will bore people*, and so forth.

None of the reasons are the truth. The truth is they are ashamed. Despite being told that the course does not work unless they can share themselves with others, they just cannot bring themselves to do it. Most of us carry with us what Bradshaw describes as *toxic shame*. It is rooted deeply in our childhood, and can be associated with all kinds of experiences.

I was deeply ashamed of my parents — the *abnormality* of my father. I hid this information from everyone, even my best friend. Somehow this shame transferred to me. I was ashamed of myself for having such a parent. Most of us carry toxic shame of some kind. Toxic shame is, as the name suggests, poisonous. We may be involved in certain areas of life that we are ashamed of, because they are damaging and destructive. Healthy shame causes us to look at them honestly and recognise that we should stop — give them up. Shame is telling us that we are not being true to our natures, and that is damaging to our sense of worth.

But toxic shame is difficult to shift because it is rooted in someone else's behaviour. Sometimes it develops as a consequence of the cultural context that we live in, for example, my own shame about my working-class origins. At a rational level I know there is nothing to be ashamed of, but at an emotional level I still feel I have no right to sit in a first class compartment or go into a *posh* department store.

For most of us, the fear of exposing our toxic shame is enormous — the consequences of being found out are felt to be too horrible to contemplate. And so we keep those things of which we are ashamed to ourselves, and in so doing keep ourselves apart from others, and deprive ourselves of the experience of love. We dare not be *real*.

In order to encourage participants to take the next step towards self-acceptance, break through their fear and let themselves be known, they are asked to complete the *Johari Window* exercise (see *Quest: a Search for Self*, Cirese, 1977)

The Johari Window

The purpose of this exercise is to encourage people to be open, in order to uncover unconscious aspects of ourselves — those aspects we have buried deeply in our unconscious — and make them accessible to our conscious minds. If you do not know yourself, you cannot make yourself known to others.

The Johari Window is a model for explaining how and why being open leads to becoming more self-aware. About ourselves, say the devisers of this process, there are certain things we know, and things we do not know (*fig* 3a). Also, about ourselves there are things that are known to others, and things about us that others do not know (*fig* 3b). If we superimpose *fig* 3a onto *fig* 3b we get *fig* 3c.

Within this matrix there is only one possible direction for the move-

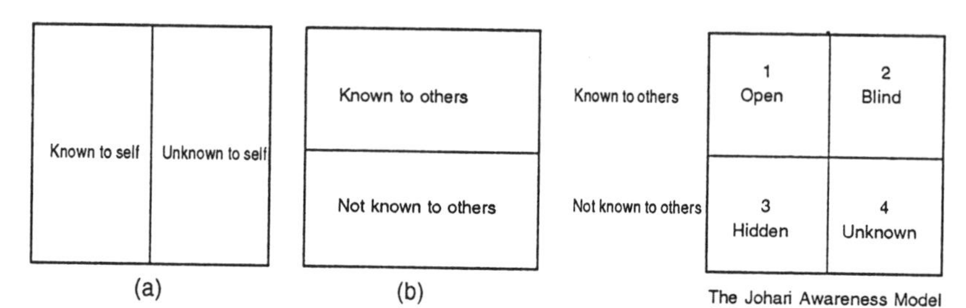

Fig 3. The Johari Window.

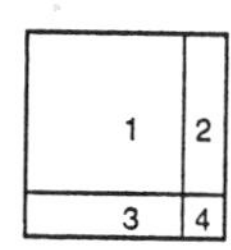

d. Movement of information within the matrix.

ment of information, That is from Box 2 to Box 1. The theory is that, by moving items from Box 2 to Box 1, you will open up boxes 1 and 3 and reduce boxes 2 and 4, like this (fig 3d):

The implications for this are that the less we hide and the more open we are, the less blind we are and the more aware (or less unconscious) we become.

How does this work? It looks as though all that should happen is that we simply hide less, but still do not become more enlightened about the *blind* and *unknown* content. It works on the principle that, when we have the courage to be more open, other people are encouraged to be more frank with us about those aspects of our personality or behaviour that we cannot see for ourselves, but which are glaringly obvious to others — thus reducing the content of the *blind* box.

Another development that occurs is that our openness provides people with a context within which they feel much safer to share their own hidden thoughts or feelings, and so they will be open with us. Very often the revelations of others enable us to recognise something about ourselves that we were previously unaware of. All people are mirrors of ourselves.

To encourage people to bring their hidden, shameful thoughts, feelings and deeds into the open, course participants are asked to write at least one of these down. The instruction is to write down a feeling, thought, or motivation (something you would like to do or have already done, thought or felt) that you know about you, but that other people in the group do not know about you, *and* you would not like them to know. Something you are ashamed of.

I will not tell you what happens to the information people have written down, as that might spoil it for you, should you ever be in a group where the Johari Window is used. Suffice it to say that people are generally very nervous about writing anything down, and mild hysteria sets in, with people giggling and talking nervously to people around them. Most people do manage to write something, however.

Exercise

Now it is your turn.

Write down three things about yourself that you are ashamed of. Ideally they should be things you have never told anybody, but if you are one of those people who tells at least one person everything, then write down something you would not like to be generally known about you, by your family, work colleagues, or some other group. If this is because it would probably end up in your dismissal, rather than that you are ashamed of it, don't put that down.

Sometimes it is difficult to know if we *are* ashamed of something, so just visualise yourself telling a group of people — family, friends, work-mates — and see how that feels.

You might consider something is not worth putting down, because it is too *trivial*, but that could be an excuse. The one I kept avoiding putting down (I do the exercise too), was *I pick my nose and eat it*. Even now I cannot write these words — knowing that several thousand people might read them — without a sense of dread. Somewhere I have picked up the idea that this is an act far worse, far more shameful than lying, cheating or stealing, because those things I will quite cheerfully admit to having done. Perhaps it is because those other things are in the past, and this is something I still do.

Anyway — back to the exercise.

Having written down your three items see if you can pluck up the courage to tell someone about it — someone that you feel might be shocked by it or angry, upset or disillusioned with you. Notice the reasons you give yourself for avoiding tackling this, and notice the reactions you have when you contemplate doing it (body sensations, feelings, emotions, thoughts).

Do some flow-writing about what you think will happen, and why you feel you don't need to do it.

Then, if you really want to move forward, do it — communicate to the person or persons you are thinking of, and see what happens.

I am frequently amazed at the variety, and sometimes the triviality (as I see it) of the items people are ashamed of. Of course, you couldn't get anything more serious than picking your nose and eating it — could you?

Our darkest secrets

Here are some of the darkest secrets people have:

* When I was ten I took my clothes off in front of other children in the woods. Nobody else did. I felt ashamed of myself. I am ashamed of my body;
* I realise I get nervous and start to talk in a situation that I don't want to go through with — I feel week and vulnerable;
* Not having done something with my life sooner;
* A one night stand with a colleague. Something I had not done before and felt very ashamed about;
* I've slept with my brother. Now I feel that I raped him. Feeling guilty about him. Keep hidden my family past;
* Got married because of pregnancy. I made her pregnant so she wouldn't end our relationship. The baby died — she had a miscarriage;
* My grandfather sexually abused me when I was a child;
* I am jealous of people who are happy;
* I devised a scheme to steal £5000 from the parents at school;
* I'm gay and I'm ashamed;
* I've been sexually abused;
* I feel like killing my step-dad;
* I used to steal money from my parents;
* I am devious, manipulative;
* Worried because I have homosexual tendencies;
* I want to kill my father;
* I slept with someone for the wrong reasons, even though I knew I was just being used. Unfortunately I made the same mistake again not long after. I thought it would be different;
* Ashamed when I have sexual experiences with women because I had a sexual experience with a prostitute;
* I had a sexual relationship with my sister;
* I had a cigarette ten days ago;
* I have an attraction to violent pornography;
* Child marked by my husband. Ashamed of having a hatred for someone whose actions damage people;
* When I was very drunk I fell downstairs, nearly killing myself. Too ashamed to admit this, I said I'd been mugged;
* Abortion;
* Hate friend;
* Stole money from mother;
* Sometimes I fantasise about sexual act with someone of the same sex;
* I feel scared of sex and I'm backing away from having a relationship at the moment;

* I'm afraid of getting old. I hate the wrinkles developing on my face. I hate my body. Feeling inadequate as a person;
* My pride wont let me change my mind about things;
* Not really knowing what I want to get out of my life;
* I think about oral sex a lot;
* At times I really hate people. I had two affairs with married men;
* Inability to do things, take action;
* Lack of progress with communication. Maintaining a veneer;
* Weakness of character;
* Missed opportunities;
* I got thrown out of the dentist because I would not open my mouth;
* If I don't get respect from certain people I want them to suffer more than I have done. I never show that on the surface because I am deeply ashamed of that image;
* Ashamed that I am not ashamed of what happened between me and dad, because I enjoyed it and felt special. Sometimes ashamed that I enjoy sex. I am ashamed of my body;
* Obscene acts. Male orgasm. Sex;
* Motivated by money. Afraid of being lonely. Hating my mother. Not being motivated to succeed;
* Being lazy. Not protecting someone. Telling mum I hated her. She didn't love me;
* Buy pornographic magazines and masturbate. This is the thing I am most ashamed about of all;
* I feel ashamed of my ego. I often put myself first at the expense of others. Feel selfish, bad and arrogant;
* Sister 11, me 14: fantasise and play games, interfere with in sleep. Sexual fantasies about any girl, woman;
* I want my lover to hit me when we have sex, and vice versa.

Well, that is it. Divulging these thoughts and actions causes people to squirm with embarrassment and sweat with fear. Once other people have heard them the reactions are fairly universal. This one from Dianne is fairly typical:

Dianne: *They are not such terrible things really. They might think other people will be shocked, but people aren't so wildly shocked by them. If anyone else were to tell you what they were ashamed of, I could forgive it, but when it comes to myself I can't do it. It seems so bad.*

And this from Harry:

Harry: *There was nothing I heard that made me feel* Oh my god, that person is terrible! *And so I don't have any less opinion of anyone in this room because of what was said. There was nothing bad there, was there? We have all got things that we have been trying to hide. There were a few duplications. Other people having problems seems less bad than if you have it yourself.*

This person was positively exuberant:

Olive: *I think it is a great experience because I realise that there are lots of people who have exactly the same problem as I have, which is very funny to me. I didn't expect that at all.*

This is the first glimpse people begin to get, that they are not alone in carrying around toxic shame. When they hear what other people have to say, and can listen to that without needing to condemn, blame, or reject that person, they begin to have hopes for themselves. When they see that being open about their *shameful* attributes earns them only acceptance and compassion—or at worst, gentle, empathic amusement—they are, at first, disbelieving, and then hugely relieved. Our *crimes* are quickly put into perspective, and recognised as *errors*, or habits which grew out of need, rather than out of an intrinsically evil nature.

Some people need a little more support in dealing with their shame, and reaching a stage when they can forgive themselves.

Wanda had already revealed to the group that she had been sexually abused by her father as a child. The abuse was not extreme, mostly taking the form of inappropriate fondling and kissing, but nevertheless, it had affected her quite severely. She did not understand why, since it was not *terrible*. *Any* sexual behaviour towards a small child is inappropriate, however, and constitutes a deep betrayal of trust — certainly in this culture, where such behaviour is taboo. She felt this betrayal when, innocently, she attempted to kiss him the way he had kissed her — but this time her mother was there. Her father was very angry. Then she knew that what they had been doing was *wrong*.

The shame came from the realisation that she had been complying with something that was *bad*. She had been enjoying the attention, and the fact that it made her feel special, and now she saw that this was *bad*. No wonder she had difficulty relating to men after that. The more *special* she felt, the more ashamed and guilty she later became, and she did not know why until something triggered off the repressed memory of what had occurred with her father. Wanda wanted to know how she could deal with these feelings, so that she could relate to men more healthily.

Wanda: *I didn't feel very comfortable. I thought I was going to burst into tears again.*

Jean: *Why?*

Wanda: *I am ashamed of it. I didn't want to tell anyone.*

Jean: *You are ashamed that you enjoyed it.*

Wanda: *I don't know if* enjoy *is the right word. I felt I was* special. *It was nice. So, I think that is more where my problem is. I think I should think it is a bad thing, but I don't.*

Jean: *If anyone should feel guilty about it, who should that be?*

Wanda: *My dad.*

Jean: *Yes, you were an innocent child who trusted that what he did was okay. But it wasn't okay, was it? I want you to get that it might have felt okay, but it wasn't okay, was it?*

Wanda: *No, it was wrong.*

Jean: *I don't know whether it was* wrong *or not, but it wasn't* okay. *What wasn't okay about it?*

Wanda: *It was secretive.*

Jean: *He got angry with you when you did it publicly. He had drawn you into an act which he knew was not right. So at that point he let you know that what you did with him was wrong. He betrayed your trust. There is something else: you said it was secretive, but there is something else as well. You are, to your father, I suspect, a surrogate wife. You inappropriately bonded with your father. He treated you as if you were a sexually mature person, and you were not. You have never been a child to your father, and he has never been a father to you. He was your husband. What you will look for in your relationships is the father you have never had. You had a lover, not a father, and that is a sad loss. It is not that this is bad. Nothing is bad.* Nothing is good or bad, but thinking makes it so — *Shakespeare. But the way your father expressed love to you was totally inappropriate, and you inappropriately bonded with your father. And you have had to be a lover to your father. You have not been his daughter. Does that make any sense to you?*

Wanda: *A little, yeah.*

Jean: *This will mess up your relationships with men, so you need to sort it out. Other people will have inappropriately bonded with their parents. Anyone else recognise this?* (some raised hands).

Many people want to have children, but they don't want to be parents. Many people want to be married, but they don't want to be a husband or wife. They want the security of that situation, but they do not want the responsibility. The same is true of parents. They want what they get from children, but they don't want the responsibility.

Revealing her shame about her *enjoyment* of the special relationship she had with her father proved to be the first step in releasing Wanda from years of damning self-judgement and guilt about her complicity in this *shameful* act.

Carol was another person who was carrying a shameful secret that she felt people would not forgive her for. Again, she was willing to address this openly with the group:

Carol: *I was the person with the child who was marked (by the husband). She was about three and my husband was violent. I noticed marks on her bottom when I was bathing her the next day, and I didn't really do anything about it.*

Jean: *Why didn't you do anything?*

Carol: *I was scared. I didn't know what to do. I didn't want to lose my husband, so I didn't do anything.*

Jean: *And what have you said about yourself?*

Carol: *That I'm not a good mother.*

Jean: *Have a lot of compassion for yourself. What position is the woman in, who lets her child get beaten? She feels powerless. If you could have done anything differently you would have done it. You felt insecure. You could not give that up. You were coming from your safety-needs.*

Carol: *I know all that and I still beat myself up about it.*

Jean: *Look around the room. Do you think the people in here want to beat you up? Some people in this room would not have put up with that, but then they know they have done other things that you wouldn't have done.* 'Let he who is without sin cast the first stone'.

The vicious circle of toxic shame

It is so self-destructive to be toxically ashamed. The way to de-tox, so to speak, is to realise that what you have done is not going to stop people loving you. The problem with shame however, is that often the thing we are ashamed of affects our behaviour in such a way that we become even more ashamed of ourselves, and produce a situation which does make it difficult for people to love us.

Many of the children I have worked with who are toxically ashamed act out their shame through temper tantrums, crime, bullying, violence and so on. All of this alienates them from other people and confirms their belief that they are *bad* and *unlovable.* It is a vicious circle whose hold is difficult to break.

It is worse than a vicious circle — it is a kind of spiral, a vortex in which there is only one direction to go — down. Maurice is a classic example of the victim of this spiral.

Maurice: *I do feel it is so destructive to keep things hidden. I was quietly crying while T* (another participant) *was speaking* (cries again), *because I felt what he was saying so strongly, and I now have someone I am really fond of, but I am really destroying any possibility of relationship.*

Jean: *You mean you feel anger, and it is to cover up your pain.*

Maurice: *Yes. I will seek out relationships with people who are like my parents. I try to cover up instead of telling people who I really am. My first sexual experience was with a prostitute, and I feel so ashamed of it.*

Jean: *Why did you do it, though?*

Maurice: *I was feeling so secretive about sex, I suppose. I wanted to have a sexual experience, and I couldn't find the right situation for it.*

Jean: *Did you feel you might make a hash of it, anyway?*

Maurice: *Yes — it was horrendous.*

Jean: *Most people's first sexual experience is pretty horrendous as a matter of fact. Anyone aware of this?* (Lots of hands are raised).

Maurice decided to have his first sexual experience with a prostitute out of the toxic shame he had developed due to the unhealthy relationship he had with his parents. He felt that it was *bad* to want sex with someone — that sex itself was bad. He sought out a situation which would confirm his feelings for him. Now he is a *bad* person who is not fit to have sex with anyone who is *decent*. If he tries, he fails, confirming to him his sexual inadequacy. He attempts to cope with his shame by getting angry, and this means that he loses the relationship, confirming him again in his beliefs that he is inadequate and *bad*. Down and down it goes. Diagrammatically it looks like this:

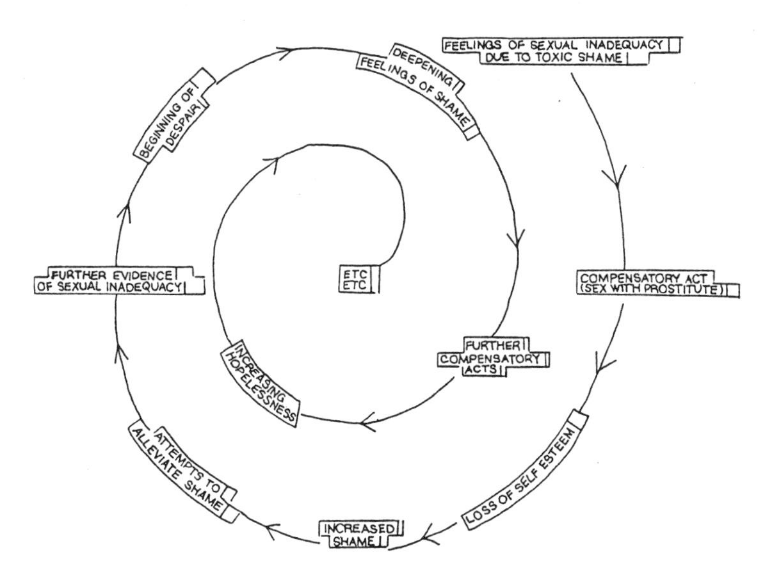

Fig 4. The downward spiral of self esteem.

as a similar problem. Her feelings of toxic shame stem from the as treated by her parents in her early childhood. This treatment ı her feeling totally unlovable and not being able to bear her own company. She became a *stimulus-junkie,* always needing to be diverted from the pain she carried around inside her. She discovered that having exciting and passionate relationships with men gave her the attention she craved, and also provided her with an amazing *buzz*.

This *buzz* derived from new and stimulating romantic-passionate relationships is addictive. It is the most addictive of all addictions, and possibly the most soul-destroying. Stable relationships are like a *drying out* period to the passion-addict, and the withdrawal symptoms are horrific, because you begin to feel the pain that the stimulation was keeping at bay. You also miss the high you were on.

So you break up yet another loving but *boring* relationship, leaving behind pain and disillusionment, only to repeat the cycle again with someone else. Since this process usually entails deceit and breaking of commitments, not to mention disruption of children's lives, if they are involved, it usually produces yet another downward plummet of the spiral of self-esteem — feelings of being *bad* and *worthless*. What you then have to offer to the new man or woman in your life is even more shame, which they will have to compensate for. Kicking this particular addiction is extremely difficult.

I had many opportunities to learn this lesson, but I fell for it time and time again. I could not believe that the passion would not last. It never did. I kicked it only when I began to see what it was really costing me, in terms of my self-respect, but the day I realised I might have to learn to live without it, I felt as though there was nothing left to live for. I will be dealing with this dilemma more fully in the next chapters.

Why do we continue to indulge in behaviour we are ashamed of? It is almost as though we must confirm to ourselves that we *are* worthless and shameful. So although we desperately attempt, through our addictions, to escape from this horrendous view of ourselves, we run around in a hall of mirrors, where there is no escape from the way we see ourselves. The very escape route we choose only serves to magnify our sense of shame. The way to reverse this downward spiral is to tell the truth, to own our shame, to be real with people. But this presents some difficulties of its own.

Being real in an unreal world

The Velveteen Rabbit in Margery Williams' story longed to be real, and was ashamed of his unrealness when confronted by two real rabbits. Sadly, in our human culture, the reverse applies. We are taught to feel ashamed of being real, in a world where most people try to disguise what they suspect are their *true natures*.

One of the considerations that people on the course have, when they have taken the risk of being open, and experienced only love and acceptance, is that, when they get back into the *real* world they will not be able to risk it. This is certainly a dilemma. Many people do not know how to cope with other people's feelings and support them in dealing with guilt and fear. They will often attempt to be reassuring: *Well, don't worry about it, or I'm sure it wasn't your fault*, or *Don't feel bad about yourself*, and more. And then they hastily change the subject. This is so crushing to the person who has found the courage to risk themselves! Nothing closes me down faster.

However, I usually realise that I made a mistake in telling someone who could not handle it, and I look for someone who can. For many people it simply reinforces the fears they had about telling someone in the first place, and they vow that it will be the last time they confide in anyone.

Maybe there is a need to be circumspect about the people we choose to be open with, or maybe we can enable them to cope more comfortably with our embarrassing revelations. I am often quite touched by the frequency with which my students will come up with excuses for me, if I own up to some weakness or mistake I have made. That is an opportunity to explain that I do not need them to do that, although I appreciate their concern. They simply need to allow me to *own up*, and to accept what I am saying, without judging me for it, or allowing it to influence their attitude towards me.

It is not only other people's embarrassment about our shortcomings, or our differences, that poses a problem, however. There is also the fear of the judgements others will make, particularly those who have the authority and position to influence our future plans, or sabotage our careers. Is it sensible for someone who is, for instance, a gay, male sports teacher to reveal this to his head teacher, or to the Local Education Authority for whom he works? Sadly, it is probably not a good idea. Prejudice abounds about gay men who have access to young boys, and such a person would probably end up losing his job, or suffering severe discrimination.

Unfortunately, our social milieu does make it very difficult to be completely open with everyone about everything, and this causes a lot of pain. I know several gay people — male and female — who do not feel they can reveal their sexual preference at work, and consequently feel they cannot form close friendships with work colleagues or include them in their social life.

I do not know any way around this problem, except to take the risk and become a possible candidate for martyrdom. I suppose social attitudes only change when people are prepared to challenge them and fight for what they believe in, but that is up to each individual to make that decision. It takes a very brave person to challenge social taboos.

The same dilemma is true for people who feel they cannot reveal certain things to their families. Issues of sexuality, abortion and crime are often kept from those who should be closest to us, and most ready to forgive and offer support. This creates a barrier to intimacy within those relationships, and destroys the potential for unconditional love and trust.

For some of those who dare to trust the power of love, taking that risk is often a freeing experience. Wanda (mentioned above) was adamant early on in the course that she was not going to confront her father with her knowledge of the abuse that had occurred. As the course progressed, however, she began to see the adverse effect it was having on her relationship with him, and on the third evening of the course she plucked up the courage to talk to him about it. She came in the following morning looking very pleased with herself.

Her father, at first, denied all knowledge of this act and then said, if it had happened, he could not remember anything about it. He then said that it could have happened, or might have happened, and if she said it had then it must have been the case. He told her how sorry he was if anything he had done had harmed her in any way. She told him how it had affected her relationships with men, and he was very upset.

What she needed was for her father to take the responsibility for what had happened. This he did, and the effect on her and the relationship with him was very releasing. The shame was put where it belonged — with her father.

For those who have different issues that they feel they cannot reveal to their parents, the same principle applies. Children do not get to be the way they are unaided. That is not to say that it is all your parents' *fault*, that you do the things you do and are the way you are, but they are certainly *responsible*. You also have to accept a measure of responsibility for how you turned out, since you were the one that developed that particular survival-strategy.

To a child, however, it looks more like 'Hobson's Choice', since it seems that they will lose, no matter what they do. For instance, children who are abused could get the abuse stopped by revealing what is happening to a responsible adult, but those who consider it often realise that this will mean being taken away from home altogether, which seems a far more frightening option than putting up with what they already have.

However, as adults, we really do have a choice. We do not need to keep colluding with the lies. And we can offer our parents the opportunity to accept their responsibility. In the case of offspring who become gay, parents must accept that they have played a role in that development. Not many gay people might realise that their sexual preference has anything to do with their parents. If they did they might not be so ashamed of letting their parents know, or so fearful of the consequences this knowledge might have for their parents. There is no reason why the offspring should carry the responsibility alone.

In case any people reading this are beginning to feel that I am saying it is *wrong* to be gay, let me assure you that this is not the case. Neither am I saying it is *right*. I am simply saying that in this culture, being gay can present difficulties when it comes to being authentic. If we do want to be real, and to feel free to express every aspect of ourselves, then looking at what makes people choose the homosexual, rather than the heterosexual, path might enable us to be authentic with our parents, at least.

Most gay women who take my courses seem to have had difficult or distant relationships with their mothers — they have never felt really accepted or loved by them. Gay men often idolise their mothers, but are kept at a distance by them. They therefore grow up finding it impossible to have sexual relationships with women, although they are often very friendly with them. This is because they do idolise them — and they also resent them. Many men with idolised mothers develop the *virgin-whore* construct of women. *If they are not pure and innocent they must be whores.*

One gay man I know does not trust his mother, who was often cruelly rejecting of him, and certainly not accepting and loving. He was constantly criticised by his step-father, and when this man physically abused him, his mother sold out on him by standing by and doing nothing to stop it. Despite all this, his mother was an object of worship. He pined for her, kept her photograph by his bed, kissing it when he went to sleep, and eagerly waited for her to ring. He showed all the symptoms of being in love. His love was unrequited.

When he spoke to me about his sexuality, he was clear he could not tell his mother because she would not be able to handle it—and yet part of him really did want to tell her, because he knew she would be devastated, and he almost gloated over the pain she would feel. He could not have found a better way of punishing this woman than to become gay. When women (*mothers*) have been a distant object of worship, and are therefore a mystery —and a threat—it must look to the survival machine inside our heads that it would be much easier to have a relationship with another male.

I am not claiming that all homosexuality has its roots in the way children are reared, but from what I have heard from the vast majority of gay people I have worked with, it certainly looks is if inappropriate or inadequate child-rearing might be a basis contributing to homosexual preference.

Laurence was a gay man who hated his mother, and yet desperately yearned for her love. He had a similar predicament about revealing his sexual preference.

Laurence: *I am gay. It is not the first time I have talked about that, but I am looking round thinking,* do I talk about that in here? *This year was the first time I realised that I have to go out and tell people who I am, because I cannot live if I don't. So you've got to accept yourself. I think it is a major problem. I went into a deep depression when I realised,* God, I have to tell it to someone!, *and I phoned a friend who came over and I told him. He said* Well — yeah? *I never expected people to accept it. Another friend doesn't really accept it. It's whether you accept it yourself. It always takes a little bit of courage to tell them, but it helps a lot to talk about things that you never talked about before.*

Jean: *Do you know why you decided to be gay?*

Laurence: *I hate to think of the Freudian side of it, but I told a friend and he said* It's all because of your mother.

Jean: *It will be impossible for you to have a relationship with women before you look at the relationship you have with your mother (*which was pretty bad*).*

Laurence: *I have had about three relationships with women, but they (*the women*) have all been depressed. When I split with my last girlfriend — that was this year — this was the first relationship that was more serious than the others. When it split, this was the time I got depressed, and I knew I had to do something. I cried a lot. I am able to do that. I've still got loads of problems. I don't tell everybody. I don't go round telling my boss, but if you trust somebody you should tell them. You go to places where there are other gays so that you feel more comfortable, more acceptable, but it is still hiding, you know.*

Jean: *It is a hard path to take.*

Other gay males have had difficulty in relating to their fathers. They have inappropriately bonded with their mother, or they might yearn for a relationship with a male, since they have never had the fathering they needed.

Whatever the reason for their choice, gay people in this culture often have much more difficulty than heterosexual people when it comes to being authentic and expressing who they are. However, having said that, most of us find it difficult — whether we are gay or not!

Reversing the spiral

For those of us who do not have propensities towards behaviour or habits that are outside our culture's tolerance level — or who are prepared to give them up if we do — there is a way out of the ever-downward spiral, or helter-skelter of life. It is *to tell the truth and handle the consequences, accept responsibility and hold yourself accountable.* It really is not as bad as it sounds.

One of the course-participants had revealed that he had *interfered with* his sister when he was fourteen, and she was about eleven. He was still carrying a lot of guilt with him about this, and did not know what he should do about it. Would he be opening a whole can of worms if he owned what he had done, and talked to her about it? Wouldn't it be better left alone? After all, she might not have realised what was going on.

I suggested to him that he address the issue with his sister and, if it was clear that she was not prepared to discuss it, he should leave it alone. After he had completed the course he told me that he did bring the matter up and, although she was quite taken aback by his frankness, she did say that she had thought for a long time that he was a bastard.

Although the thought of addressing the issue with her was terribly frightening, he did find the courage to do it. He was relieved of a burden of guilt that he had been carrying around with him for years, and he was able to ask her to forgive him. It was not easy for her to allow him to clean it up with her, but I suspect it will make a huge difference to their relationship. It has certainly made a difference to him. He cannot, of course, put the clock back and undo what was done, but he can let her know that he too has paid a price for involving her in his sexual explorations.

I have made some major mistakes in recent years, and at one time I would have lied or made excuses for myself. Now I do not do that — never, no matter how tempted I am to find the easy way out. There is no integrity in it, and my relationships will suffer. I know, in the end, I will come out losing my self-respect, and losing the relationship.

I remember one occasion when I was conducting mock-interviews for my final-year students. They were all entering into the spirit of it, and one girl made a special trip to Cornwall from Coventry (250 miles) to pick up her best 'interview suit' for the occasion. I had invited four head teachers, who had agreed to give up their precious time and (for one of them) travel a long way. Everything was arranged. On the Monday morning everyone turned up punctually. Everyone, that is, except me. I was in a school supervising a student on teaching practice, having totally forgotten about the session.

When a colleague rang the school and told me that my students were scouring the countryside because they were convinced I had been knocked off my bicycle on the way there, and was lying dead under a hedge, I thought it might have been better if I had been! In fact I wished I could die, right there and then!

On my way back to see my students, all sorts of creative excuses ran through my head. It was an emergency, and the school had called me in — insisted that I go . . . But in the end I told them: I had forgotten. They were hurt and angry (some of them). *How could I just forget? I was supposed to care!* I told them that forgetting didn't mean I didn't care. It didn't mean I didn't value them — it just meant I forgot, because I am human and I can forget things. People like me who lead complex lives frequently do forget, despite double-entry diary-keeping, and all sorts of other memory-joggers. I listened to all they had to say, and told them I thought they were justified in feeling angry. In their situation I would have felt the same. In the end they forgave me.

The forgiveness of the students and the head teachers, who all agreed to come back another day, helped me to forgive myself. I can think of that incident now without any sense of shame or embarrassment, but I am sure if I had lied about it that would not be the case.

The problem with all of this is that it goes against all our survival instincts. As small children we had no shame, but we soon acquired it. Many of us were taught to be ashamed of our bodily functions, of our enthusiasm and sense of wonder at life. Curiosity about our bodies was seen as an unhealthy, *bad* act. Innocent childhood explorations into sexuality were given a sinister significance.

But it was even worse than that. We were taught to be ashamed of succeeding too well — and, of course, of losing at all. We were damned if we did, and damned if we didn't. Phrases like, *getting too big for your boots*, being *puffed up* and *too clever for your own good*, were all designed to make us ashamed of our accomplishments. Actually, they were really designed to protect the ego of parents from offspring who had the benefits of superior educational opportunities, but they had the effect of making those of us whose parents suffered from feelings of academic inadequacy feel ashamed of our own ability. If we were accomplished we must play it down and hide or disguise it.

We were taught to hide our defects, cover up our deficiencies and make sure our mistakes were attributed to someone, or something, else. If we did not do this we would be in deep trouble. Disapproval or anger would follow the revelation of any of these *defects*, or worse, disgust or derision would ensue.

I remember needing desperately to go the toilet one play-time, when I was about twelve. I pulled down my pants and sat on the toilet with huge relief and started to pee, when suddenly I realised that I had sat on the cover of the toilet and the pee was running all over my pants! They were wet through before I could do anything about it! Being the regulation *navy-blue knickers* they were heavy and sodden. I could not tell anyone about it, and I lived in dread, all the rest of the day, in case someone could smell it. I agonised about leaving wet patches on the desk seats and someone else spotting it. I was terrified of the scorn that would follow from my classmates. I also had to suffer the discomfort of sitting in very wet, very cold pants for the rest of the day. That was a small price to pay for saving my dignity! I did not even dare to tell my mother, because she would have shouted at me for needing another clean pair of knickers. So I took them off and went *knickerless* — another major crime, if discovered!

Stephen King in *IT* describes how Eddie, as a child, comes to realise the threat that his mother poses to his identity. Eddie's mother is totally possessive and manipulative. Eddie is *delicate*. She makes sure he is. At this point in the novel he has broken his arm and is lying in a hospital bed, half-conscious. He has had all sorts of encounters with deadly and unearthly creatures. He hears his mother's voice, dimly in the background:

> Eddie saw the leper, the mummy, the bird; he saw the werewolf and a vampire, whose teeth were Gillette Blue-Blades set at crazy angles like mirrors in a carnival mirror-maze; he saw Frankenstein, the creature, and something fleshy and shell-like that opened and closed like a mouth; he saw a dozen other terrible things, a hundred, but just before the clown washed out completely he saw the most terrible thing of all: his Ma's face.
>
> *No!* he tried to scream. *No! No! Not her! Not my ma!*
>
> But no one looked around; no one heard. And in the dream's fading moments, he realised with a cold and wormy horror that they couldn't hear him. He was dead. It had killed him and he was dead. He was a ghost. (King, 1990, p782).

Eddie's mother achieves this annihilation of her son's sense of self by manipulation and total control. When all else fails, she attempts to shame him into submission by being *upset by him*. This is the scene King describes when Eddie attempts to assert his right to have friends, something that poses a threat to his mother's security-needs:

> She felt safer in her tears. Usually when she cried, Eddie cried, too. A low weapon, some might say, but were there really any low weapons when it came to protecting her son? She thought not.
>
> She looked up, the tears streaming from her eyes, feeling both unutterably sad, bereft, betrayed . . . and sure. Eddie would not be able to stand against such a flood of tears and sorrow. That cold, sharp look would leave his face. Perhaps he would begin to gasp and wheeze a little bit (he has asthma) and that would be a sign, as it was always, a sign that the fight was over and that she had won another victory . . . for him, of course. Always for him.

I have had many people on my course who resorted to subterfuge and lies in order to avoid upsetting their parents. Old habits die hard. If we cannot be truthful and unashamed in front of our parents then who on earth can it be safe to be *real* with?

School is another place where toxic shame is re-fuelled. I will never forget the pain I suffered from being humiliated by a teacher who exposed my *crime* to all my friends and classmates. The gross offence I had committed was to make what I thought was a friendly gesture, by chalking a cartoon picture of a little first-year girl who had a bit of a crush on me, on the blackboard in her classroom. She had thought I was sending her up and was very upset, but I knew nothing of this. Instead of drawing me aside and letting me know how upset this child was and letting me clean it up with her, the teacher held me up as an example of a thoughtless and cruel person who was only marginally short of criminal.

The pain of this exposure lasted for far more than the few minutes it took to 'dress me down'. I felt as though she had put a placard around my neck which everyone could read — people throughout the school, people on the bus going home, everyone. It hung there for weeks. I could not take it off. Maybe it is still there. I never could read the chapter in *Jane Eyre* where the girl is made to wear such a placard without feeling incredibly upset.

I am sure that many of you have suffered in the same way. The golden rule we develop from all this is *Thou must not be found out!* And so we become adepts at disguise and secrecy. Another worm goes into the already-squirming can, to eat away at our sense of worth and wholesomeness. Then comes the fear that, if we let them out, they will consume what is left of our remaining self-esteem. How many times have people said to me that the work I do is dangerous, because it will *open a whole can of worms*? But the worms are illusions, woven by lies. Letting them out allows them to escape and leave you free of them. I have often wondered why people want to hang on grimly to their cans of worms. It can't be good for the digestion! It certainly is not good for the soul.

But the memory of those initial feelings of shame and fear of isolation — being cast out — are very strong in all of us, and it requires a powerful force to persuade anyone to take the risk of being *real*. The only force powerful enough is love, and the realisation that, when we know who we really are, when we can reach beyond the shame and the guilt, we reach a place where we can never be alone.

> The impeccable practice of truthfulness is said to serve several functions. It encourages ethicality, requires precise awareness of speech and motivation, enhances clear perception and memory of events which might otherwise be distorted by lying, frees the mind of guilt and fear of discovery, and consequently reduces agitation and worry.
> The fully enlightened individual, freed from greed and anger and other unskilful states, has neither desire nor need to distort the truth, or act unethically. Those who are fully ethical have nothing to hide, and truthfulness, like all the other perfections, is said to ultimately become a spontaneous and continuous expression of the Arahat's (enlightened being's) essential nature.
>
> (Walsh, 1984)

7. *To thine own self be true*

It is interesting that contemp orary research has found evidence that psychologically-mature people contribute more to charity than do the immature, and that their lives tend to be more orientated towards service . . . Human survival is going to require tremendous psychological resources and maturity, and the techniques which cultivate them may be crucial.

(Walsh, 1984).

See yourself in others:
Then whom can you hurt?
What harm can you do?

(The Buddha).

As a teacher, I was quite clear about what people needed to do in order to develop cognitively, or intellectually. I knew there were progressive stages through which they needed to pass, in order to reach the level of abstract thought. I also knew, mainly from studying the works of Jean Piaget, that children go through progressive stages of social development, but I had never considered that there might be stages of *psychological* development through which we need to progress in order to reach *psychological maturity*. Now it seems patently obvious that this must be so.

I can also see *now* that, just as people who do not mature intellectually are very limited in their capacity to communicate and understand life at an abstract level, so people who are psychologically-immature find it impossible to live self-expressive, creative and expansive lives.

All the people who have featured in this book so far have either been the victims of others who are psychologically immature, or they have damaged others out of their own psychological immaturity or ignorance. I remember reading *Black Beauty* by Anna Sewell when I was a child, and being puzzled by the anger expressed by one of the characters towards the stable boy who almost killed the horse out of *ignorance*. Ignorance, said the horse's owner, was the next best thing to wickedness. "If people can say 'Oh, I didn't mean any harm', they think it's all right." Of a woman who killed her baby out of *ignorance*, he said, "A woman should not undertake

e a small child without knowing what is good and what is bad for
.. is made such an impression on me that I have remembered it all these years. It had never occurred to me that ignorance was no excuse for damaging people. I always thought it was.

I think we all have the responsibility to know what is good and what is bad for us. Because people are *ignorant* of the unconscious thought processes which dominate their behaviour, they do inflict pain and suffering upon others or upon themselves, or they do nothing about the pain and suffering that is going on in the world.

A few days ago, I woke up feeling angry — yet again!. I realised, almost instantaneously, that I was in fact *looking for something to be angry about*. As usual I wanted to focus this on Tim, since he was the nearest target. He asked me if I would like a fruit juice, and I told him not to *pester* me! This was so unreasonable that I had to warn him that I was looking for someone or something to be angry with. "Do you mind if I ask why?", he asked, tentatively. I had to look at this for several minutes.

It seemed as though Tim was intruding on my *space* — he was making demands on me, just by being there. I felt I just needed to be left alone — but he was not really bothering me. So, left alone by whom, or by what? What I came up with was that I needed to be left alone by all the responsibilities I had — marking essays, student references, requests for more courses, introductory talks, tutorials, individual sessions, writing this book, cooking meals, shopping. Again, I was into my *I'm inadequate, I can't cope . . . It will all end in disaster* movie.

That realised, the anger went. I could share my anxiety with Tim, then see that all I had to do was whatever was next on the agenda. I did not have to work out how I could cope with all this all at once, and reach a place where I had it all handled and had nothing else to do. Then I would really panic! I was so delighted that I had managed to complete this process *before* I started to be destructive towards Tim. That was a real joy. I could see definite progress. Because I have learned to access my deeper thought-processes, and therefore tell the truth, I am more able to be of service and less likely to be destructive in the world.

What I have begun to see is that I have a responsibility to achieve psychological maturity, and reach that point where I do become charitable, generous and oriented towards service. This has certainly been happening to me over the last ten years. I am becoming much more aware of my responsibility as a member of the human race. I sometimes feel overwhelmed and burdened by the impossibility of the task facing us — that of moving ourselves forward towards a consciously responsible level of existence, before global warming and other problems threaten the survival of present life-forms. I also see that there are other forces operating which might accelerate this process.

The Hundredth Monkey Phenomenon

The forces I am referring to are those described by Sheldrake (1987) as *morphogenetic fields*, or M-fields. Talbot (1988) describes these as 'a mysterious force that connects each individual with all other individuals in its species past'. Sheldrake implies that each species has a *group mind*. Talbot explains, 'Before we go into what M-fields are, however we need to look at *morphogenetics*. Morphogenetics derives from *morphe*=form, and *genesis*=birth. It addresses the mystery of how living forms come into being.'

Scientists know that the DNA in each of our cells is the blueprint for putting a human being together. The problem is that they do not know how each part of a human being knows what to become and where to go. Why don't we grow arms out of our heads and fingernails on our elbows? Talbot explains this in highly understandable terms. I can do no better than use his own words:

> Think about this for a moment. Imagine that in an empty lot you come upon a pile of building materials, and on each and every piece of lumber is a tiny list of all the materials that will ultimately constitute the house. Imagine that as you watch, the lumber, the nails, the roofing tiles and the door knobs all begin to assemble themselves into the structure of the house. The question is, what force allows all of the building materials to read the blueprint, discern their own special niche out of thousands of possibilities, and then align themselves into a house? This is one of the problems of morphogenesis.

Morphogenesis also enables living organisms to regulate their own design if something unexpected should happen to the original development plan. Talbot describes a situation where, if we tie up part of a dragonfly's egg, the egg will still grow into a perfect, if much smaller, dragonfly. He also talks about the way in which creatures have the power to regenerate all or part of themselves — newts can grow new limbs, and starfish, if split into pieces, regenerate into several whole new starfish.

With regard to human beings, the research undertaken by Lorber on the human brain, which I have quoted in chapter two, appears to fit into this pattern. It seems that when people's brains do not develop *normally*, other parts of the brain take over the function of the bits that are missing. It seems, says Talbot, that living organisms, 'possess a curious property of *wholeness*'. For a more detailed explanation of this, and other fascinating phenomena, I recommend you to read Talbot's book.

Sheldrake (1987) maintains that M-fields govern both the structure of living organisms and their behaviour. The past habits and behavioural patterns of living organisms build up and affect the habits and behaviour of members of the same species which are in existence now.

One of the most famous examples of this is a phenomenon described by Lyall Watson (1980). In 1950, on the island of Koshima, a group of researchers were observing a population of *Macaca Fuscata* monkeys. They started to feed the monkeys sweet potatoes, and dumped large consignments of these on the beach. The monkeys took to this novel food, but did not like the sand and grit they were covered with. Eventually one of the females solved the problem by taking her sweet potato down to the sea and washing it clean. She taught this trick to her family and soon a small group of the colony were rushing down to dunk their sweet potatoes in the sea.

The researchers then observed an inexplicable phenomenon. At one moment only a small group were dunking — suddenly the whole colony began to dunk as well. Stranger still, at exactly this time, on other islands that had no visual contact with Koshima, and on the mainland, all the monkeys began to dunk their sweet potatoes in the sea. It was as if the monkeys possessed a *group mind*. This phenomenon has become known as the *hundredth monkey effect*.

Although Sheldrake acknowledges that this evidence is purely anecdotal (not subject to rigorously controlled experimental conditions), he does cite other incidents which were conducted in a more scientific way to support his M-field hypothesis. One such experiment was conducted on national TV, and produced significant results.

So what has this all got to do with psychological maturity, or enlightenment, if indeed they are one and the same thing? Well, as I said, the task of developing worldwide psychological maturity before the human race exterminates itself seems impossible — there are so many human beings still living in darkness, and more and more keep being born. But, if Sheldrake is correct, and if more of us who *are* here become psychologically-mature, then we could (would) create a morphogenetic field sufficiently powerful to enable the human mind to evolve, so that future generations will be born at a more enlightened, or psychologically-mature level than we were. As Satprem (1984) puts it 'We are the result of an evolution, not of a succession of arbitrary miracles'.

Levels of consciousness

The question now is, what does it mean to be *psychologically-mature*? It certainly entails going a step beyond where we have reached so far. It goes beyond the ability to be aware of those unconscious thoughts that hitherto have been unavailable to us. It means accessing higher levels of consciousness than those we usually accept are there. Becoming truly self-accepting involves reaching the level of reality where this '*I*' we speak of is 'the voice of all men fused into one cosmic consciousness, and we are all the sons of

God' (Satprem, 1984). After all, if you discovered you were the offspring of God, would you need to wonder if you were lovable?

I have already suggested the model of psychological maturity described by Abraham Maslow, but that is not so detailed as the one developed by Assagioli (1991). Assagioli proposes that there are several levels of consciousness, one of which seems to correspond with the M-fields referred to above. Assagioli called this the *collective unconscious*. Hardy (1987) believes that both these models depict the human being as a kind of receiver. She says we are like a TV set that is picking up past historical and geographical areas of human experience — 'in fact all the experience that has ever been or is, is now'.

This, and the other six levels of consciousness, are described by Assagioli in the egg-shaped diagram below.

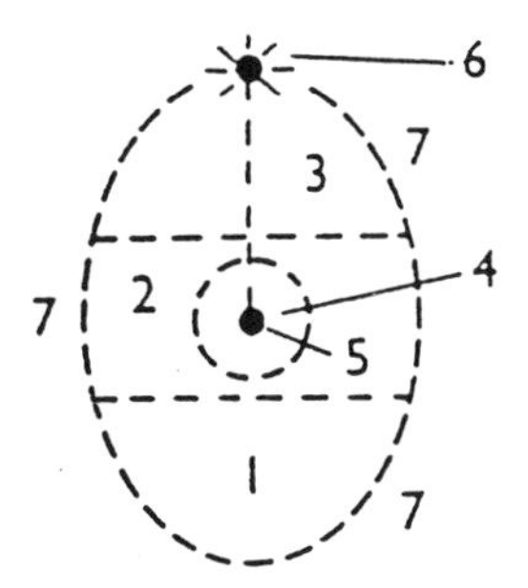

Fig 4. A Map of the Person. 1 The Lower Unconscious; 2 The Middle Unconscious; 3 The Higher Unconscious or Superconscious; 4 The Field of Consciousness; 5 The Conscious Self or "I"; 6 The Higher Self (or Soul); 7 The Collective Unconscious (*From Assagioli (1987)*.

For a more detailed description of the states of consciousness, please refer to Hardy or to Assagioli. I will describe them briefly — not an easy task.

The outside of the egg is the *collective consciousness* or M-field. Assagioli believed that we should be as concerned about making the collective unconscious conscious as we should about becoming aware of our personal unconsciousness. We need to illuminate the workings of the group mind, otherwise our strivings for personal peace and harmony will constantly meet with collective unconscious resistance. If we do not influence the collective unconscious we will experience difficulties and will feel alien to our context.

What seems to happen is that the collective unconscious influences the mind of the individual — sets limits on it, or pre-determines its function. That this does happen is evident from the experience of people who are on this path. This is verified by Marilyn Ferguson (1982, p123):

> To the individual whose gate of change is well defended, the transformative process, even in others, is threatening . . . Those who cannot communicate their own liberating discoveries may feel polarised at times from those closest to them. It is a lonely path.

However, should a sufficient mass of minds progress beyond this limit they influence the collective mind (or unconscious) which, in turn, communicates on a mass scale with all other *receivers*. To use the TV analogy, the person has an idea, persuades several other people to accept it and this is then *broadcast*, at some level, on a national scale, becoming available to the whole population. I suppose this is the principle on which advertising works.

Erich Fromm (1985), in his outline of what is needed for social transformation, asserted that 'Human solidarity is the necessary condition for the unfolding of any one individual'. In a survey carried out on people who have involved themselves in transformative processes, 44% of the respondents considered the greatest threat to widespread social transformation to be 'popular fear of change' (Ferguson, p123). However, Ferguson also maintains that there is a vast support-network which those on the path of transformation can tap into. Without this the journey would be intolerable. In my experience it is my friends and fellow-travellers on this journey who have kept me going, and allowed me to experience the tremendous joy that comes from pursuing increased awareness of different levels of consciousness.

The other levels described by Assagioli are as follows: the lower unconscious (no 1 in *fig* 1) is what has been well described by Freud. It consists of *demons* that we have suppressed or repressed — events, thoughts and motivations that we have buried — since they are usually associated with painful and damaging experiences. As Sue Patman says, 'what *was* is the lower unconscious'. It consists of 'fundamental drives and primitive urges'. Freud described it as the 'cellar' of the house of the personality.

If the lower unconscious is the cellar, the middle unconscious is the ante-room of consciousness, or the *pre-conscious*. It is the area of unconsciousness that we can be aware of if we are sufficiently *awake* to focus on it. Perhaps this is best illustrated by example.

I often think I am angry with somebody or something — that is, my anger is what I am immediately conscious of. If I allow my consciousness to spread a little wider I can see that really I am hurt, or anxious about something, and that is what the problem really is (level two). It then takes another step to move me down to the cellar (level one) and see what the true origins of the hurt and anxiety are — that I feel inadequate, and that means I will be out of control, and I have to be in control because my father's illness made me feel so powerless, as did my mother's anger. I have addressed this in depth in earlier chapters, and I hope that you will already have had some realisations of the need to integrate these aspects of ourselves, so that we can begin to recover the self-love that we lost.

Number five in the diagram is the *conscious self* or '*I*'. I will explain the differences between levels five and six, the *self* and the *higher self*. The *self* or *I* is, according to Assagioli, the centre of body, mind and feelings. It is, in Krishnamurti's (1982) words, the *observer*. The *self*, or *I*, is the still centre of the human being. It is that part which can be still enough, and sufficiently removed from thoughts and emotions to become aware and access other levels of consciousness — such as the middle and lower unconscious. At the personality level, says Assagioli, the *self* is 'stable, sure and indestructible'. It is, he says, a 'reflection of the *higher self* or *transpersonal self*, and it reflects, however palely, the same qualities as its source'. It is that which can observe the working of the mind. 'This (higher) *Self* is above and unaffected by the flow of the mind-stream, or by bodily conditions'.

I am not sure where the *ego* fits in here, but I assume that much of the contents of the mind are associated with the ego, and in order to *observe* these contents, we must be able to go outside our ego. But this is where we — or I — get into deep water. So I'll dog paddle out of it by quoting yet another expert! Moore (1973) speaks of the human being's relationship with the *mind* in this way:

> It is known 'within' undeniably that in reality one is not the contents of mind; these contents are the agents through which the process of creation, maintenance and dissolution take place. Hence one of the cardinal injunctions is *Know Thy Self*, the One to whom the body and the contents of the mind belong.

If you are wondering why this all matters, I can say that, in my experience, it is very important, since I agree with Assagioli that the *Self* 'is the source of light and love'. The *personal self* is actually connected to and part of the *higher Self*. It is through the *I*, therefore, that we are able to connect with, and perhaps unite with, the *Source*, (number 6), which is the still centre of the *superconscious*. It is that which perceives the whole, the universe. It is the *transcenders*, those who have this experience of connectedness with the *Source*, who are described by Maslow (1987) as being:

> more prone to a kind of cosmic sadness . . . over the stupidity of people, their self-defeat, their blindness, their cruelty to each other, their short-sightedness. Perhaps this comes from the contrast between what actually is, and the ideal world the transcenders can see so easily and so vividly, and which is, in principle, so easily attainable.

This leaves us with the level of the *higher consciousness*. This I can only describe as the area of vision, of what is possible if we lived 'more from the soul and less from the personality. It is the window into the sky' (Hardy, 1987). This is where we get in touch with our creativity, unconditional love, true generosity, self-acceptance, humanitarian and heroic action (Assagioli). We cannot have access to these forces, which are always available, if we are not willing to 'descend to the basement' and re-integrate the lost and suppressed parts of ourselves. It would be like trying to walk upstairs without our legs.

Many people realise that this level of consciousness is available to us and, I think, try to take shortcuts by attempting to attain it without starting, as Alice did in Wonderland, at the beginning. I have met many 'enlightened' individuals who just seemed to me to be too good to be true, because, I think, they were behaving as they thought an enlightened person would, or should, without having completed the journey; a bit like someone who eulogises about how wonderful a place is without having been there.

In *Siddhartha*, Herman Hesse (1973) describes the central figure's search for enlightenment, and how this takes him through all sorts of adventures, debauchery and *hell*. When he finally arrives at what he was looking for, he realises that it was available to him all the time, but he needed to learn some hard and difficult lessons before he got there — namely to express his emotions, to experience pain, to realise the futility of avarice and greed, and to develop humility. Perhaps the greatest lesson was that he was trying too hard to find it. This effort to find enlightenment, so that we can find peace, and all suffering will end, is still embedded in the ego, and it does not work. Some people try to skip a grade — or even two or three, but this is like learning something by rote, rather than acquiring the concepts that support it through direct experience. Sooner or later the mechanically-acquired learning breaks down.

> The layers upon layers of God-denial (denial of the Higher Self) that encrust most souls in physical form cannot be removed all at once as in a surgical procedure. They require the gradual wearing away of resistance through experience . . . Be patient then, and allow yourselves to see the eroding of the layer upon layer of defence that exists in the human cycles. You will see that what is thought of as dire straits is an opportunity to learn.
>
> (*Emmanuel's Book*, p21)

'I'm an urban spaceman, baby'

This could explain why we have to be *embodied beings*. Emmanuel (1987) describes our bodies as the space-suits we need because they are necessary, where we are on Earth. He says:

> Your physical bodies can be symbols to you of restriction, of ultimate pain and death, of surprising and alarming needs and of unexpected triviality that knows no bounds of denigration. Or they can be seen as chosen vehicles that souls are inhabiting because, rather like space-suits, they are necessary where you are. It is within your humanity that you will learn to recognise your divinity.
>
> (*Emmanuel's Book*, p3.)

Well, I had never considered my body to have the functions of a space-suit before, but I really like this analogy — I find it fun. And when I take my space-suit off, who is inside? Why, *me* of course — *I* am. The sad thing is, I feel, that most of us wait until our bodies are worn out, or damaged beyond repair, by accidents, careless living, addictions, before we can discover who we really are. We have created an illusion of separateness, and think that we really are who we think ourselves to be. Descartes should perhaps have said, not 'I think, therefore I am', but 'I think, and therefore I become what I think I am'.

It is hard to let go of the notion that we are not the identities we have constructed by what we have, do, think, or feel. Through your space-suit you can *see* what you want, have the *concept* of ownership, your mind or ego can become *attached* to relationships, possessions — but the mind is only the space traveller's computer, and all the other stuff is the life-support system to sustain — what? Who is the *urban space-person*?

Again I say it is *you*, and it is only you-in-your-embodied-form that needs all this paraphernalia. Once you have completed your journey you can leave it behind. If Emmanuel is correct, you need your space-suit to come to school on planet earth. The lessons of the next grade are to be found here — nowhere else — although he says there *is* a somewhere else. In fact there are several somewhere elses which we have graduated from or will graduate to. However, the thing to do is to make the most of this learning experience. Don't be too worried about the next — that will come in time.

Now I must say here that I know this kind of thinking is a new departure from how we normally view life on earth, and it seriously challenges currently-held belief-systems, so I don't ask you just to believe it, unless it appeals to you. On the other hand I don't want you to 'not believe it' either. I would suggest you practise the capacity to live in the question, rather than *wanting answers*. The longer you are willing to keep asking the questions, the more truth is likely to be revealed. Or as Krishnamurti (1978) says,

> Question-and-answer is a most extraordinary movement of enquiry, till you reach a point where your brain cannot answer. Then that question has its own vitality, its own energy. It's not you answering it. It self-answers.

I had an interesting conversation with a man on one of my courses who was a genetic biologist. This is what he had to say about beliefs and *understanding*.

Steve: *I was talking to a physicist, and I was trying to say we actually live in a Newtonian universe, but that view of the universe was not right. Then Einstein came along. I asked him if he understood the Einsteinian universe, and he said, 'No, no-one understands it — you just get used to it.' And I think we are used to the Newtonian universe. It makes sense to us. The Einsteinian universe makes no sense to us. It is the same in my field, the genetic field. You have to say, 'Okay, it doesn't make any sense to me'. But you just have to let it run for a while, live with it — and then you can see* Oh yes, it makes sense. *You can progress then . . . This is what Einstein did with it — he just saw it first, and now a lot of other people run with it. He modified our view of the universe. That is the problem — we think we need to understand things. We don't need to understand things, we just accept them, and we test it and see — is it right?*

At another point Steve pointed out that we still do not understand the mind, although we certainly know we have got one, and we use it.

Steve: *I can tell you what life is, but then something happened which we cannot explain. There is a big difference between human beings and the chimp; not biologically, not genetically, but at this level — that we are stood here talking about all this strange, weird stuff. The* mind *was born that could comprehend the universe. We don't understand what the mind is, we don't understand what thought is. Did that evolve from an organic source? Did organic life-forms tap into something that already existed — the mind — or is the mind a by-product of this need to survive?*

Jean: *So is it an evolutionary process, or is there a universal mind — a universal intelligence?*

Steve: *Yes — God. You can have both of those, and every one of you is right, whichever you feel most comfortable with.*

Jean: *The truth is, we don't know.*

Steve: *There could be a God. I used to be an evangelical atheist (*laughter*).*

A few years ago, I would never have entertained the thought that a *disembodied spirit* would be a possibility, let alone that he, she or it could communicate through a human *channel*. Now I say — how, or who, am I to know? Also, experiences I have had lead me to embrace the possibility. I will talk about these shortly. I realise that, in my space of disbelieving, I could see only what my limited perceptions and senses would allow me to see. Because I was fearful and ashamed of the aspects of me that were hidden in the cellar, and wanting to keep them there, I could not begin to ascend to the attic, and so I experienced myself as separate, isolated, cast out. As Satprem (1984) puts it:

> We have separated from the world and beings across the millennia of our evolution; we have *egotised*, hardened some atoms of this great body, and asserted *we-me-I* against all the others, similarly hardened under an egoistic crust. And having separated ourselves, we could no longer see anything of what was *ourself*.

Our eyes, Satprem says, are not 'organs of vision, but of division' and if we can get back to a recognition of our true selves,

> . . . this is joy — *Ananda* — for to be ail that is, is to have the joy of all that is.

Because we do not know who we are, says Aldous Huxley (1984), we behave in the 'generally silly, the often insane, the sometimes criminal ways that are so characteristically human'.

Understanding is the booby prize

I must digress a little here — or maybe it is not a digression, more like a *con*fession. This chapter is written in a different style to most of the others. It is much more theoretical and relies heavily on the work and words of other experts and writers. This is because I find it extremely difficult to *get a handle* on all of this *consciousness* business. Again perhaps I can use Moore's (1973) words to say it for me:

> One person cannot tell another what consciousness *is* because of the limitations of the spoken and written word . . . Consciousness cannot be defined nor described because it does not have the properties and limitations of a sensorily-perceived object. It is not possible to describe what consciousness *is*. All confusion in philosophy and religion is due to one adopting the interpretation of another or rejecting the interpretation of another, forgetting that *experience* of the indefinable and indescribable cannot be conveyed by the spoken and written word. (p.9)
>
> (Moore, 1973, p9).

It is not that I do not *know* what I am talking about, it is just that I find it extraordinarily difficult to put into words, because my knowledge of quantum physics, M-fields and the like are very recent and limited, and experience of my *Self* has been fleeting and intermittent. I cannot claim to have ready access to the *Higher Self*, although I am able to be more in touch with my *I*, or *personal self*, these days.

Steve put it beautifully. There are things we know which we cannot understand. There are different levels of knowing. Mostly we operate at the level of *understanding*. If we can't understand something, and we are supposed to be experts or intellectuals, we dismiss it as rubbish, since it threatens our reality, or if we know we are not very clever, we dismiss ourselves as being unintelligent — *thick*. This is what Audrey did with the conversation that went on between Steve and myself:

Audrey: *When I went home last night, my son was waiting for me. I told him that I had not understood anything that was said in the last session. He asked me if I had stood up and said I didn't understand it. He said, "You are going to tell the same old story, that you are not clever enough to understand it, and I won't have it". I said, "I'm not clever enough to understand it", and my son said, "It is just a story". I just didn't want to stand up and say I didn't understand it because I didn't want to feel stupid in front of everybody.*

Jean: *Who else didn't understand it yesterday?* (Everyone's hand goes up!)

Mike: *It is just a story.*

Audrey: *I just panic and then I can't listen.*

Now I will explain the heading of this section. When I took the *EST Training* I kept hearing the trainer say, "Understanding is the booby prize". I smiled, knowingly, along with all the rest, but I had no idea what he was talking about. As an academic, or *sort of* academic, I thought understanding was *it*.

Gradually I came to see that many people are existing at a level where they are satisfied with an intellectual grasp of things and never graduate from that to the level of *experiential knowing*. Reading books is great, and very worthwhile, but if you stop at the level of understanding what you read, you will not find it ultimately useful in your dealings with the universe — you must *be* it.

I think there are many times when my *Self* gets expressed in my interaction with life. Those are the times when I, as *ego*, cease to exist. I am aware only of *me* and *other* being one and the same. This happens with me often in my individual sessions with people, and on the course I teach. Somehow we fuse, and their suffering and pain are my suffering and pain, and their joy is my joy.

I am much better at sharing pain and suffering than sharing joy. I wonder why that is? Actually there *is* joy in sharing pain with people — paradoxically enough.

One thing that might make this chapter more accessible, though, is to have a direct experience of the *Self* — now that would help, wouldn't it? Most accounts of this happening are fairly mystical and seem to occur through years of practice, or through near-death experiences. Now, I do not want to wish that on you — it is a little drastic. Maybe that is why I like

Krishnamurti. He says you do not have to go to a hermitage or become a monk — which is a great relief — you merely need *constant vigilance*.

That means that the whole of your daily routine life needs to becomes a meditation. You observe yourself in every situation, and be aware of thought. I go along with that, but even when I can do it, it does not put me in touch with the *Self* in the same way that the following simple exercise did. Why don't you try it for yourself? You will need to tape the instructions, so leave yourself about three quarters of an hour for the whole process. Please make sure you leave plenty of pauses on the tape so you can follow the instructions. The pauses come where you see this symbol: *.

An exercise in contacting the *Self*

First of all carry out this relaxation process.

Sit in a relaxed position, with your back as straight as possible. I bought myself a meditation stool, because I cannot sit cross-legged on the floor comfortably. Alternatively you could use a pile of cushions.

Focus your attention on every part of your body in turn, beginning with your neck, then focusing your awareness on the front of your body, chest, ribs, diaphragm, etc. As you focus on each part, become aware of any tension, tightness, or discomfort that is there, and just have it be okay for it to be there — just experience it and then let it go. So let your awareness go into your abdomen and belly, into your pelvis, then your thighs, knees, front of your legs, ankles, feet and toes. Bring your attention back through the soles of your feet, heels, achilles tendon, calves, backs of knees, backs of thighs, buttocks, each bone of the spine and all the muscles attached to the bones, shoulders, neck, back of head, scalp, and face. As your awareness travels over your face, feel the skin on your forehead become very smooth and let your eyelids go loose; as you get to your jaw muscles, let your mouth fall open and your jaw relax. Now just let your body feel very very relaxed.

Now begin the next part of the exercise:

Simply imagine that in front of you is an enormous, clear container. *

Start to put into it all the material possessions you have — the contents of your home, your garden, gardening equipment, books, records, furniture, kitchen equipment, shoes, clothing, jewelry — everything that belongs to you — don't forget your car, or other mode of transport. *

Then put your pets in, make sure the house is empty — then put that in too. *

Now put in all the people you know — relatives, friends, lovers, work mates, business associates, tradesmen etc. — put everyone you know in there. *

Now put all the roles you play in life in there — your role as a husband, wife, lover, friend, daughter etc. Put your career in there too. *

Now put all the judgements you have about yourself in there — that you are this kind of person, or that kind of person. *

Put your emotions in too — anger, fear, happiness, excitement, boredom — put them all in the container, and see them as colours floating in there. *

Now put all your mind in the container — all your thoughts, beliefs, attitudes, opinions, ideas — put them all in. *

Now put your body into the container. Watch your body go into the container. *

Now observe everything in the container — just observe it. *

Now ask yourself, 'Who is observing the contents of the container?'

Now look for your body in the container and put it back on.

Climb out of the container and look around. You will see a radiant light. Walk through the light and down a corridor to a door.

Open the door and you will see the room you are sitting in.

Go and sit in the chair, or position you were sitting in when you started this exercise.

Feel the pressure of the seat on your buttocks . . . Be aware of the rest of your body . . . When you are ready, open your eyes.

Most people who carry out this exercise to the end have a variety of experiences which I will describe for you later. Some people, however, cannot/will not complete it. They get *stuck* at some point — usually when they are asked to put something into the container that is very tied up with their identity. They are also suspicious about what is going to happen to the contents of the container. It seems to escape them that there is no container and no things inside. It is all happening in their mind. However, the mind is a very powerful force. Perhaps they are right to be cautious!

Some people have a whale of a time with this exercise, throwing things in with careless abandon, freed from some huge burden. Possessions and relationships can make us feel *solid* and *secure*, but they can also imprison us in need and attachment. I certainly notice that as Tim's salary rises, my anxiety-level rises correspondingly. You would think the reverse would be true, wouldn't you? But the more you have, the more you have to lose. The problem is not the having of possessions and relationships, but the attachment we develop to them, and the identification of ourselves with things and people. Money, status symbols, relationships, job titles and qualifications become the validation of our existence. To see that we are not all of that can be a relief — and a release. To have an experience of our *Selves* that is not rooted in physicality or psychology, or the mind, but is of the spirit, can be a significant moment in life.

When I tried this exercise on myself it was the first time I allowed for the possibility that the essential *me* might be eternal and universal. Up to that point I had never understood this higher consciousness stuff. I had put it into the category of *airy-fairy, mystical clap-trap*. I still do not know whether the experience I had was simply my mind playing the movie I wanted to see, but I certainly experienced something that caused me to suspend my previous cynicism. As I delve more and more into questions of existence, I realise how arrogant it is of any human being to assume that we can know for sure that this is all there is, and our own level of existence is all that is available. These are some of the experiences that people shared who carried out the above exercise:

Dorothy: *I think I missed something. When you asked us what was looking, there was nothing, void — inability to describe.*

Jean: *You can't describe it, but the closest you can get is* — 'It was nothing'.

Dorothy: *It was nothing that I recognised. There was* something *there. There was no form to it. Was it of this planet? I have no concept of it at all.*

Sarah: *The emotions . . . I saw them as colours. The biggest one was confusion, which was a horrid mustardy-yellow, and it sort of went* Yuck *into the container. It was horrible . . . I would have liked a bit longer to look around. I enjoyed it. I tried to see myself, and I could see a woman standing there, and she looked totally peaceful. All I could get, all the feeling I had, was one of generosity. Total ability to give.*

Adam: *I was probably a child of five or six, very inquisitive and unquestioning and taking things in.*

Gwen: *The one who was left was a clear, all-knowledgeable me. It was* okay.

Various people: *It didn't look like anything . . . Presence, no form . . . A space . . . light . . . That's it — it was weird . . . Awareness . . . Consciousness.*

The conversation continued. I explained to the group that those who found it almost impossible to describe, as did Dorothy, were finding it impossible because they were attempting to describe the *ineffable*. It is that of which we cannot speak.

> Because the Self has no definable properties,
> The Self is indefinable.
> Because it cannot be said how large or how small the Self is,
> The Self is limitless and infinite.
> Because the Self is formless,
> There is only One Self. (Moore, p45.)

The word Dorothy used to describe her experience was *Nothing* — and yet, she said, *there was something there*. It was not something she recognised. Is the *Self 'nothing'* then? Is that what we are? It does not fill most people with enthusiasm and hope to think that they might be *nothing*. However, if we examine what *nothing* is, things might look more hopeful. What would happen if I wrote it this way: 'NO THING'.

This conversation elicited the following response from one of the participants:

Sarah: *If it is No Thing, then it is everything.*

Jean: *How did you arrive at that conclusion, Sarah?*

Sarah: *I don't really know — it just seemed obvious.*

Well, it might have been obvious to Sarah, but it was not obvious to the other participants. Perhaps this extract from Moore (p48) will help to illuminate the thinking behind this:

> Nothing is the only indivisible absolute
> which the mind is capable of appreciating and understanding.
> The only qualification of *Nothing* is that there is only One;
> there cannot be two Nothings.

I suppose it follows that if there is only one nothing, then that must be everything. If the logic of that escapes you, as it does me, then try it the way Emmanuel [Rodegast, 1987] suggests:

> Close your eyes. Concentrate on the forefinger of your right hand. Experience its dimension. You are familiar with that finger. You know its size, shape and how it feels.
> Now extend your awareness of that finger as far as it will go, as far as you are able to feel comfortable, still feeling "yes that is my finger".
> Now expand your finger beyond that familiar feeling. You notice that the self fills that finger-space too, pushing out the boundaries of the familiar without loss of self.
> That is what you are all about . . . extending into the greater Self . . .

If you imagine expanding your finger to fill the whole universe, then it becomes the whole universe, or everything — but at the same time, it is No Thing. You cannot identify it as anything separate from, and having a different identity to, anything else. We are only able to identify something as a particular object by all the *not that thing* around it. So if you are No Thing, then you are everything, and as such, there is no real separation between you and other things, or beings.

When I was sitting in the jacuzzi at my health club recently, I tried another exercise: imagining that I was rubbing out my body-outline bit by bit, starting at my toes. I had the amazing sensation of *being* the water, the bubbles. It was really quite weird. So our experience of this division between ourselves and the rest of the world is an *illusion*. When you were born you did not suffer from that illusion — you were everything, or No Thing and, as Moore says *'Nothing is God'*, and God is the Creator:

Man finds fulfilment in dis-covering Nothing.
That Nought out of which All Things appear . . .
All Things that have been, are, and ever will be
Are contained in the void and chaos of Nothing,
Where shines the light of the Self, pure Consciousness . . .
God manifests, through Man, to HimSelf. [Moore, 1978]

The *Self*, or Nothing, is where we started, and it is from that space of possibility — everything-nothing, that we can and do create ourselves. And what do we do with that space of possibility? What do we fill it with?

The space of possibility

From the moment we are born we are already filled with potential. Given the correct environment and nurturing we would simply fill up the space of possibility with the potential we have — just as the acorn becomes a mature and magnificent oak, providing nothing happens to stunt its growth — so also we can become a human being, fully mature in every sense, physically, socially, emotionally and spiritually. However, the human being has one draw-back that the oak does not have — we have a mind!

It is the mechanisms of the mind, our psychology, which closes down the space of possibility and limits our potential. As far as I understand, the oak tree does not spend time wishing it was a willow, or comparing itself unfavourably with other oak trees, nor does it give up when it is damaged by a storm. It does not complain about the misfortunes that befall it — it simply carries on growing to the best of its ability.

Not so with human beings. Gradually the space of possibility gets filled in with the beliefs we develop about ourselves — the fears, the needs and all the other aspects of being human which we have discussed in earlier chapters. We close down our opportunities and cripple ourselves — with, of course, some help from our friends, parents, enemies, and our culture generally.

Eventually we are so cut off from our outer perimeter, so encapsulated by our walls of defence, that we cannot feel our connectedness to Oneness. We completely forget who we are. It was this isolation that I used to feel before I began the process of opening up that space again. Now that I feel I am nearer to my perimeter, I do feel a strong sense of connectedness to other beings and to nature. In so doing I know that I cannot operate in isolation from the rest of the world.

Diagrammatically it looks like this:

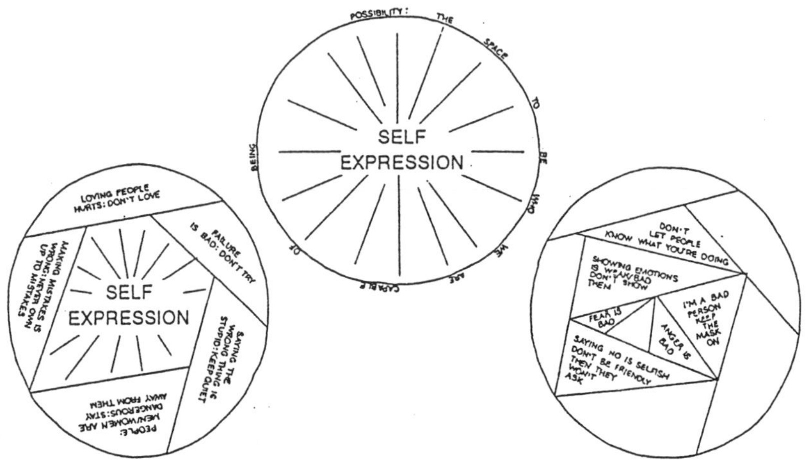

Closing down the space of possibility.

I am inextricably connected with everyone else — I *am* everyone else. Their pain is my pain and their joy is my joy. Their misfortune is my misfortune, their mistakes are my mistakes. When I know that, I also know that whatever I do affects them also. Someone said this centuries ago, and probably said it much better than I could, so I will share his words with you — I am sure you have heard them before:

> No man is an iland intire of itselfe;
> Every man is a peece of the continent, a part of the maine;
> If a clod bee washed away by the sea, Europe is the lesse, as well as if a promontorie were, as well as if a mannor of the friends of thine owne were;
> Any man's death diminisheth *me*, because I am involved in mankinde.
> And therefore never send to know for whom the bell tolls:
> It tolls for thee.

This was written by John Donne, poet, clergyman and religious writer in the 17th century. I regret we still have not got the message!

I saw the effect that my brother had of the experience of his *Self*. From being a completely isolated, closed-down individual who could not, or would not, communicate with anyone, who despised the human race and took the same attitude that Scrooge did about poverty and hardship — '*Let them die and decrease the surplus population*' — he became a warm and concerned person. He put on a *Walk for the World* event in Whitby and raised in excess of £4,000 for people in Third World countries.

To me that was nothing short of a miracle. If that could happen to him, it could happen to anyone. If we all began to realise that we have a *responsibility* to commit ourselves to our own growth and well-being, and that we therefore have a responsibility to the growth and well-being of everyone else on the planet, then we might indeed find hope for the survival of our species and for the regeneration of the Earth.

Of course, my brother did not only begin to appreciate and do things for other people, he began to experience that other people loved and appreciated *him*, for the first time in the 58 years of his life. Although my brother died with shocking suddenness two years later, he died having really *lived*, for the first time since he was about three. His brief, two-year *real* life and his death are a memorial to what it is possible for people to overcome, if they are really determined to do so. He had to overcome enormous fear, covered over by layer upon layer of defences, to begin to set foot on the path. I admire the courage and commitment it took for him to do that, and I admire all other human beings who take the courageous decision to do the same.

Although my brother's death was a great shock and a terrible loss to me, the fact that I had come closer to an experience of who I really am enabled me to experience his death in a very powerful way. Once I had stopped feeling terrible grief and let this out fully, I began to feel incredibly connected with my brother. I meditated for ten minutes or so every day, and really got a sense that he was a source of benevolent love, that he was there to guide me and protect me in a way that he had never been when he was alive. I felt one with him. I know now that *my brother is me*, that he has not ceased to exist, only in his bodily form, and that he learned an invaluable lesson while he was here this time, that I perhaps had helped him to learn. I feel very grateful that I was able to do so, and very joyful that he has possibly moved up another grade in the school of life!

On death

'Death', says Emmanuel, 'is like taking off a tight shoe'. Well, we will have to take his word for that! But I can see that, if the preceding statement were true, then death is a transformative process from one expression of life to another, less restrictive form. Death, when viewed in this way, gives life meaning. It is a marker for the end of one cycle and the beginning of the next.

If we did not die then there would be, literally, no *deadline* for us to work towards, no motivation to find out what we could make of our lives. Rather like my students, who put off their assignments until the last possible moment, we might well delay putting our utmost into life until we could see an end to it. The uncertainty that surrounds death — the fact that we never know when it might come—sharpens the intention. I remember when I was a teenager and in my early twenties, I used to stay in bed all morning — and sometimes most of the afternoon, because there was always tomorrow. It seemed that time went very slowly, and I was always waiting to be somewhere else, or someone different, before I started to really plan and shape my own destiny.

I also remember that when my brother died so suddenly, someone who had been close to me, but who had been holding a grudge against me for months and refusing to communicate, instantly let go of it, because he saw that I could die at any moment too, and his grievance would pale into insignificance if this happened. He would never have forgiven himself for letting his hurt get in the way of our relationship. So death, especially the unpredictability of it, can be a great motivator.

It is not death that I fear, but *dying*. I find pain hard to tolerate, and hate to think that I might have a lingering and protracted death, as indeed my father had. But I also see that *we only get the lessons we can cope with* — and that I will probably know how to cope, should this situation arise.

Maybe what makes dying so fearsome is all the speculating we do about it. If we could simply trust the process of life — and death — we would not spend so much energy trying to work out how we are going to handle it! We are as addicted to making dying easy as we are to having living be a *piece of cake*.

As my life unfolds I am beginning to trust the process of it more and more. I am beginning to be able to 'meet with triumph and disaster, and treat those two impostors just the same', as Rudyard Kipling puts it. I don't think it will make a *man* of me, but I know it demonstrates a progression towards psychological maturity.

Nowadays, when disaster threatens, or even when it strikes, I seldom despair, or panic — well, only for a brief while! I usually know that *universal intelligence* has simply set me another test in the curriculum of life, one that we can only fail by refusing to take it — running away or opting out (suicide). Even then, Emmanuel tells us that suicide is the only action that is left to people, when they have put together a curriculum-package that is too advanced for them this time around. They need, he says, to *come home*, get regenerated, and design a curriculum for next time that is not so challenging. We need to have, he says, the utmost compassion and understanding for people who take their own lives.

I could see this when an ex-university student of mine took this way of solving her problems recently. I saw that she was perhaps too fragile to cope with the problems of life in this culture at this time. It is too destructive. As David Smail implies, we have to fight a long, and sometimes seemingly futile, battle in our attempts to heal ourselves, because we are surrounded by destructive forces which are alien to our *Selves*, and which created the damage in the first place. Fromm (1985), and Smail (1987), both argue for changes in the structure, attitudes and values of our culture, in order to provide an environment where we can develop without being deprived of the nurturing we need.

David Smail implies that, without some major social reform or revolution, the human condition is hopeless. But *revolution* is only the turn of a wheel — it simply puts power into different hands, not hands that are necessarily kinder or more humane. What is required is *evolution* — the *inner revolution*, as Krishnamurti puts it. The evolution of the individual is the only thing powerful enough to overcome the destructiveness of human beings. You cannot fight force with force. Martin Luther King maintains that you can only fight it with *soul force*. You cannot fight hate with hate, you can only 'fight' hate with love.

This is the way in which Martin Luther King inspired his followers to overcome the hatred, prejudice and violence perpetrated against the black population in the southern states of the USA, which were rooted in deficiency-needs (psychological immaturity). I cannot do better than to use his own words:

> To our most bitter opponents we say: "We shall match your capacity to inflict suffering by our capacity to endure suffering. We shall meet your physical force with soul-force. Do to us what you will, and we shall continue to love you . . . Throw us in jail and we shall still love you. Send your hooded perpetrators of violence into our community at the midnight hour, and beat us and leave us half-dead, and we shall still love you. But be ye assured that we will wear you down by our capacity to suffer. One day we shall win freedom, but not only for ourselves. We shall so appeal to your heart and conscience that we shall win *you* in the process, and our victory will be a double victory.

Like Gandhi, Martin Luther King saw that the forces of evil were more to be feared than death. Death is not destructive, it is simply a transition, but hatred, and the fear from which it grows, which stems from a total lack of understanding and awareness, are totally destructive. They can only be overcome or transformed by love. Not, however, by what normally passes for love in our cultural experience. That is the problem — we cannot, as a rule, utilise the transformative power of love because we do not know how to access it. We have hardly any direct experience of what love is! Until we know what love is, we are powerless to act against the forces of fear.

8. *Love: the compass to our potential*

Our cultural concept of love's possibilities has been so limited that we don't have the proper vocabulary for a holistic experience of love . . .

Ferguson, 1982, p433.

All we need is love

When my relationship with my second husband ended, it left me with a lot of questions, perhaps the most significant of which related to *love*. I was so sure I had loved him and that he had loved me. It certainly *felt* that way — it definitely *looked* that way. He did and said all the right things — and so did I. Why did I stop loving him? I had all sorts of reasons, but something did not ring true. Were any, or all, of those things sufficient to change that magical *something* we had?

Another thought began to creep into my mind. Did I *ever* really love him in the first place? What did that mean anyway? Had I ever loved anyone? Could I ever love anyone? Did *anyone* love anyone?! I almost drove myself crazy with all this. How was I to ever find the answers? Luckily I had Krishnamurti at my side (in book form), reminding me that I did not need answers, and perhaps these were really good questions. I began the process of exploring them.

My oracle, Krishnamurti (1978), was certainly clear what love was not:

> It is not fear, it is not dependence, jealousy, possessiveness, domination, responsibility, duty, self-pity, or any of the other things that conventionally pass for love. If you can eliminate all these, not by forcing them, but by washing them away, as the rain washes away the dust of many days from a leaf, then perhaps you will come upon this strange flower man hungers after.

Well — could I *wash them away*? I never saw a soap powder labelled 'need and fear remover'. I suppose I had already taken the first step towards discovering love — to begin to question my constructs of it. I remember realising one day how my hunger for a particular type of love devalued the love that was available to me. I made a list of people who loved me. It was a long list. I realised, in the light of this exercise, that it was quite irrational to feel unloved, that I was surrounded by an abundance of it, but it just was not the right kind, so it would not do.

In the name of love, and to keep men around me (because I thought they were the only source of it) I have gone through a lot of self-denial. I used to be proud of the fact that I was so adaptable; now I see that I was simply operating out of the need for love. I would have done anything to have love in my life, and I did. I almost took up shop-lifting, because I lived with a marxist who thought 'property was theft'. I can laugh at it now, but at the time I could have put myself at huge risk. My judgement was so clouded by the need to have him approve of me and love me, that I was willing to risk my career and my integrity to stay in the relationship.

Some people will kill themselves rather than lose the source of satisfaction of their need. They will kill themselves because they feel they cannot have it. One young man I knew dropped out of school and came very close to committing suicide, because he fell in love at the age of fifteen, and that love was unrequited.

Deborah made her sacrifices too, in order to keep the man she loved in her life. It brought her to the verge of suicide, and is still causing her tremendous problems. When, on one of my courses, I made a rather flippant remark about the lengths we will go to in response to unrequited love, she became very upset:

Deborah: *I was very angry when Jean made light of the fact that he wanted to kill himself. I got to that point myself, and although I took the tablets, I didn't feel it was* me *doing it. It took me about an hour to realise it was me, and that it was a damned silly thing to do.*

Jean: *Why did you want to take your own life?*

Deborah: *Because I had had something taken away from me — my baby. And as a result of that my boyfriend walked out too. He wanted me to have the termination, and I didn't want it. I didn't stand up for myself. I believed everything he said. I believed his lies. He was saying if I did this thing for him we would have a relationship afterwards.*

Jean: *And if you didn't?*

Deborah: *I chose him. The baby had to go.*

Jean: *How do you feel about it now?*

Deborah: *I feel guilty, because I sit here listening to other people say they can't have babies and they want them, and I could, and I didn't have the strength to do it.*

Jean: *And do you think you can forgive yourself for that now?*

Deborah: *No.*

Jean: (To everyone) *Do you think she should forgive herself?*

All: *Yes.*

The source of need

Is this love — this suffering, this pain? Obviously not — it is *neediness*. But washing it away, as Krishnamurti suggests we might do, is not easy. It might even be impossible. Where does this neediness come from? Where would we derive a need so strong that the unfulfilment of it would drive us to suicide, or extreme self-denial? Out of this desperate yearning, those of us who do not try to physically destroy ourselves murder our souls by denying them expression. We become what we think other people will find acceptable, and we deny our own truth.

When what we perceive as the source of our need does not provide it, we anaesthetise our pain with all those tranquillisers I have mentioned previously: alcohol, TV, food, sleep, diversions.

Why are we so desperate for this 'strange flower'? For many people, this is obvious, for others it is not. In Deborah's case her mother had sent her to live with her grandmother soon after she was born until she was four, and then, when her mother re-married, she was *farmed out* to a succession of child-minders. Her mother had essentially abandoned her. Deborah was yearning for something as a child that was not there.

Her mother was the person to whom Deborah should have been special. She was absent. This created an unsatisfied craving to be special to someone. When it looked as if Deborah had found the special 'one', in an intimate relationship, the scenario with her mother was replayed — she was abandoned. It looked completely hopeless to her. For the rest of her life the person with whom she should have had a special relationship, the source of love, was going to reject and abandon her: there was no escape. What was the point of living, only to have this pain reactivated over and over again?

The problem is that as adults we can be reasonable. We might see why Deborah's mother (a single parent) could not cope with her and sent her away. We might see why she put her out to child-minders, and Deborah, as an adult, certainly can — but a child cannot reason, a child can only feel, and what she feels is abandoned, unloved. What has she done to deserve it, she wonders? She must be *evil*. Adults are always right, adults are always perfect — the child must therefore be the bad one who is being punished for something.

This line of emotional response is fairly obvious in a case like Deborah, and in the cases of sexual abuse cited earlier, but in some cases it is not so obvious. Some people have really nice parents, who do not abuse them or abandon them. They are not treated badly or neglected. Do they escape unscathed? Sadly, they do not. Although I have covered this in the previous chapter on parents, I need to re-iterate this because it is the people whose parents were *nice*, and not obviously damaging, who have as much toxic shame as others, but have more difficulty in identifying the source of it. Take Charles for instance. Charles was the person I referred to earlier who dropped out of school due to unrequited love. He had very nice parents who treated him very well. What did they do when he refused to go to school?

Charles: *They were a bit disappointed, but they felt they didn't want to push me in a particular direction.*

Now this is perfectly *reasonable* isn't it?

Jean: *How did you feel about the fact that they did not want to push you?*

Charles: *With hindsight I feel that is a shame. But it was . . . it has been a nuisance.*

Jean: *I want to say what a pair of limp-wristed twits your parents were! If you were my kid and you dropped out of school, I would say "What the hell do you think you are doing? Get out of here and back there right now. Don't sit there feeling sorry for yourself, get off your bum and get to school."*

Actually, I hope I would not speak like this, but at least my outburst has some passion! I would certainly want to know first of all why the child did not want to go to school. I would make sure they were not being bullied, that they were not afraid of someone or something, but I would not meekly accept that the child did not want to go. Reasonable parents do not do us any favours! At least when my mother shouted at me when I came in late, or when I gave up jobs, I knew she cared, even if she had a funny way of showing it. When parents are so reasonable, many children feel that they simply do not care.

Jean: *Do you have an experience of being let down by them, Charles?*

Charles: *But it feels as though there isn't anything I can do about it.*

Jean: *Now you are being reasonable. I don't care whether you can do anything about it. Do you have an experience of being let down by them?*

Charles: *That would be the one that came to mind, yes.*

It was very difficult for Charles to say this. I realise that this could sound as if I was putting words into his mouth, but Charles was not the kind of person who would agree with me, unless he really did agree. He liked argument and debate, as long as it was intellectual. He is a very controlled individual, very unemotional. I certainly got the picture that he came from a home where emotions were not expressed, and everyone was *nice*. It was not easy for him to criticise his parents, because they had always encouraged him to do what he wanted and they had always been *reasonable*. What more can you ask? Isn't that love? No, it is *not*.

'If you really loved me'

From these types of model we pick up an idea of love that is distorted. What we see as love, what we are told is love, is actually an expression of parents' neediness, or their fear. In Charles' case his parents were presumably afraid of emotions. There was, to use the terms of Skynner and Cleese, a convenient *screen*, behind which unacceptable emotions were carefully stacked away.

From my interactions with Charles I would guess that almost anything that could be classed as an *emotion* would be shoved behind the screen. Consequently, Charles, who is a young man who should be full of energy and *joie de vivre*, felt, to quote his own words, 'very empty and sad'. He intellectualises everything to cut himself off from his feelings. He told me that he wasn't like that once. It obviously took him a while to learn.

The title of Alice Miller's book, *For Your Own Good*, is a sinister one. Hitler's father beat him almost to death *for his own good*. Out of an inability to distinguish their own needs from a true expression of love for their children, parents manipulate their offspring and attempt to fit them into costumes that are of parental design — the costume they would be happy to see us wearing. No matter that it is not what their children want, or feel comfortable in. They must represent their parents' efforts and be a reflection of their parents success in that role. Charles' costume had to be one that was devoid of emotion. He had to be (as he is now) a nice, polite little boy, a reasonable person, someone who would not create waves or draw attention to himself.

Despite the fact that children know that the costume does not suit them and does not fit, they contort themselves to fit into it in the hope that, then, they will retain their parents' love and get a sense of their own worthiness. But that is tantamount to someone loving you because you buy your clothes from the right sort of store — you are not being loved and valued for your uniqueness, and for the fact that you are *you*.

Of course our parents do not intend this, nor are they aware that this is what they are doing. If they were aware, they would stop, because they do not mean to harm their children, they want to love them — but that is impossible if you do not have, and never have had an experience of love. Most of us think we have had love, and we are sadly wrong.

So some of us dutifully don our costumes, and from time to time we become aware of their hateful restrictions and try to take them off. But discarding costumes makes us feel exposed, ashamed. Only the costume, we think, earns us love — without it we are worthless.

Tricia is a perfect example of a parent-pleasing, tailor-made child, who kept desperately trying to feel at ease in her costume and failed.

Tricia: *I feel very evil at times. I am a door-slammer. I feel the overwhelming compulsion to throw things. I feel really* evil.

Jean: *You are angry. You need to find out what you are angry about.*

Tricia: *I can pinpoint things within my marriage which undermine my self-esteem. It goes back further than that. My father tried to mould me to what they thought I should be. He still manages to make me feel really inadequate.*

Jean: *That is a killer. If you think back to* Emmanuel's Book, *he suggests you once put on a costume that doesn't fit. That is where the rage comes from. You need to burst your way out of there.*

Tricia: *I did rebel. I drank a lot, and slept around with people. Although I was quite a* good little girl, *too.*

Jean: *Yes, it's* 'Let's let the bad girl out of here'. *Of course the bad girl isn't bad, it is someone who wants to say "Look — this is me! I don't want to be* you: *I just want to be* me!"

Tricia: *When I go and visit my parents I make a resolution that I won't let my dad get to me. He always gives you the impression that he can do everything better. He does it as a joke, but I think he* means *it really. He has no idea the effect that has on me.*

Jean: *Are you doing what you want to do with your life now?*

Tricia: *I have got wonderful ideas of selling up and taking off somewhere — and I think mum and dad would be upset if I did.*

Obviously Tricia has learned to be a *people-pleaser*. She thinks she will not get love if she does something that goes against the wishes of other people. She must live her life in a way that other people approve of, otherwise she will be worthless. She also seems to have married a man who replicated her parents. It is as though we need to keep repeating the experiences of our childhood, until we discover how to deal with our parents and not allow them to invalidate us.

Perhaps the practice we get finally enables us to affirm who we are — or it doesn't. We have to keep banging our heads against a brick wall, until we see that the only thing that changes is our own heads. It certainly provides us with the opportunity to see that we do not need to find our validation from someone else — that we do not need to keep being dominated, manipulated, abused, rendered emotionless — and whether we learn or not is up to us.

Derek learned a lot from his (*nice*) parents about love. What he learned was that *you never get anything for nothing,* and that *love comes with strings attached,* and *you had better watch out, because if someone loves you, there is a price to pay.* He could not really see that there was anything amiss with this line of argument. He was extremely reluctant to acknowledge that his parents were anything other than *good, loving people.* The problem is they were also *needy* people.

Derek: *But surely you owe your parents something? After all, they brought you into the world.*

Jean: *People want children, but they don't really want to be parents. Your mother wanted children — she took on that job. You don't owe your parents anything. Where does that come from, that you* owe *them something? They don't owe you anything and you don't owe them anything! This is not some kind of* Monopoly *game we are playing here.*

Derek: *They have given me* life! *I am not able to look after myself at first, so they look after me, therefore I owe them for looking after me.*

Jean: *I would hate to be in a relationship with you, Derek. Boy, are you going to cash up things in your bank account, and are you going to want payment back for it!*

Derek: *How do I change this? What do I do?*

Jean: *I will give you this pen, Derek. (*Takes pen from table and gives it to him*).*

Derek: *Oh. What do you want?*

Jean: *I don't want anything — I just gave it to you.*

Derek: *Oh, (*slightly embarrassed*), guilt, indebtedness . . . Do you want it back?*

Jean: *I gave it you.*

Derek: *It's not a short-term loan?*

Jean: *I gave it you.*

Derek: *For ever and ever?*

Jean: *I gave it to you.*

Derek: *Yes, I do find it hard to accept gifts.*

Jean: *Furthermore, it wasn't a pen, it was love.*

Derek: *Looks like a pen to me.*

Jean: *It was love, and it was a gift.*

Derek: *Point taken. Love is a gift.*

Jean: *You don't really know that.*

Derek: *I'm struggling towards knowing.*

Jean: *If it is not a gift, it is not love.*

Derek: *Yes, you do not want to love in the expectation that you are going to get something back.*

Jean: *If it is not a gift it wasn't love, it was* trade. *When people give you love, say* thank you *and accept it.*

Derek: *But giving love in return is a way of saying* thank you.

Jean: *In return for love? People do this, they say, "Oh, what can I give them back, otherwise they will think I am dreadful. I really ought to give them something". If you want to say thank you, say thank you!*

Derek: (Still talking about giving love back) *Not because you* ought *to, but because you* want *to thank the person who has given you that.*

Jean: *Then just say* thank you. *If love is an obligation, it isn't love. Are you trying to justify that you ought to give something back? Are you trying to have your construct of love be right?*

Derek: *Yes, I can see that. I find this so difficult to get round.*

Jean: *It will destroy your relationships, Derek.*

Derek: *It has done.*

Jean: *You say* I love you? (places hand to ear to hear the expected reply 'I love you too'). *And this is what your parents have done with you, otherwise you wouldn't have learned it* "I love you and what I want from you is . . . I love you too". *They don't spell it out, but you get the message anyway.*

Derek: *I would really like to get rid of this* love as a duty *thing. If I could free myself of that and look at my mother as a person! The word* mother *brings with it obligation and duty. I do love her, but the other things are there.*

Derek's love for his mother is obscured by the feeling that he has a *duty* to love her. That love is something he owes her, and if he doesn't pay her back for what she gives, her love will cease. There is, in this system, a constant weighing and measuring to see, *how much have you given me and what do I owe you*? I suggest to you that this is how people *normally* interact with 'love'. We are constantly weighing up the evidence, adding up the score to see if, or how much, we are loved. What a lot of energy we expend on this game!

We fail to realise that the acceptance of love is a gift, too. Giving love automatically returns it to the giver. Only if the gift is not valued, not allowed in, can it feel wasted. And why would not people simply accept love — let it in? There seems to be a deep suspicion of 'love', which was illustrated by the conversation with Derek. He is not the only one: most of us seem to have difficulty with love. Deep down, when people offer us love, in whatever form — gifts, help , support, sympathy, attention — we wonder *what is behind it? Why are they doing it? Do I deserve it?*

One of my clients is deeply depressed because she desperately longs to get close to people, and yet she is also desperately afraid to do so. When she was small her parents paid her very little attention — they were hard-working, busy people. She had an uncle who played with her, was fun to be with, sat her on his knee and had physical contact with her. He was the only person who did. When she was eight her uncle went away. She does not remember him telling her he was going, although her mother maintains that he did tell her. Since that time, she has decided that loving people is dangerous. When you let someone get close to you — they leave. This has left her in a depressing place where her fear of love is as great as her longing for it. She wants closeness, and cannot cope when it is offered. Love stays tantalisingly out of her reach.

Love, in our culture, can become a game which we all play by different rules, and then wonder why we never seem to win.

This became very clear to me one evening when Tim took me out, on our wedding anniversary, to a special restaurant that we normally would not think we could afford. We sat there in the candlelight, music softly playing and Tim took my hand, gazed into my eyes and said "I really love you". I had a feeling that he thought that this was the appropriate script for the occasion — this is what he *should* be saying — and so he had dutifully obliged. I also know that, at that moment, he was in touch with loving me.

Being in a somewhat playful mood, and feeling that Tim was perhaps 'hamming it up' a bit, I told him I loved him too, and then added, "But if you *really* loved *me*, Tim, you would have bought me flowers as well, and found a restaurant where I was serenaded by the waiter". Entering into the spirit of the game, Tim replied, "Well if you really loved me you'd have skipped dinner and gone to bed with me and made mad passionate love". "Ah", I replied, "If you really loved me you'd have booked us into a hotel for the night, so that we could have done both". And so it went on, until, in the end, we were laughing hysterically at this funny game we had discovered.

The tragedy is, of course, that for so many people, it is a deadly-serious game that they see as the truth. Most people know precisely how to play this game. They have played it all their lives and they believe it is the only way to play the game of love. When I invite them to demonstrate the rules of the game they can do so with alacrity. This is how we play it on the course.

The phrase, *If you really loved me you'd . . .* is written at the top of the board and the participants are asked to complete the sentence. They have no trouble at all complying with my request! With increasing humour they shout out the ending of the sentence. The completed list looks like this:

give me space; give me affection; treat me as an individual; not mother me; not lie to me; wouldn't treat me as a possession; want to be with me; let me make mistakes; wouldn't be jealous of people I go out with; let me meet your family; not say nasty thing; want to be with me all the time; go to bed with me; be as unhappy as I am; care about me; tell me you love me; love me as I am; wouldn't do courses; be responsible for yourself; support me; let me be bad sometimes; not keep secrets; tell me everything; respect me; share everything; be friends; not isolate me; not make me feel guilty; let me go; let me be free, but know *you* can't be; know I was equal; have a child; come and see me; notice me; know what I am thinking; know what I want without me telling you; not send me to school; trust me; be honest; listen to me; buy me flowers; support me financially; understand me; remember my birthday/anniversary etc. not make me feel guilty; not criticise me in public; not hurt me; not leave me; would leave me; give me your last toffee; entertain me; wear fish-net tights; marry me; divorce me . . .

I could go on. The lists from each course are similar. How tragic they are! What do they say about our relationships with each other, and with love? The manipulation, the possessiveness, the pain, the guilt, the imprisonment, the unrealistic expectations in those words! And yet this is what we do in relationships. Who wants to carry on playing this game? When I ask this question I do not get any volunteers. It is a game that has no winners. Both people end up losing. They lose their identity, their self-respect, their dignity — they lose love.

Sadly, most of us do play this game to the hilt — or even to the death. Many of us are still playing it, determined that one day we are going to win — find someone who fits the bill. Or we have given up and decided we cannot win, and we are never going to play again.

Looked at this way, the game of love is clearly madness. We learned to play it at a very early age, and then took the advanced course from the media — popular love songs, romantic novels, films and television soaps all provide us with more pieces for the jigsaw of love. We play the game *s/he loves me, s/he loves me not*, using people instead of flower petals. One by one we pluck out of people what we need, looking for evidence of love, until there is nothing left, only emptiness. And then we say *you see, I knew you didn't love me*, or *I just don't love you any more*. As Stuart Emery (1978) says, 'Most people's relationships are based on need, and they are disasters'. All the items in the list above can be traced to the need for security, for belonging, recognition, validation, and identity. They are certainly not about love.

Love is all there is

The above list indicates that we hold love as a *concept* — something with definable and measurable properties, something we can identify. Only when we take it out and look at it, can we begin to see that this notion that *love is conceptualisable* might not work too well. If it is not a concept, however, what on earth is it? Maybe we should not be looking on earth!

In fact, the answer to this conundrum is extremely simple. *Love is what is there when we take away fear. Love is you, without your costume. Love is who you were, and who you are. God is love, love is God. Love is everything and no thing. Love just* **is**. When you have an experience of the *Self*, then you have an experience of love. When you experience the being of another, then you experience love. Everything else is not it.

When I experienced loving my brother I saw his encrusted soul, his essence struggling for expression. I saw his pain, his loneliness, his fear, and inside all that I saw *him* — I connected with him. In order to do so, I had to relinquish my resentment about his inadequacy as a brother, his failure to meet my expectations, and to be there for me when I needed him. I had to handle my fear of rejection and love him anyway.

Let me take you back to the plastic container exercise (chapter seven). This was designed to enable you to have an experience of the *Self*. It was also an experience of love. People described it as peace, oneness, being. That is love.

I cannot do better than to use the words of Emmanuel to clarify the whole issue of 'love'. When asked 'how can I learn what love is?', he replied 'By knowing who you are':

> You will not exhaust the love in the Universe if you were to absorb it from now until the end of time.
> Love is all that exists.
> Love is the universal communication. It is the energy that has created the universe and is keeping it going. God is love. All matter is formed by love. A leaf holds together for love . . . There is nothing but love. Don't let masks and postures fool you. Love is the glue that holds the universe together . . . Love requires no practice. Love is. One cannot practice is-ness. One can, however, practice the decision to love . . . Love is not mastered, it is allowed . . . You yearn for love as the flower yearns for the sun, and you have as much right to it . . . Love is eternal. It passes through every illusory barrier, such as time and space. Love is an unbreakable connection.
>
> [Rodegast, 1987]

When we experience a sense of connectedness with another person's being, then we know what love is. Love is the *space of possibility* — it is who we are, and who we can be.

When we encounter life, we begin to close the space down (see *fig* 6, in chapter 7). We learn that love — being ourselves — means that we can be hurt and damaged. We get the message that being ourselves is not good enough to please the people we rely on, and who are our source of survival and love, and so we build the layers of protection. Charles, Derek and Deborah all learned that LOVE = PAIN, and said, *I won't do that again*. I won't trust again, get close again, depend on someone again. I will build a wall around love, and wait and see if someone is brave enough and persistent enough to get inside it — but I will employ all my weaponry to make sure they do not manage it.

The problem with this is that the other part of the equation is NO LOVE = PAIN, also. The truth of it all, as Guy Claxton (1984) points out, is LOVE = PAIN SOMETIMES . Of course, when we are very small, and the people who purport to love us are causing us pain, it is easy to feel that the only solution is to cut ourselves off from love, or re-create it by experiencing the feelings of anguish that it caused us in our childhood.

Robin Norwood, in *Women Who Love Too Much*, suggests that this is what many people do. This applies to men as well as women. We have equated love with pain, with feelings of frustration and anxiety, or we have equated it with deadness, with being safe, with staying inside our *costume*. This leaves us in a quandary, because something within us, the *Self*, recognises that we are being led up the garden path — not to a bed of roses, but to either a cabbage plot or a tangle of thorns. Where then does the path to *real* love begin?

Some of the problems we have with love arise because our human vocabulary is too limited to encompass it. Robin Norwood points out that the Greeks were streets ahead of us in this respect. They had two names for it, *Agape* and *Eros*. This is quite useful, since it does help us to distinguish what love is not, even if it does not tell us what love *is*.

Eros was the name the Greeks used for *passionate love*. Those who think that passionate love is *true love* measure the intensity of their love by the intensity of their suffering. *Passion*, Norwood points out, literally means *suffering*. Therefore, *it is necessary to suffer in order to be in love*. Being in love, according to this yardstick, means that you constantly yearn for the object of your devotion and their prolonged absence brings about a a state of torment and anguish.

The more obstacles that are put in the way of *true* love, in this model, the more the person suffers, and the more ardent they feel about the object of their desire. One person on the course said that he had finished a relationship because he thought he did not love his girlfriend — she was not the right one. But, when she found someone else he realised he still loved her, because he had this terrible yearning.

Jean: *We are looking for the one*. The one that is going to come along in the shining armour or the flowing sequinned dress, and rescue you from this predicament called life. And when they don't do it they are not *the one.*

Derek: *I broke up with my girlfriend a year ago. On the face of it we had a good relationship, but in spite of our almost-happiness, she was not the right one for me. She was the first one, so she couldn't be the right one. What a waste. You couldn't expect the first one to be the right one.*

Jean: *No, of course not. You have to shop around, don't you? Make sure there isn't a better bargain hiding somewhere.*

Derek: *When I realised this, it was like being hit on the head with a mallet. How stupid I feel about this! It really was fear and more fear that made me think in this way . . . I'd like to stop loving her, as she has moved on, and has found someone else.*

Jean: *I think what you mean is you would like to stop yearning for her. Loving people is fine. It does not hurt. What often happens is that we are not in touch with how addicted we are to people, until they are not available any more. You can break off a relationship, but as soon as the other person finds someone else, you think, 'hang on a minute, there might have been a bit of meat left on that bone, and that was mine, and now someone else has got it'* (laughter).

Derek: *I was paralysed for three months, simply through realising I had lost this person I loved. Crazy!*

Well, yes, *crazy* is the word to describe it. Don't we say we are '*madly* in love'? 'I'm *crazy* about you'? Absolutely true. What we should say is 'I'm madly *addicted* to you'. 'I am madly addicted to the high I get, to the rush it gives me, to the adrenalin-flow that happens around *being in love.* I certainly remember all those symptoms only too well.

If the object of my undying devotion was late, I would work myself up into a frenzy of anxiety. Had he *gone off me,* or *found someone else*? Or was he *lying dead on the road,* or *badly injured in hospital,* or, worst of all, *had he forgotten*? I would much rather he was in hospital — or even dead, than have simply *forgotten* that he was going to meet me. If someone *really* loved me, how could he possibly forget? It must mean *he doesn't care enough.* When he finally did arrive I would give him hell, especially if he did not crawl in on all fours begging abjectly for forgiveness.

When all this anguish and passion subsided, and the non-appearance of the loved one ceased to cause such intense concern, merely mild annoyance, then it seemed I must no longer be in love, and so should move on to pastures new. I used my feelings as a barometer to measure the intensity of my love for many years. I firmly believed that when I stopped being filled with desire every time I saw my loved one, then love had died.

I would have dismissed as arrant nonsense the notion that, as Erich

Fromm suggests, love is not created by the *object* — the other person — but by myself. I thought falling in love was like having a careless accident, like tripping over something, or falling into a hole. Once you bumped into *the one*, there you were in the grip of this obsession. What did it have to do with *me*? Subsequent experience has taught me that Erich Fromm might be correct.

A few years ago a carpenter came to the house to do some work for us. The weather was warm and sunny, and after he had weighed up the job we sat outside drinking tea. I found him interesting — a *Jack the Lad* type who had travelled widely, was witty and yet obviously beginning to think about *life, the universe and everything*. As we talked he became more interesting and I began to think he was quite attractive. The conversation became prolonged and led to the fact that he was at a loose end that evening.

Taking pity on him (my mind, my 'parrot' said), I invited him to come with me to a student function I was attending. At the party he wooed me with fruit juice cocktails, wheedling the woman behind the bar into fishing out pieces of fruit from the salad to decorate it with. He also persuaded a woman at a motorway service station, in the early hours of the morning, to gift wrap a box of chocolates for me, which he presented with a flourish. I was extremely impressed. He then said what a pity it was that I had to drive him home at that time of night (he had no car and it was a distance of about twenty miles round trip). I agreed. I said that would not be necessary as he could stay at my house. His face lit up. I said it was perfectly okay as Tim and I had a spare room he could use. His face fell!

I began to realise that I was falling into a very old pattern of mine — one that I thought I had given up years ago. I had been *flirting*. I realised my thoughts had been running along the lines of *who would know?*, and *what's the harm?* I am sure many of you know the type of thoughts I am talking about. I turned to him and said, '"I think you are very attractive and I like you very much. I might even be falling in love with you a little bit — and I have no intention of doing anything about it, other than to say, thank you for a lovely evening; I've very much enjoyed your company."

It was a revelation to see that I had been indulging in a *game* I was not aware of playing — or perhaps more accurately, did not *want to be aware* of playing. Fortunately for all concerned (Tim, the carpenter and myself, not to mention all the other people who would have been let down and damaged by me indulging myself in this way), I became aware of what I was doing before it went too far. I had been leading myself and the carpenter up the garden path. Our carpenter was baffled by my sudden withdrawal from the game, but I did apologise for my lack of integrity and he took it in good part.

This experience presented me with a very concrete illustration that *falling in love* is not an accident. It is a step that we can take, or not take. We have the choice from the beginning. I realised that I would have been using this man to feed my parrot (or 'boost my ego', if you prefer), but that would have hurt Tim and damaged our relationship, and for what?! For a bit of excitement and stimulation. The whole episode demonstrated to me how important it is to live according to principles, not according to feelings. It was quite frightening to see how easy it was to be tempted and to come up with thoughts which would make it okay. Maybe I needed to go through this so that I would learn, once and for all, that *falling in love* is not such an attractive proposition and that it is something over which we have total control.

The *pay-offs* for *Eros*, then, are excitement, stimulation, heightened awareness and sensitivity, feelings of well-being and being in love with the world. This could be a description of someone taking stimulants or narcotics, and it is as addictive. The drawbacks to *Eros* are anxiety, depression, withdrawal symptoms, mood-swings and feelings of being out-of-control. Norwood suggests that the safe alternative to *Eros* (passion), is *Agape*.

Now after looking at what *Eros* constitutes, *Agape* might seem to many of us to be a better bet. *Agape*, says Norwood, is the stable, committed relationship, based on companionship and friendship that two people have, who really respect and admire each other. Each gives the other a lot of encouragement. The two people mutually support each other in making it through life. There are a lot of common interests and shared values and goals. Associated with *real* love in these terms are feelings of 'serenity, security, devotion, understanding, companionship, mutual support and comfort' (Norwood, p43).

Many aspects of this description would have applied to my previous marriage. I notice, however, that when it looked as though I was becoming capable of standing on my own feet, the encouragement and support I received from my husband changed to criticism and discouragement — because he was scared of me realising I could do without him. He thought that would make him redundant.

Apart from this, and other possible drawbacks, *Agape* does not sound too bad to me, but Norwood suggests that it might be a bit boring compared to the passionate and heightened emotional state of the alternative. The problem, she believes, is that, in this culture, we are led to believe that:

> A passionate relationship (*Eros*) will bring us contentment and fulfilment (*agape*). In fact, the implication is that with great enough passion a lasting bond will be forged. All the failed relationships based initially on tremendous passion can testify that this premise is false. In a

> passionate relationship, fraught as it must be with the exci suffering and frustration of new love, there is a feeling that something very important is missing. What is wanted is commitment.
>
> (Norwood, p44.)

Norwood goes on to say that if we do eventually get the commitment, and people start to feel safe and warm towards each other, they will also feel cheated because the passion has gone.

> The price we pay for passion is fear, and the very pain and fear that feed passionate love may also destroy it. The price we pay for stable commitment is boredom, and the very safety and security that cement such a relationship can also make it rigid and lifeless.

All this looks like 'heads we lose and tails we lose', doesn't it? Is there any point in having relationships, and is there such a thing as *true love*? I think this is where we started this chapter. Do not despair, dear reader, as Jane Austin might say, all is not lost. Norwood touches on another alternative which she calls *true intimacy*. True intimacy is, however, only achievable when we have gone through *recovery*, this meaning the healing of the afflictions caused through our early childhood experiences.

If this makes us all sound like casualties in the game of life, it is probably quite accurate. We are. It seems that the prospect of true intimacy, far from being desirable, actually fills us with dread. Is it any wonder? Those with whom we were once most intimately connected, our parents, exploited our innocence and violated our trust — even those who did it ever-so-nicely — and we are definitely not going to try that one again, even if we knew how to, and most of us have long forgotten.

Love is an act of will

Falling in love is, Erich Fromm (1966) suggests, an *act of will*. It is a decision, a judgement, he maintains, and moreover, it is not constituted by the *object* — the other person — but by the *faculty* — the mind. Furthermore, he asserts, if we concentrate all our love on one person, then it is not love, it is a 'symbiotic attachment, or an enlarged egotism'. He is saying that it is a manifestation of need for security or feelings of self-worth.

> Love is not primarily a relationship to a specific person; it is an *attitude*, an *orientation of character*, which determines the relatedness of a person to the world as a whole, not towards one *object* of love.
>
> [Fromm, 1966]

Adopting the position that it is the other person who is generating the feelings and state of *being in love* is, Fromm says, as ludicrous as someone thinking that, if only they could find something really beautiful to paint, the *right* object or view, *then* they would become an artist. Finally he concludes that 'love is exclusively an act of will and commitment'.

Scott Peck (1989, p82) offers another definition of love, albeit acknowledging that giving definitions cannot be satisfactory, due to love's mysterious nature:

> The will to extend oneself for the purpose of nurturing one's own or another's spiritual growth.

He also maintains that love involves *effort*. I would add that the act of love also requires courage.

There do not seem to be many examples of 'love' around, for people to experience, or use as a model. Life is full of examples of *Eros* and *Agape*, some of which present pretty convincing evidence that they are *it*. Having been involved in that kind of relationship (a cross between *Eros* and *Agape*) that was the envy of people, who thought that what we had was *true love* — and knowing (from the inside) how far removed from 'love' it was, I cannot recommend it as a model.

I am sure that, when people do observe and experience demonstrations of 'love', they do not identify it as such, because they are looking for something different. In order to truly love each other, two components are necessary: 1. we need to be able to let go of our fears; and 2. we need to love ourselves.

Love is letting go of fear

Jerry Jampolsky devoted a whole book to this idea. Where there is fear in our hearts, there is no room for love. This knowledge has been available to human beings for millennia. One of my participants drew my attention to the fact that this whole idea was in the Bible:

Ann: *I looked in here because it was to do with fear and love. It says 'There is no fear in love, but perfect love drives out fear because fear has to do with punishment. The one who fears is not perfect in love.'*

When we want to love people, fear steps in and says, *look after yourself, protect yourself, get things for yourself, otherwise you are not going to survive.* I want to make it clear that I am not writing a recipe for martyrdom. I never again want to hear the phrase, *after all I've done for you . . .* People need not to come from a position of sacrifice in their relationships. That is not love. Love should contribute as much to the giver as to the receiver. If people really want to contribute to you, to give you love, then they will not use their generosity to manipulate you. Loving someone should not, does not, deplete the one who loves in any way. It should feed you, not take something away from you — but not because of anything the other person does. However — back to fear.

What are the fears that stop us loving? I have given you some examples above — for example, the fear that people will make us dependent upon them and then let us down, or the fear that people will want something back for their love.

You could take a few minutes to jot down some of your fears. I will start you off with an example of mine.

When I feel powerless, I cannot express love. I am too busy trying to control everyone, so that I get back some feelings of power. At this moment of writing Tim's job is threatened. I am feeling very vulnerable. The school where Tim works was closed down due to complaints brought against staff by pupils. The Local Education Authority are, very properly, examining all the statements made by pupils which could imply that professional mishandling of situations could have occurred. Tim has been waiting for two months now to have his name cleared and, although I know that this is a formality and that Tim would never do anything to harm anyone, I am afraid that justice will not be done. So many people recently have been wrongly accused and punished for crimes they did not commit.

Despite the fact that I love Tim dearly I find it difficult to be supportive and loving when my security is threatened. Tim can be so innocent, so trusting and naive. In these ways he is very similar to my father. I found myself getting irritated and wanting to control everything around me, including Tim. Once again I looked for things to be angry about. It felt as though I had regressed — slipped back to a familiar and horrible way of being. My fear was driving me to do anything in order to feel that I was able to control what was happening. The truth was I could do nothing about it.

After a week or so I woke up one day feeling really ill and dispirited. Life all seemed too much to cope with. For once I allowed Tim to hold me and comfort me. I say 'for once' because I have a huge resistance to feeling my vulnerability and allowing someone to love me makes it difficult to avoid doing so. I started to sob. I was scared; part of me knows that I am not my house or my possessions, but the frightened child in me wants to feel secure. I suddenly got in touch with how I had felt as a child. I told Tim "When I was small I *so* desperately needed to know that I could rely on my dad to keep me safe and protect me and he couldn't even protect himself, let alone look after his family as well." I suppose I was projecting or transferring those feelings I had about my father onto Tim. If I feel he is disorganised or does not seem to be coping the frightened child in me cries out for re-assurance and protection and I want to make him conform to my ideas of how he should be behaving. "If I can get angry enough I can get back into control", is the strategy I employ.

Can I love from this dark and chaotic place? I cannot. I cannot love myself either, since I know that I am damaging someone else out of my fear and that is not what I stand for.

When I can quiet the anger, when I can hear the frightened child, when I can say, 'look, Tim is frightened too and he needs love, not anger', then I can begin to see the enemy within — fear. I talked to a loving friend, who told me to have compassion for myself: 'You are in a frightening situation'. Somehow I do not allow myself to feel afraid. When I realise that there are people around me who can support and love me, then I can put fear where it belongs and love Tim through this crisis we find ourselves in. Somehow, in that way the crisis diminishes and gets put into perspective. So love serves us both.

It is important to have people around who can give you love in times like this. When you speak to some people with fear they fuel your fear with their fear. Some people might want, unconsciously, to undermine my relationship with Tim, perhaps wanting it to fail so that they can say, *there you are you see, she couldn't make it work either*, and so they will discredit Tim and imply that he is a waste of time. As long as you are speaking to people who are committed to your growth and well-being, you can deal with your fear and put it to rest.

As I learn more about love, I can learn with and guide others. I have learned about commitment, responsibility, integrity, truth, openness and many other things, but 'love', that is a *biggy*! Leading my courses teaches me a great deal about love and gives me plenty of opportunity to 'practice the decision to love', as Emmanuel puts it. *And* it does not always look like love to the unpracticed eye!

Deborah had made it clear from the start of the course that she did not want to speak. Normally I respect people's right to remain silent, but I knew that Deborah needed to experience love and forgiveness in order to heal. She also needed to forgive herself. She had already told me in private that she was angry that I had made light of Charles' remarks about suicide. After I had apologised to people in the room for being somewhat flippant, perhaps offensive, I invited Deborah to tell people why she had been upset by my comments.

Deborah: *I don't want to.*

Jean: *That makes me feel very sad. I feel that if I allow you to go out of here without saying what you need to say, it would not be an act of love, it would be an act of irresponsibility on my part, just like Charles' parents. Not finding a way for him to share his pain with them, and then by not insisting that he met his commitments, they abdicated their responsibility. It was not an act of love. I feel I cannot meet my commitment to you because you are not allowing me to love and support you. You are shutting me, and everyone else, out. By coming on this course you have paid me to facilitate your growth, and now you are saying I am not going to be able to do that. Is that right?.*

Deborah: *I just don't want to share this with people.*

Jean: *Charles did not want to go to school, and it could have ruined his life. Should his parents have just let him do what he wanted? Maggie* (another participant) *did not want to share what she shared, but she did.*

Maggie: *Part of me did, part of me didn't.*

Jean: *Maggie knew 'this is the cross-roads'. It graphically illustrates the point at which we can take the fear-choice or the growth-choice. Every time you take the fear-choice, something in you dies. It is not an act of self-love.*

In your work with disturbed and abandoned children, Deborah, doesn't something in you die every time you see someone take the fear-choice and not the growth-choice? Do you know you cannot support someone in taking the growth-choice if you do not do that yourself in your life? You thus have a responsibility in your work to push through your own fear, to recognise it for what it is, because you are asking your clients to do that. We are never going to enable people to push through the fear that we ourselves fail to address.

When we attempt to facilitate the growth of others in an area where we are stuck, they will know. Words of the utmost wisdom will not make a difference, because they know that you do not really know what you are talking about. You only know the theory. Something will say to them *do not trust this person.*

Jean: *So if you cannot do this out of love and commitment to yourself, do it out of a commitment to the people you work with, whom you love, and who love you, who are relying on you to support them. Sometimes it seems easier to do things for other people than it does to do them for yourself.*

Deborah: *I feel very pressured at this moment.*

Jean: *That's okay.*

This conversation illustrates Peck's definition of love. I will repeat what he said:

> The will to extend oneself for the purpose of nurturing one's own or another's spiritual growth. (Peck, p82).

I was willing to make myself unpopular with the group in order to nurture Deborah's spiritual growth, and I did! William seemed to think I *forced* Deborah to talk, and he did not approve. I told him that normally I would not do that, and I am beginning to think that, by not doing it, I have sometimes let people down, sold out on them. If I had made a mistake in handling Deborah that way, I told him, then it was a mistake. I would rather err in that direction, however, than do nothing and then think later on, 'why on earth didn't I make sure she got it off her chest?'

I suppose I might be saying tomorrow, 'why on earth didn't I wait until she was more ready to do it?'. But she might never have been ready to face that fear without a great deal of encouragement, which some people would see as pressure. It is important for everyone to be willing to make mistakes, because if we are not willing to take that risk, we will do nothing. It is also vital to be willing to own up to our mistakes. If Deborah comes to me in a few months time and says that sharing with the people in the room did nothing for her and I should have waited, then I will apologise deeply. And of course, she did not need to comply with my request. Deborah was quite clear that she did have the choice. She felt pressured, but she could have stood her ground and said 'No'.

When I see that someone needs to forgive themselves, love themselves, if they are to move forward developmentally, then I have to exercise *ruthless compassion* — strong love, in order to support them. I find it extremely difficult. I would far rather say, *okay, don't bother*.

The problem with this is that it is difficult to distinguish between manipulation and domination — control of people — and supporting them and nurturing them in their spiritual growth. It is easy to do the former and claim it is the latter. That is why it is extremely important that people in a position of authority-management-responsibility, or even friendship, make sure that they *know themselves*.

Even then there needs to be room for self-doubt. The motives behind our interactions and support must be other-centred, not self-centred. They must be love-based, not fear-based. This conversation with Eileen might serve to illustrate the difference. Eileen's father is 82, and she does not feel she has ever had a relationship with him. He sits watching television most of the time, and behaves as if she were not there.

Eileen: *My dad has built this wall around him. If I insisted on communicating with him, the flood-gates might open. I don't know whether I could cope with all his years of sadness.*

Jean: *Could you cope with all* your *years of sadness?*

Eileen: *I don't know. I think it is better to leave well alone. Just let him be; let him live his life in his little capsule. This is my predicament. Do I approach him, try to break down the barrier, or do I let things go on as they are and take the easy way out?*

Jean: *What do you think?*

Eileen: *I think I might be opening the Pandora's Box. He has always been a recluse.*

Jean: *The only thing that gets in the way of your connectedness is fear.*

Eileen is afraid that she will not be able to cope with her father's pain —

and her own pain. She cannot predict what will happen to herself, to her father and to the relationship. This uncertainty is difficult for human beings to cope with. It brings up a lot of fear. I told Eileen that the only thing that gets in the way of her loving him, and him loving her, is fear.

There is so much fear involved in opening up and being vulnerable to other people that the mind will come up with all sorts of reasons why you should not do it. When people open themselves up to love in the room they sometimes sweat and shake, but when they have actually managed it people feel overwhelming love for them. There is an amazing feeling of connectedness, and this communicates to people.

Jean: *If you could possibly be brave enough, don't keep yourself from your father's love, and don't keep your love from him any more. It is not necessary to say to him you* really hurt me, *for it will only send him further away. All you need to say is,* Dad, I need you to love me, I want you to love me.

Eileen: *I haven't called him Dad for years. Too much resentment.*

Jean: *What is the resentment about?*

Eileen: *I wanted him to be a father.*

Jean: *You wanted him to love you and he was too scared?*

Eileen: *Too selfish.*

Jean: *Too scared. Selfishness is about fear.*

Eileen: *Isn't it self-indulgence?*

Jean: *Don't we all live out of our deficiency-needs? We all live out of there, and out of those deficiency-needs we destroy each other, and we destroy ourselves and we can't see it. But until we see it we will continue to destroy each other, not only on an individual scale, but on a world scale. We will keep taking until there is nothing left. And still our egos won't be satisfied. Out of your father's fear and selfishness, he hurt you, and out of your hurt, he hurt you, and you will hurt him back, and it doesn't work. You need to release your father from his prison with love, so that he can release you from yours. That is an act of true generosity.*

Eileen: *And courage.*

Jean: *Yes, generosity and bravery.*

Eileen: *There is a possibility that it will back-fire, and then I will look a real fool.*

Jean: *This is fear speaking. I'll wait for him to get off his fear before I get off mine. Nothing is going to happen if you do that.*

Eileen: *There was a time when I put it all in a letter, and he said 'why did you write all this to me, I don't need this'.*

Eileen had obviously felt very rejected by his response to her 'cry from the heart'. Her letter was accusing and, I suspect, coming from a desire to get back at him. It is not very palatable to the recipient. It has to be handled with love and compassion if people are to be held accountable in a way which enables them or empowers them to come clean about what they have done. Eileen's father obviously cannot handle pain very well and, I suspected, neither could she. She said that was possibly true.

Jean: *If you want to move forward, you have to let go of your attachment to your father one way or the other.*

Eileen: (eagerly) *What is the other?*

Jean: *If you really did not need his love, and did not care whether you had it or not, he would not annoy you. You could let him be. Get him out of your psychological space. You could look at him with love and accept him just the way he is. You could be free of him. It requires a shift within yourself. It requires you to discover the capacity to love yourself, and then it really will not matter whether other people love you or not — they will anyway.*

Eileen: *What is the first step?*

Jean: *Well, first of all you need to get that you really are love, and you are connected with people, and then you need to be generous with yourself (your love), which will include your father. Deal with your fear. When your fear speaks, set it gently aside. Fear speaks to you a lot. You tried communicating once and it did not work. Most of us live from the philosophy,* if at first you don't succeed, give up.

Eileen: *At 82 you don't have many more chances, let's face it. You can, say, give it a year or so, and you just don't know what will happen.*

Jean: *You can either have all the reasons why you shouldn't do this, or you can just do it. Because these reasons are bottomless. If one doesn't work you just come up with another one. Do you get it?*

Eileen: (Laughing). *I get it.*

Speaking to Eileen reminded me of the game we played as children, when one person put their hand on top of the others', and then that person put their hand on top of yours, and so on. It was move and counter-move. Some people can go on like this for ever. In the end, if you really want to support them you must stop playing the game.

Perhaps the worst fear people have about extending themselves, in order to contribute to the growth of others, is that the people they are attempting to contribute to will resent the intrusion and be angry. Sometimes this happens. There have been occasions when people have been angry with me, but it was usually when I was not sensitive, when I did not appreciate how afraid they were, and did not make allowances for it. The other aspect of this is, of course, that they need to have *given you permission* to support them.

By coming on the course, people have given me that permission. It is usually a tacit agreement with close friends that there is permission for mutual support. If people do get angry, it is useful to consider what you might be doing to trigger their anger and, if it *is* something you are doing, stop it. As I pointed out to William, you have to be willing to make mistakes, and then be willing to own them.

In my interactions with Charles I was very blunt and forthright, but he was far from angry.

Jean: *I want to waken you up somehow, Charles, and I don't know what is going to do it. You are very controlled. I would like to see you go bananas. There is a naughty boy in you somewhere who wants to dash about and scream and just be free.*

Charles: *Er, yes. I need to acquire a greater range of modes of behaviour.*

Jean: *Yes, and ways of speaking. You need to learn to say* shit *and* fart, *and things like that, and don't be so terribly intent on working out what to say, and how precisely to say it, because it makes you sound like a dictation-machine. I don't want to insult you, Charles.*

Charles: *No, no I agree with you.* (He is looking very cheerful).

Jean: (To others). *He likes it! Do you know why you like it? Because it says I care about you. That is why you like it!*

Charles: *Yes.*

Jean: *This might dent your ego a little, but you know, that is love speaking. Is that right?* (He nods). *I do care about you, Charles. I would like to set you free. You are a bit like Leslie really, he just has a different kind of costume. His is a military one. Yours is vicar-like. You are young, and setting yourself free might be scary for you. You might have to kick over the traces.* (One of the assistants offers to help him). *See, he loves you too.*

When Charles was little he could not stamp around and scream and shout and have fun, and that space of possibility got closed down. *Don't get close to people, don't lose control, don't trust anyone.* If he wants to get close to people he has to face all those fears, and eliminate them, and then all that will be left will be *him* — and love.

I am a little concerned that people reading this might lose the context in which this was said, so I want to emphasise that Charles really got a strong sense of being loved. His face lit up, and he looked alive for the first time in the two weekends — maybe for the first time in a long time.

It does take a lot of courage to support people in this way. I know it is painful for people to hear things like this. I know other people feel uncomfortable with it, and I sometimes feel sure that they will not like me, or they will walk out of the course. That is frightening. It is not easy to love — it is effortful. Most people could not cope with doing this, largely because they do not feel loved themselves, and they operate out of fear of losing the love of others. Loving yourself, then, is a very necessary component in the task of loving and supporting others.

Loving yourself

Sonia did not love herself, and did not know where to start in order to do so. She was deeply ashamed of herself and guilty about something she had kept hidden from people for many years. Sonia had given birth to a handicapped son. When he was born she really loved him and was determined to keep him and care for him, feeling sure that her love would overcome any difficulties that would arise.

Unfortunately, she could not foresee that other circumstances would occur, which would make it almost impossible for her to cope with the situation. Her son was severely retarded and she unexpectedly became pregnant with another baby. Around the time the second baby was born, her oldest child had to have an operation which left her in need of constant attention. They also moved to an area far from relatives and friends.

Sonia found it extremely difficult to share her secret with people in the room. Her fear was enormous, but she managed to do it, which in itself, was an act of love, because she let us see her pain; she trusted us with her shame and guilt:

Sonia: *When he (*her son*) was born, I loved him very much, but my love just didn't last and I don't love him any more. People think that to be a mother means to love your child. I love my daughters, but I don't love my son. I've done this terrible thing . . . one has to be responsible for one's actions.*

Sonia had been trying to cope with her son and her baby at a swimming pool on a very hot day, while her husband looked after the other child. Her son filled his nappy and Sonia felt she had to go back home and bath him.

Sonia: *I just did not want him any more. I had to go home leaving the other three by the pool, and I had to bath him. Something just snapped inside me. I held him down under the water, and he struggled and I held him down, and then I realised what I was doing and I left him. I have always felt so terribly guilty and ashamed of it. I wanted him to die.*

After this incident Sonia and her husband realised that she simply could not cope, and they had the child put into a home. She did not want to go and see him, and did so very infrequently. She currently had not seen him for eighteen months.

Jean: *Is that because every time you see him, it reminds you of the guilt and pain?*

Sonia: *Maybe. I don't know. When I see him — I didn't see him for two years, and then when I saw him they had to prise him off me, but he is like that with everyone.*

Jean: *Do you feel guilty that you produced a handicapped child?*

Sonia: *I did. I thought I had given him a booby prize. I brought him into the world, and what kind of life have I given him?*

Jean: *If what Emmanuel says is genuine, your son* chose *you. Maybe you chose him, too.*

Sonia: *He was the only one of the three who wasn't a mistake.*

Jean: *Then you chose him very carefully.*

Sonia: *And I let him down.*

Jean: *Maybe you didn't let him down. Maybe you did the only thing you could do at the time. Maybe that is what he needed to have happen to him, too. Who on earth knows? I don't. You made a mistake. When we damage someone, whether we do it accidentally or deliberately, what we need to do is clean it up. You may say he doesn't understand, and I say it doesn't matter. You don't know what he understands. Complete it with him. Even about the way you feel about him — the guilt that you don't love him.*

Sonia: *Surely if in his own way he could understand, that would further harm him. If he understands that I am his mother, and I don't love him, that would be terrible.*

Jean: *It is not the truth that you don't love him. You don't* feel *anything for him, but love has nothing to do with feelings.*

Sonia feels that she cannot be honest with her son because he is *fragile*. I have to say that he sounds pretty tough to me. He is a survivor. Sonia feels that it is because he is well cared for where he is. The truth is he is better cared for where he is than he would have been with Sonia, because she was too afraid and inadequate, but that is not a crime. Most of us would be inadequate in those circumstances. The brick wall that exists between Sonia and her son consists of fear, the fear that she could not handle the situation and let him down, letting down all the rest of her family too.

Jean: *Fear builds the wall. Fear says,* I can't handle this; got to cut myself off emotionally. *But you can't do it. If you go and tell your son the truth, which is not that you did not love him, but that you could not cope with everything, then you may get that you love him, and loving him does not mean that you have to look after him. Loving him may mean that you leave him just where he is, knowing that he is safe and cared for, knowing that you have done what you can do. But you need his forgiveness, actually, don't you?*

Sonia: *Yes.*

Jean: *It does not matter if he cannot hear this at a cognitive level. He may get something. You are not doing this for his sake, you are doing it for yours. You need to forgive him for being the way he is, but you don't need to do it for his sake. Forgive him and forgive yourself, then you can begin to love yourself.*

As long as Sonia feels guilt and shame she cannot love herself, or her son. It is essential that we love ourselves if we are to love others. Similarly, before we can contribute to the growth of others, we must be committed to our own spiritual growth — practice our decision to love ourselves.

In order to do this we must deal with our guilt and shame. We must stop beating ourselves up, and criticising and judging ourselves. Would you speak to a close friend the way you speak to yourself? Of course you would not. Why do you tell yourselves you are stupid, useless, worthless, bad and wrong? What is that going to do for you? Speak to yourself with compassion, kindness and love.

Sandra: *I don't know whether I have got love for myself. I looked in the mirror last night and thought,* who is that person? *I did not feel anything.*

Jean: *Love is not about feelings. Coming here is an expression of love for yourself. All of you coming here was an expression of loving yourselves, because it was an expression of commitment to your own growth. You need to keep making that commitment. Take the growth-choice, not the fear-choice. That is an expression of loving yourself. Do what will facilitate your growth and move you forward along the path of your journey in life. Give up the things that don't support you.*

When I am beating myself up I know I am not loving myself. I know that what I need to do is have compassion for myself. I can be harder on myself than my mother ever was, if I am not careful. I have to be very vigilant with myself in order to get balance in my life. I have a tendency not to allow myself to play enough and then get resentful about 'having' to work so hard. When I do play it would be easy to feel guilty. My mother used to say, "What are you doing, you idle devil, sitting there with your nose in a book, while I'm working my fingers to the bone..?" Now I have got an internal driver, my critic, the internalised mother, saying, *What are you doing? How dare you enjoy yourself!*. I can get into it in a big way. It is tempting to impose this work ethic on people around me.

Loving ourselves requires us to learn to say 'no', taking time for ourselves, telling people what you want from them, allowing them to do things for you. If we give out all the time and put nothing back for ourselves, we will deplete our energy. That is different, however, from giving out with the expectation that others will repay us. I know that it is my responsibility to replenish my energy supplies and find support for myself, and it might not come from the people to whom I am giving the support. There is another aspect of loving yourself though, which I have mentioned in previous chapters. That is about how you express love, who you are in your life.

Sandra: *I look after myself. I go to the gym.*

Jean: *But I wonder what you do to express yourself in life. To let people know who you are. What of yourself do you put into life?*

Sandra: *I don't know.*

Jean: *That is an act of love too. I suspect you feel dead about life don't you?*

Sandra: *When you said 'how many commitments have you got?', I thought 'I haven't got any'.*

Jean: *That makes for a dull life. We fill our lives up with things, and it can be full of nothing in particular.*

Life can look pretty full, but when you look closely, all you have is the wrapping paper, so we need to put something in there, otherwise it is all pretty, but empty. What is needed is a vehicle that will enable people to put themselves into life, so that other people can recognise who they are. Only then will you start to get a true sense of yourselves.

Most of us do not have a sense of purpose in life. We drift through life aimlessly with no direction. Life is *done to us*. There is no sense of our own power in that. In order for a person to love themselves they need to get a sense of their own power, to get back in touch with who they really are, the source of love and energetic self-expression. It also helps if we relate to other people who know that we are not our costume, and who can support us by relating to our centre, and making sure we express ourselves fully in life.

This brings me neatly to the next question. If we can — and do — love everyone, because love is who we are, on what basis do we select someone to have a relationship with? This posed a real problem with me after I left my previous husband. I remember feeling really scared, as if I had fallen into a great void. I thought I was doomed to live a celibate and lonely existence for evermore. If we cannot base relationships on feelings and we cannot base it on need, what do we use as the basis for intimate relationships — and where does sex come into all this?

9. Sex: the final frontier

Sex is the beginning, not the end. But if you miss the beginning, you will miss the end also.

(Bhagwan Shree Rajneesh)

Up to now it could sound as though relationships are hard work, if not impossible. Successful relationships certainly do demand effort. As Scott Peck (1989) says, love is *effortful*. The source of joy in relationship is true intimacy. I think this is where sex comes in. I say *I think* because I want to make it clear that for me, at this point, this is largely a theory. However I have begun to put it to the test, and I have checked it out with other people who are putting this theory into practice, and they seem to think it works. I share this with you as a fellow-traveller, not as a guide.

I know this is an area to which I need to give considerable attention in the immediate future. I think that, without a satisfactory or satisfying sexual relationship — and that does not necessarily entail penetration — relationships are in danger of being joyless. Without this element in a partnership, two people can certainly seek and have pleasure together, but that is a different matter.

Sex as a source of pleasure and joy

I would like to divide sex into two sections, one labelled *sex for pleasure*, and one labelled *sex as a source of joy*. Neither of these two experiences are better or worse than the other, but they are different. Pleasure is usually short-lived and appealing to the senses. Joy is a spiritual experience being, as Erich Fromm (1985) says, '. . . a concomitant of productive activity . . . Joy is the glow that accompanies being . . . Joy in sex is experienced only when physical intimacy is, at the same time, the intimacy of loving . . .'. By *being*, Fromm means the experience of connectedness at a spiritual level. Fromm's statements find support from an unexpected source. The *Report of the Commission on Human Sexuality*, compiled by the Methodist Church (1990), states:

> We wish to begin this report with an affirmation of the joy of human sexuality, a subject for thanksgiving . . . The purpose of sexual inter-

> course is to form, develop, reinforce and renew a bond of love within the context of a committed, personal, loving relationship . . . it is an expression of unity between two persons . . . So the mystery of our sexuality is the mystery of our need to reach out to embrace others, both physically and spiritually. Our sexuality expresses God's intention that we find our humanness in relationship; as such it expresses to others both our incompleteness on our own, and our relatedness to other people. This requires a willingness to be known and to be loved.

If we engage in sex for pleasure, Fromm (1985) asserts, it is not conducive to joy. Pleasure derives, he suggests, from excitement, and people think this will give them joy. It does not do so, however, and the lack of joy leads us to seek ' . . . ever new, ever more exciting pleasures'. This is perhaps why many couples *go off* sex after a few years together — or even a few months. It could also explain why people get drawn into more unusual sexual activities, 'wife-swapping', or extra-marital affairs. Presumably if they are looking for excitement (pleasure), they have to keep varying the stimulation since we soon habituate to the same, or similar, familiar stimuli. I want to emphasise here that I am not saying that having sex for pleasure is *wrong*. If that is what people want it is okay with me. I am simply pointing to a different dimension of sexual activity that is definitely available, but not widely broadcast or practised.

I wonder how many of us really experience *joy* in our lives. Very often we are so focused on pleasure that we are not aware of the possibility of joy. There is absolutely no harm in sex being pleasurable or exciting — I am simply saying that it is difficult to sustain pleasurable or exciting sex within a long-term relationship. It might not be impossible, but most people I speak to own to it being highly unlikely. Focusing on pleasure might be stopping people from experiencing something deeper and more sustainable and fulfilling — joy.

The next question must obviously be *how do we derive joy rather than pleasure from sex*? Before I address that, I would like to look at why many of us find fulfilling sex difficult to achieve, even at the pleasure-level. I wonder if I can do this without devoting a book to it!

Sexual games people play

I am frequently surprised, when the topic of sex comes up on the course, to find how many people — women in particular — feel that sex is given far too much significance in life. I used to say that I would far rather play squash, or go to bed with a good book, than make love with someone, and I got a lot of agreement about that. I thought for a long time that the agreement came from women aged thirty-plus, but I have begun to realise that it is not the case, for many younger women also have this attitude. There are plenty of men, too, who do not give sex high priority in their lives. There are also men and women who do feel sex plays a significant part in their lives, so I do not want to give the impression that it is not, and should not be, important.

I think many people are astonished to find that they are not alone in finding sex a problem, or unimportant, and they are also quite relieved. What makes it particularly problematical is when one partner does not think it is important, and the other does. The one who does attach importance to it sees the other person's lack of interest as a personal rejection, and the one who is not enthusiastic experiences their partner's anger or hurt at being rejected as pressure to perform.

A couple I spoke to recently had been experiencing this type of problem. Kevin and Julie had been married for seven years. For both of them it was a second marriage. Kevin was delighted that Julie was so giving and spontaneous sexually at the beginning of their relationship and for several years into their marriage. In his previous marriage his wife had been quite scathing about his sexual performance. He had been very careful not to upset her and felt, as a result, quite inhibited and incompetent in bed. With Julie he felt relaxed and his sexual confidence began to grow.

After a few years, however, the situation deteriorated. Julie began to feel resentful about Kevin. She could not think why. Kevin was always considerate and respectful of her wishes, but still the resentment grew. At the time of our conversation their sexual relationship was non-existent, and Kevin was extremely depressed. Julie, on the other hand was becoming increasingly angry and feeling very pressurised and guilty.

During the course of our conversation she began to realise that Kevin had been trying to get his sense of worth and re-assurance that he was a *normal* male from their sexual relationship. There was, therefore, no space for her to say 'no' to him as this resulted in him feeling bad about himself. This had led to her feeling that she had no real choice in the matter, whether she felt like it or not she had to 'perform'. This is death to a joyful sexual relationship. Resentment and guilt were the inevitable outcomes of this situation for her. Resentment at the pressure she was feeling, and guilt because she felt responsible for her husband's unhappiness.

Guilt also came from her being 'dislodged from her role' as Kelly [1955] puts it. She had always thought of herself as having a healthy sexual appetite and being a 'sexual' person. When she could no longer be like this she felt she was not being herself. This leads to people feeling that they are, in some strange way, betraying themselves.

In order to deal with the guilt she began to affirm more strongly her right to abstain from sex if she did not feel like it. Of course, with all those negative emotions going on she rarely did feel like it.

The effect on Kevin was to plunge him back into all his doubt and fears about his inadequacies. In fact he was not inadequate and never had been. Julie had been exploring the possibility that she had been the victim of sexual abuse at some stage of her childhood and, not surprisingly, this was bringing up very strong emotions around sex and reactions that were unexpected and nothing to do with her current partner. She realised, however that Kevin's experience in his previous marriage had made him very vulnerable and susceptible to sexual rejection. She had felt she had to protect him, and yet this meant that she could not listen to her own preferences when it came to sex. This replicated for her the situation she was in when she was abused.

When we uncovered all of the unconscious, and hence undelivered communication that had been going on about sex, it became clear to Kevin and Julie that what they had really been saying to each other was "I'll supply your needs if you supply mine". Julie's needs had been for security and love. Kevin's had been for reassurance that he was an okay guy. Julie felt that she was paying a high price for Kevin's love. When they had a sexual encounter there was a conflict of interests. Julie wanted to be loved for herself, not for her performance in bed.

In Kevin's case, and for many many other people, *I don't want sex* is heard as *I don't love you*. That's it — no argument. Well — is it? It certainly was not true for me, because it looked as though sex had little to do with love, as far as men were concerned. Most women that I have spoken to who are not enthusiastic about sex feel that they have been used by men as objects of pleasure. I thought sex would get me love, and it only got me sex! The men I played this game with never realised that there was a condition attached to my willingness to go to bed with them and, when they failed to come up with what I wanted I felt cheated. Had I realised at the time, the game I was playing in life might have been a little more fulfilling on the relationship front and I might not have felt so bitter about the male of the species as I did for many years. In spite of this, I still kept going back for more. I must be a slow learner!

Having something someone else wants is a position of power, especially when you do not need anything from them, and do not expect anything back immediately. What women get from this is control of the relationship. What it costs them is the feeling that it is a one-way, unsatisfactory process. I am sure it happens the other way round, too. This is only one of many games that get played in the sexual arena.

Some men play the game called *if you talk about it and brag about it often enough and loudly enough, everyone will think you are normal*. Some women, on the other hand, play the game of *I don't know what all the fuss is about, I'd be quite happy if I never had it again*. I think what they would really like to say is *I'm very disappointed about sex. There seems to be little in it for me — there is always something missing*. These roles can be reversed, too.

Bhagwan Shree Rajneesh (1975) — a teacher perhaps unjustly discredited by the media — quoted Masters & Johnson who said that 90% of woman never have an orgasm during intercourse. This, he says, is why women are angry and irritated. He expresses the view that, because women are not fulfilled sexually, they become anti-sex. That would certainly echo my experience.

When one of my previous partners asked me why I was not interested in sex, and I told him that it was probably because I did not have an orgasm, he said, *what do you mean by an orgasm*? He was in his forties at the time. The Bhagwan goes on to say that women feel they have been used.

> They feel after it . . . that they have been used. They feel like a thing which has been used and then discarded.
>
> (Bhagwan Shree Rajneesh (1975))

Many women have told me that they cry after sex. They often tell their partners that they are *crying for happiness*, but it is not so. One of my friends told me that she feels, *like a used receptacle. He could have used one of those blow-up dolls. He just isn't there — I am not there for him.*

I think that women must take some responsibility for their experience of being used. I felt like this for years, but I was an equal player in the game as I said earlier. I don't ever remember communicating to my partner that I felt this way. 'Lie there and think of England' is a female attitude that must stem from Victorian values and mores. Many women (especially of my generation) are deeply culturally conditioned to think of sex as a 'duty' — something we do to keep men happy. I am sure that some men would be appalled if they thought that women were making love to them for this reason. Some women will fake orgasms to keep the male ego intact and then talk about the ineptitude of the men they have bamboozled. I think some women can get quite a kick out of doing this. Sadly it is a pyrrhic victory. Men have no way of knowing they are not satisfying their partner and so never learn how to do so. Nobody wins in this game. Men and women seem to have been set up by the culture to make a mess of something that should be a natural act and could become a joyful and spiritual experience — or even just good fun!

Why is sex, for so many people, a fairly mechanical act? Why do so many people have to fantasise in order to bring themselves to a climax when they are making love? Why do we find arousal so dependent on fantasy or calculated stimulation? I think there are several reasons.

Barriers to intimacy

As we ingest messages about our bodies, personalities and behaviour from the culture and the environment, so we take on broad messages about sex and about our sexuality. I am sure I do not need to spell out the damage that is done to our sexual self-image by being told sharply not to *play with ourselves*, to *cover ourselves up*, and so on, when we are very small. We soon get the message that nudity is shameful and sexual organs too awful to be spoken about, except euphemistically.

In our teenage years sexual exploration is often treated as a *sin*. In my case, if I came in late after having been out with a boy, my mother would accuse me of being a whore, a dirty bitch, loose, and I would certainly *come to no good*. I now know that this came from her fear that I would get pregnant, and it also came from her belief that sex was bad and wicked — but *I* thought this was true. Any exploration of sexual relationship was a sin. I was dirty and immoral. Sex was never spoken of by my mother except as something bad, dutiful and unpleasant.

My excursions into sex were, as I have said before, prompted largely by a need for *love*, but there was also a degree of defiance there too, and a wish to state that sex was okay. Unfortunately, I never quite managed it. Promiscuity (for women, of course, not men) was culturally unacceptable, and I do not think that has changed much despite modern trends towards sexual liberation for females. We still have white weddings, with all that they symbolise, and the female who has many male partners is still not held in any esteem. This was certainly true among the student population at the University where I worked and I don't think this was unusual. Women students who slept around were the subjects of gossip and to gain such a reputation was not considered advisable.

I realise that there are many men who do try to be 'fair' about this. I know a 26 year old who is fighting his prejudice in this regard in his present relationship. His partner is very honest about her sexual history prior to meeting him, and he found this admission of her promiscuity difficult to deal with. He had the idea that *decent* women do not screw around. He also subscribed to the fairly common conditioned male view that it is okay to have affairs with *indecent* women, but you only make commitments to *decent* ones.

I can also see that men who do not think it is particularly clever or *manly* to have numerous sexual partners might be made to feel ashamed and pressurised to conform to a more *macho* image by their contemporaries. I was speaking to a client recently who felt that he had to cover up his sensitivity and vulnerability around other men by pretending to be 'one of the boys'. In fact he hated being like that, but did not realise that there were men around with whom he could express different values. Mostly he avoided men and felt quite isolated and lonely. I recommended him to join a men's group in the area where he would find men with whom he could be authentic about his feelings and his sensitive attitudes towards women.

It says a great deal for men like Tim and many of his friends who have the courage to express their respect for women and to treat sex with some reverence.

The appearance of AIDS on the modern scene has, I think, provided a justification for those who moralise about sex. The old prejudices and attitudes have never really gone away. They had simply gone underground. Mary Whitehouse has a large following; 'fornication' is seen as sinful in some religious circles, and 'adultery' is still punishable by death in some countries. So there is, historically, a cultural climate that attaches a stigma to sex. Many men still think women are *fair game* if they have a reputation for sleeping around. No — nothing changes much, it seems.

There are men who find it impossible to make love with women whom they respect and admire. These men have to persuade their partners to dress up in the sort of clothing that is associated with prostitutes and women in servile positions, with slave girls and waitresses. Even then they have great difficulty in becoming sexually aroused around women whom they cannot avoid seeing as *equals*. They often marry women whom they consider to be stupid or *dumb* for this reason, but this is a recipe for disaster, as far as other aspects of relationship are concerned. Simone de Beauvoir (1972) said that she thought sex was a degrading act as far as females were concerned.

These cultural and parental messages about sex, and how wrong and immoral it is, seriously affects our attitudes to sex and our involvement in it. I know one young, successful and very attractive man who finds sexual relationships extremely difficult, because in his family sex is a taboo, and therefore, by implication, undesirable subject. Since his main motivation is to gain the approval of his parents, he cannot involve himself in sexual activity without experiencing feelings of guilt and shame. These feelings make it difficult, sometimes impossible, for him to get or sustain an erection.

Many of us are toxically ashamed in the area of sex. It is small wonder that I was raped and did nothing about it, when I had been led to believe that I was nothing better than a prostitute anyway. I am sure there was a part of me that really believed I had been treated the way I *deserved* to be treated.

Not only did my mother imply that sex was dirty, but that it was also *dutiful*. She also gave me the message that men had all the pleasure, and women had to suffer it. I certainly bought that one! I won't say I never derived any pleasure from sex, but if I did, it was always a bonus. The main priority was making sure *he* enjoyed it. This was deeply-embedded in my sexual psychology.

Even now there seems to be something quite wrong about concentrating on myself when I am making love. That seems selfish and unjustifiable. Of course I know, intellectually, that it is not, but that is not how it feels. It also means that I must, logically, feel ashamed if I do enjoy it, because it is not my role. This sounds like madness, but people are insane in the area of sex. Cultural attitudes are in opposition to our natural instincts, and this produces an inner conflict which can only lead to bizarre or inconsistent behaviour, followed by feelings of shame — a case of *damned if we do and damned if we don't*.

So it is shame that produces barriers to intimacy and true fulfilment in sexual relationship. Because we are ashamed, we cannot be fully present to someone else, and so fantasising is the alternative to real experience, and it also provides us with an excuse to avoid intimacy. Although, for many years, I stoutly maintained my right to be a liberated sexual female, underneath my shamed child was saying *you are bad, wicked, wrong, you will be punished for this. You must not do it.* I don't think my inner child is very different to that of many other people.

If women receive the message that sex is *bad* and *awful*, men receive the message that to be a *real man* they must be virile and sexually very active. A *real man* lays any female he can persuade to co-operate, can and does perform several times a night, and lives up to the heroes of pornographic or sensual literature who have *pricks like iron bars* and eject *rivers of semen*. These are actual quotes from a book my friend and I picked up and read (avidly) when we were about seventeen. We did wonder how the two managed to avoid being washed away in the flood of semen and *pussy juice* that apparently oozed out of them!

Many women enter into the spirit of this marvelling about the size of men's penises, and being very admiring about men who are *well-endowed*. This is tough on those men who carefully shield their penis from view when using public urinals, because they feel they are far from well-endowed — whatever that means. Men derive their shame, then, from falling short of the sexual hero, the macho model that other men seem to emulate so readily.

I know that, for some men, using a public changing-room is a humiliating experience, as they feel they do not measure up to this image. In fact, it is a myth that women *need* large penises in order to be satisfied. Many women find it painful to be penetrated by a large penis. The one and only time I had an orgasm by intercourse, the guy had a very small penis. On this occasion I was on top of him. This is often the best way for women to achieve orgasm. The 'missionary' position is not a natural position to assume and was apparantly unheard of in the third world and in the East until they became 'civilised' by the Western World.

So 'big is better' is a myth that causes many men to feel ashamed, but women can also have concerns about their sexual organs and the rest of their bodies. Some have ideas that their genitals are abnormal, and so avoid oral sex and make sure that they make love in the dark. Some, like me, feel that their breasts are under-sized, others that they are too large. We worry about being under- or over-weight, about being a seven stone weakling, about stretch marks, knobbly knees, fat thighs, body odour and numerous other attributes, or the lack of them. And that is before we even get into bed! We are ashamed of our bodies, inhibited by lack of experience, afraid of our ineptitude, scared of being *boring*, worried that we won't have an orgasm, worried in case we come too quickly or not at all, concerned about putting the other person off.

Come to think of it, it is a wonder any of us make it into bed with members of the other sex at all! For those of us who worry about sexual ineptitude, or our ignorance about it, there are multitudes of books we can read. It is astonishing to think that we have to consult experts in order to perform a *natural* act. But this seems to be necessary in a culture that can pervert our perceptions of an act of love and turn it into a vice.

Other fears derive from unfortunate and unpleasant, perhaps frightening, experiences that people have had in their lives. Sexual abuse will obviously produce a lot of fear in the area of sex, but it could also produce promiscuity. Where children learn that this is a way to get love and attention, they will use it as a means of getting more, and they may well develop an attachment to sex that becomes an obsession. They will also see it as a means of regaining their power. I have dealt with this in chapter one. Exposure to 'flashers' or other sexual offenders will also instil fear into people.

But men who are inept and inexperienced, ignorant about sex, can often colour women's attitudes to sex early on in their sexual development. I suppose that if women were more educated about it they would not put up with this treatment, but we are not. Even now, in schools, sex education is sketchy. Teachers are aware that they have to be very careful how they handle this *sensitive* area, because they could and do get complaints from parents who object to their children being *subjected* to such knowledge. Perhaps they are afraid that teachers will tell children that sex is okay.

Women are not blameless, either. Women can be extremely insensitive when men have problems sustaining erections or ejaculating prematurely, or not managing to ejaculate at all. I remember one partner telling me that his previous lover had become very angry and hugely upset when he lost his erection after a long period of foreplay. As a result of this he was so nervous about losing his erection he could not manage one for months. Luckily he was underlyingly confident about himself in the area of sex and so he was able to overcome this problem.

Women who have fragile egos will find it difficult to deal with such incidents, but men need to realise that the problem belongs with the woman, not with themselves. The trouble is it ties into all the cultural stereotypes of the *real man*. Ellis and Becker (1982) state that we have many irrational beliefs in the area of sex, and it is these which cause us difficulties. In the case they cite, of a man who experiences impotency, the beliefs which are causing the problem are, they say, *intercourse is the only way to achieve satisfactory sex,* and *I should be able to have intercourse and would rate as a rotten person if I couldn't.* The authors go on to state:

> When you accept another's definition of how sex must be, you are often setting yourself up for failure.

I have a great deal of fear around sex, and a lot of resistance to it. I think I have said before that I used to use sex as bait, and having landed the fish I usually went off it. The motivation to avoid sex becomes stronger than the motivation to engage in it, or to put it another way, the cost becomes higher than the pay-off.

I once carried out a process in a course I was taking which was about sex. We were told to close our eyes and think of a time when we had sex, and then think of subsequent times. What I *saw* was a series of pictures, a bit like a *what the butler saw* machine. I realised that sex, for me, was a performance. I think it is for many of us. We perform, and our inner critic judges the performance. We are our own most critical evaluators. Some men are almost paralysed by their concern about whether they have or haven't got it right for the woman they are making love with. Bhagwan puts it beautifully:

> You are thinking about the result. And how many modern books have created many new problems? You read a book on how to make love and then you are afraid over whether you are making it rightly or wrongly . . . The wife is worried whether she is helping the husband to relax totally or not. She must show that she is feeling very blissful. Then everything becomes false. Both of them are worried about the result and because of this the result will never come.

My performance in bed centred around getting men to ejaculate and, if I am honest, having that happen as quickly as possible. For one thing, it proved how irresistibly sexy I was, and for another I didn't have to put up with it for very long. No wonder I never had an orgasm! The first time I did feel very safe with a man, safe enough to think about myself and my own pleasure, I did have an orgasm, only to be told off because he had had to hold on so long and he had found it a strain. So that was the end of that. To refer to Bhagwan Shree Rajneesh again, he says, of this attitude:

> (In such a case) your sex act is to relieve. It is just like sneezing out a good sneeze.

I have allowed myself to be subjected to the most humiliating sexual situations, and I have been compliant — Why? 'All part of the service', I suppose!

ɔose in writing this is for readers to realise that sexual problems y more the *norm* than the exception. The problem lies in cultural conditioning, sexual stereotyping and a conspiracy of silence. Men do not usually discuss sexual problems, only sexual prowess. Women have developed a jokey cynicism about sex, but they rarely share the fear, upset and sadness they have about it.

If we seek advice about sexual difficulties, it is usually treated as a behavioural problem, and behaviour-modification techniques are employed, designed to eradicate the old response and substitute a better one. However, the mechanical problems of sex are often deeply embedded in life-problems — problems which have their roots in our early conditioning or experience, and so are not easy to solve. When we can identify the life-problems concerned, and find a partner who is committed to discovering connectedness and intimacy in the relationship, these problems can be overcome.

When it comes to taking on a new venture or tackling anything similarly fearful, I seem to be able to over-ride, or transcend, my ego by being aware of what it says and remaining focused on my organising principles (which I will come to in the next chapter). In other words, fear does not stop me, because I have found a motivation that will enable me to confront it and overcome it. 'Use your fear to go forward'.

Why bother?

It seemed until about a year ago that there was nothing in sex for me that would make it worthwhile tackling all the fear and conditioned shame I had about it. After all, it does take effort and energy to do that. Also it was supposed to be something good, something pleasurable. Why go through all that agony of fear for something that was, to coin a phrase, an anti-climax, or even a non-event?

I then discovered *tantric* sex, or a form of it that was acceptable to my Western psychology. I will not go into this subject in great detail here, but just enough to whet your appetite. The difficulty I had with sex was that the context I saw it in was negative. It seemed like a fairly pointless activity; much ado about not very much. Then I read this:

> Approach the sex act as if it is prayer, as if it is meditation. Feel the holiness of it.
>
> (Bhagwan Shree Rajneesh, 1975)

So far removed was this statement from my concept of sex that I almost dismissed it as arrant nonsense. I read this in the aftermath of the Bhagwan's ejection from the USA for tax evasion (they said), so I had every justification for being deeply suspicious of him and of it. In fact, I think it has provided the key to the door which has so far kept out much of the joy in our relationship.

Tim and I have begun to explore this meditational approach to sex with the aid of books like those of Daniel Read (1989) and the above-mentioned article by Bhagwan. We have also done some work with James Holland of *Creative Interactions*. I cannot say that I approve of much that Bhagwan seemed to represent, but I do feel that he had something of value to teach in the area of sex.

The best part of this practice, for me, is that it is so simple, and demands that there are no expectations, no focusing on *results*. It also advocates bypassing the mind. For me that was terrific. That is where I have all the problems. My body functions perfectly well if my mind will let it. Isn't that true of most of us?

To many people this description of *meditational* sex may sound bizarre, because it is so far removed from the cultural image of sexual activity. The culture tells us that we should be *turned on* by our partner's bodies, stimulated by sexy underwear, titillated by sexual fantasy. Sex shops thrive and they are full of erotica and implements which will enhance or sustain sexual performance, and stimulate sexual arousal. The sex therapists I attended advocated reading pornography, looking at photographs, fantasising or smoking marijuana in order to become sexually-aroused and uninhibited. They meant well!

In fact doing all of this stuff did allow me to get to the point of having intercourse, but I was left with a feeling of annoyance, that I should have to go through all that performance for what should be a natural impulse. It might have been a formula for getting down to it, but it certainly did not tackle the root of the problem. It also took a lot of commitment and, to be honest, the thought of all that frightened me even more, because it felt *dirty*. I am not saying it is, I am simply saying I did not like the thought of getting off on literature that could be seen as offensive and degrading to women, or to men.

One of the books we were recommended to read was Nancy Friday's *Secret Garden*, a book of female sexual fantasies. Some of these fantasies place women in very servile and humiliating roles. Some put men in the same position. Okay, they are only fantasies, but they contain strong messages about males and females that I now feel are unnecessary and unhealthy.

I am saying that this did not work for me, nor did it work for the person who was my partner at that time, because it did not tackle the life-problems — it treated our sexual difficulties as a mechanical problem, which was only part of the story. I had no commitment to sex for the reasons I have stated previously.

What Tim and I have discovered is something really incredible and wondrous, and so amazingly simple. If I lie close to my partner and allow myself to fully experience the contact of his body against mine, the beat of his heart, his body contours, his breathing, and if I, at the same time, can be aware of my body sensations, synchronising my breath with his, I discover that my body becomes aroused. Not only that, but to use Bhagwan's words:

> When the two become one rhythm then their breaths have become one; their *prana* (life energy) flows in a circle. The two have disappeared completely, and the two bodies have become one whole; the negative and positive, the male and female, are no longer there.

We have had no *foreplay*, nothing, and yet we are both highly aroused, not in the urgent, frantic way of previous experience, but gently and warmly glowing with sexual energy.

What happens then is — wait for it — a loud-speaker switches on in my head, which goes something like: *he'll get ideas — he'll want to have intercourse and it will hurt. Anyway, it will all be over in five minutes and I won't have an orgasm anyway, so why bother?*. Or, *See, you are thinking about the shopping now — I knew this would be hopeless, might as well get up and get on with things — I've got too much to do to lie here messing about*. Or, *This is getting boring, nothing is happening, I'm only doing this for him anyway, and why should I* . . . ad infinitum.

At first I thought the loud-speaker was talking a lot of sense, but I tried an experiment: I switched it off and focused my attention back onto my body-sensations.

> Do not talk, do not say anything, because that creates disturbance. Do not use the mind, use the body. Use the mind only to feel what is happening. Do not think, just feel what is happening, the warmth that is flowing, the love that is flowing, the energy that is encountered, just feel it.
>
> (Bhagwan Shree Rajneesh, 1975).

This is, of course, meditational practice, the practice of watching the flow of the mind and focusing on the now. Meditation should, in fact, be part of day-to-day, moment-to-moment existence. It is only through meditation that we are truly alive — living in the moment, right now — otherwise we dwell on, and therefore in, the past, or live our lives anticipating the future. No wonder we derive little satisfaction or joy! Joy can only result from being here and now.

The result, for me, of adopting a meditational and *holy* approach to sex was sensational (literally!). Of course, the parrot piped up again from time to time, and it was tempting to respond to it, but I resisted the temptation. Eventually I experienced what I can only describe as a total body-orgasm

of the type I had never felt before, and had never realised was
least I think it was an orgasm! Whatever it was, it was okay b,
importantly, I was totally at one with my husband in the process, completely aware of him, not having to be with some fantasy figure and shut him out. I have never felt such a deep sense of connectedness and love with Tim as I did on that occasion.

The importance of intimate communication

One of the obstacles that frequently gets in the way of any sexual experience is the level of communication that is available. I speak not only from my own experience, but that of others, when I say that when there is a communication *block* in place in the relationship, it is extremely difficult to engage in deeply intimate sexual activity. It is as though you have to open up a penetrating channel to your soul, and I do not think that the soul finds it a very satisfying experience to open up to someone who is coated in armour. I know that when I feel that someone is blocking me out I play the same game, almost automatically. In this space there is no room for making love, particularly in the way I have described above.

There was a time when Tim and I set aside time for true and deep communication, simply saying everything that came to our minds to say for ten minutes, while the other person listened, and then allowing the other person to do the same. I found this very powerful. Unfortunately we stopped doing it before it became a habit. The cold war sneaks up surreptitiously, and for long periods of time we are locked into it. There is no conscious intention to do this, and I think the psychology behind it is complex, and perhaps does not need to be understood. What is important is to have a commitment to breaking out of it.

The strange thing is that I always feel that, although Tim is the one who initiates the ice age phase (he finds communicating in this way extremely difficult, or perhaps uncomfortable), he is the one who feels hurt by my apparent lack of love and interest in him. So both of us are locked in our pack ice, feeling neglected and ignored by the other. Well — *there's nowt so queer as folk*, they say in Yorkshire, and I guess they are right. Tim and I are just as queer as everyone else!

I think many people (Tim and myself included), are afraid of this depth of intimacy in relationship. It is almost as though it gets too good. I don't think we can cope with it. Maybe deep down we believe that relationships cannot work, that they will end in disaster or that they have to be a constant struggle. Maybe, also, we are afraid that if we managed to sustain such depths of intimacy we would be desperately afraid of losing the relationship. To know that level of connectedness and lose it might be unbearable.

The problem is that the human mind always operates from the illusion of *scarcity*, and from predictions of doom. Perhaps I am operating from the position that *what you have never had, you do not miss*. That, I feel, is sad, because I think we have known true loving connectedness, and we do miss it. We knew it when we were, as Emmanuel puts it, 'part of the oneness', and intimacy in sex is the nearest we can ever get to 'coming home'. And perhaps, if Emmanuel is correct, Tim and I are justified in being afraid of love.

> Since love is the most powerful force in the universe, it is also the most frightening, until it has been entered into completely.
>
> (Emmanuel, 1987, p203).

Emmanuel also says (p204):

> Sexuality is a wonderful door to oneness. It is the willingness to see and to be seen, to share as completely as you are able, through each and every part of your dear self, so that you can be known and cherished . . . It is perhaps the most direct means of unification when it is experienced on all levels, not only at the physical, of course, but not only at the spiritual either. Sexuality is a biological doorway into truth.

This does seem, then, a very big step to take, and yet I feel we have dipped our toes in the water, and are looking longingly at the ocean, plucking up our courage to dive in and ride the waves throughout the rest of our life's journey.

I feel like saying now *watch this space for the next exciting episode of transcendental sex*! We are on a journey, and each new opening demands of us the courage to step through and discover another dimension of life. We are on the threshold of an opening and it is time we just got on with it!

The moving story of the wizard who thought beautiful thoughts

I want to add this story as a sort of afterthought. When I was small I was really clear that I wanted to be a *princess* and live in a beautiful palace. Well, I already was a princess, and all I wanted to do was inherit my birthright! My favourite fairy story was *The Princess and the Pea*, but when I was twelve I read another fairy story which enchanted me even more. I cannot give credit to the author for this story, for the book is long since lost, but the story is not.

In this story the princess, Melissa, lives with her father and mother in a palace in their kingdom. Unfortunately, her parents are thoroughly broke. Her clothes are in tatters and the palace is falling apart. She has three suitors who are all pretty unprepossessing, and by this time you are thinking, what kind of a deal is this? What is the point of being royalty if you are that poor? However, there is one redeeming feature in all this. They have a court wizard, but even he is no great shakes, because he only has one spell up his sleeve — he thinks beautiful thoughts and puts them into people's heads. So they are all poor but no-one is miserable. They all think each other is the 'bee's knees', and they have all they could ever wish for.

Then along comes — yes — it's the *bad guy*! He is a regular wizard who woos them with promises of lots and lots of goodies. They are convinced. Off goes Goliath (the good guy who thinks beautiful thoughts) and the whiz-kid prevails. Naturally, they are at first enthralled with all their new toys, but Melissa finds she is extremely irritated by her suitors, and begins to find them really stupid and ugly. Arguments break out and misery prevails. They would have given anything to have good old Goliath back. Well, you've guessed it: back he comes. They welcome him with open arms and throw the used-car-salesman-type wizard out. Melissa realises that she has always been in love with Goliath, so they get married and — yes — live happily ever after!

For some reason I was thinking about this fairy story the other day. I realised that my Goliath was Tim, who thinks such beautiful thoughts, and what I have been doing is thinking that I needed someone who had all the goodies: someone successful, organised, responsible, strong. All this time I have been missing the point and failing to recognise what I have got — someone who has a precious gift. Will we live *happily ever after*? Maybe!! We still have a lot to learn.

10. *Choose your partners for the dance of life!*

Only in relationship can you know yourself, not in abstraction, and certainly not in isolation.
The movement of behaviour is the sure guide to yourself, it's the mirror of your consciousness; this mirror will reveal its content, the images, the attachments, the fears, the loneliness, the joy and sorrow.
Poverty lies in running away from this either in its sublimations or its identities.
(Rodegast *et al*, 1987).

Many of us spend more time and thought on buying a car than we do on selecting a life-partner. Those of us who, when we buy a car, do not make sure we know what we are getting, soon experience the consequences, and then we usually blame the person we bought it from, for conning us. We do similar things with our relationships. How foolish it would be to buy a car solely on the basis of liking the colour and/or shape! We would be sensible to thoroughly test drive it, check out its previous history, discover what the faults are, and see if we are willing to accept that no car is going to give us everything we want, unless we pay an extremely high price for it. In the end we have to accept that we chose what we got, and if we did not notice some defect, that's tough, and we have three choices — put up with it, get it fixed, or trade it in for something else.

I have done all three of those in a relationship, usually in that order. I have put up with it until it reached the point of breakdown; or if it couldn't or wouldn't get fixed I have traded it in or exchanged it for a different model which simply had different types of defect — or, worse still, the same kind again! In terms of relationships, all of us are *used models* that are going to come with defects created by the wear-and-tear of life and misuse by previous drivers (parents, teachers, employers, lovers, etc.) We have been driven too fast, too soon, before we were *run in*, kept in the garage too long, or simply abused through ignorance of how we worked.

That has about exhausted that analogy, but I hope you get the picture.

The problem is that we do not really know what we are looking for, so we wait until something, or someone, catches our eye. We may think we know, but most of our looking is, in fact, motivated by deeply-buried emotional needs that we are completely unaware of. And so, we may find something we definitely were not looking for, but may be irresistibly drawn to it, despite our better judgement.

These needs are so embedded in our emotional experience that it is extremely difficult to identify them. To do so would mean accessing the layer upon layer of pain and shame associated with them, that living has inflicted upon us. Most of us get into relationships so that we can avoid having to do this, rather than getting into them to facilitate the process. It would seem ridiculous, at one level, to get into a relationships so that we can get in touch with our pain — that sounds like masochism.

However, my experience of life so far has taught me, and keeps teaching me, that until I can open up the flood-gates and let out the pain I have accumulated throughout my life, I cannot support other people in getting in touch with their pain and, perhaps more importantly, I cannot express my own power in such a situation. It is difficult, therefore, to feel that you can have any influence over what happens to you, or to others, and the probability is that life will end with you feeling that it was all *much ado about nothing*.

So could this be what relationships are really all about, or is that only a part of it? Is this notion complete nonsense? Aren't they really about walking hand-in-hand into the sunset with someone, and living happily ever after? Aren't they the answer to all life's problems? I don't think so. I think the major purpose they can serve is the working out and/or working *through* of the problems we accrued as a result of our early-childhood experiences. Maybe, as well as that, they are about remembering our connectedness, as I indicated in the last chapter.

I have just had a conversation with someone who is averse to the idea of getting into a relationship where she feels she would be put in a position to care about anyone or anything, because she feels so inadequate and empty — she feels she has nothing to give. And yet she desperately wants someone to care for her. The problem is that, if she were to become involved in the pain and suffering of humanity and of the planet, she would get in touch with her own pain — and that is something she has been trying to avoid for years.

So the answer seems to be *don't care, batten down the hatches, shut it out*. That way, however, we simply lock pain in. It does not kill us to let the pain out, as long as we have someone who can hear it too. It kills us to keep it in and, furthermore, it kills the people around us, who are dying from care-deprivation. Extreme examples are those in countries where there is large-scale starvation, or those who commit suicide because they have no one who seems to them to care enough to listen to them. But these are the worst cases in a generally-deprived world.

I do know how this person feels, since talking to her brings up my feelings of hopelessness and inadequacy — too much pain, not enough of me to go round — and, in this state, I feel I do not know enough to be really effective. This is when it becomes clear to me that I need partners — people with whom I am aligned, who are able to work with me to remedy the destruction that those who dare not care are wreaking upon the planet, and on their fellow human beings. Without a network of committed partners, it would indeed be hopeless. This applies to all workers in this and related fields.

And perhaps, whatever I do, or you do or don't do, with or without aligned and committed partners, it will all turn out the same anyway. The truth is, we will never know, but we might as well create a good snakes-and-ladders game to play whilst we are here, and decide what the *ladders* will consist of, that will take us to square 100 on the game-board of life. We also need to recognise that the *snakes* are essential too; without them there would be no game, or it would very soon be over.

My relationship with Tim seems like an endless game of snakes-and-ladders; just when we get close to *Home,* we hit the biggest snake on the board and down we go again! All there is to do is pick up the dice and throw again! We could quit, of course, but then we would simply have to find someone else to play with! As it is, both of us play pretty fair and that is really all you can ask.

Many people, however, seem to hate the idea of snakes-and-ladders in relationship. They want to play a game where every move takes them closer to the winning post, and all they get along the way are the *goodies.* You know — *you have found Mr/Mrs Right, move to 'Bliss' and stay there, until you both die simultaneously, do not want for anything, and collect a nice fat pension and a gold clock for your blissful retirement*! I am not saying there is anything *wrong* with this, but where is the opportunity for growth and development, excitement and adventure in that scenario?

What seems to happen is that people look for partners, not in order to play the game of life to the hilt, but to avoid losing. The sort of person to look for in order to avoid losing might be very different from the sort of person who would enable you to thoroughly throw yourself into the game, and help you to become a better player.

Can you see the difference? One is selected on the basis of *how do I make it through life as safely as possible?* and the other is chosen for their ability to empower us to take risks and pull out all the stops. The first would rush around helping us to shore up our defences, pull up the drawbridge, prime the cannons, stock up the provisions and line the walls with satin padding. The second would be planning the party, sending out the invitations and preparing to celebrate life with the whole world.

If the latter sounds like hard work, look at the energy it takes to keep the ammunition checked, and to patrol the ramparts twenty-four hours a day!

The basis of relationships

So if life is to be a glorious, if somewhat taxing and challenging adventure, whom should we choose to share our journey? I have had many relationships with men, and only with my current partner did I seriously examine what I wanted, in terms of support and empowerment, from a relationship. Mind you, prior to leaving my previous husband, I probably would not have considered using those words in connection with intimate relationships. I did not know what they meant, and I would not have wanted to find out, especially about *empowerment*, which I would have dismissed as jargon.

My previous relationships were all based on very unconscious needs, several layers of them, and because of this they did not work. None based on need will work, and this is also true for those that *look* as if they are working. This is because people involved in such relationships work hard at giving the relationship the appearance of being a *good* one, based on commonly-agreed criteria. They never argue, they *really love one another*, they are inseparable, and each is all the other person wants or needs.

One couple I spoke to fitted this description exactly, apart from the fact that they did have separate holidays, so were not *inseparable* in that respect. However, in other respects they were inseparable, since they made sure that certain functions were performed by one partner, ensuring that the other person felt incapable in that area, and could not cope if the other was not around.

I saw this many times when I ran a singles group — one partner had never learned to drive a car, change a plug, do the ironing, or cook a basic meal, and so depended heavily on the presence of the other for those functions. My proposition is that such relationships are founded on staying safe, and they are so safe that both participants are anchored to the spot, in a state of suspended animation. They consist of what Eugene O'Neill calls the 'spiritual middle-classers of life', those, he says, who, having succeeded, do not move on to *greater failure*.

Although people in such relationships do no apparent harm to each other, they die a slow death, as their potential, or their spirit, gasps for breath beneath the security-blanket they have wrapped around themselves. Please do not hear me say there is anything *bad* or *wrong* about this. If people really feel that what they want to do is climb into a nest with someone and never test out their wings, that is their choice — as long as it *hoice*, and not something they do because the alternatives are felt to be too threatening. Even then it is okay, as long as they both are happy to accept the consequences, and they are both fully aware of what the consequences are.

Being safe is not the only basis for most relationships. Some partners are selected because they will supply the love we have always wanted and never felt we got in our childhood. Some give us a sense of importance — of being *somebody*, rather than nobody. So the deficiency-needs identified by Maslow are often at the basis of our choice of relationship. But on what do we think we are basing our choice, and why?

Top of my shopping list when looking for a partner was *intelligence*. I always thought it was because I do not 'suffer fools gladly', and I want some stimulating and intelligent conversation with the person I live with. Today I learned something else.

I attended the first session of an Intermediate French Conversation class. For the first half hour I was quite happy, as I could make sense of most of what the tutor was saying. Gradually, however, it became more difficult, and I realised that most of the other people in the class were understanding more than I was. My spirits started to sink and a familiar syndrome appeared. I began to feel very tired and to yawn frequently. My chest started to feel tight and I could not take in enough breath. This was something that used to happen to me a great deal. It is very distressing, the more so because it seems so trivial and does not constitute a legitimate illness. It is, however, very debilitating.

The day before, I had been to see a healer, who said to me 'If there was one basic thought that was driving you in life, what would it be?'. I tried very hard to filter out, or reject, what came immediately into my head, which was *I'm not good enough*. I did not want it to be that, because I already know that it is nonsense, and of course I have to accept that I *am* good enough, and *I'm not good enough* is just a thought I have. In other words, I thought I had that one flattened. In fact it seems that it is still the whole foundation of my survival.

I think I realised as a child (at a deep level of consciousness) that being a *clever girl* was the only way I was going to escape from the horror of my existence. It got me praise, attention, it singled me out from amongst the crowd. Furthermore, the heroines of all my favourite books were always *clever girls*, and they always commanded respect and admiration in the end. When my academic progress was halted by the family's economic circumstances (and my mother's attitudes to females) the way became clear: attach yourself to an *intelligent* or *clever* man. That way, because someone intelligent wants a relationship with you, you must be seen to be intelligent yourself. Not being a *clever girl* spells out annihilation for me, and the effects on my health are disastrous and immediate.

What is there to do about it? I observe it. Today was probably the first time I have had a direct emotional experience of this driving survival-force. As I began to realise what was happening in this French class I saw several interesting things. One was that I was very happy to sit and say nothing — a very unusual occurrence for me in groups, and very useful, since I can become very impatient with people who say nothing in groups. I now have more compassion for silent group members.

Another thing was that this was not just an interesting insight, I was in the presence of a horrific *demon* that was destroying my health and affecting my relationships with everyone. The demon's name is *I'm not good enough*. This demon is so malevolent that when the healer I went to see woke it up, so to speak, I felt a pain in my throat that I thought would kill me. She simply put her hand round my face, and I felt as though I needed to expel an evil force that did not want to come out, and was hanging on grimly in the region of my throat.

I now begin to see what people might be saying when they talk about exorcising demons. The language used is off-putting to some people, but I can see that these forces that arise out of the unconscious, rooted in the vulnerability of childhood, exert a force over us that can sometimes be experienced as a *presence*, something with a personality of its own.

I feel that the growth processes I have been involved in have been driving this force nearer and nearer to the surface, so that now it is identifiable or tangible, and therefore more vulnerable and determined to hang on. It is still in there, as I discovered from the French class three days after visiting the healer! Maybe all I can do is be very vigilant about its presence, and keep recognising that it is not really *me*. Only love will drive it out, love and compassion from me, and acknowledgement of the pain and fear it causes.

So we look for a partner to quieten down the demons, and the demons fight back, determined not to be disestablished, as they are very committed to doing their job — which is to ensure our individual *survival*, even if it kills us! Finding the 'right' partner does not work. Most of the partners I found who were *intelligent* seemed intent on showing me how clever they were in comparison to me, which really defeated the whole object of the exercise.

Sophie's demon was made of different stuff to mine. She chose a husband who physically abused her consistently over a long period of time. Why would she want to stay in a relationship with him? The motives were complex indeed. Sophie had been abused as a child and thus she felt vulnerable, weak and powerless. The obvious person to seek if you are *weak* is someone who is *strong*, who will protect you. Unfortunately Sophie confused strength with bullying and domination (which is truly a sign of weakness).

Jean: *When you have been treated the way you were treated as a child, it gives you a sense of not being able to be instrumental in changing things, Then you have a huge obstacle to overcome. Everything looks impossible. So it looks as if the best thing to do is attach yourself to someone who looks strong. Your husband is not strong, he is a bully. Did you think he was strong?*

Sophie: *Yes.*

Jean: *People who have inner strength do not bully people. You picked someone you thought was strong so you wouldn't need to cope with the difficulties of life. But you are as capable as anyone else. You just told yourself a lie a long time ago, because you were thrown into circumstances which made you give up. You became resigned to the situation. You carry this with you through life.*

Sophie: *Yes, I* belong *to him (*in his own thoughts*). He would prefer me to be in the house and have no friends.*

Jean: *Take yourself away.*

Sophie: *I know that he will go anywhere and do anything to find me. He won't give up.*

Jean: *Yes, and there is a bit of you that likes that, Sophie.*

Sophie: *It's nice to be wanted.*

Jean: *You like that game, otherwise you wouldn't have got into a relationship with him. That is not love, that is ownership — possession.*

It is clear from the last part of this conversation that Sophie also enjoys his possessiveness, since she interprets this as being *wanted*. She has convinced herself that this *strong* bully cannot manage without her. Power indeed, to have someone so strong be needy of you! But what an incredibly high price she is paying to get her love and security needs met!

Jean: *The only thing keeping you there is you — you have no intention of leaving.*

Sophie: *Do I have to be dead before I realise that?*

Jean: *I sincerely hope not.*

Sophie: *I don't want to stay.*

Jean: *You do. If you want to know what your intention is, look at the results you produce. What is the pay-off for staying in this relationship?*

Sophie: *I don't have to take responsibility, do I? (*Laughs*) I don't* have *to do anything?*

Jean: *Yes, you don't have to do anything with your life. That is a huge responsibility. 'I have all this creativity, but I can't do anything while I am with him'. The next thought is, 'if I do leave him and I do try to do something, would anyone want me to do it anyway?' It seems better to be a failure and have someone else to blame.*

As you can see, in addition to allowing her to feel powerful, this relationship gives her permission to abdicate responsibility for her own growth and self-expression.

Another underlying motive for the selection of a partner is the unconscious need to perpetuate the *family system*. Peter had a 'very loving family'. His father and mother gave him lots of love and a lot of freedom — so much so that, at the age of eight he was raped by a stranger in an alleyway as he wandered around the city alone. He never told his parents about the incident. Why, I asked him, if his parents were so loving, why did he not instantly run to them for protection and consolation after this horrific thing had happened to him? He had many reasons: they would curtail his freedom, and he felt *dirty*, bad. They would be angry with him.

I pointed out that if his relationship with his parents had been a truly loving one, he would not have avoided telling them. The initial instinct of any child who is frightened or in pain, hurt, is to run to someone with whom they have a loving, trusting relationship, so that the pain and hurt can be shared and they can be protected. The fact that he did not do so indicates to me that the family system was set up to project an image of a *nice* family, where no-one had any problems and no problems arise. But they did.

Peter did say that he had conflicts with his parents in adolescence. I am not surprised. The need to present the image of a *normal* family is often so strong, that a system is devised to convince all within and without the family that everything and everyone is *normal* and *okay*. If any member of the family strays from that line, then the whole system is thrown out of balance, and the survival of the group is threatened. There was no permission for Peter to express his pain, and so he had to pretend that it was in his best interests to keep quiet.

Peter had been in only one long-term relationship, which he had never really let go of. He and his ex-partner wanted to complete the unfinished business in the relationship. As they addressed the problems that had arisen and had never been resolved, it became clear to me that they had both come from a similar family system.

Rose: *I wasn't completely honest with Peter, because I remember walking into his flat and thinking 'Shit, I don't know whether I should be here' — and I just used to swallow those feelings, because they didn't fit. So I wasn't able to say 'I feel really uncomfortable', so he didn't get all of the messages.*

There was no permission for problems to arise, and therefore no opportunity for them to be addressed. When Rose told Peter she was unhappy, he dismissed this as being unimportant. He told me 'I thought if I ignored it it would go away'. *It* did not go away, but eventually Rose did, and she never came back. It left Rose feeling guilty and Peter feeling betrayed. Peter lost the person he loved, just as, in his adolescence, his parents lost him. Later in life the suppressed pain of the abuse caused a severe and prolonged breakdown. This could have probably been averted, had Peter's family been able to allow for the occurrence of disaster and problems, within the structure of their relationships.

There is an endless supply of unconscious drives and motives which impel people into disastrous relationships. Accessing these is difficult, but not impossible.

An exercise on drives and motives

Make a list of people with whom you have a 'committed relationship'. Do not start looking 'committed' up in a dictionary, or thinking about it for any length of time, just put down whatever or whoever comes into your head.

Now ask yourself: to what am I committed in that relationship? Again, do not wonder what that means, just write down whatever comes to mind initially.

Keep asking yourself the question: what else am I committed to in that relationship? until you feel you have reached the bottom line.

If you want a tip on how to do this effectively, look at what you actually *do* in the relationship, to find the answers.

For instance, in my relationship with a friend of mine, I looked at how I *am*, in the context of the relationship, to find out what I was committed to. This is what I came up with:

I am committed to:
* finding fault with her, but not letting her know I do this.
* having her like me;
* keeping her around;
* avoiding confrontation;
* having her advance in her work;
* having her do things the way I think she should;
* having her be really powerful — but not too powerful, because she might get to be more powerful than me;
* supporting her in having her marital relationship really work;
* putting her well-being (eventually) above my fear of losing her.

Perhaps you can see from this that I have a major unconscious commitment to keeping the relationship in its present form.

I value her friendship very much, so much so that I have, at times, allowed the fear of losing her to stop me being honest and letting her know when I think she is doing something that is not in her best interests. In this way my unconscious commitment to keeping her around stops me from being a true friend and having her well-being be the main priority. I don't trust her, always, to know what she is doing and to go through her own process, so I am unconsciously committed to being in control of that, and to feeling good about myself at the expense of her power. Having said all that, I know that I do not let these unconscious commitments stop me for long, from the commitment I have to her growth, but sometimes they are serious contenders in terms of priorities. You could say I am committed to getting my love-needs met through this relationship.

Some of the other participants found they operated from security-needs in their relationships:

Barbara: *I am committed to feeling secure. A place where I can stay the same. Security is fairly superficial. I don't hang on to that one particularly hard.*

Jean: *To the parrot* (the mind), *it is vital. Actually it is a very strong motivating force. It takes a lot of courage to step beyond that.*

Barbara: *It would do, but it is not a step that can't be taken. The main part is for me to stay the same* (the need to be consistent, in Guy Claxton's terms).

Jean: *But that is safety too, in a way. Safety is consistency. What would happen if you change? What is the fear?*

Barbara: *If I change, I think one of the fears is that I would actually achieve things, and then I would have to stand on my own feet, and then I might not be able to fulfil the responsibility.*

Jean: *What is the cost of not changing?*

Barbara: *Massive.*

Jean: *Denial of yourself, frustration, anguish, despair?*

Barbara: *Yes to all of them. I know what it is costing me. I also know that I have got to do something about it now — well not right now* (empathic laughter as other participants recognise that she is still procrastinating), *but soon now.*

Jean: *Change is scary . . . You need a lot of support.*

Barbara: *I don't know where to get it from.*

This is the problem that we are often faced with when we undergo a transformative process. There seems to be no support from the sources that we previously relied upon for our survival. But as Marilyn Ferguson assures us in her book *The Aquarian Conspiracy,* there is a vast support-network growing up for those who find that they need new partners to join them on their journey, as it frequently means leaving behind those who are too afraid to step out into the unknown.

Most of the people who take courses of this nature find that they quickly become surrounded with like-minded people who are heading in the same direction. I now have far more support and many more committed and loving friends than I have ever had — and I had to let go of some of the friends I did have in the process!

Rose discovered that her longest-lived friendship was based on a commitment to getting her friend's approval:

Rose: *I recognise this feeling with her that I have to prove how glamorous, intelligent, deserving of respect, efficient, successful, I am.*

Jean: *You are committed to getting her approval?*

Rose: *Yes, it is bizarre.*

Jean: *You have too much attachment to keeping it going. You have to be willing to lose it for it to be worth anything. If you are committed to the longevity of the relationship, there can be no integrity, no openness.*

Rose: *It is painful. It feels as though I am going through a divorce.* (There had been a quarrel, and the other person was not speaking to her). *I don't need her. I have lots of friends.*

Jean: *You obviously do, or you wouldn't hold on to her. You need her approval. I think in some ways you think 'If I can have this person as a friend, I must be okay.'*

Rose: *At the moment I want to punish her, because I feel betrayed.*

So busy is Rose attempting to get her friend's approval that she neglects to communicate to her friend the level of openness and trust that she requires in a relationship. That is not the point of the relationship, as it stands: the point is to make sure that Rose does nothing to upset her friend.

Other 'unconscious' commitments that emerged from the exercise were: *validation, sex, being comfortable, acceptance, rescuing, being needed, status, more sex, protection, security, respect, and keeping a distance.*

Another one that arose was similar to the one Rose came up with: *keeping the longevity of the relationship going.* Not surprisingly, perhaps, it was Rose's ex-partner who had this one in his relationship with her:

Harry: *The strength to keep it going was my commitment to her.*

Jean: *You died when you made that the commitment. The relationship died. She died.*

Harry: *It was worth it. There were good times as well as bad times* (he is still keeping the relationship going in his head).

Jean: *You lost the relationship because of it, because you would not address the problems.*

Harry: *I didn't understand the problems.*

Jean: *You didn't understand the problems because you didn't want to know there were any.*

Harry: *I wanted them to go away.*

Jean: *You bought the lie that people can be happy all the time. The whole culture gives you the message that you can be happy all the time, or most of it, and the way to do it is be in a relationship. Part of you believes that if only you could find the* right *one, then you would be happy. No, you won't. You could instead acknowledge and celebrate the problems in a relationship. They present opportunities for you to grow.*

Participant: *Is that what you do?*

Jean: *Eventually! I do, because I realise that out of those problems I learn such a lot. At the time, no, it does not feel like cause for celebration, but very rarely do I think of giving up, because I know that, eventually, we will work something out. When you are where Ron and Marie are, it is desperate, you are stuck. You cannot get through it and you cannot see any way through. That is awful.*

Ron and Marie came on the course together. It was clear from the outset that their relationship was in crisis. Marie's job was a demanding one, which took her abroad for long periods of time. In the past Ron had always gone with her, giving up his employment, sometimes at a point where he could have been promoted. He had always looked after the children while they were abroad, and did so very well, but he had realised that, gradually, he was losing his sense of his own worth. He probably never had much anyway. He began to blame his partner, and, in an attempt to regain a sense of his own power, he constantly found fault with her and was angry much of the time.

She, of course, was not happy with his constant criticism and angry outbursts, and both of them were at a point where it looked as though there was no way out of the predicament. There was great attachment, certainly on Marie's part, to the remuneration she received for her work, and the life-style it could buy, and there was great fear on Ron's part of losing a relationship where he was cared for (or rather looked after) and felt secure. I suspect it provided him also with a great excuse for not 'succeeding' in his work, and not even needing to attempt to succeed and find out what he really wanted to do with his life. He could always say 'If it wasn't for my wife's job, I would have . . .'

Their predicament reminded me of an experience I had the previous week. Tim and I went for a walk on a disused railway line. The path was grossly overgrown with nettles, brambles, briars and other unfriendly undergrowth. Several times, from where we were standing, it looked impassable. On two occasions one or the other of us decided that we should give up, because there just was no way through. However, we are both pretty determined people under certain circumstances, and because we had committed ourselves beyond the half-way point, we pressed on, only to find that there was, after all, a way through — difficult, requiring patience, but there.

This seemed very analogous to life and the difficulties people might encounter, especially in relationships. Only commitment to something worthwhile will get you through. Most of the things we are committed to in relationships, however, are more self-defeating than empowering. The inevitable result of basing relationships on a commitment to getting the other person to meet your needs is the breakdown of the relationship, or the breakdown of the people within it.

On the second weekend of the course it occurred to Ron that maybe his wife was not to blame for his lack of success. He began to take responsibility for the situation he had bought into, and to realise that he needed to 'find himself'.

Ron: *My inner self is not happy. I want to change — there is something else I want to do. The price we have to pay in this case is that we will be splitting up. So that is unfortunate. I am just trying to get happiness and peace of mind for myself.*

Ron got into a relationship to fulfil a need, that of security, safety. To a degree the relationship fulfilled that need. He did feel safe, but at what cost? The cost was the other levels of the needs-hierarchy, those of love and self-esteem. Presumably at present he does feel that his love-needs have been met, and then the esteem needs arise, the need to 'find himself'.

Ron: *I need to stand on my own feet and feel stable, balanced. Maybe then I will be able to look at things in a more rational way.*

Ron realises he has paid a high price for the fulfilment of his safety-needs. It has become intolerable.

Ron: *I am hungry, and over the years the hunger has become anger.*

Jean: *Hungry for what?*

Ron: *Ambition. Over the years the frustration has turned the hunger into anger.*

Jean: *You are hungry for recognition.*

Ron: *Marie is a brilliant person. I have come to terms with the fact that I am the shadow, and I do not want that role. I do not like it . . . Maybe I am shutting down all communication. I can be manipulated into doing something I don't want to do.*

Jean: *Yes, and your fear of your lack of strength is causing you to run away.*

Ron: *I want to face myself.*

Jean: *Face yourself in this relationship, because if you run away from it the same problem will come up again, and next time it will probably be worse. Everyone will have lost out, including your children, and you will take yourself with you into your next relationship. The problem with people who are not in touch with their own power is that they are desperately afraid of being controlled or manipulated by other people. Actually no-one can manipulate you unless you give them the means to do so.*

The situation for Ron and Marie is not so unusual. We get into situations for convenience or comfort, and then find we are trapped. But it is not, as we think, the *other person* who has trapped us, it is *our own neediness,* and that is what can be used to manipulate us. Actually the other person does not need to do anything. You will do it all. You will resent needing someone and accuse them of manipulation when they tell you that the alternative to staying under those conditions is to leave, or to work it out.

For Ron and Marie there are several possible solutions. One is to call it a day and split up. If they do this, however, before they have thoroughly explored the roots of the problems, they are likely to repeat the whole scenario next time around. The second solution is to stay as they are — obviously not a happy or a healthy situation, and one that Ron says he is not prepared to accept. However, when the chips are down, and the reality of *standing on his own feet* hits him, he could scuttle back into his safe nest.

Thirdly, they could both do what they want to do with their lives, start to work with the difficulties in the relationship, and see if they can reach a satisfactory compromise which will enable both of them to have what they want. The problem is, of course, that neither of them knows what they want. Marie is probably doing her job for the status it confers, and Ron has never allowed himself to have any vision of what he want to do with his life.

Ron: *You see, I don't know what I want. I am not sure.*

Jean: *That is the problem.*

Ron: *I want to be myself, and then I will be a much better partner.*

Until they both look seriously at these problems they will have no way of knowing whether they can mutually support each other in fulfilling their growth-needs.

I have a feeling that, providing they really want to put some effort into working through their problems, they will learn much and grow much and eventually enrich and enhance each other's lives and those of their children — if they do stay in the relationship for the foreseeable future.

Very few relationships fail if both partners are committed to their own growth and well-being and that of the other person — providing they are both willing to expose themselves to being vulnerable, and are willing to seek support from an unbiased third party.

Jean: (to Ron) *From where you are standing there is no way through. But it is like I told you about going through the undergrowth on my walk with Tim. You need to have commitment and trust in the process. Just keep walking, and if it really gets too frightening and too tough, find a guide who can show you the way.*

Ron might find that true power in relationships comes from looking at what you are doing, acknowledging your mistakes, cleaning them up or taking correction and moving on. To do this we sometimes need the assistance of an unbiased *witness*.

The role of counselling in relationships

This is really an aside, but I think it needs saying at this point. Many couples seem to dislike the idea of eliciting the aid and support of professionals in addressing the problems in their relationships. Some of those who have sought help have not been happy with the process. I suppose, like every other occupation, there are more and less effective counsellors. My advice would be to go to someone who has been personally recommended, from a trusted person's own experience, if at all possible. There is, however, a book which tells you what to look for in a good counsellor and offers all sorts of other useful advice. It is *The Counselling Handbook* by Quilliam and Grove-Stephensen (1990).

Several problems seem to arise for people in the counselling situation. To sit and listen to your partner trotting out a list of your *faults* and misdemeanours to a third party is not comfortable. Furthermore, your perception rarely fits with your partner's and there is a tendency to *squabble* about who said and did what and when. A good counsellor will not allow this situation to develop, setting ground-rules from the beginning: no interruption, and establishing that although prepared to listen to everything, they are not necessarily taking what is said as being factual but merely that person's interpretation of events. Where counsellors or therapists do appear to be biased, or more inclined to favour one person's version than that of the other, then think about changing them for someone else.

The other difficulty or discomfort that arises from counselling is the necessity to explore the basis of our conflicts in the presence of our partner. I recently worked with a couple who seem to have been enmeshed in conflict over a long period of time. It became clear eventually that each was attempting to use the other person to ease the pain of their *wounded inner child* (Bradshaw, 1991). When I began to address the pain that Mandy had been carrying around with her for so long, for which she could find no balm, she began to sob, but, suddenly, finding herself in a *weak* position in the presence of the enemy (her husband, and perhaps me) she began to build up her defences again, getting back into the *he did* and *he said* level of the conflict. I know what it is like to reveal my vulnerability in a relationship where I am normally *the strong one* and my partner is the one who depends on me. It feels as though there is nothing to rely on and we will both sink.

In many cases people use their anger to protect their wounded child. They build a wall around their pain so that no-one can exploit their vulnerability. Exposing that to the person who is their constant companion and (it seems like) constant opponent, is tantamount to letting the Trojan horse inside the walls of the citadel. The only thing that can penetrate those walls is love, unconditional love that recognises the isolation of the guarded heart.

But many enemies have come along before in the guise of love and only inflicted more pain, and so there is a deep suspicion of anyone who seems to have the power to penetrate the defences, and a deep fear of those who are there to witness it. Maybe it will give them the key so that they will, in future, have easy access to the guarded heart and have the means to damage it further.

So counselling is threatening to our defences — it has to be if it is to work. In order for wounds to heal they need to be uncovered. Once the healing process begins people do not feel the need to defend themselves so fiercely. Can you imagine allowing anyone to get near to you if you have a great, gaping wound on your body? Most of us have gaping wounds in our hearts and we do not want people to get close to us, particularly those who are stamping around blinded by the pain from their own wounds. That is especially so when they are the people who have the power to inflict even further hurt.

There are times when I feel that people need to undergo a personal healing process before they can address the issues in the relationship, as often these stem from individual damage that is being irritated by rubbing up against another person. This does not mean you should not be in a relationship until you have dealt with your own agenda, as Ron proposes — indeed the relationship can allow us to see what that agenda is, if we let it.

Once we can begin to fully *own* the reactions that are responses to our own life problems, it is then possible to address the mechanical problems which arise in the relationship. It is extremely useful, I find, to draw this distinction between *life problems* and *mechanical problems*. If, for instance, two people differ in their standards of tidiness, it should be possible to look at the problem quite objectively and devise some ground-rules which will provide a satisfactory solution to the problem for both people, by negotiation.

Unfortunately, this does not happen often. As a rule, both people stubbornly adhere to being right about their preference. One will defend the untidiness by talking about the right to do your own thing and be free, and will criticise ridiculously high standards, amounting to obsessiveness on the part of the other person. The other will rant about the selfishness, slovenliness and ineffectiveness of the partner.

What could, in fact, be going on here at the *life problem* level is, on the one hand, a fear of domination and a determination not to be crushed, and on the other hand, a fear of chaos resulting in inadequacy and total annihilation. *Mechanical problems* then are the surface issues that come up in relationships, and *life problems* are those reactions which are embedded in our survival and took root, probably, in infancy.

It is our life problems, therefore, which keep us stuck in rigid patterns and do not permit any flexibility. These are the issues that a perceptive counsellor will quickly uncover. Once unearthed, however, some of them can, I believe, only be dealt with at a very deep emotional level. All the talking in the world will not do it. It then might require the services of a particular kind of therapist or healer, or perhaps both.

I know there is a trend these days for experts to say that people can be their own therapist (*eg* Miller, Stettbacher (1991) and Masson), but maybe this is people's survival-strategies at work in a subtle way. I know, for sure, that my healing is not complete, and I am currently working on my energy-levels with a healer who really does not go in much for talking, but something is happening which by-passes my very alert and agile mind.

I can now spot any real threat a mile off and work out how and where to build the barricades without letting it appear to my consciousness that it is happening. The healer I am seeing at the moment sees for herself what is going on. She does not have to ask and she uses healing techniques that my mind cannot block out. I know I could not do this alone. It takes her energy and insight, or her channelling of that energy, to move me. The 'enemy within' is extremely powerful and needs the extraordinary power of love if it is to be brought to rest.

Communication in relationships

When the presence of life problems is acknowledged and the healing process is under way, the issues which seem to dog relationships can be addressed with more hope of reaching a satisfactory agreement. These issues, in my experience are as follows:

* **load sharing**: who does what, and how much;

* **responsibility**: who responds to what is needed and wanted in the relationship;
* **boundaries**: how much time is allowed for individual and shared pursuits, how much is personal space respected, do partners respect your personal possessions, how much consultation is there about inviting other people around and arranging social occasions?
* **openness/communication**: how much of yourself do you reveal, and how much do you expect the other person to reveal? How much do they let you know about what is going on in their life? Do they let you know what they are thinking about you or the relationship? Do they let you know how they are feeling? Do they withhold emotions or love?
* **fidelity**: what constitutes infidelity, and where do you both stand on that issue? Do you have agreed-upon rules about fidelity?
* **money**: how much are you in agreement about credit/overdrafts/loans? Do you agree on savings and spending — for what or on whom? Do you have joint bank accounts or do you have 'my money' and 'his money'?
* **leisure time**: does it have to be shared, or can you pursue separate interests? Does one, should one, have more leisure time than the other?
* **sex**: is sex a way of reassuring each other that the relationship is working? Is it really okay to say 'no' to sex? Who really decides when, and when not to, have sex?

I am sure this list is not complete, but these are the main issues that seem to me to appear in our relationships. Perhaps you could make your own list of those areas which cause concern or conflict in your relationship. And then you could complete the exercise which follows.

An exercise on relationship issues

Divide a sheet of paper into two columns. On the left hand side write down a list of *mechanical problems* that crop up in your relationship — for example, 'he/she does not put the top back on the toothpaste, despite the fact that it drives me mad'. In the second column write down, as far as you are able, the *life problems* which might be associated with this issue.

An example is given below.

MECHANICAL PROBLEMS	LIFE PROBLEMS
Getting ready for holidays. I always have to think what to take, and end up doing the packing. This annoys me immensely. Looks as though he does not want to take responsibility.	I have a great deal of anxiety about getting lost which means I have to start out dead on time in case we miss ferries etc. He does not want to go on holiday as he associates leaving home and going away with rejection and loss.

e identification of the life problem takes the heat out of the nd enables a more cooperative and compassionate transaction to take place. When I realise that Tim is not *deliberately* leaving everything to me, I can talk to him at a different level. When he realises how extremely anxious I get when he procrastinates, he can see that I am not trying to dominate him by getting him to do things my way; he can help me to acknowledge the anxiety beneath my anger and perhaps avoid adding to it unnecessarily. This situation persisted for several years before we both realised that there was more to it than met the eye. We had to sit down and ask *what is really going on?* Prior to that we had both assumed the other was just being *difficult*.

Tim's early childhood experiences of 'going away' were when his mother left his father, taking Tim with her. The excuse given was that they were going on holiday, but the atmosphere was one of hostility and upset, and so Tim unconsciously associates any going away with this climate. He managed to fulfil this prophecy with me for many years, leaving things to the last moment so that, in the end, the climate was one of hostility and upset.

My own experience of going on holiday was that my mother worked herself up into a frenzy, probably because she felt she had to do all the organising and packing for everyone, and the atmosphere was filled with anger and anxiety for a week, if not a fortnight, beforehand. It is almost compulsory for me to panic before we go away, and Tim's life problem only feeds into this. We found the perfect partners to keep our patterns going, did we not?

Discovering the life problem behind our trivial disagreements cannot always be done in the heat of the argument or in the midst of the dispute, but it can be done retrospectively. If both partners were to make a list similar to the one described above it might enable them to identify areas of potential conflict in advance and discuss them beforehand, so that the crises can be averted. Now that Tim and I are aware of the life problems associated with 'going away', we remind each other about the potential difficulties beforehand and plan well in advance. Our *disease-entities* are appeased.

Load sharing and responsibility

Many couples seem to keep a mental inventory of who does what around the house, and what each chore equates to. Is cooking equivalent to washing up? Should you, to be fair, swap around these tasks each day or each week? Does looking after the children count for as much as working all day from nine to five? Does mowing the lawn and cleaning the car add up to doing the cleaning of the house and clothes?

These issues seem so trivial, and yet they often lead to major upsets and resentment within couples. Many people fall into the male/female stereotype trap of thinking that men should do particular chores and women others. My ex-husband, for instance, was extremely resistant to hanging out washing, as he felt he would be considered to be *less than a man* if someone were to see him doing it. He also used to volunteer to clean the windows for me, the implication being that the responsibility was mine, but he would relieve me of it for once.

When challenged he would say it was purely *semantics*, but that is not the case, for the language represents the way in which such attitudes are historically transmitted in our culture and embedded in our unconscious, influencing our perceptions and expectations in relationship. My present husband has none of those constructs — he will do whatever is needed in terms of domestic chores, and he does it of his own motivation. I cannot acknowledge him enough for this. In fact he often does it more willingly and certainly more cheerfully than I do!

It feels uncomfortable to be addressing such practical issues after dealing with the profound and deeply emotional and spiritual areas I have been discussing up to now. However something tells me that it might not be so obvious to some readers, who may find it liberating. These areas certainly still cause huge problems amongst many of the couples I work with and associate with.

A constant complaint I hear from female friends is that their partners will not take responsibility for anything (or almost anything) in the home. This is not, of course, true for all men about every task. My ex-husband organised and planned everything we did, except the day-to-day chores of shopping, cleaning, cooking and laundry. There is frequently a split, I find, where women are expected to cope with the day-to-day domestic chores while men do the *important* stuff like paying bills, looking after the maintenance of the garden and appliances, and doing the decorating.

I think the problem with this is that many men fail to realise what a grind it becomes to constantly think what needs buying, to plan menus and do the same things day in and day out — often on top of other work. It is not an even split, and leads to an unhealthy co-dependency, where one partner cannot survive (or thinks they cannot) without the other. In a healthy, empowering relationship people share their skills and teach each other, so that both are competent, and responsibility for tasks is interchangeable. This does not necessarily mean that you both have to do everything. Tim likes cooking and I enjoy wallpapering and tiling, so Tim tends to cook more than I do and I end up sticking the wallpaper on more frequently, but this is by *choice*, not by expectation.

Responsibility is often taken away from men at a very early age. Their mothers are often reluctant to insist that boys learn to look after themselves, believing that mothers must do things for their children. Not so with girls. Many men, therefore, see this as evidence of love, and feel cheated and unloved if women do not continue this *looking after* process. In fact, it is disabling to look after people, and the people doing it usually end up resenting their role.

I have been wracking my brains to work out what to say next, to give the magic key which will allow people to tackle the issue of shared responsibility, but I do not think there is one. It is a matter of uncovering the associated life problems — fear of domination, fear of not being good enough, sense of not being loved, expectations deriving from role-models of men and women which are rooted in cultural history. Once you have identified life problems, it is necessary to keep addressing them (because they will persist) and consciously allocate tasks and routines between involved parties — children included.

Of course the immediate difficulty that then arises is that one partner does not like or trust the way the other person does it, and wants to keep something to themselves. A good example that comes to mind is driving the car. Some of us hate being driven by someone else, and yet we resent being the person who always has to drive. I struggle with this one sometimes. One gesture which might work is *surrender*.

The first time I rode on the back of a tandem bicycle with Tim, it was horrific. Tim (at the front) had total control. I had no way of steering, no brakes, no gears, no nothing — all I could do was pedal. Tim wove in and out of traffic while I screamed and shouted, along the High Street of Leamington Spa. I was terrified. I felt totally and utterly out of control. And then I got it — surrender! There was nothing I could do unless I wanted the front seat (which I definitely did not), except surrender. So I did just that. I placed my life in Tim's hands and peddled. We got home in one piece (and at peace) and I enjoyed the fresh air and the scenery.

So often we give people responsibility for doing something, and then interfere with the way it is being done. Obviously offering tips if someone is struggling, or doing something ineffectively is okay, but *offering* is the operative word. I get really shirty if Tim turns down my helpful suggestions or ignores them. Why? Because *I know best, and I have to know best to give me a feeling of power* (a life problem).

If you do have fear about handing over responsibility for something, then do it — hand control to the other person completely for a month and see what happens! For example, if one person normally handles all the financial transactions, give that to the other person to do for at least a month, and both of you observe your reactions. Make sure you keep in constant communication about them without blaming and criticising each other.

Money

People are crazy in the area of money. Money represents security, power, love, survival, status — *all* the things on Maslow's hierarchy. Most of our interaction with money is rooted in life problems rather than mechanical problems. Take away the life problems and money is simple. Charles Dickens' Mr Micawber said it all a century ago: *Annual income twenty shillings, annual expenditure nineteen shillings and sixpence — result, happiness. Annual income twenty shillings, annual expenditure twenty shillings and sixpence — result, disaster*. Simple isn't it?

It is simple for Tim and myself because, thank goodness, we have similar life problems with regard to money, and so there is little conflict. I suspect, however, that we do not grow a lot in the area of money because we collude. I have learned from Tim to be more generous with money (and with other things too) and I managed that because he did not scare me to death by being reckless or irresponsible with it. Tim and I share bank accounts and communicate very well and clearly in this area. We seldom have a dispute. We consult and negotiate and respect each other's fears in this area, because we each recognise them in ourselves. If only we could do this with other issues — but we are learning!

All the rest

I need to devote a whole book to the subject of partnership rather than attempting to deal with these important issues hurriedly. Suffice it to say that couples or partners need to devote time and energy to making it clear to each other what they expect, where the boundaries are on issues such as fidelity, reliability, privacy and time to oneself, inclusiveness (including other people in the relationship, rather than excluding them and practising 'togetherness'), sharing of leisure time, and so on. So often we have expectations that are not communicated because *they should know*. But people come from widely different experiences of relationship; they therefore bring vastly different defence-strategies with them.

The beauty of relationship lies in exploring these mysteries, unravelling the complexity, sharing the joy of insights and unlocking of the pain. In this way the context of the relationship becomes one of growth rather than one of need.

The context of relationship

What does the *context* of relationship constitute? Context, according to the Collins dictionary, derives from the Latin, *contextus*, a putting-together or 'writing-together'. It is that from which meaning is derived. If we want to know what a word means, for instance, we look at it within the context of the words around it, and those words can change the meaning or emphasis — for example, 'This is very dear for something so badly made', or 'Oh, dear, what have you done?' or 'Hello, my dear', or 'What a dear little ring'.

Now take the last sentence: 'What a dear little ring', could mean 'what an expensive little ring', or it could mean 'what a sweet, pretty little ring'. The meaning would depend on another context — the circumstances within which the statement was made. A female shopping with her prospective fiancé might hear it as a signal that a ring was too expensive. The male might hear it as a signal that his partner wanted it. He would be operating within the context of *nothing is too good for her*, and she would be operating out of the context of *I must not ask for too much, or he will think I am greedy, and go off me . . . Another possible context that could be affecting the listening of the two could be that of one coming from scarcity* — an *I don't deserve it* attitude, and the other from *abundance* — a *where there's a will there's a way* attitude.

A context is, therefore a framework, or orientation which we put around events or interactions, which influences or distorts the perceptions and judgements of those events and the people associated with them.

What we are told about people, or are led to believe about them, influences our judgements and reactions. The context in which we perceive people influences our experience of reality. Another example would be that, when I walk into a psychiatric ward, I want to categorise people into patients, visitors and staff. Psychiatric patients frighten me, visitors do not, even when the 'visitors' turn out actually to be patients, and vice versa.

I am reminded of an experiment which was conducted by two psychologists (Hiroto and Seligman, 1975). Psychotherapists were shown a video of a man who was being asked about his feelings about his work experience. Half of the psychotherapists were told that the man was a job applicant; the other half that he was a psychiatric patient. The videos they watched were identical. They were then asked to write a description of the man. The half who had been told he was a job applicant used words like *realistic, fairly sincere, enthusiastic, relatively bright, pleasant*. The other psychotherapists, who thought they were looking at a patient, described him as a *tight, defensive person, dependent, passive-aggressive, frightened of his own aggressive impulses, considerable hostility, repressed* or *channelled*. Spine-chilling isn't it? Seligman (1978) explains:

> the psychotherapists in the context of a mental hospital expect to see behaviours that signify underlying pathology. This expectation biases them to interpret 'normal' behaviours with the labels and diagnoses they are trained to use.

A context then is something which holds the content of something and shapes it in a particular way. A context within relationship usually from some need or expectation we have about the nature and func relationship and the roles of the people within it.

An exercise on context

Try out this exercise.

Draw a circle, and put around the edge of it the context of relationship, taken from the unconscious commitments you discovered in the last exercise.
Now fill in the middle of the circle (the content of the relationship) from the list below (it is not exhaustive — add others of your own if you want to).
Leave out any that are in the list that do not fit into the context you have put around the edge.

Having fun, sex, intimacy, romance, affection, arguing, hostility, responsibility, commitment, rearing children, taking risks, experiencing pain, developing a successful career, developing many different relationships, contributing to other people, developing individual qualities (self-confidence, power, inner strength, self-worth, independence, generosity, ability to fail, valuing others), developing skills normally associated with the opposite sex, being able to be totally open and honest with someone, learning to be vulnerable, learning to love unconditionally, owning up to our mistakes, learning to forgive, learning to share, identifying our basic fears, learning how to surrender (give up control), the joy that comes from all of this.

Here is an example. Some people actually have a commitment to the belief that relationships cannot work — every relationship will fail. They set impossibly high standards for relationship, like *there must be no disagreement, no need for other people, no faults in the other person in meeting criteria of the perfect partner,* and so on. With this as a context or framework for relationship the content (or possibility for action and interaction) will be severely restricted. If the perfect woman is 'lady-like' and virginal, then activities like *having fun* and *sex* might prove problematical. Arguing and hostility would certainly not feature, and if the perfect woman was also a picture of health then there would be no room for her to be sick. This may seem far-fetched, but it actually happened to me in one relationship. There was certainly no permission for me to be ill. I was supposed to be the one who looked after people, not the one who needed looking after.

If the perfect woman is stereotypical, then (in the case of the former) she would not find approval if she showed evidence of becoming independent or powerful and wanted to develop lots of friendships outside of the relationship, because the ideal of the *perfect woman* might be that *all she wanted was her man*. This might sound ridiculous. I assure you it is not. I hear this sort of expectation voiced frequently.

As a rule, people who operate out of the context that relationships can't or don't work do so because they have a huge fear of intimacy. If you believe that something has no chance of working then you have the perfect reason for avoiding it altogether.

One man, Derek, realised that he had built failure into his relationship, by his unrealistic expectations of how relationships should be. He was the person mentioned in chapter eight, who could not accept love as a gift, but saw it as manipulation. The context of relationship for him was a commitment to *avoiding domination and manipulation* — the safety level (being in control) of Maslow's hierarchy. This, as a context, would cut out unconditional love, vulnerability, openness and honesty, experiencing pain, allowing the other person to argue or be hostile, intimacy, affection, forgiving, sharing, owning up to mistakes, and surrendering and commitment. Commitment is seen, in this case, as the *taking away of choice* — therefore putting oneself in a position to be manipulated.

As a result, personal growth would be unlikely to occur, nor would the other person be allowed to grow and develop independence or self-confidence. Sex would also be likely to cause problems, as someone who cannot give of themselves (someone very controlling) is in trouble sexually — to the degree where they cannot manage to climax or enjoy climax, or they are so afraid of closeness and feeling out of control that they become impotent and cannot even begin the process.

In short, the context of a relationship can and does pre-determine the fate of it and the state of it. Imagine what happens when two people have contexts which are totally different — the first person might be into being in control, and the second might be intent on being looked after. Both come from safety-needs. Many unstated *deals* are made in this type of relationship. *You look after me and I then don't need to develop myself, take risks, widen my skills, seek out other relationships, develop inner strength and self-worth, because I will get all this from you*. Or, *You can develop a successful career so that you can provide for me (as long as that doesn't mean that you start caring for other people). You cannot, however, fail, or take too many risks*. Or, *You can't be vulnerable or share yourself with me because knowing how you really feel will scare me*. Or, *You must never be out of control (never learn to surrender) because I can't cope with responsibility — that was not the deal. You must be strong. I must be weak*. This looks as though the two people should be ideally suited — the contexts are complementary, but I think you can see that it eliminates growth — indeed growth is threatening, as it will upset the balance and rock the boat. Although it is the perfect dance, it is the dance of death in relationship.

So if the context of relationship is *feeling safe*, however you have that set up, and if something occurs within the content of the relatio does not fit that context, we say 'that does not make sense (fit in), the... this relationship is bad' — not working.

If the context of the relationship is about getting love, or feeling good, or having life be easy, then you can see how many of those factors above would either have to be eradicated, or would cause huge and irresolvable conflict.

This is an era of rapid evolution in the psychological and spiritual growth of humanity. It is almost inevitable that one or other of the partners in a relationship will begin to feel the impelling desire to listen to their inner self — the angel who says, *Let me out of this prison of fear and let me show you love.* At that point, the other person, if they are still operating out of fear and need, will become the jailer of your soul. There is only one context that will liberate the spirit in a relationship, and that is one of growth.

Growth as a context for relationship

So relationship is a mirror in which we can see our deepest selves, if we look hard and long enough. To many of us that prospect is horrifying. We choose our partners so that they will reflect back at us how wonderful, successful, intelligent, attractive, worthwhile, hard-working and lovable we are, don't we? Well, yes we do, and that is the problem. We definitely do not want our partners showing us our blind spots, pointing out our weaknesses and spurring us on to take risks and *change*. That would mean that we were *not good enough* the way we were. We want someone who will help us build a cosy, armour-plated nest, not kick us out of it.

Talking this over with a friend of mine, she realised that she wanted her husband to mirror back to her that she was worthwhile and lovable. His behaviour towards her told her exactly the reverse — that she was not worth the time of day. But if this is a mirror, then our partners are simply reflecting back at us what we are expressing to them. My friend realised that she had actually been expressing her worthlessness and unlovableness, and the mirror had dutifully reflected it back. The opportunity was, therefore, to see why she was presenting herself as worthless and unlovable, and how she was doing that.

It reminds me of the mirror in *Snow White and the Seven Dwarves*: 'Mirror, mirror, on the wall, who is the fairest of them all?' At the beginning of our relationships the mirror dutifully replies 'You are, oh beautiful princess'. Further on into the relationship the mirror says, 'Well I don't know, maybe you're not so great after all'. It might be that we are trying to convince the mirror how ugly we are at that time.

The *mirror*, or partner, might be doing us the greatest favour in reflecting the way we really feel about ourselves back at us. It is the beginning of awareness, and therefore the opportunity for growth. Unfortunately it does not feel good and it does not feel safe. Nor does it feel safe to be encouraged to grow in a relationship.

Growth often feels unsafe to the partner of the person who is growing. They had a good reason for seeking you out too. Very often someone who mirrors back to you that you are no good has an investment in keeping you that way. They want a mirror that tells them they are superior, to counteract their feelings of being just the opposite.

In nature, the mother bird knows that the nestling does not want to jump out into space and fend for itself. But she also knows that, if it does not do so it will not survive. Spiritually a human being will not either. We need to fend for ourselves psychologically and spiritually, and we need a lot of support in making those leaps.

In a relationship which has *mutual growth* as the context, all content is permissible, providing it is used as an instrument of developing awareness and mutual support. Even violence could be seen as an opportunity for growth. If this sounds a bit *over the top*, consider the next paragraph.

One woman came to see me because her husband frightened her. She had been sexually abused, although she did not know this at the time — she remembered it when she took my course. Because of this early history of abuse she put up with violent outbursts from her husband, feeling paralysed with fear when this occurred. She also put up with sexual violence or abuse from him, again because she felt paralysed and felt she could not stop him. Her husband was, essentially, a man committed to loving and caring for people (we all are, actually). Why was this going on?

One of the reasons why this behaviour persisted was because he did not know that he frightened her so much, and took her lack of objection for compliance. She did not put clear boundaries around his behaviour, and let him know what the consequences of subsequent acts of violence would be — she simply put up with it. Much of this comes from the belief that develops as a result of childhood abuse, namely that you are powerless to stop anything happening. Some of it also stems from the belief that you are so worthless that you are lucky to find anyone who would want a relationship with you, so you had better stick to someone who does.

On his part he had been abused also as a child, although his abuse was more difficult for him to see. His parents had, like many caring parents, wanted only the best for him, but *the best* had to be the way *they* saw it, not the way he wanted it to be. He had been all but crushed, and so was determined to assert his power over someone else. Where better to demonstrate your power than in a sexual encounter?

For the female, facing up to the history of her abuse was extremely confronting, but she realised that she did have a commitment to her own growth and to that of her partner, and that, until she addressed her problems, she was unlikely to be able to support him in addressing his. She bravely went through several sessions relating to the childhood abuse, and then was able to persuade her husband to come to see me too. He came, with some reluctance, but he did not run away.

Eventually these two people learned how to communicate and support each other, and these particular problems no longer occur. I am sure they have others, but their commitment to their own growth and that of each other will, I am sure, serve them in addressing any other issues that arise in their relationship.

The factor that was really crucial in persuading the female partner to address the violence in the relationship was the realisation that it was severely hampering her work with deprived children. In this day and age, people who work with children who are at risk are required to teach such children how to protect themselves and say *No*. How could she do this when she found it impossible to do it for herself? She was increasingly aware of the hypocrisy and ineffectiveness of this, and so was determined to do something about it. That she grew, and that her relationship was enhanced, was a by-product of her commitment to her purpose in life. She might not have put it this way at the time, but I think she realises now that this is, in fact, what happened.

She used the relationship as a mirror to tell her what was stopping her being a *force of nature* in the work she had chosen. The mirror told her what she thought of herself, and in working out why she held herself in such low esteem, she discovered how she had been abused in the past. Now I am not advocating that we deliberately get into relationships with people who are harmful and destructive, but I do say that, if those are the kind of relationships you choose, you should look and see what they are telling you about you, and about the context you have put around the relationship.

If we are need-centred in our relationships we become at worst destructive and, at best, limiting. Need-centredness, despite the fact that it can look self-sacrificing and humble, is in fact *ego-centredness*. Hungry egos are demanding and dispiriting. They do not allow us to follow our hearts, but demand that we listen to, even deify, fear. Fear becomes our master, and all those who enter into relationships with us must become its servants.

To have our relationships be powerful requires us to know what we really want to do, and then to be true to that calling. In that way our partners can serve and support us in our growth. The difficulty many people have with this is in knowing how to live their lives *authentically*, following a path that will lead them to remembering who they are.

11. *Joyful participation in life — principle-centredness*

You come at a most exciting and unusual time in the history of the human race . . . It is not your wondrous human self that I address . . . but it is the soul of you that has chosen to walk in the costume that you wear to heal the wounds of society's illusion. Oh, not all by yourself. Do not let my statement bend you down in fatigue or exalt you beyond human capacity . . . You have come to heal, to sew up the tattered fabric of human misconception . . . When you pick up the needle and thread and begin to say, 'All right, I see this tearing here and I don't know what I am doing but I will begin to make the first stitch' you will find you belong to a community of magical beings that have walked in their self-disguise at least as cleverly as you . . . There is a need for those of you who are willing to begin the seeing . . . remove the lens of illusion and move forward. And never doubt your dreams, never doubt your vision.

(Emmanuel, Bromsgrove, May 1992)

I have no spur to prick the sides of my intent, but only a vaulting ambition which o'erleaps itself and falls on the other.

(Macbeth, Shakespeare).

I studied *Macbeth* at school and I have been haunted by this character ever since. I felt a bit sorry for him, as I thought he was tricked, first by the witches and then by his wife. But I suppose they had to have his cooperation and the witches certainly spotted him as a likely candidate for mischief-making.

By the pricking of my thumbs,
Something wicked this way comes. (Act 1, Scene 1).

Macbeth was a man who operated out of deficiency-needs, if ever there was one. He allowed his thirst for power to come above everything — integrity, loyalty, love, friendship, all went out of the window, and he became a slave to ambition. Eventually life, to Macbeth, became a *'tale told by an idiot . . . signifying — nothing'*, and yet he got what he wanted — he

became king. But at what cost? He obviously decided it wasn't wo
and so did his equally ambitious wife.

Does this mean that to be ambitious, to want success, is wrong and will inevitably lead to disaster? I don't think so, but perhaps a better question is, *will it lead to joy?* And if not — what will give us joy in life? One thing is clear — living out of fear-centredness will not. Had Macbeth consulted a therapist, instead of the witches, he would have probably discovered that he had very little sense of his own worth and had felt extremely powerless as a child. He probably had a huge fear of being out of control, and needed to be in a position where he could be totally controlling of everything.

In his favour, he definitely struggled with his conscience when considering whether or not to murder Duncan (the current *thane*, or king). Perhaps Shakespeare was trying to say, *look what happens when you allow your ego-needs to dictate to your heart*. Macbeth did indeed 'yield to that suggestion', which his whole being told him was evil, and he paid the price for doing so, losing everything in the end, including his own self-respect.

How to live successfully

Looking up the words *success* and *ambition* in the dictionary yields interesting data. *Ambition*, according to Collins, derives from the Latin *ambitio* — a striving to please.

This would imply then that anyone who is ambitious is looking for approval. In order to please they must be successful, the present-day meaning of which is, to be famous or wealthy or achieve some desired outcome or goal. So, while there is nothing wrong with ambition or success, does it really get us what we want? Who are we striving to please — and why? How successful do we have to be before we have succeeded in achieving our ambition? In my experience it never ends. There are those of us (most of us) who are never satisfied even when we achieve outstanding results in life.

A business associate and I recently undertook some work for a government organisation. We handed out evaluation sheets at the end of the course and 19 out of 20 people who took the course made favourable, even flattering, comments about the standard and quality of the teaching. All of them reported achieving all of the objectives, except for one person who felt he had achieved all but one of the 17 or so we had set for them. One other person had made a slight criticism of the way we worked together. This was not substantiated by any of the other comments.

Despite all this the two points we focused on were the negative ones. The others, we thought, were okay and *wasn't that nice of them*, but the ones that stayed with us were the criticisms. We had to work hard at realising that we had worked well together (this was the first time we had worked as a team), that we had obviously made a difference to these people, and we had actually had fun and found it a joyful experience. Both of us seemed to have a compulsion to see only the evidence which would confirm our firmly-grounded belief that we are not (and never will be) *good enough*.

The Collins Dictionary turned up more interesting information, in that the old and obsolete meaning of *success* is, *any outcome*. Now this is surely good news for those of us who want to succeed. All we have to do is enter into an activity. Whatever the outcome of that activity we will have succeeded. Now doesn't that turn the mind upside down? As long as you enter the race and start to run, you will have succeeded. You may not win, but you will have succeeded, and the very act of participation is enough.

Are you, like me, wondering why this definition is now obsolete? Well you don't have to wonder for long. It does not fit into our cultural construct of what is needed in order to be *seen* to be successful. In this culture success is about winning, coming first, getting acclaim, achieving some socially-recognised result. Can you imagine someone saying 'Yes I was totally successful at work — I was made redundant', or, 'I succeeded at university — I failed my degree'. And yet there was an outcome, and that outcome could have been far more beneficial to that person's psychological growth than one considered to be *successful* by the rest of society.

If we could live our lives out of this now-obsolete definition of success, we would all be successful. No-one would be *better* than anyone else — but of course, in the ego's perception, this will not do. We must be able to measure ourselves against others to see where we stand in the approval stakes.

What is the way out of this 'striving to please'? Do we have to die before we see a different way to live, that will free us from the treadmill of ambition — daring to dream — or the chains of hopelessness — giving up the idea that we could ever do anything with our lives, other than carry on feeling that we are nothing and nobody.

Sadly many of us do seem to wait until it is too late to do anything that we consider worthwhile. We live in fear, striving for recognition, trampling over others in our reaching for fame and riches, scurrying into the bunkers of comfort, to the exclusion and neglect of those less fortunate, or killing and torturing in our acquisitiveness and our need for more power or territory? Does it get us what we really crave for? No. 'The point of death', Emmanuel tells us, 'is the moment of truth':

> As you leave your bodies, what is made available to you is the entire panorama of your human existence, and because, at that moment of releasing yourself from illusion, you move back into your angelhood,

you see all things with the eyes of love. Do you scold yourself? No, for you see from where your cruelty came. You do weep for yourself and for all of humanity? There is no such thing as punishment in the open compassionate heart. There is only profound caring that sees behind every facade of behaviour the frightened, abandoned child.

(Emmanuel, Bromsgrove, May'92)

When the veil of illusion is removed we see all that we did, for what it really was, and we realise the opportunities for love and self-remembering that we have lost. I see my mother now, and my heart aches for her. At the age of 89 she is waiting to die. She cannot see that love comes from giving — even now, and I have tried to show her often enough! She is still trying to get love from people by manipulation (although this is not deliberate or conscious). She sulks, regresses, accuses us of neglect. She keeps saying that she wants to die, but I can see she is afraid of death also, because there is a part of her that knows she has not remembered who she really is, and without that there is no peace.

She is still trying to accumulate and hang on to money and all her possessions — for what? Why do we need to cling to pathetic mementos that we think say who we are — that keep us stuck in the past, rather than living in the present? We cannot store up joy; we cannot harbour a collection of monuments to our worthwhileness. We can and do try to, though. In my mother's case the sum-total of her belongings adds up to the value of a few hundred pounds. It is very upsetting for her to realise that this, in her view, is all her life has amounted to. Of course it is not, but that is how it looks to her.

My mother could live for years yet, wanting death because life has no purpose and she feels *useless*, that there is no point in her being here. And yet she lives in fear of death also, because she knows she has not expressed or experienced who she is. Perhaps she has not learned the lessons she came to learn in this life.

My mother cannot *take it with her*, and yet she hangs onto *it*. Why do we bother getting *it* all in the first place? Well we know all that now, don't we? We think having things will give us a sense of identity, make us feel safe, have us feel loved, get people to accept and be pleased with us. But that does not give us a sense of who we really are, the love that we are, the *angels* or beings of light that we are. So why bother acquiring them?

Does this mean that we should take a vow of poverty? No — I don't think so. I enjoy my comfortable home and I find it useful to have a word-processor and time-saving gadgets in my kitchen, but these objects are no longer symbols of security or status. They are there to nurture me and free my time to do the things I really want to do, to be the person I really want to be, and am capable of being.

I like my surroundings to provide a harmonious setting for my life. When I am close to nature I feel nourished by the environment — the song of the birds, the beauty and wonder of life in all its different and amazing forms — I find this very uplifting. Since I do not have this available to me normally I do my best to create a pleasing and harmonious context for my life in my home and in my garden. At one time I would have furnished and decorated my living accommodation to impress my friends and visitors, rather than to nurture myself and my family. This shift in attitude requires the creation of a very different context for life from one of *approval* or *safety*.

You can't take *it* with you, but you can and do take *yourself* with you, and the more you honour who you really are the more you will discover your self-hood in this lifetime and create joy and love in your life.

We can honour who we are by living authentically, by expressing love in our lives, by standing for truth. If we have as our life-purpose that we will bring light into the darkness of the world, we do not, as Emmanuel reminds, need to do great deeds. We can live according to certain conscious principles, or standards, in our daily lives, but this is not easy.

Getting out of the ego trap

Surrounded as people are by social structures which create competition, comparison, subterfuge and inequality, it is difficult, if not impossible, to sustain our authenticity without some form of constant reminder from the higher self — something that allows us to recall who we are and why we came.

It is so tempting to be pulled back into listening to the voice of fear that says, *don't listen to that, you'll lose everything, you'll end up in poverty, you'll die and no one will care or even know you existed*. We dread ending up like the flowers in Gray's *Elegy*, that were born to blush unseen and waste their sweetness on the desert air.

However this is a very human construct of reality. Does the flower feel unfulfilled? Although it is unseen by humans it is doubtless *seen* by many other life-forms who appreciate its usefulness and its nurturing presence. It does not have to win prizes at the Chelsea Flower Show to serve its purpose in life. It is easy to see that other life-forms serve a purpose in the overall plan of nature. We can see what happens if species disappear — all of nature has to make adjustments. Each unit in a species or genus plays a vital part in the continued evolution of life on the planet, and this is obvious. It is much more difficult to see how, or where we human beings play our part.

The ego is constantly at work trying to figure out how to keep us *insignificant and safe*, or how to make us look *bigger and better*. We have no organising principles to our lives other than these, it seems. Ah, but what about growth? Yes, there is the possibility of growth as an organising principle, but how do we do growth? 'Taking risks', you may say, and that would probably be true. But what kind of risks, and doesn't the mind then rush in and say 'well, if I take a risk I want a reward. Where is the status-power-money-fame I will get for taking the risk?' And if the reply is, 'maybe you will get nothing, except the lessons that came from taking it — lessons in love, humility, acceptance, courage, commitment, integrity, trust, responsibility', maybe nothing but that, the mind then says, 'no deal, not enough and too much. All of that will get me nothing.'

In fact *all of that* will get you your *Self*, but it is impossible to work out in advance what that will mean. And when you do achieve it there is the danger that you will almost immediately forget how it was to be you beforehand, and you will say, 'that's no big deal'. Yet something in you may sing and say, 'yes — I remember now'. My editor offered me this quote to illustrate this point. It is from John Ruskin, *It's not what you get for it; it's what you become by doing it.*

If flowers could speak and tell you what their purpose was in life they would probably say something like 'to contribute to the well-being and development of the planet'. And they would carry out their purpose (as they do), quietly and unassumingly, gradually unfolding and blooming, growing into what they were intended to become. And having served their purpose they would sink back into the soil from whence they came, so that other plants could grow and be nurtured out of their dying. Most human beings, though, have forgotten why they are here.

So what would you say about your purpose? What principle could organise the content of your life and give it meaning? What purpose could you create that the mind, or parrot, could not latch onto and turn into more food for its ever-open beak?

What if it was something that could not possibly be achieved, or could not be achieved in the foreseeable future — certainly not by you alone? How would that be? Or would the mind immediately say 'what's the point of having it, then?' We are so used to considering our lives through the lens of self-interest that the mind cannot grasp that any benefits might accrue from taking on something unattainable, or something that would not necessarily be attributed to us — or something that would present us with the dilemma of not knowing how or where to start.

Yet so many people live with the agonising hopelessness of not knowing what they want to do with their lives, with the fear that when they reach *retirement* age, they will not know what to do with themselves — life will be effectively over. They think 'would it not be wonderful to be this or that, or to belong to this or that profession?'. But people then come to the conclusion that they are not clever enough, bold enough, young enough, old enough, that it would be too difficult, too much trouble. There is some reason why we cannot do what we would like to do. Perhaps ıld start to consider who we are, rather than what we want to do.

I suggest that one way to do this (the only way I have found so far), is to create for yourself a purpose in life that you consider to be a *mighty* one — one worth getting out of bed for in the morning! A purpose that is bigger than your ego, and one which honours the *Self* — one that is compatible with light, truth and love. I invite you to find a purpose for your life that will enable you to bring light into the darkness, as Emmanuel puts it.

Many of the people who take my course are thrown into confusion — and dismay, perhaps even anger, at this point in the proceedings. By the time we get around to addressing this issue, many of them are feeling unburdened and free. They definitely do not want to get into something that they see as *heavy* and serious. They want to go out and play. They think that the aim of the course has been accomplished for them — they have become free of their fear, and they want to bask in the delight of that. And that is wonderful — no harm in that. Except that I know that this will not persist.

In my experience that will not be enough. Something in you will say, 'what can I give of myself, now I have remembered who I am?'. 'Where can I take this — what can I do with it?' 'Where is the darkness I can illuminate with this light I have found?' These questions are asked not so that we will be acclaimed, but so that we will be able to do what we came here to do, to make our contribution to the well-being of the planet and of all who occupy it.

This is, in fact, the most powerful part of the course, but it is difficult to hear that — just as it might be difficult for you who are reading this to take it seriously. However I invite you to try this out, not for a week, but for a good period of time in your life. Just try it and see what happens. It is an act of faith, a leap into the unknown. You, like myself, will have no way of knowing what the outcome could be, or could not be. But if you do not try it, then it is certain that life will go on pretty much as before — except that, having got thus far in your growth, it might prove easier to tackle problems that come along.

One person who felt totally liberated by the experiences she had on the course came to the final session and told me that she did not want all this 'purpose stuff' — she just wanted to retire from her job, which she disliked intensely, and work in her garden.

Carla: *I couldn't cope with the pain of all the cruelty in the world. I just want to crawl back into my shell.*

Jean: *You have to cope with the pain of humanity and of being human every day.*

Carla: *Yes, but I think this means I should be doing something wonderful and I don't want to do it.*

Jean: *You are entitled to crawl back into your bunker of course, and you can spend you life working in your garden, but the danger is that you won't live very long.*

Carla: *I don't want to get old anyway, so I might as well die.*

Jean: *I will tell you how to avoid growing old. Keep living!*

Carla said that she did not want to end up living in an old people's home — that would be worse than death. I could see that, in wanting to bask in her new-found happiness and turn a blind eye to suffering, Carla might be jumping out of the frying pan into the fire. She might soon become disillusioned and bored and be back where she started — feeling that life was pointless and she might as well not be here. I suggested to her that the danger of not finding something to live for, that was 'bigger than her ego', was that she might end up as a vegetable in her own garden. I did not want her to go through all that pain again. She had suffered enough. Carla was not willing to accept this possibility and I had to allow her to walk her own path.

Of course there are people who do get into 'good works' and Carla was one of them, but this, she said, gave her no satisfaction. I feel this is because, very often, when we have some spare time and are bored with our jobs, we look for voluntary work as a way of getting recognition and feeling good about ourselves. We feel bad about doing nothing, so we take on some unpaid task. The underlying motivation in doing this task, however, significantly affects the outcome.

If we enter into the task as a true act of love, as a gift, or contribution to something we really consider to be worthwhile, then, I suggest, we will be extremely powerful in our execution of it, and it will give us joy and a great sense of our own power. Having a purpose in life is not about doing *good works* — it is actually about putting yourself first — not putting the ego first, but putting the *Self* first, and that means expressing your power. Even when you have not formulated a specific purpose it is still possible to operate out of an unconscious commitment to an undefined vision and when you do it creates a distinct improvement in the quality of interaction with life.

Many people, however, do not want to be powerful, and I think this was at the bottom of Carla's desire to forget all about 'purpose' and stay in the bunker. People realise that they cannot be *powerful* and *safe*. The two things are incompatible. Once they feel happier, they want to retreat again into their shell and be happier inside it. This is a trap . . . I think!

I say 'I think' because since I visited Emmanuel I am not so sure. When I asked a question about purpose in life and whether we needed one or not, I was told:

> Birds do not sing so others will hear them, and yet if they do not sing they could not live.
>
> (Emmanuel, Bromsgrove, May 92)

Presumably, what Emmanuel meant by this was that we should do what we do because it is in our nature to do so, and not work out what we should do so that it will get us the attention and admiration of others. Nor should we do *nothing*, because in doing nothing, in expressing nothing of ourselves, we will die.

Emmanuel also went on to say that there are beings of light who have never forgotten who they are, who are the most ordinary people. They work in butchers' shops, or own the tobacconists down the road; they are farmers or factory workers, but, he says, because they have never forgotten who they are, the planet is in no danger of destruction.

> Greatness rests in the most ordinary of beings. There are those walking the planet now, many of them, that are called from the oneness because humanity, in its cry of love, has bid them to come and they have come. And they are masters — they are beings of absolute remembering. They are angels and they have never forgotten that — and yet do you see them walking with magnificence down the street? No. Because they know who they are, they know their power, they know their worth and they know their purpose. And so they come, to be in their perfect loving, and perhaps they run a tobacco store or are butchers, perhaps they drive a street-car or are farmers, perhaps they are crippled children. Perhaps they are seemingly the most unremarkable people, and yet their nature shines so brightly that our world is kept in the hands of love and absolute safety, because of their presence and the danger of global destruction has long since passed because they are here.
>
> (Emmanuel, Bromsgrove, 92)

I have to confess that I find this difficult to believe — or is it that I just do not want to believe it because it does not fit in with the theory I have constructed about life? Perhaps it means that I can stop trying — and then what would I do with my time on earth? I also wonder how all the poverty, destruction and violence in the world is going to stop, if we all get on with working in a shop, or garden? I cannot see it as a solution, but I am willing to accept that it could be.

A couple who had taken my course sent this observation to the magazine which is supplied to all course participants. I think this illustrates clearly what Emmanuel is saying.

> It was at breakfast in a large, second-rate hotel in Buxton that a small, middle-aged lady came to ask what we would like to have. This waitress was so bright-eyed and open-faced, and spoke with such a

cheerful voice, that we immediately had a sense of well-being. We were served and she went to table after table, but we couldn't help but notice that she gave pleasure to each group of people, winning smiles and cooperation from all.

I don't remember much of what we ate, but I can still feel the warmth and friendliness that abounded in that very large room. We were loathe to get up and leave, even though we were in a hurry . . . but we knew we were each getting the same sense of joy from this woman.

When we eventually got up to leave, I just had to say a 'thank you' to her for being so special. In my inadequate way I went close to her and smilingly said I'd enjoyed the breakfast. Ken, however, was far less inhibited. He gave her a hug and thanked her for being so radiant. I don't expect she gets that treatment very often, especially from someone whose only words were to order egg and bacon! She will never know what a wonderfully happy beginning she gave to our holiday. Nevertheless, I want to say how lucky we are that there are people like her who really do make the world a better place. Thank you, little waitress, and thank you to those of you who have enabled Ken and I to be delighted by these people now.

I suppose if everyone did spend their lives creating wonderful gardens, or serving people in this loving way, then there would be no time for destruction, no expression of greed, no wars, only beautiful gardens. Perhaps that is all there was, once, the Garden of Eden. Then fear arrived in the guise of the serpent, and gardens were no longer enough.

So what do I know about life-purpose? I do know that it is healthy to know that you do not know, so I will continue to play the game I have been playing so far with life until I find a better one to play, and I will make room for new possibilities. I know that once I think I have found the answer, I am in trouble. So Emmanuel did me the greatest favour in instilling doubt in my mind on this issue. I was also reminded of the danger of thinking that I have to wear myself out changing the world, when really all I need to do is remember who I am.

One of the interpretations that people can put on this is that they can be complacent about the plight or problems of others. That those are 'their problems' and nothing to do with us. So this presents me with a dilemma. Do I work on finding the light within myself, and leave everyone else to their own problems, or do I intervene when I see injustice, treachery, genocide, starvation, abuse? Do I teach what I have learned? Do I nurture others who need care and attention? I think Emmanuel would say '*yes* — but not motivated by the need to be seen by others to be *great*.

All I can do now is share with you something that I have found to be a most powerful way forward, and one that does not seem to allow the ego ch control. It also leads me to engage in joyful activities with fellow-travellers, who make my journey through life delightful, exciting and challenging. Maybe I am not ready to dig gardens yet — or maybe it is not my way.

For those of you who know you are not living life in a way which produces joy and satisfaction for you I suggest you create a purpose for your life — an *organising principle* that will enable you to find a direction for your energy, and have your ego be your servant rather than your master. Where do you start? I suggest you take a look at what is happening in the world that bothers you, that makes you say (compassionately, not righteously) *that should not be*. Something that you feel moved to want to *do something* about, which has, perhaps, in the past, made you feel defeated by the magnitude of it. In other words, *where do you see a tearing in the fabric of life?*

It might be that you see how destructive or inequitable the economic system is, and how it creates poverty. It might be that you would like everyone to be educated in a way which will lead them to understand more about the world and how it works, and more about each other, so that we develop better communication and cooperation between individuals and nations. You might feel that, if only people could communicate effectively and trust each other, much of the evil in the world would end. Perhaps you find it devastating that people and young children should die of curable diseases and starvation in the Third World. Perhaps you long for world peace and a planet with no borders or divisions of language. It might be that you feel that if people lived in communities again, many of the problems we have would be solved. You might be appalled at the amount of crime in the world, and the involvement of our youth in drug-taking and criminal activity. You might be appalled at the way the old are treated and want to do something for the quality of their lives.

I could go on and on. I have not even mentioned the environment! Do you get the idea? I have to warn, though, that as soon as you begin to play this game the parrot will fall off its perch with panic. 'How can you expect me to take on something like this — are you mad? I don't have any qualifications, I don't have any time, I have a job I do not want to give up — it makes me lots of money — anyway I will never get another one. I refuse to get involved in some crack-brained mission to save the world. This all sounds like some kind of religion to me'.

The mind is looking through the lens of fear. Notice how we manage always to find reasons why we *cannot*, or *should not* do something, before we have even begun? Emmanuel was reassuring on this issue of 'purpose':

> If you find your dream, it does not mean what fear says it must mean. It will not call forth enormous change. You will not lose your friend or

> lose your mate, and move to some mountaintop or palace. Remember who you are, and your change may be unrecognisable to those who you know with great intimacy. And that does not in any manner belie the truth of your remembering. When the mind is looking to find the costume, the form in which greatness, angelhood, can be represented upon the planet, of course fear says, 'well, there must be this greatness, or this more-than-selfness. That is illusion. You know it — you just wanted me to tell you so.
>
> Follow your heart: if it be modest and unassuming then praise the heavens for that, and if it wants to turn around and roar, then praise the heavens for that as well. Do not squeeze yourself into anonymity, neither thrust yourself into the eye of the public. Be who you are, and trust the ebb and flow. Greatness comes sometimes to those who are simply walking their path. They turn around one day and say, 'what is everybody doing here? Why are they following me? I hadn't noticed I was so engrossed in the loving of my own life.'
>
> (Emmanuel, Bromsgrove, 92)

Follow your heart. If you feel there is something missing in your life, and that what is missing is *you*, then you need to start looking for it.

In the *Wizard of Oz*, the lion, the tin man, the scarecrow and Dorothy all had a mission. Although their missions were differently-worded, they had strong connections. The tin man wanted to be able to feel love for people; the lion wanted to overcome his fear; the scarecrow wanted to feel competent, and Dorothy wanted to feel loved. Their purpose, or mission, in other words, was to discover who they really were. They decided to support each other in pursuing their missions. Or to put it another way, they realised that in order to find out who they were, they would be better off enabling other people to do the same.

In order to accomplish their mission they set themselves a goal — find the Wizard of Oz, because he could work miracles — or so they had heard. They had no idea where to start on this journey, they only knew it was somewhere, 'over the rainbow' — somewhere that was beyond their present reality. They did not know how to get there, but off they went, happy in their comradeship. Soon, roads (yellow brick ones) opened up to them, and all sorts of people came to their aid, enrolled by their courage and determination.

What they discovered at the end of their journey was that, *in the process of seeking their goal, they had found what they were looking for*. They had conquered fear, experienced great love, given love, demonstrated ingenuity and cleverness. Despite the fact that the Wizard was a fake, and therefore their purpose in going to see him had always been unattainable, nevertheless, having somewhere to aim for — generating the will to set out and making a commitment to others — enabled them to reach their heart's desire. I find this a most inspiring story.

So, having a purpose is not a *cranky* idea. Nor is having one that is not attainable, stupid as it sounds. It does not have to be attainable, and you must journey towards it as if it were!

The will-to-power

Whatever you choose as the aim or focus for your life, make sure that you can commit yourself to *accomplishment*, that it is not just a *nice idea*. I suggest you meditate on it. Try stating, in a few words, what you would like the focus of your life to be. It might sound something like these examples given by people on the course:

* To create a world where people are safe and where people are kind to each other without being afraid;
* to create a world where people truly love one another and can express themselves;
* to create a world where people are allowed to be themselves;
* to create a world where people can be accepted and loved; where people can and do communicate effectively; full of peace, love and harmony; where people are able to share and be open with each other;
* to have a world where everyone recognises their prejudices and can live in harmony;
* to empower people to communicate fully and celebrate their oneness;
* to enable people to live in harmony with their natural environment;
* to have a world where everyone has access to or the right to health;
* to have a world where everyone is spiritually prepared for death or another life;
* equality and respect for people and nature;
* to have a world where people are released from the constraints of their own egos;
* to have a planet that is unified in its purpose;
* where every being feels equal, regardless of colour, creed or race;
* where human beings live in harmony with nature and the universe;
* a world of simplicity, creativity and spiritual enlightenment;
* a world that is ecologically-balanced and sound;
* a world where everyone can achieve their potential;
* in all the universe, inner satisfaction for all beings;
* bring about world peace and world unity.

When you have formulated your own vision of how you would like the world to be, sit down quietly for a few minutes, close your eyes and see how the world, or life on the planet, would look if that mission were accomplished. My own purpose is to have a world where people live in harmony with each other and with nature.

When I tried out this meditation exercise, I saw people tearing up their passports and rushing joyously across borders to embrace each other and celebrate their oneness. Children played safely and freely in the streets, fields and parks. People took the locks off their doors and windows. Communities sprang up, where everyone looked after children and cared for each other. People exchanged their skills out of love for one another, so there was no need for money. Those who were in need were helped by those who had plenty. Weapons were destroyed, armament factories dismantled, natural alternative energy-sources were developed, and people smiled.

Then I drew a picture. Not a graphic representation of all of this, but a 'mood' picture. For this a box of pastel crayons is the best medium, because you can mix and 'smudge' the colours. A sheet of A5 paper is nice too, although A4 will do. Do not worry about 'not being an artist' or not being able to draw. Many people have a lot of beliefs about their artistic ability, and these beliefs are not the truth. This does not have to be a wonderful work of art that is worthy of being hung in the Royal Academy, or even in your living room. This is for you, and it does not matter what it looks like, as long as it represents your vision in some way.

Put your pastel crayons in front of you and, keeping your vision in mind, take out the first crayon that your eye is attracted to. Now let your hand do whatever it wants to with that colour. You might find it easier to use your left hand, or the non-dominant hand, whichever that is, to trick your mind a little. When you feel you have done all you want to with that colour, choose another one and work with that until you feel you have done what you want. Continue this process until the picture is complete.

When I did this I kept thinking I had finished, and then feeling that it wasn't really right, and adding more and more. I suddenly realised that I was doing one of my *this isn't good enough* routines, so I stopped. I am still not satisfied with the result, but I intend to give this picture a title, and hang it near my desk, so that I can be reminded of what I am here to do and be every day. I can also be reminded that I do not have to be *perfect* or *good enough*. Whatever I produce is okay, as long as I do what I can do.

So now that you have a sense of a purpose — an organising principle for your life — I can assure you that your life will become extraordinary. So many of us compromise our principles for money, for what we think is love, for status, or because we have no organising principle in our lives that allows us to create a context of principle-centredness. To pursue any of the purposes stated above would entail addressing those issues within yourself first. Held before you as a beacon to illuminate the darkness, your purpose will transform the most mundane tasks into acts of love and commitment. Washing up can become a way of expressing your love for the human race (and that always includes yourself first). If I wash up the dishes in the context of my purpose, I do this with a sense of excellence and high quality, with regards to hygiene, the environment, and the cleanliness of the dishes.

In my everyday life I attempt to be aware of my responses and reactions to provocation and complaints. I try not to be drawn into disputes unless it is to act as a mediator. I also try not to join in gossip sessions — but I do find this difficult! Having such a purpose does, however, make me far more conscious of what I am doing, and therefore I have more choice about whether I do it or not. I do practice communication, love and forgiveness as much as I possibly can. I do not find this easy. I think you will have realised by now that I frequently forget who I am, unlike the beings Emmanuel talked about, who never forget that they are beings of light. However, for me, having a purpose does jog my memory before too long.

Commitment to a purpose is a very powerful tool in creating possibilities in life and conquering fear. Once you have stated your intention, opportunities seem to open up to enable you to address yourself to your purpose. People seem to be drawn to you, and doors that seemed closed suddenly stand ajar. How and why does this happen? Perhaps we have ways of communicating that are just as powerful as speech that we are unaware of. With clear intent we send out clear instructions to people and the universe. If we are expressing one intent at a conscious level, but operating out of another, conflicting intent at an unconscious level then confusion abounds and nothing comes of it. If, however, the whole psyche is aligned then, as W H Murray says, "Providence moves too, all sorts of things occur to help one that would never otherwise have occurred". Just as people mirror back to us what we are putting out, so the universe reflects to us the intentions that we are expressing. When I have strongly held a vision I have been amazed at the events that have occurred to move me forward on my path.

Sometimes the things that occur do not look like opportunities, they look more like disasters — but if you look at them in the light of your purpose in life, and respond to them accordingly, it becomes clear that they have occurred to serve you — it just doesn't look that way at the time. I do not see anything that happens to me in my life as a 'mistake' or a 'disaster' I see it as an opportunity to re-appraise the situation and look at where I am going wrong. When things get really difficult this is not an easy thing to do, but any other way of coping with it does not work for me.

So you have a purpose and you can, within this context, make the filing, the sweeping up, the shopping, the shopkeeping, and other apparent chores, an expression of your love and commitment to the quality of life on the planet — and that might be all you need to do.

If you would like to do something else — perhaps have more exciting adventures — go further afield: try making a ten year plan. Within the context of your purpose, write down where you would like to be and what you would like to be doing in ten years' time. Do not allow the mind to step in at this point, with its reasonableness and caution. You do not have to do all this — it is only a game to play. Sit with your eyes closed and conjure up a vision of you and your life in ten years. Who will be with you? What will you be doing? Where will you be living and working? It does not matter how fantastical it seems, let it emerge and do not edit it.

Write it down. Now look at what you would have to be doing in five year's time in order to bring that about. Then look at what you need to do each year from now until then, to achieve your five-year aim. Do this in detail so that it looks something like the one below, which was based on the following purpose: *to empower people to participate fully in life and celebrate their oneness.*

Bob: *I put my personal life first.* (Bob is an architect). *I gave myself some terms of reference. The way to achieve that was to put the effort to working in the community, rather than working on commercial projects.*

In 2002: I will be encouraging communities to set up their own planning practices, and will have expanded into Europe; I will be re-appraising community practice and encourage communities to set up their own practices. Complete a book on community education projects and publish it. Give more time to lecturing and sharing knowledge. Get out of my original practice by giving more control to staff. I will be starting to pull out, because I will be getting to 61. I would do more lecturing. Review aims and self-growth, and put into practice whatever comes out.

2000: specialise in community education projects. Consolidate practice as community practice. Develop a model for independent community practices so other people will do same thing. Continue to lecture. Work on self-growth and take an active part in supporting others. Pass on what I learned.

1998: expand practice. More emphasis on community education projects. Reappraise aims and practice aims. Give lectures in the community. Encourage more community participation in self-building projects — encourage the community to plan their own environment. Continue own growth and review aims again.

1996: move offices and consolidate architectural practice. Continue study of educational needs. Start giving lectures on community architecture.

1995: move to a new home. Start a special study of educational needs. Give informal talks on this.

1994: set up a practice and concentrate on community architecture. Take an active part in Jean's seminars.

1993: study community architecture. Join public-speaking club to learn how to project myself.

As you can see, Bob did not follow the ten-year and five-year process I suggested above. He felt it was better to plan in two-year stages after the first four years. That is perfectly okay. Whatever works for you is fine. Actually this plan makes more sense if you look at it from the bottom to the top, but he did develop it the other way round. My own ten-year plan looks like this:

2002: I will be taking part in operating a holistic healing and educational centre, in an area just outside a large town, surrounded by woods and hills, and close to water. This can be a river, or lake, or both. The main building would be early Victorian or Georgian, giving a feeling of space and serenity. The centre will offer residential courses, and individual healing sessions offered by a variety of practitioners. It would incorporate a shop selling wholefood and organic products and a wholefood restaurant.

In the grounds there will be a school for psychologically-damaged children, and any other children who want to come, and a centre for old people which focuses on giving them a purpose for their lives. There will be a conference facility for businesspeople who want to develop ethical business practices. There will be a drop-in centre for anyone who wants support, and various groups operating to support people with specific problems — such as sexually-abused men and women, or couples having relationship problems.

Some people would live and work in the centre and others would work outside and live in. Other people would work in the centre and live elsewhere. Each living unit would have their own self-contained accommodation and there would be communal sitting, meeting and eating areas, so that the whole community could meet and eat together at least once a week. There would be a community meeting once a week to encourage open and effective communication.

I have put in my goal for ten years' time because I want to emphasise that it should be as detailed as you can make it. You need to be able to see it clearly and visualise how it could work. You do not have to be able to see exactly how you can do it at this stage, nor should you begin to feel that now you have written it down, it is a matter of life-and-death that you bring it about. Although I have written down my plans for the years prior to this, which include building up my business with my partner so that I can finance the development of this project, and applying for charitable status — not to mention writing and publishing more books, and adapting my work to the area of business (which we have already begun to do), I do not feel that I have to complete them. In fact I suggest that, once you have written down in fine detail what you intend to do, that you throw it away, or at least put it somewhere out of sight!

If this sounds contradictory (since I suggested you keep your purpose somewhere in view), I can assure you it is not. I do not want to give your mind more ammunition with which to criticise you, and put you under pressure. It really feels threatening to put my ten-year plan into print, because I feel it gives the people who read it the opportunity to test me out. I can imagine someone writing to me, or ringing me up in ten years' time and saying, 'Well — did you do it then?' and if I say *no*, replying, 'Well you are not much of an example, are you? No point in listening to you!'. Well I guess I will just have to take that risk, because, although I have every intention of making this happen, I have no *investment* in it — no attachment to the outcome.

My ten-year plan in 1982 was to become a professor at the university. Instead, here I am in 1992, no longer an employee of that establishment, let alone a professor. Having that as my ten-year plan was, however, very useful, as I soon realised that it was not the direction I really wanted to follow. Because I wrote it down, and declared that it was my intention, I was motivated to find out what I needed to do in order to become a professor — and when I found out, I soon saw that I was not willing to do it! The reality was that writing research papers, attracting research money and sitting on numerous committees (the functions of university professors) was not my cup of tea at all. It would have driven me insane! I wanted the influence I thought the position would bring me, without all the trouble of doing what it would take to get there. So I gave up that one pretty quickly!

The next ten-year plan was for Tim and I to own and run a private school — a therapeutic community which would be based on similar principles to the courses I now run. When we went into it, however, we realised that we were not willing to take the financial risk involved. We did not want to do it enough, it seems, and so that dream came to nothing. But it was all a useful experience.

It showed me, for instance, that I had to enrol a lot of other people in the project — we could not do it on our own. That meant that we would have to consider sharing our lives with a group of people and, for me, it meant relinquishing the notion of *being in charge*. We also learned a lot about what it would take to set up a school and finance that sort of operation. We learned a lot about ourselves too! So both these plans were 'successful' in the obsolete meaning of the word, since there was an outcome. The major outcome was that I gave up my job at the university, and am now concentrating my energy on developing this work for the general public and for businesses.

Many of us do not want to dream, and if we do we are careful to keep our dreams to ourselves, in case we fail and end up with egg on our faces. However, as I said above, in order to succeed with our dreams we need to be bold enough to share them with others, who might want to support us in having them come true. As Goethe said, *'Whatever you can do, or dream you can do, begin it. Boldness has genius, power and magic in it. Begin it now.'*

Changing your purpose and ten year plan

As you can see, I have changed my ten year plan twice over the last ten years, and this might look as though I had no real commitment to it in the first place. That is not so. It was only because I had a commitment to it that I discovered it would not work. I could have spent the next twenty years at the university, declaring that I wanted to be a professor and moaning because *they* would not give me promotion. This is what many people (including me in the past) spend their time doing.

There is no harm in changing your ten-year plan, once it becomes obvious that it is not what you really want. However, here is a cautionary note: be really clear why you are abandoning your plan, and tell the truth about it. If you are abandoning it because you are too frightened to tackle it, that is okay, as long as you know that this is the reason. It is important to be authentic in your approach to this exercise, and that requires that you search for your true motives.

Tim and I were clear when we abandoned our school plan, that we did not have the knowledge required to set up a business, and that we did not have the courage to borrow a very large sum of money at that time. We also saw that we were not willing to find out how to set up and run a business either. It would probably have been very foolish and irresponsible of us to do so under the circumstances. I was really clear that I only thought I wanted a professorship, but I had not really considered what that meant in terms of the type of work I would have to do, first of all in order to get promotion, and secondly in order to carry out the job.

It might well be that I will discover in a few years' time that my current ten-year plan is inappropriate too, but at the moment I have a total commitment to bringing it about. It is that commitment which makes the difference.

Something at stake and nothing at stake

One of the many things that could get in the way of bringing your dreams into reality, apart from life-problems that could intervene, is that we do not make an important *distinction*. In one of the seminars produced by the *Centres Network*, Werner Erhard drew attention to the fact that there are two areas of operation which we need to define and identify. The two domains are headed *Something at Stake* and *Nothing at Stake*. A great deal of pain and upset in people's lives comes from the failure to draw this distinction. This is because of the very different nature of these two domains, and the behaviour that is appropriate to each of them. I think you will see what I mean as I proceed.

In the domain of *Nothing at Stake*, what is appropriate is to do exactly what you feel like doing, and do not do anything you do not feel like doing. Various things would come into this category — taking a vacation, leisure time, or sex, for instance. These are situations where you should do only what you feel like doing, and do nothing that you do not want to do. I had to laugh when I heard this. I wonder how many people do sex that way? Most of us seem to do what we think will please the other person, or what we think the other person wants us to do, or what we read in a book is the right thing to do.

Vacations do not fare much better. I remember going on a cycling holiday and thinking that I must go out on my bicycle, whether I felt like it or not, because that is what I said I would be doing. How many people, I wonder, sit baking on beaches, sweat pouring off them, risking skin cancer and suffering blisters, because they have to go back with a tan? Isn't that what you are *supposed* to do on holiday?

How many times have I gone to parties because I thought I *ought* to, even when it was the last thing I felt like doing? We human beings are crazy — aren't we? Of course, like everything else, it is not that simple. In going to a party there might well be something at stake. If someone has gone to a great deal of trouble to make arrangements, hire rooms and make food, it is disrespectful to cancel an arrangement because you no longer feel like going.

In those circumstances I would say there was *something at stake*. What would be at stake would be the time and commitment that the other person was giving to me. My reliability would be at stake. My word would be at stake. *Who am I?* would be at stake. If we could not rely on anyone to keep their word if they had accepted an invitation, then I guess not many of us would entertain people.

However, what we can do is seriously consider whether going to the party is something that we really *want* to do, and if we don't, then we should not accept the invitation in the first place. Most people do accept invitations because they do not want to say *no*. What is at stake is the other person's opinion of us. So we say *yes*, and then let them down anyway.

In the domain of *something at stake*, feelings are irrelevant. We do what we said we would do, what we made a commitment to do. We take a stand that something at stake, something that matters, is significant, and then we keep our word, and feelings do not come into it. It is a matter of ignoring the parrot and taking the next step, whatever that might be. According to Werner Erhard:

> People devoted to spontaneity think it means something that they don't feel like doing a particular thing. They think it means something more than the mere fact that they don't feel like doing it.

This penchant we have for allowing our feelings to dictate our actions is often devastating to our relationships. It leads to people losing trust in others and becoming isolated and unsociable. It is also disempowering, because we have no faith in our own ability to fulfil the promises we make, or carry out the tasks that we have committed ourselves to undertake. This becomes very clear when people are asked to make the promises we ask for at the beginning of the course. People do not trust themselves to make promises because they know how easily they can be seduced into breaking their word — mostly by their own feelings and thought-processes.

Many people I deal with — students, children, course participants — are amazed when they 'reasonably' tell me they are not going to do something, because they don't want to, or don't feel like it, and I say, 'Yes, so what? What difference does it make that you don't feel like it? Why do you think your feelings are significant?' I assure you that I would never get out of bed any morning if I considered my feelings, because, these days, I never feel like waking up, let alone getting up!

So in the domain of *something at stake* you are authentic only when you are principle-centred — you live according to your organising principles and are true to yourself. In my experience, when I do not draw this distinction between these two situations, I do not derive much pleasure or joy from life.

I should point out here that both these domains are necessary, and each supports the other. It is necessary to go on vacation sometimes, otherwise life could get very draining. However if life was one long holiday it would probably become pretty meaningless. I once read a play in which a man was granted three wishes, and wished, carelessly, for a month of Sundays. By the time the month was up he was extremely bored. So balance is what is needed, and the awareness of the difference between these two areas of our lives.

Pursuing a career

Another problem, which arises when people are creating a purpose for their lives, is their livelihood. It is often too daunting a prospect for many people to consider changing their job, particularly if it is one that required them to study for specific qualifications. Many of the purposes outlined above are obviously compatible with the 'caring professions'. But what if you work in a factory, or in insurance? How do you heal the world from those positions?

It is not impossible if you come from a position of *service*. If you begin to operate within your business in a completely ethical manner, several things will happen. You will influence others, and you will attract customers. If you do it *in order to* attract customers, it will not work. It will not work, because no matter how hard you try to convince yourself that you are serving others, if that is not the case, people will smell a rat. If you consider how best to serve your customers in the sense of honouring them and doing for them what is in their best interests, then you will automatically attract people to you, because you will be living authentically.

In the work-place you can also live authentically and serve those who are your managers or employers, as well as your peers or helpers. This does not mean that you become *servile*, but that you honour those you are serving and do for them what is in their best interests. It is not in their best interests to allow them to exploit you and manipulate you, so you do not allow this to happen. If you worked in a factory you might turn your attention to the way in which the factory disposes of waste, whether they use re-cycled paper in their offices, or how much responsibility they give to the work force. There are many many ways of participating in work which could be aligned with a life-purpose.

If this is not enough many people find it satisfying to get involved in voluntary work of some kind. This is a very good way of finding out if you do want to change your direction and train for something else. One accountant I know became a *Relate* counsellor. He did this for quite a while, on a part-time basis, and then decided that he really did want to continue in accountancy and look at how he could have his business truly serve people.

So, as Emmanuel says, you do not need to give up everything and do great deeds. It is possible to carry on your lives in pretty much the same way. Having a purpose will change your whole orientation to life and the way in which you participate with others. Your life really can become a splendid torch that will light the darkness of the world, and allow you to leave life feeling 'thoroughly used up', knowing that you put everything you had into the time you spent on the planet, this time around!

12. *Out of the chrysalis — the continuing process of evolution*

I have written a book called Grist for the Mill. *It is a book which specifically talks about how to use all of our daily-life experience in order to awaken. It's all 'grist to the mill'. All of your life, all your social roles, your physical illnesses, your losses, your gains, all is grist for the mill . . . Each of us not only has our own karmic predicament, but we have our own way of awakening, and I can't tell you my way is any better than any other way. My way is a way of loving service, but the loving service must be done without any attachment to the fruits of the act . . . You take your existential situation, your children, your loneliness, your sickness, your age, and you use it all as the vehicle for becoming free, because that is the only reason you are here . . . The end result of a being that is free of attachment is not someone who doesn't look like anyone else. You are not going to end up looking like Buddha, or Christ or St Theresa, you are going to end up being just who you are, except with no clinging. It's not that you get rid of your neuroses, it's just that they become irrelevant. Keep in mind that the end is nothing special . . . You are it — you are just busy thinking you are not.*

(Ram Dass, 1977)

This is it!

'The end is nothing special', says Ram Dass, 'You are it!'. He could have added, 'and this is it!', because I know that to be true. There is nowhere to get to, this really *is it*. As he says, the problem is, we are all busy thinking we are not and it is not — *it*, that is. In other words everything that happens and everything we do is what needs to happen, and how it needs to be in order for us to get to the next step in our journey. All this may seem to be enlightened smart-talk — one of those truisms that we all agree to sagely, without really having a clue what they mean. I would like to explore this a little by talking about my students at the university.

When my students carry out their final teaching practice they usually can't wait until the end of the eight weeks or so they are in school. They are quite shocked when I remind them that finishing their teaching practice is only the beginning of the next forty years or so of teaching. Like everyone else they are busy waiting for the learning to be over so that they can get on with life for real.

Well, there is no practice for life and there really is no practice for teaching, or anything else. You are doing it for real, no matter what you call it. And the way you are doing it is the way it is. For me life does not get any better, nor does it get any easier, it just makes more sense and seems more handleable. When I realise that everything that happens is simply part of the learning process, then I can stop trying to get it right and be perfect — when I can realise this, of course!

I am constantly being reminded, however, that I still have a mind that functions in much the same way that it learned to function, all those years ago in my childhood. I recently had a letter from a client (who has become very dear to me), thanking me for the work I had done with her. It made me cry. I feel extremely sad when I realise that I cannot always be so generous, so loving, so committed to people. But, when I am generous, it makes such a difference in the world.

I spend much time comparing my day-to-day self with my working, much more conscious, or spiritual self, and the everyday me does not come out too favourably. In particular I find it difficult to be my spiritual self with the one person I am committed to most of all — Tim. My relationship with him sometimes does not feel like *it*, at all!

I read Susan Jeffers' book *Opening our Hearts to Men* with resistance which bordered on anger. I found myself refusing to believe that this woman could be so loving and non-judgemental of her partner all the time. What was she, some kind of saint, or something? I guess I felt pretty inadequate as, once more, I ran my comparison tape. Was I fit to write books if I could not be as enlightened, as compassionate? Mind you, Susan Jeffers had received a great lesson — she contracted cancer of the breast and that is what enabled her to address her anger with men, and 'open up her heart' to them.

Is it going to take that degree of suffering to make me learn? I sincerely hope not, but I am slow in this area — although I am learning. I have noticed that I do not always have to point out to Tim how he is doing things and correct him — not always. And not nearly as often as I did only six months ago.

Instant enlightenment — *from time to time*

There was a time when I felt totally enlightened, just after doing the *EST Training*. I was in love with the world and I felt totally loving and open. It did not last. I think, in some ways that this euphoric experience did me no favours, as I have been inclined to compare my life with this phase ever since, and think that nothing else is *it*.

So the statement from Ram Dass at the beginning of this chapter gives me heart, because it reminds me that I do not have to live up to a formula for the enlightened being in order to be perfect. I am perfect already, just the way I am — and it is very hard to remember that!

I had a really good lesson in this respect only yesterday. Tim and I made love — and, guess what, it was not perfect. In fact it was hugely disappointing for me. I notice I do not want to go into the details as it is too *personal*, not to mention the fact that I do not come out of it looking *enlightened*, or on a par with Susan Jeffers — but I will carry on anyway.

We were practising our tantric sex, *being* with each other, breathing together and so on. I was just beginning to really get into this, when a delivery man knocked at the door and we had to stop in a hurry! He was an hour earlier than he had said he would be. I remember thinking, 'Oh well, that's it, we are just fated where sex is concerned. We were obviously not meant to do this'. I recognised that this was not exactly enlightened thinking. Total victim stuff, in fact — *the world is doing it to me*. So when Tim suggested that we could get back into bed and resume, I agreed.

Minds being what they are, I was busy being in bed with Tim *and* thinking about the piece of furniture that had just been delivered. What would I use to strip it with? How could we replace the marble top that he had broken during delivery? Didn't we do well to get it for that price? You know how the parrot goes. Instead of saying, 'look Tim, I don't think this is working for me', I carried on — or the bit of me that wasn't working on the piece of furniture did.

Tim suddenly started to get excited and carried-away. I remember thinking at the time, 'I could stop him and should stop him, because he isn't with me at all', which is small wonder, because I certainly wasn't with him, but I let him carry on to a climax. For the rest of the day I was angry. I started to find fault with Tim and snap at him. I started to wonder what I was doing with him. Finally I had the thought that I clearly wasn't capable of having a sexual relationship with anyone, and I should release him from his contract with me. I said as much.

He was not too happy with this news. It took me another two hours to get round to saying to him that I was actually very hurt, and felt very used during our session that morning. The problem I had with this is that I know Tim is extremely sensitive about sex, and I did not want him to start beating himself up for being selfish. Of course that is just what he did do. However I knew that I could have stopped him, and so I pointed this out to him. It is almost as though part of me wants to make men wrong, and find an excuse for not participating in sex.

Tim looked at what he had been doing, and acknowledged that, at the time, he had not been in touch with me, he was carried away with his own bodily responses. I did a lot of crying, probably not enough, as I told him how *used* I felt, acknowledging, at the same time, that I could have stopped that happening and did not do so. How can I expect Tim to know how I am feeling if I am determined not to tell him or indicate this to him in any way? Maybe that resistance comes from the hopelessness of my past history: *'here we go again, this is what it is all about, men only think about themselves . . .* '. I am heavily programmed with all that stuff and sometimes I give in to it. This is progress, because at one time I gave in to it constantly. I felt better when I had told him, but something in my head said, 'no more'.

The following morning Tim turned to me and said, 'Let's have a hug'. At this point I wanted to be cold and rejecting. Didn't he get the message? Instead I noticed all those thoughts and turned to him and hugged him. I had to smile. You see, my body was harbouring no resentment about sex, about Tim, or about anything else. I noticed I did not want to let myself be aware of it, but my body felt really sexy, it was just my mind that was saying, 'no way, I'm not going to be turned on around this man, or any other, ever again.'

No, we did not make love, but I let go of all my resentment, and I have opened up my heart to the possibility that maybe sex is not a thing of the past for me, and that perhaps I don't need to encourage Tim to go and find a relationship with someone who is not screwed up about it — if such a one indeed exists! So it is truly, all *grist to the mill*, as Ram Dass says. But it would not be so if I had not learned that my thoughts are not *me* — it would be disaster, tragedy, the end of 'another beautiful friendship'!

I find Ram Dass encouraging, because sometimes I find myself wondering who I am, whether I am kidding myself, whether all of this work I do is necessary, and what on earth is it all for? I am reminded by Ram Dass that it is about being free. So do I know what he really means by that? No I do not, but I do have a *sense* of it, and from time to time I have an experience of freedom from attachment.

As he says, I do not experience having dealt with my neuroses — I just experience that they, at those moments, hold no significance. I also know that I can disengage my thoughts, and live in the moment without allowing myself to be dictated to by my parrot-mind. Those are moments when I feel truly powerful. Those moments are becoming more and more accessible to me.

In fact they became available to me the morning after the hug with Tim. We did make love, and I assure you I had to be extremely clear that I was not my thoughts — since I was deeply into the thought that I should not be trying this again, as it would all lead to disappointment, and end up like it did the previous time.

Well I won: Jean 1 — Mind 0. And we had a great time!

Oh, of course there are still many times when I am still trying to be *somebody*, as Ram Dass would put it. My *somebody training* was pretty thorough — as with many others. You know, that *somebody* that you were taught you ought to be, in order to get the love that you needed. But those times are diminishing. Lots of situations come along that are tempting: writing a book is one of them. Now I might really get to be *somebody*!

But I can laugh at myself for my fantasies of fame and fortune, and get on with the job of sharing my journey with you, in the hope that you will benefit as much as I have from the wisdom I myself have learned from others. And added to, in my own way.

So, healing the wounded inner child, dealing with the toxic shame, recovering from the damage we have incurred in our passage through life — it all takes time. Do not be impatient and do not give in. Simply see that everything that happens is, as Ram Dass says, *grist to the mill.*

Some experiences from felslow learners

Originally, I thought I would end this book by including some statements from people who had taken my courses, or who had had other, similar learning experiences, to demonstrate the benefits that can accrue from following this path. I felt that a useful source of information would be the magazine that I produced for people who have taken my courses. Most of this consists of 'shares' from people who want to let others know how they are getting on.

There are those, of course, who speak only of the good things that have happened, and how they are feeling great, but somehow those did not seem appropriate. I do not want this to sound like an advertising slot for my work. I want, instead, to demonstrate the courage that it takes and the commitment that is necessary if we are to begin to realise who we are and what our journey in life is about. What it takes, in other words, to start to be free.

This extract comes from someone who took my course after years of therapy, having been an alcoholic for quite a while. I make no apology for the length of it, or for the length of the other extracts I include. Some of these 'shares' are, I think, brilliant, and express far more explicitly than I can the experiences of the people concerned, as they deal with their frustration and the dawning realisation that healing is a delicate process which does not always yield the results we think we ought to have.

I would like to share with you the singer's words that have been echoing in my head all day: Don't push too far, your dreams are china in your hands . . . *The more I hummed to the wisdom of this sentiment the more I realised how powerful it is.*

If anything that is precious and of real value is held too tightly, it can so easily be crushed and destroyed, especially if it is caught by the grip of fear. Like the gentle

breath of a silent wish, a dream is a fragile entity. Part of its purpose must surely be to exist as a course of great inspiration.
In truth I have been extremely disappointed with myself, for having achieved so little of what I dreamed possible after completing the level one course of the Seminars, in September 1989. Where, pray, is this person that I hoped and dreamed I was capable of becoming? Still hiding in her chrysalis — that's where! Nice and safe.

This person goes on to say that in the process of applying for a new job (which was a breakthrough for her in itself), she had to look back on the last few years of her life.

The full horror of those empty, cold, lonely and painful journeys fills me with a sense of great unease even as I write.
However, I have accepted that I cannot have a 'psychiatric history' that spans 25 years of a 35 year life and suddenly kiss the sorrow goodbye and be a free spirit. At least I *can't — it would take more strength and courage than I possess to do this!*
I ceased to feel frustrated with myself when I was recently guided towards re-understanding that the whole *adult cannot emerge unless the damaged child within has been healed. I had been* pushing too far, *trying desperately by conscious reasoning to force myself in a direction that my wounded subconscious was not yet ready for me to take. What was it Othello said, 'How poor are they that have no patience — for what wound did ever heal except by degrees?'*
I have always known and understood that we are all in pain. The nature of its infliction matters not. Pain hurts, however it may be caused. To live, *by definition, means to incur some damage along the way. Whether it is in the form of a physical disability, or the emotional turmoil caused when our most intimate relationships are not working as well as we hoped. Be it the grief caused when someone dear to us dies, or the inescapable mental torment we might experience at times . . .*
I would like with empathy and humility to acknowledge you all. Moving within the circles that now surround my life enables me to enjoy a wealth of compassion, understanding, tolerance, kindness, support — more unconditional love than I have ever known. It is thanks to you that the 'healing process' has begun. After all is said and done, it is only by watching other butterflies that I can learn how to use my own wings — once I have found them, that is.
So if there are those among you who may be feeling angry or despondent with yourselves for not moving forward *as fast as you would have wished, please join in the chorus so we can sing in harmony:*
'Don't push too far, your dreams are china in your hands . . . '

This person can trace most of her problems to being sent to boarding school, where she tried desperately to be who she thought she ought to be, true to her *somebody training*. Susan Jeffers (1992) suggests that we should take the *Everybody Training*, where we learn that our sense of self can only come from what we can contribute to others, rather than from trying to get a sense of *somebodiness* from our relationships. This is not a task that can be accomplished by reading one, or even several books, and/or by taking courses — no matter how profound or how effective. Some of these books and courses can and do offer the wisdom we need to nurture ourselves back to health or wholeness, but using this wisdom in our daily lives — remembering, consistently who we really are — demands constant practice, with large doses of humility and compassion for oneself.

Another of my course participants describes his journey over the last nine or ten years and, as you can see, he has not found it easy, but he does get a sense that he is progressing, slowly and sometimes painfully. What I like about this letter is that it possesses the other vital ingredient to the recipe for development: humour!

It is about nine years since I went to a pub in Kenilworth and met a woman who wore tight denim jeans that showed off a very nice bum. During the evening she engaged me in a weird conversation about some kind of course she had just completed in London . . . What she had to say made very little sense to me, but memories of her bum stayed with me over the next few days and I phoned her. One thing did not lead to another, but instead to an invitation to her home to hear more about the course she had been on.

*My main problem in those days was the inability to say 'no', especially to attractive women. Weeks later I went on a workshop at Warwick University which she set up for the Centres Network in London. For days after this course I walked round in a daze, sporting large eyes and a silly grin. In the months and years that followed I did many more Centres Network courses. Jean Bond (*she of the lovely bum) *had also established a support group for the victims of these courses; more, she began to develop her own personal development courses. I stayed on the periphery but was occasionally ensnared into doing more courses, sometimes assisting, occasionally leading support group meetings. As personal development goes I suppose I must now be somewhere around the Ph.D. level!*

But never once, during these nine years, have I experienced enlightenment.

Very often during these nine years I have experienced depression, even despair. Worse, certain aspects of my personality, which had hitherto remained insignificant to myself and others, began to appear all too often. I became known as Mr Angry. One friend who I'd made via the support group told me that he had never ever witnessed such a degree of anger without it resulting in physical violence. My health suffered. Until 1983 I had never been inside a hospital except to visit. Since 83 I have been hospitalised three times. The last nine years have been, by and large, the unhealthiest of my life. Prior to these courses my marriage had been rather like a comfortable room, the walls covered in thick, clever wallpaper,

comfortable, spacious, but somewhat empty. Now it began to deteriorate, cracks began to appear, not only in the wallpaper but in the floor and ceiling.
Whenever I tried to 'enlighten' my family, my wife especially, to point out where I thought they were going wrong, the reactions and responses just caused rows and made me very . . . ANGRY! *I drifted away from old friends. It seems they found me difficult to understand, or I saw for the first time how sad, desperate, even tragic their lives were. I was happy for them to drift away because I no longer knew how to communicate with them in a way that was not threatening or uncomfortable on both sides. I stopped playing the guitar, stopped writing songs, poems; creatively I felt in a barren desert.*
But recently I have had a sense of it all coming together.
I used to say that once you have experienced one of these personal development courses, your life will never be the same . . . My own experience has been that the initial courses gave me a sense that there were alternative perspectives available to me; that my psychology was so deeply ingrained that I could and would regress without ever realising it; that there were people around who I could trust. My first course, therefore was just the first step.
Over the years I have sought and found other people to support and guide me. In addition I have the very real friendship and support from so many lovely people connected with the support group. Every course, every consultation, every call for help, when I have been lost and stuck, has been just another step along the way.
Nine years of slow and painful progress. I don't mean the shouting and the crying when I've let go *or got in touch with some trauma of forty years ago. Small potatoes that. No. I mean the pain of months and years of very gradual change. No longer the highs of music and affairs to lift me from the seeming desert I thought I was in.*
Most of these nine years I have felt just that — in a vast, endless, barren desert in which the few oases only served to indicate how vast that desert was. These years of 'breaking through', bit by bit, of never feeling that I was in sight of peace, tranquillity; never able to make sense of who I was or what I should do. All that pain and never a sense of enlightenment.
But recently I have a sense of it all coming together. No miracle. No stupendous breakthrough. Just connecting much of what I have learned about myself these last nine years. I know now where the anger, the frustration, the resentment come from. I understand why it is that I protect my inner self from the outside world. Why it is that I walk in perpetual fear. I know too what a tremendous loss I have suffered by hiding away the person who I once was, all these years.
For the first time I see the possibility of transcending my ground of being, that I may not have to remain the victim of my psychology and its tyrannical grip. I don't know how to do that — I just sense the possibility, and even that, right now, lightens me a little. I know that no-one, not any of the teachers or therapists I have had, is ever going to hand me the magic elixir, rid me of my psychology. Only I can do that. But I know I can never do it (or anything else for that matter) alone.

They, and all the lovely people I've met and befriended via *courses and groups can and will help me. They do it by nurturing and nourishing me, by reflecting back my anger, my resentment, my frustration, through their love, wisdom, experience and learning. Eventually, I even realised that I am worth all of that, worth it because we are all one. So don't ask me what 'enlightenment' is. I haven't a clue!*
Nine years on I wonder what my life might have been if I had not phoned back the owner of the lovely bum. I don't think I've achieved anything particularly significant. I don't feel fulfilled. For most of that time I haven't felt any different. Only recently have I felt different, when some of the pieces have started to connect. But I can see that, for me, there was no other way than the way I chose. For me, once I'd taken that first step there was no turning back. Perhaps one day I'll look back and feel glad I took that step!
And the next nine years? More open, I think. Open to allow more of the real me *to come out — that gentle loving person, that awe-struck exuberant child. Even those close to me haven't seen either of those. Open to allow people in, especially people like my gentle loving and oh-so-patient wife. Perhaps a book of all I've gone through this last nine years* — From Fuck to Stuck to Luck with Pluck.
I experience the possibility.

When this person met me he was impressed by my 'bum'. When I met him I was alarmed by his appearance. Although attractive, his hands shook perceptibly, he chain-smoked and he looked as though a good night's sleep would not do him any harm. He seemed a permanent *cheerful Charlie*, although I know now that is not how he really was — that was just his *act*.

As he suggests in the letter, he was also consistently unfaithful to his wife and happily disregarding of the way this hurt her. He swooped from hyper-highs to extreme lows. I think he will not mind me saying that he is now more real, more honest, more *him* — and he doesn't smoke any more. So I am glad he took that step, and I think that he is too.

So is the next person I include in this section. It is someone that I wrote about earlier in the book, Ruth, who had been severely sexually abused as a very young child. This person suffered excessive damage and, as you will see, thought that she had little chance of leading a 'normal' life. I felt that letting you hear from her would give encouragement to those of you who feel that you have a long way to go and a great deal of healing to do.

In the past year she has married and had a wonderful little girl, who is, without any shadow of doubt, an angel. I saw her when she was a few hours old and she is definitely a 'letter from home', as Emmanuel would say. What a gift my client has given us all in this child! I think that the message contained in this letter is evidence for all of us that it is possible for the most severe damage to be healed, and that it does not have to take a lifetime before we are healed sufficiently to allow us to lead effective lives.

I've sat here for half an hour — thinking and reflecting on where I am and I've drawn a huge flow diagram with 'ME' in the middle and all sorts of arrows shooting off — me the teacher, me the new mother, me the wife . . .
And I'm really feeling quite proud of myself — for being all of these for other people. Before I worked with you I really had reached the point of believing life wasn't worth struggling with. Now I see one word in letters six feet high, CHOICE— *that's what working though all my past history has shown me. I have a choice — no, thousands of choices, or opportunities and freedom in my life. Before, I was trapped — trapped by my guilt, my shame and my denial of who I am. I am an adult who was abused as a child. Now that I can* own *my past, I am free to embrace the future — truly a wonderful gift. Thank you.*

Sometimes it seems that it is difficult for us to see how we have changed. I know that it is difficult for me to remember how I used to be — the aggression, the control, the need always to be right, the constant anger about everything. Above all, the unawareness of all that. My client has the same problem it seems, as she needed to ask other people whether they thought she had changed.

When I asked other people, friends and my husband, how I've changed, if they think I have, I was delighted by the overwhelming 'yes' as an answer. Everyone I spoke to said I am more relaxed and a lot more fun, I laugh a lot more — at myself mostly! For my part I feel more centred, more in touch with life. I no longer observe *life and* plan *it like I used to. Beforehand, I was terrified of being* found out *— or of making a mistake. Now I'm too busy living life to worry (well, 80% of the time, anyway!). Of course there are still* bad days, *when I feel insecure, inadequate, unlovable, but these pass quicker, and I am at least aware of them for what they are — ghosts from the past. All around me there is evidence of the true me — now — and I'm learning to believe in myself.*

This next person, however was in no doubt about the changes the course had made to her life.

I'd like to share with you my thoughts on the course. In short it has proved both revelationary and revolutionary.
Revelationary because you have helped me see myself and others as they really are for the first time ever, and revolutionary because my relationships with everyone have completely changed. In fact, it's only now I feel I'm actually engaged in true relationships with all the people in my life.
The knowledge and insight I've come away with from the course is something I've been desperately seeking for probably the last 22 of my 26 years. I've known for this long that 'something' wasn't quite right — either with me or with the world

— 'something' that was almost impossible to put into words. The words which went some way to explain were 'longing', 'hurting', 'aching', 'misery', 'desperation', 'self-hate and disgust', 'withdrawal', 'living at the North Pole', 'is this all there is?' These feelings formed the basis of any others I allowed myself to have, such as happiness and sorrow, and were impossible to shake off.
It's only now that I can be properly free of these feelings and understand why I couldn't escape them before. I now see myself and everyone around me totally differently. I can now be honest, fair and respectful with myself and treat others in the same way. The results of this have been amazing. I'm relating to people and they to me just as — in fact probably better than — I'd always wanted, and now I see why it couldn't be like this before.
Since the first weekend on the course, all this has seemed so easy, effortless and natural. The whole experience has been quite joyful. I have only just started on my journey, but I am determined that my lid's never going back on!

Support groups and networks

One thing I want to emphasise is the importance of support. I know I have said this earlier, but I want to repeat it. Almost every letter I receive, telling me of the progress people are making, the problems that they conquer, the fears they overcome, the successes they experience, all reiterate the importance of having people around them who offer unconditional love, who listen, who care and who give them effective support.

I don't know why it is, but we *civilised* human beings seem to be deeply suspicious of *groups*. When I set up a social group for single and divorced people many years ago, I was quite surprised by the sneering condescension that many people had towards belonging to such a group. A typical comment was that it was 'all right for those who needed it, but I have friends of my own'. Men especially seemed to think that joining a group indicated that you were socially incompetent and inadequate as a male. *Let's face it, all you had to do was go down the pub, wasn't it?* That's where you met your mates. Women were a little more accepting of the need for a group set-up. It was not so easy for them to *go down the pub*, even in this liberated era. They were still seen as *easy prey* by many of the men who were there.

I have not heard many supportive conversations taking place between men in pubs. I don't think now that the group I set up was particularly supportive either, but people did care for each other, especially when members were ill, or had experienced rejection.

I am a strong advocate of support groups. I know that the support I have received over the years has enabled me to keep on growing and learning in an atmosphere of love and concern that has made the process much less painful. In times of fear and pain I have always had many people to turn to, who somehow enabled me to move forward and tackle the obstacle in front of me. I want to say now, *thank you* to them all! They know who they are; my friends, my clients, my students, my teachers, my relatives and of course, definitely not least, Tim.

And I want to urge you all to consider the importance of developing for yourselves a network of support around you to assist you on your journey. It is not difficult. One way is to do a few of these 'weird' courses, make sure you tell your friends and neighbours about them so that they have the opportunity to do them too, and, lo and behold you will find that you belong to a community of wonderful, supportive and loving friends!

That is what happened to me and it is what happened to many of the other people that I am now associated with. Marilyn Ferguson (1982) mentions the emergence of support networks as a significant feature of the present age of spiritual growth, and she similarly stresses the importance of making new connections as some of the old friendships we had no longer seem appropriate to the new direction of our lives.

The next extract from the *Quest* magazine comes from someone who has seen the need for a strong support network. She is part of my support system and it is extremely helpful to me to have her around. Prior to taking courses of this nature she was extremely suspicious of *groups*, and still is, of course! But now she does not pay much attention to her suspicions.

Within eighteen months of taking the course I had transformed my dead-end job into a rewarding career, and doubled my income. I recently gave it up to become an undergraduate student, in order to further develop my career. I got married, and my partner and I between us have built a supportive, loving partnership which brings us fun. My sister, who I hadn't seen for over twelve months, turned into the best friend I've ever had. I totally committed myself to my little nephew, who has since brought me more joy than I ever expected life could hold for me. Not bad value for a two weekend course!

For those people who don't know me I must stress at this point that I am not some kind of wonder-woman who achieves with ease, and people who do know me will laugh at the very idea! I am someone who manages to work diligently and conscientiously to maintain an air of depression in even the most euphoric of environments, and I can be relied upon to perceive the negative in the most positive of situations — in short, where gloom is, I am to be found. What I am trying to say is that if my *life can work then* anybody's *can.*

However I did not achieve my present, dare I be rash and use the word 'happy', life from the course alone. The difference was made from being involved with people who had also experienced the course. Day-to-day sharing of experiences of life, and day-to-day love, compassion and empathy can heal even the deepest and most painful of wounds. I know this is really possible because it has happened for me. That's not to say that people can only be supportive friends if they have done courses; I was lucky enough to have several wonderful friends and I still have them. But people brave enough to tell the truth about life don't grow on trees, and doing courses and being involved in support groups is one way of meeting lots of them. The more people we have around us who are willing to share their experiences of life, the more we can learn, and thus have a happy stay while we are in this world.

The next person whose contribution I include also recognises the power and importance to his growth of support groups, despite the fact that he lived alone for many years. He was extremely sceptical about doing a course with a large number of people, especially people he had nothing in common with. He is an extremely intelligent, well-educated man who found himself on a course with people who were unemployed, not exactly *well read,* and obviously *not his cup of tea* at all.

I think this letter demonstrates not only the transformative power of such groups, but the speed with which people can get in touch with their connectedness, no matter how resistant and cynical they might be initially. I know that working with a group is far more effective over a short period of time than working in a one-to-one situation, although the latter is sometimes necessary. The person who wrote this next contribution had, in fact, been having individual therapy sessions for two or three years prior to taking the course.

I did the first course in June 1989 and found it one of the most moving and rewarding experiences of my life. I remember that when I first joined the group my heart sank into my boots; did anyone seriously think that I was going to bare my soul to a group of people who seemed to have nought to the power of nought in common with ME?

It just goes to show how wrong you (I mean I, *don't I?) can be. I wouldn't have believed it possible that during two weekends I would see people's lives change before my eyes, nor that in such a short space of time I could come to feel lasting ties of friendship and respect for each and everyone, in what had started out as a random group of strangers; still less that I could have shed tears in public in front of them, without feeling the least ashamed.*

Nonetheless I can't say that I now walk serenely possessed of wondrous new powers of love for my fellow beings; obviously I haven't achieved the same breakthrough as some other people I know. The period after the course is particularly difficult; it's as if I have been shown the key to a new life, but can't quite work it by myself yet.

After experiencing the power of the group it's agony trying to recreate that sense of empowerment within myself, by myself. In fact I feel as if I'm having to pull myself up out of a swamp by my own bootstraps. It's easy to lapse back into all the old habits, and so difficult to generate that dynamism I found in the group that made me believe — really believe — that I could break free.

So what's to do? I've noticed that the best way to recharge my batteries with purpose and energy is simply to contact other people who have done the course. The support groups that Howard has organised in London and that Ken and Eileen run in Worcester have been lifelines for me. Now I'm trying to set one up in my own area — I find just phoning and talking to people who have done the course terrifically exhilarating; there seem to be so many unspoken ties linking us, before we have even met.

This, I hasten to add, has thoroughly selfish motives too. I found that the course worked for me because, by contributing to the group, I was helping myself; in committing myself emotionally to others I was receiving back immeasurably more. For me, the healing lies in the giving (not something I'm much practised in, I'm sorry to say).

So I'm trying to recreate that pattern in my life outside the course, but it's hard. My mind knows how it's done, but I need to feel *it too. So I've enrolled on another course. Perhaps then I'll find the power source that will make those other bits of me come fully alive again. Watch this space!*

I hope the above letter will be useful to those of you who are suspicious of groups and who feel, as I did, that you can do all the growing that you need to and want to, on your own. Of course that is true, you can, but do make sure that it is the most effective way and that it is not really your mind trying to keep you safe. I know that, for me, doing it on my own, and doing it *my way*, is a guarantee that I will stay strictly in control. Nothing can take me by surprise, or penetrate the barriers. I am in charge.

In groups I find that I cannot predict what is going to happen. I can, of course still resist the lessons, I still have that choice, but somehow it seems a little stupid to do that since I obviously want to learn. There are really hundreds of courses to do. So why not leap into the abyss? There will be me and many thousands of others to catch you, I promise.

And if you don't, *tant pis*, as the French say. You really are perfect just the way you are and whatever you do is what is right for you. This is, after all, not about being somebody different, it is not about being anybody at all, other than *yourself*.

The end!

So why have I written this book? Why have I exposed myself to the world, made myself so vulnerable? Partly, of course, it is the ego at work — the part of me that still wants fame and recognition, that wants to be able to say, 'I'm an author', especially now I cannot say 'I'm a university lecturer'. But there is another reason.

It is to invite you to walk this path, in whatever fashion is right for you. Be part of the adventure of discovery, of remembering who we are and what we came here to do, of having this planet be a place where we can find ourselves and experience our connectedness with each other, and with everything else on this beautiful earth. It is an invitation to open the door to freedom and to the oneness that we came from. I invite you to join me, and many others, to play wholeheartedly in this game of life. Thank you for participating with me in reading this book. I hope that you found in it what you were looking for.

Here is some 'before and after' poetry, contributed by people who have taken my courses and who wrote these for the *Quest* magazine. I leave you with their inspiring words.

Before Inertia

Everything inside is locked up tight
Just like a bank in the middle of the night
I'm safe.

I've got blankets
I've got food
I've got gin
to help my mood.

I've got Mills and Boon
and chocolate sweet
and days and days
of endless sleep.

I've got loads of time
- and it's all mine.

I've bandaged my hurts
and closed up my mind
I've blocked every way in
that others *could find . . .*

Can't see much though.
Perhaps I've gone blind.

Still, it's safe in the dark
No-one can get me,
or push me about,
or try to upset me.

Perhaps I'll look out
let life in — a chink.
Whoops, I can't feel my body!
Can't seem to think.

What's happened now?
I've been very careful.
Whatever's gone wrong?
The others *have gone.*

I'm all on my own.

Hello . . . I'm here.
I'm here . . . I was only hiding.

I'm here.

Valerie Ann Lester

After Power

I saw power as clouds,
dark, grey and looming.
Power to me was 'Power Over'.

But I saw also that there was another power, another cloud,
and this cloud was green and pink and blue and silver,
and instead of looming over me
it was beneath me and around me.
When I sank into it,
it shimmered gently, radiant with pearls.
This was the power to Be.

This was the power of gentleness and compassion
and absolute love, for me and for all.
This was the power that said,
'You are whole, you are perfect',
'You are the power in your world
and you are as you choose to be.'

When I knew this,
the Power sparkled and crackled with diamonds,
set me on my feet and settled around me as a cloak, and was
the Power to Do.

When I spread my cloak like wings,
its brilliance illuminated all around me,
and by its light I saw that it was
the power of energy and inspiration
to accomplish anything I chose
and that
both Powers were mine.
Now.
And that 'Power Over' had no power over me.

Barbara Blades.

Appendix 1. Postscripts

The following letters indicate the effects that the course had on the lives of those people whose conversations feature in the book.

Sandra (chapter 8)

I have addressed the situations we discussed on the course. I am quite a lot closer to my parents. Although my relationship with them is not perfect, it is better. I told my mum about the sexual abuse that I was subject to as a child — I found this very hard to do. She cried and I cried and then she came to the Police with me. They were very nice to me and treated the situation very seriously. They went round to his house and took him away for questioning.

He admitted it all straight away and also admitted abusing my sister as well. The case went before the Crown Prosecution, and they decided, due to the fact that I would not want to be put through a gruelling court case and that it happened 20 years ago, that he should get a very stern warning, or a 'bollocking', as the police put it, and he assured them that it was a short phase he went through in his life, and has never abused anyone else. I am very happy that I have dealt with it.

I have also left a dead relationship and now have my own flat, which I have decorated really nicely, and now I have friends around for meals and chats — the sort of thing I always dreamed of doing! I met someone really nice-looking, and went out with him for a couple of months, but he was all looks and not a lot else — he thought the world revolved around his index finger! I am glad that I went out with him though, because I had never felt good enough, and I have proved the point that my sex drive is certainly intact — wow! I have joined the Samaritans and am training to be a counsellor and have started giving blood.

I am glad you are using extracts about me in your book — it makes me feel heroic!

Clare (chapter 4).

Thank you for your letter inviting me to respond to how the course has affected me. Pre-course I would have put your letter in the chicken-shit file, or binned it, and that would have been the end of that!

I find it very painful to look at how I was before I met you — I've started to cry — I was so lost, there was so much darkness, there was so much fear. Recognising my fear is a major breakthrough and very liberating. I don't feel smothered by it any more.

Only recently I looked back to last year's crap, and said, 'What the hell was I doing in that miserable, manipulative, desperately-seeking love for that bullshit relationship?' Although I know why, and have learned from it, I remember my reply to it then. I was defensive, 'Well there are some good bits, life is meant to be like this. It's not that bad — it could be worse'. God, it was worse than worse, I was stuck at the bottom of a pit. I had no idea I could get out and bring so much light into my life!

By taking care of myself and taking life at a more leisurely pace, and noticing how and why I respond to some situations, is a good way for me to tune in to myself. I am beginning to feel more centred, I am becoming more decisive, to know who I am. (It's very difficult to buy clothes for yourself when you don't know who you are). I recognise most of my old survival-patterns and am changing them.

At the moment I am going through the first anniversary syndrome of last year's events. My partner going, discovering he was leading a double life, my father-in-law dying, frantically studying for my anatomy exams, while trying to fight off flu and fatigue!

By January of this year I wanted to get flu very badly and go to bed for a month. I wanted my body to eliminate all the gunge of sadness, anger, resentment and blame. It didn't really happen.

During a recent check-up at my clinic a lump was discovered on my right breast. During the last two weeks I've felt my life was on hold while I awaited the results. I had two cysts. The Doctor drained the fluid from them with a syringe. Although the results show they are non-malignant I will only know for sure later.

Having been through a similar experience yourself, you can imagine how I felt. It was panic, fear, complete shock, numbness. Then as I sat in the overcrowded waiting room of this cancer hospital I managed to get a hold of myself. It was a clear message. Whatever the result, I need to work more on this. To heal myself, to get support, and quickly. I could sense the panic from everyone in the room. I couldn't believe I was there.

The nurses were wonderful, they held my hand when I cried from the syringe going in. I saw the fluid from the cyst in a glass bottle. Yesterday I lay in bed and felt that all the build-up of emotions from past traumas that had all come together and condensed into a cyst, which had then been drawn out as fluid and put into a glass bottle in front of me. I visualised all the pain and anger that had been taken from me in that little glass bottle. I am making changes to my diet and have found a wonderful healer. I feel a sense of relief at being given such a clear message.

Although I have mentioned positive aspects in my life, I have also had down times, feeling stuck in the past — the frustration of it. Maybe they are bubbles that rise up from time to time to be looked at and healed. So all this happens for the right reasons. I have just realised that when the lump was first discovered I had a sense of letting go *— letting go of over-mothering, over-worrying about other people — it was quite freeing.*

That's all I have to say for now. There will be more.

Duncan (chapter 4).

I am writing to let you know how things have developed in my life since attending your course.

First of all I would say that I attended the course out of curiosity. 'There's nothing wrong with me', I told myself, and it was only after exploring my relationship with my parents with you, although briefly, that I discovered that perhaps things weren't all they seemed.

As you will recall I had stopped going to church (Catholic) but had been unable to discuss this with my parents. In fact I had developed quite a nice little routine by visiting the church the week before they ever came to visit me, finding out what was going on, and then I could talk to them quite comfortably about parish events as well as attending Mass with them when they were here.

As you told me I was living a lie, unable to have a full relationship with them — all of which I thought I was doing for their benefit. It was something I knew I had to address, but how, when?

As I told you, a close friend suggested that I couldn't really expect to attend your next course until I had dealt with the problem discovered in the first one. However my concern had been about upsetting them, making them ill, but I decided to go ahead anyway in November 1991.

I was surprised at the reaction I got. Having expected anger, uncontrollable tears, what have you, we actually had, and still have, at regular intervals, reasoned logical discussion about my faith, why I still feel a Christian without going to church, without any drama or upset. Whilst my mother is upset at the decision her reaction in particular has surprised me. Perhaps she's mellowed in old age, or perhaps she's just appreciated my honesty.

Perhaps more uncomfortably, since these events I have also seen the same 'dishonesty' to my parents by my brother and sister. Both have frequently told me things and then said, 'But I'm not going to tell mum and dad, because they'll only worry', or 'because they'll only get upset'. Needless to say I've encouraged them to just be honest, and on one occasion my brother admitted how surprised he'd been at the reaction.

I've learned a lot about honesty in the last two years, not only with parents, but in all aspects of my life. The result has, I suppose, been that I somehow feel more relaxed, at ease with myself, and more confident. I don't know why, but there you go. Perhaps you can tell me!

Vera (chapter 10).

The course did make a lot of difference to me and I have made very significant changes in my life:

1) I left my job (end of contract anyway, but a choice I would have liked to have made myself);

2) changed my relationship with my husband — we are planning to live apart and then see what happens — what a sense of freedom for me! — and how terrifying!!

3) exploring the possibility of a mid-life career change to law — very ambitious, and I have no idea about how realistic I'm being, but it's now or never for that type of change;

4) still working on the 'tidy the house etc.', but several rooms have been done, and most significantly, if very sad and nostalgic — have got rid of all maternity and baby clothes — well I'll keep one or two little bits for old times' sake!

So that's the result of being 40!! A new life! I wish it wasn't so painful!

John (chapter 3).

I think the problem I have in trying to relate how the course affected my life is that it was so successful. I now have to force myself to remember how I used to be, and even then feel that I am only getting a flavour rather than the essence of my old self. I think I should qualify that: I still retain the qualities, ethics and values that I held, but now I am much more effective in seeking to attain these goals.

I went into the course believing I trusted people, but not doing so really. I would share my possessions, but not my feelings, thoughts and ideas — myself. The actual process of the course allowed me to address that problem, which I think was fundamental to achieving change in the rest of my life.

The most obvious difference in my life is that I now do things that I believe should be done, rather than moaning to myself about them. I actively campaign for the rights of tribal people. I am in the process of helping to set up a credit union — a community banking system. And I now have a job working with people with learning disabilities. Before the course I worked unpaid as a gardener. There is nothing wrong with gardening, I still enjoy it, but I was a gardener so I didn't have to be with people and I didn't get paid because I didn't value myself.

Life is by no means perfect — perfection is unattainable, but I have a much more positive attitude to life which makes it a pleasure rather than something to be endured.

Appendix 2. Recommended Reading

Emmanuel's Book & Emmanuel's Book II,
Pat Rodegast and Judith Stanton.
These books will never become obsolete for me; they contain eternal wisdom which I know I will refer to for the rest of my life. They are books to be 'dipped into' and used at times of crisis and times of joy. They give sense to the process of life and have a feeling of spiritual fun that I find comforting and uplifting. They have enabled me to 'lighten up' about life and the spiritual journey. I do not feel the need to believe that they are the words of a disembodied being, but it is difficult to know who did produce them if they do not come from a being more evolved than we who presently inhabit the planet. (Century, 1991)

The Aquarian Conspiracy,
Marilyn Ferguson.
Marilyn Ferguson has written a serious and informed book which is fascinating and encouraging to the person who is on a spiritual journey. I was heartened to discover that the transformational process is taking place in all walks of life and in all places on the planet. The author covers the changes that are taking in place in education, health, business, communities and individuals. It seems to be gathering momentum and moving towards the point of a paradigm shift or quantum jump, so that the focus will be no longer on *having*, but on *being*.

The Fear of Freedom,
Erich Fromm.
This is a slightly more 'academic' book, but well worth reading. It spells out clearly the necessity for individual freedom from the unconscious needs that drive us, the pursuit of which leaves us feeling unfulfilled. 'Destructiveness', is, he says, 'the outcome of unlived life.' In this book he emphasises how essential it is for our wellbeing to live life fully and how, paradoxically, we are afraid of doing so. (Ark, 1984)

Beyond Fear,
Dorothy Rowe.
The nature of fear is fully explored in this readable and fascinating book. Dorothy Rowe takes a very eclectic approach to exploring and explaining human behaviour and the nature of fear. She spells out what we do to avoid facing our fears and the problems that this leads to. Mental illness is, she believes, only an exaggeration of fear based behaviour. In saying this she moves away from the medical model to a more empowering explanation of anorexia, obsessive behaviour, depression, schizophrenia and manic depression. (Fontana, 1987)

The Drama of Being a Child
For Your Own Good
Banished Knowledge
Alice Miller.
Alice Miller turned away from practising psychotherapy and is now a full-time writer. She feels very strongly that orthodox psychotherapy denies the damage that is caused by inadequate parenting and 'poisonous pedagogy' — the cultural attitudes that prevail towards childhood. In *The Drama of Being a Child,* Miller explores the myths of 'wonderful parents'. Using her own childhood as an example she reveals how difficult it is to expose the harm that 'nice' parents cause by the expectations they have for their offspring. People who feel that they must be defective since nothing 'bad' happened to them in their childhood will be liberated by reading this book. In *For Your Own Good,* Miller explores the childhood experience of Hitler and of various serial killers, to examine the links between violent parents and psychopathic personalities. She also points out that cruelty can be mental and children made to believe that they are *bad* in very subtle ways. These books are a must for people who wish to understand why they have developed and behave in the way they do. *Banished Knowledge* (1992) continues to spell out the dangers of 'poisonous pedagogy'. Although the first book mentioned above contains psychotherapeutic language which is difficult to grasp at times, it is worth the effort, and her subsequent books seem to have dispensed with jargon and are lucidly and powerfully written. (Virago 1987–1990)

Bradshaw on The Family
Home Coming
Healing the Shame that Binds You
John Bradshaw.
These three books were the best find of the year for me. In terms of my own growth and that of the clients I work with, they have been invaluable. They are simple to read, contain fascinating details of John Bradshaw's own dysfunctional childhood, and have some useful exercises to follow. From Bradshaw I learned the term 'toxic shame', which has been extremely illuminating from the point of view of explaining otherwise

inexplicable behaviour. Bradshaw explores the basis of 'toxic shame' and spells out its effect on our relationships, working lives, feelings and emotions. Living in the constant grip of our wounded inner child contaminates our adult lives. Until we can heal the wounds of childhood we will never function as responsible and fully functional adults. In order to mask our 'toxic shame' we develop a false self which prevents us from knowing who we really are or what we really want out of life. John Bradshaw demonstrates ways of reclaiming this wounded inner child and becoming our true adult selves. These books are very empowering reading. Although they are a little repetitive it is probably worth reading all three, since, if you are anything like me, messages take a lot of repeating before they sink in!

The Road Less Travelled
M Scott Peck.
A very readable and inspiring book. Using examples from his own life and from his professional experience, Scott Peck explores the spiritual journey and spells out the difficulties that ensue from being human in today's world. He illustrates the necessity for taking responsibility for, owning, our problems, rather than being resigned to them and thinking that we can do nothing about them. He discusses the nature of loving relationships; how to recognise true compatibility; how to distinguish dependency from love; how to become one's own person and how to be a more sensitive parent. (Century, 1988)

Opening our Hearts to Men
Susan Jeffers.
My initial reaction to this book was to throw it across the room. I did not want to hear the message it was carrying, which was *stop dumping your anger on men and deal with it responsibly*, although Susan Jeffers says it much more compassionately than that, in a way that enabled me to hear it. This book made a lasting impression on me and a great difference to the way I relate to my husband. I recommend this for all women who are carrying anger around with them and looking for somewhere to put it. (Piatkus, 1990)

Beyond the Quantum
Michael Talbot.
This is a fascinating and exciting book which explores the inexplicable. Reading it can be a mind-opening and even mind-blowing experience. Michael Talbot deals with complex scientific phenomena in a highly readable and understandable fashion. The mysterious communication system of bees, experiments which question the whole concept of reality, people who function adequately or effectively, but who have 'virtually no brain' are all examined in this book, which reminds us that our capacity to comprehend the universe is limited, to say the least. 'There are more

things in heaven and earth, Horatio, than is dreamt of in thy philosophy', Shakespeare said, and Talbot puts us in touch with some of them. Highly recommended for testing your belief-systems and encouraging you to be more open to the inexplicable.

Women Who Love Too Much
Robin Norwood.
Obligatory reading for women who cannot resist destructive relationships. Women who are attracted to and cannot get away from alcoholics, workaholics, compulsive gamblers and men who are violent or abusive will find this book extremely liberating. Although the title implies it is for women, it is of equal value to men who find themselves in abusive relationships. It offers an explanation as to why we consistently search out partners who will enable us to continue the experiences of our childhood, and offers solutions to change these addictive relationships. (Arrow, 1986)

Appendix 3. Courses

Jean Bond offers a number of courses and workshops for the general public, commercial and public sector companies. She also conducts individual sessions for people of all ages.
For further information about prices, dates and venues, contact Jean Bond at: *Aecern House, 57 The Riddings, Coventry. CV5 6AT, or call 0203 678107.*

INDIVIDUAL SESSIONS

Jean Bond sees people on an individual basis, specialising in young people (adolescents, particularly those experiencing difficulties at school, men and women who have been sexually abused, and marital problems. She does, however deal with a variety of other problems involving relationships, difficulties at work, anxiety and a general desire to grow and learn more about life and human beings generally. People have experienced increases in self-confidence and assertiveness as a result of these sessions.

EMERGENCE: a Breakthrough in personal power. ***Duration: 2 consecutive weekends and one evening. Fee: £125 at time of going to press.***

Until recently this course was entitled 'Discovering your potential' The content of this course is largely covered by the book.

LETTING GO: Breaking through to action. ***Duration: 2 consecutive weekends and one evening. Fee: £125 at time of going to press.***

This course is a follow up to 'Emergence' and completion of the Emergence course or equivalent is a pre-requisite.

This course focuses on living in the *'being* rather than the *'having* mode and on group interaction. The themes of self-acceptance, love and meaning in life are pursued and extended.

LEADING THE WAY. ***Duration: One day a month for nine months. Fee: £20 per session.***

Participants explore leadership qualities and look at how they can influence their environment and take initiatives that will empower groups. It provides ways of creating personal satisfaction in life and enabling people to express themselves.

HEALING THE WOUNDS OF CHILDHOOD. ***Duration: one weekend. Residential(Friday evening to Sunday evening). Fee: Varies according to location, but from £105.***

This course is open to anyone. It focuses on the exploration of the basis of 'toxic shame'; the effect this has on our view of ourselves and our relationships to others and on our effectiveness. Family roles are explored and participants discover the limiting effects of these roles. The emphasis is on discovering hidden shame, developing self-acceptance and healing the deeply buried wounds of our early childhood experiences.

INTIMATE CONNECTIONS. ***Duration: One weekend. (Friday Evening to Sunday Evening, Residential). Fee: Varies according to location, but from £125).***

This course recognises the dilemma of ever growing numbers of people who find it difficult to establish, re-establish, or sustain an intimate relationship. It explores in depth, the formulation of our constructs of relationships and releases people from the necessity to undertake relationships on a 'trial and error' basis. Participants are given the opportunity to develop a different, more empowering context for intimate relationships. This course would suit people who are single; who have been married, but feel they cannot risk another committed relationship; those who are in a long term relationship but feel that the communication and intimacy could be improved.

'HAPPY FAMILIES'!! Duration: One weekend. (Friday evening to Sunday evening). Fee: Varies according to circumstances and location. Could be residential or non-residential.

This course is for all the family, with the exception of children under 8. It is designed to produce more family harmony, effective communication and flexibility of family roles. Family members can begin to develop more empathy with each other. It addresses issues of sibling rivalry and effective parenting. It would be possible to run a course for parents and children who are below the age of eight.

PERSONAL EFFECTIVENESS IN THE WORKPLACE FOR (a) Support staff and (b) Middle Management. ***Duration: 3 working days. Fee: Negotiable.***

This is an 'In House' course which aims to develop the effectiveness of staff so that they derive more satisfaction from their work and become more efficient. It also addresses relationships and team work in the workplace and explores the personal experiences that affect our interactions with those who manage us and those we manage. The course enables people to create a more harmonious and satisfying work environment.

This course can be adapted, by means of a prior needs analysis to cater for the needs of a wide range of businesses and organisations.

OUTER LIMITS: Challenging the future.

Jean Bond has also designed a course for 'disaffected' youth. This course addresses issues of current concern to communities across the Country, *eg* the soaring crime rate, especially in the younger section of the population, increasing drug abuse, vandalism, violence and general disillusionment and aimlessness of the nation's youth.

The aims of the course are: to provide the participants with inner strength and self-knowledge, thereby enabling them to see the possibility of overcoming the obstacles life places in their path, however insurmountable these may appear to be; to develop a sense of dignity and self-worth; to provide ongoing support for youngsters so that they can put the tools and insights they have acquired on the course into practice in their lives.

The course is of two year duration, the last year consisting of individual support by volunteers of the youth involved. At the moment it is designed for youth aged 16–20 of both sexes. It entails community involvement and training of volunteers and would require the setting up of a management committee for its implementation. Coventry Youth Challenge (a registered charitable organisation) intend to put this course on in 1994/95.

ANY SUGGESTIONS?

Jean is always willing to develop courses (within her capabilities) to meet any perceived needs for development that people may have. She would be willing to do courses for community groups, or specific age groups, *eg* the elderly. She has recently run training courses for staff of Residential Care Homes for the elderly.

Bibliography

Assagioli, Roberto, *Transpersonal Development*, Harper Collins, London, 1991.
de Beauvoir, Simone, *The Second Sex*, Penguin, Harmondsworth, 1972.
Bhagwan Shree Rajneesh, *Sannyas*, Vol 2, No 4, The Rajneesh Foundation, 1975.
Bradshaw John, *Healing the Shame that Binds You*, Florida Health Communications Inc, 1988.
Bradshaw, John, *Home Coming*, Piatkus, London, 1991.
Bradshaw, John, *Bradshaw on the Family*,
Child, D, *Psychology of Teaching*, Holt, Rinehart & Winston, London, 1986.
Cirese, Sarah, *Quest: A Search for Self*, Holt, Rinehart and Winston, New York, 1977.
Claxton, G, *Live and Learn*, Harper & Row, London, 1984.
Coopersmith, S, *The Antecedents of Self-esteem*, Freeman, London, 1976.
Donaldson, Margaret, *Children's Minds*, Collins, Glasgow, 1982.
Ellis, A, and Becker, I, *A Guide to Personal Happiness*, Willshire Book Co, California, 1982.
Emery, S, *Actualizations: You don't Have to Rehearse to be Yourself*, Doubleday, New York, 1978.
Ende, Michael, *The Never-ending Story*, Penguin, Harmondsworth, 1985.
Erhard, Werner, *Centres Network Seminars*, 1988.
Ferguson, Marilyn, *The Aquarian Conspiracy*, Granada, London, 1982.
Frankl, Viktor, *The Will to Meaning*, Meridian, Canada, 1988.
Fransella, Fay, & Bannister, D, *A Manual for Repertory Grid Techniques*, Academic Press, London, 1977.
Fromm, Erich, *The Anatomy of Human Destructiveness*, Penguin, Harmondsworth, 1987.
Fromm, Erich, *The Art of Loving*, Unwin, London, 1966.
Fromm, Erich, *Fear of Freedom*, Ark Paperbacks, London, 1984
Fromm, Erich, *To Have or To Be*, Abacus, London, 1985.
Glasser, W, *Schools without Failure*, Harper & Row, New York, 1969.
Hardy, Jean, *A Psychology with a Soul*, Routledge & Kegan Paul, London, 1987.
Heider, J, *The Tao of Leadership*, Wildwood House, Aldershot, 1989.
Hesse, Hermann, *Siddhartha*, Picador, London, 1973.
Hiroto, D S, and Seligman, M E P, "Generality of Learned Helplessness in Man", Journal of Personality and Soc Psych, 31, 311-327, 1975.
Hubbard, L Ron, *Dianetics*, New Era Publ, 1980.
Huxley, Aldous, "The Perennial Philosophy", in White, J (ed), *What is Enlightenment?*, Tarcher Inc, Los Angeles, 1985.

Jampolsky, J, *Love is Letting Go of Fear*, Celestial Arts, California, 1979.
Janov, Arthur, *The Primal Scream*, Abacus, London, 1976.
Jeffers, Susan, *Opening our Hearts to Men*, Piatkus, London, 1991.
Jeffers, Susan, *Dare to Connect*, Piatkus, London, 1992.
Kelly, G A, *The Psychology of Personal Contructs*, Norton, New York, 1955.
King, M Luther, *The Strength to Love*, Gollancz, London, 1959.
King, S, *It*, Hodder and Stoughton, London, 1970.
Kleinke, C L, *Self-perception: the Psychology of Personal Awareness*, Freeman & Co, San Francisco, 1978.
Krishnamurti, J, *The Impossible Question*, Penguin, Harmondsworth, 1978.
Krishnamurti, J, *The Penguin Krishnamurti Reader*, Penguin, Harmondsworth, 1982.
Leidloff, Jean, *The Continuum Concept*, Penguin, Harmondsworth, 1986.
Lewin, M, "Is your Brain Really Necessary?", *Science*, 210, December 1980, p1,232.
Lorber, R, in Talbot M, *Beyond the Quantum*, Bantam New Age Books, New York, 1988, pp87-88.
McLuhan, M, in Postman, N, and Weingartner, C, *Teaching as a Subversive Activity*, Penguin, Harmondsworth, 1971.
Maslow, A, *Motivation and Personality*, Harper & Row, New York, 1987.
Masson, J, *Against Therapy*, Collins, London, 1989.
May, R, *Existence*, Simon and Schuster, New York, 1958.
Methodist Church, *Report of Commission on Human Sexuality*, 1990.
Miller, Alice, *Thou Shalt Not Be Aware*, Virago, London, 1989.
Miller, Alice, *Banished Knowledge: Facing Childhood Injuries*, Virago, London, 1990a.
Miller, Alice, *For Your Own Good: the Roots of Violence in Childrearing*, Virago, London, 1990b.
Millman, D, *The Way of the Peaceful Warrior*, H J Kramer Inc, California, 1984.
Moore, J (ed), *Make Believe: A Meditation on Individual Philosophy*, Turnstone Books, London, 1973.
Norwood, Robin, *Women Who Love Too Much*, Arrow Books, London, 1986.
Overstreet, B D, *Understanding Fear in Yourselves and Others*, 1962.
Patman, Sue, internally published article by the Psychosynthesis Research Foundation of New York, in Hardy, J A, *Psychology with a Soul*, Routledge and Kegan Paul, London, 1987.
Peck, M Scott, *The Road Less Travelled*, Rider, London, 1989.
Peck, M Scott, *People of the Lie*, Rider, London, 1991.
Postman, N & Weingartner, C, *Teaching as a Subversive Activity*, Penguin, Harmondsworth, 1971.
Quilliam, Susan & Grove-Stephenson, I, *The Counselling Handbook*, Thorsons, Northants, 1990.
Ram Dass, "The Seasons of our Lives", talk given to AHP Conference, Monmouth, Living Dharma Tapes, 1977.
Reid, D, *The Tao of Sex, Health and Longevity*, Simon and Schuster, New York, 1989.
Rodegast, Pat, et al, *Emmanuel's Book*, Bantam New Age, New York, 1987.
Rodegast, Pat, et al, tapes of *Emmanuel*, Bromsgrove, Monmouth, Living Dharma Tapes, 1992.
Satprem, "Oneness and the Teaching of Sri Auribindo", in White, J (ed) *What is enlightenment?*, Tarcher Inc, Los Angeles, 1984.
Schneiber, Flora R, *Sybil*,
Seligman, M, *Helplessness*, Freeman, London, 1975.

Sheldrake, R, *A New Science of Life: the Hypothesis of Formation Causation*, Paladin Grafton Books, Glasgow, 1987.
Skynner, R & Cleese J, *Families and How to Survive Them*, Methuen, London, 1984.
Smail, D, *Taking Care: an Alternative to Therapy*, Dent, London, 1987.
Smith, M, *The Mind*, Viking Press, New York, 1984.
Smothermon, R, *Winning through Enlightenment*, Context Publications, San Francisco, 1980.
Stettbacher, J K, *Making Sense of Suffering*, Dutton, New York, 1991.
Stone, H, & Winkelmen, S, *Embracing Ourselves*, De Vorss & Co, California, 1986.
Szasz, T, *The Myth of Mental Illness: Foundations of a Theory of Personal Conduct*, Paladin, London, 1972.
Talbot, M, *Beyond the Quantum*, Bantam New Age Books, New York, 1988.
Walsh, R N, "Exceptional Mental Health", in White, J (ed), *What is Enlightenment?*, Tarcher Inc, Los Angeles, 1984.
Watson, L, in Talbot, M, *Beyond the Quantum*, Bantam New Age Books, New York, 1988.
Watts, Alan, *The Book on the Taboo about Knowing Who You Are*, Abacus, London, 1982.
Williams, Margery, *The Velveteen Rabbit*, Carousel, London, 1985.
Winnicott, D, *Playing and Reality*, Simon and Schuster, London, 1971.

A Gradual Awakening
Stephen Levine
This is about Mindfulness, a very simple, ancient and do-able meditation form, with Buddhist origins. A reprint from the 1970s, *A Gradual Awakening* has been important to thousands of people, as a frills-free, clear, basic meditation guide, covering both the method and the surrounding issues arising from it. Exceptionally written, this is a welcome republication, and perhaps the best existing text on Vipassana meditation. For anyone seeking clarity in dealing with their own mind!

216 x 138mm, 174pp. ISBN 0–946551–90–1, p/b, £5.95.

Moon over Water
Meditations Made Clear, for Beginners & Initiates
Jessica Macbeth
Many would like to try meditation, but don't know where to start. Here, in a simple and straightforward form, are the basic techniques and detailed information that you need. Written with gentleness and humour, and without dogma, it is packed with clear and practical insights into the practice and theory of silent meditation. Jessica is an American living in Britain.
"Safe, sound and sane advice from a caring and trustworthy guide. The book fully lives up to its subtitle" — *'Yoga & Health'*. A very popular book, pleasant to work with.

216 x 135mm, illus, 192pp. ISBN 0–946551–56–1, p/b, £5.95

Sun over Mountain
Jessica Macbeth
Sequel to the bestseller *Moon over Water*, it teaches us to use imagery to heal ourselves, change old ways and generally transform our lives to live more fully. Jessica has a readable style, and she goes into all manner of different kinds of creative imagery for exploring the inner world, seeking guidance, overcoming obstacles, finding healing, broadening the mind and creating new paths. Useful both for beginners and the initiated.
"The most fulfilling book of creative visualisation I have encountered" — *Muz Murray*.

216 x 135mm, illus, 288pp. ISBN 0–946551–67–7, p/b, £7.95

How to be Happy
John Pepper
An exhilarating and simple guide to the most complex of tasks, changing our lives for the better. Pointing out that happiness is no escape into a fantasy world free of misfortune, John Pepper leads us toward the centres

of ourselves where the secrets of happiness lie. He shows us a well-being built upon compassion, understanding and social conscience which needs neither worldly success, groups, gizmos, ideologies nor institutionalised religion to sustain it. This book celebrates the possibility of love and renewal for us all.

215 x 135mm, 172pp. ISBN 0–946551–79–0, p/b, £5.95.

Getting Through to You
A Self-Help Course in Communications Skills
Alex Howard
An essential course in sharpening communication skills in daily life. It explores the simple ways in which we succeed and fail in our efforts to communicate. Can we find 'human touch' in the way we make contact with others, to create win-win outcomes? This book could revolutionise your relationships at home, at work and with friends. It aptly quotes the statements we make which destroy our 'getting through': and ways of correcting them. Useful as a reference text for interpersonal relations groups as well as individuals. The author offers the fruits of 16 years' experience in teaching practical psychology to a wide variety of people.

216 x 135mm, 25 illus, 224pp. ISBN 0–946551–60–X, p/b, £6.95

Anatomy of Errors
A Self-Help Course in Problem Solving
Alex Howard
Life is never problem-free. But the work of problem-solving only begins when you realise that problems are self-created. Alex arranges problems arising from lack of courage, lack of love or lack of wisdom. He helps you identify where you're going wrong (and right) by providing key statements which pinpoint critical errors. This is an unthreatening and commonsense approach to making changes in your life, new strategies for succeeding.

216 x 135mm, 242pp. ISBN 0–946551–44–8, p/b, £5.95

Finding a Way
A Realist's Introduction to Self-Help Therapy

Alex Howard
"This exceptionally helpful and down-to-earth book is a revealing, teach-yourself course in removing those masks we hide behind... providing many practical guidelines and a deeper spiritual understanding of who we really are... I strongly recommend this valuable book". *'Science of Thought Review'*

216 x 135mm, 224pp. ISBN 0–946551–13–8, p/b, £5.95

The Fruits of the Moon Tree
The Medicine Wheel and Transpersonal Psychology

Alan Bleakley
This book is about becoming. It takes us on a journey to discover the masculine and the feminine within, buried by modern 'education'. The author eclectically connects ideas from Jungian psychology with ancient traditions such as the long-forgotten Celtic tree-lore, viewed through the teachings of the Medicine Wheel. It has a strong alchemical flavour, with themes such as transformation symbols, rainbows, the symbolism of plants and animals, and the world of the imaginal, the Dream. Very absorbing.

216 x 135mm, 320pp, 120 illus. ISBN 0–946551–10–3, p/b, £7.95

Something is Happening
Spiritual Awareness and Depth Psychology in the New Age
Winifred Rushforth
Dr Rushforth, known in UK for her radio broadcasts, here communicates her optimism about the fundamental changes taking place in society. To her, the spiritual and psychological ways of understanding are one — both bound up with the healing process that must take place before we can become mature and whole human beings. She speaks, from 70 years' experience of helping people, of the need to understand our childhood, to forgive wrongs, and to own what is truly ours. There is a profound wisdom here, about human passions, the meaning of illness, working with our dreams, and love and aggression.

216 x 135mm, 160pp. ISBN 0–946551–05–7, p/b, £5.95

Men and Friendship
Stuart Miller
Most men have had a close male friend, yet we're taught to keep a distance, be bravely stiff and independent, to our eventual detriment. This book is about meaningful sharing, sensitivity and getting past empty macho pretences. An open and very feeling book about the understanding New Man beyond the hand-shake and competitiveness. Based on hundreds of interviews with men in USA and Europe, and on the author's own loneliness after a mid-life divorce. For men of all persuasions and lifestyles: a book for men without being anti-female.

198 x 216mm, 224pp. ISBN 0–946551–02–2, p/b, £5.95